READING POP

READING POP

APPROACHES TO
TEXTUAL ANALYSIS IN
POPULAR MUSIC

Edited by

RICHARD MIDDLETON

2000

OXFORD
UNIVERSITY PRESS

*This book has been printed digitally and produced in a standard specification
in order to ensure its continuing availability*

OXFORD
UNIVERSITY PRESS

Great Clarendon Street, Oxford OX2 6DP

Oxford University Press is a department of the University of Oxford.
It furthers the University's objective of excellence in research, scholarship,
and education by publishing worldwide in

Oxford New York

Auckland Bangkok Buenos Aires Cape Town Chennai
Dar es Salaam Delhi Hong Kong Istanbul Karachi Kolkata
Kuala Lumpur Madrid Melbourne Mexico City Mumbai Nairobi
São Paulo Shanghai Taipei Tokyo Toronto

Oxford is a registered trade mark of Oxford University Press
in the UK and in certain other countries

Published in the United States
by Oxford University Press Inc., New York

© Oxford University Press 2000

The moral rights of the author have been asserted
Database right Oxford University Press (maker)

Reprinted 2003

ISBN 0-19-816611-7

Preface

In its eighteen-year history, the journal *Popular Music* has published well over 200 articles on a wide variety of topics—a substantial contribution to the fast growing field of popular music studies. In the nature of things, essays on a particular aspect are scattered around the forty-odd issues. This is the first anthology of *Popular Music* writings. It is designed as a collection of articles on a particular theme—textual analysis—with the hope that it will serve as a focus for work in this area, useful both to students and teachers, and to other readers.

There is no single stance in the book—rather, a range of views and approaches applied to a wide variety of subjects. However, if overall there is a sense of a dominant intellectual tendency at work here, it is probably delineated by the intersection of Anglo-American cultural studies with the 'new musicology'. This describes reasonably well the general stance of the journal—at least in respect of the work on textual analysis (sociology and ethnomusicology feature more strongly in some other areas). And it might plausibly be claimed that it also describes the most fruitful approach to analysis within popular music studies over the last couple of decades.

A book on 'Reading Pop' might be organized in many different ways. The one chosen here comes partly out of the nature of the material; at the same time, the tripartite division does reflect important facets of the topic, following a route from the music, to the relationship of music and words, and then to ways in which the text as a whole can be regarded as representing aspects of social and cultural identity. Each part is introduced separately. The Introduction, written specially for this volume, stands back somewhat from the specific contents of the subsequent essays. It attempts to trace the outlines of the intellectual project of textual analysis within popular music studies, setting the main approaches in context, comparing and evaluating them, so that the perspectives found in the individual chapters can be located against a broader background. The Introduction, perhaps unavoidably, takes a particular view of this project and develops a particular argument, and it must be emphasized that these are the editor's, any flaws and eccentricities being his alone.

The latter would certainly be greater were the help and advice received from friends and colleagues to have been less. Special thanks are due to members of the *Popular Music* Editorial Group—Barbara Bradby, Sara Cohen, Jan Fairley,

David Horn, Simon Frith, Dave Laing, Sarah Thornton, and Lucy Green—both for their assistance with the planning of this book and comments on drafts of the new material, and more generally for their generous and inspiring intellectual comradeship over the years. Thanks also to all those at Cambridge University Press—especially Rosemary Dooley, Penny Souster, Penny Carter, Gwenda Edwards, and Ella Harris—whose support and hard work have been indispensable to the journal's success. And to Bruce Phillips at Oxford University Press, for taking on the proposal for this book and seeing it through. Lastly (though by no means least) I am grateful to my secretary in the Open University's Newcastle upon Tyne Centre, Kath Avery, for help with many tedious details—especially communications with music publishers (about which concern for my blood pressure forbids further comment).

R. M.

Contents

CONTENTS

Notes on the Contributors

ALF BJÖRNBERG   received his Ph.D. in Musicology from Gothenburg University, where he is currently working as Senior Lecturer. His research interests include music semiotics, popular music, and music in the media, including music video.

DAVID BRACKETT   is a composer and guitarist who teaches in the Music Department at the State University of New York, Binghamton. He has written extensively about the analysis and aesthetics of a wide range of twentieth-century music. His book *Interpreting Popular Music* was published by Cambridge University Press in 1995.

BARBARA BRADBY   is a sociologist at Trinity College Dublin who has a research interest in gender and popular music. She has published work on the musical and verbal texts of songs, as well as on fans' interpretations of songs and stars. Her work has appeared in *Popular Music, Cultural Studies*, and in various edited collections.

SEAN CUBITT   is Reader in Video and Media Studies, and Head of Screen Studies, at Liverpool John Moores University. He has published extensively on contemporary arts, media, and culture. His most recent book is *Digital Aesthetics* (Sage, 1998).

UMBERTO FIORI   lives in Milan. In the 1970s he was lead singer and lyricist for the Italian progressive rock group Stormy Six, and also began publishing articles on popular music. In the 1980s he worked with the composer Luca Francesconi (an opera based on Coleridge's *Rime of the Ancient Mariner* was produced in 1999). He has published four books of poetry, and a selection—*Talking to the Wall*—has been translated into English.

DAI GRIFFITHS   is Principal Lecturer in Music at Oxford Brookes University. He has published articles on songs by Elvis Costello, Bob Dylan, Michelle Shocked, and Anton Webern. He has written an article on words in pop songs for the next *New Grove Dictionary*, and is working on a book on the pop song as art form.

CHARLES HAMM   is Emeritus Professor of Music at Dartmouth College, where he taught for many years. Among his many publications in the fields of American music and popular music are *Yesterdays: Popular Song in America* (1979), *Music in the New World* (1983), and *Putting Popular Music in Its Place* (1995). An edited collection of Irving Berlin's early songs appeared in 1994.

STAN HAWKINS   taught at the University of Salford from 1987 to 1995, and founded the Popular Music Research Unit there. Currently he is Associate Professor in Musicology at the University of Oslo, where he teaches and researches within the field of popular music.

ELLIE M. HISAMA is Visiting Assistant Professor of Music at Connecticut College. Her current research explores the music of Joan Armatrading, The Cure, and *Miss Saigon*, and she is writing a book about popular music and the politics of race.

RICHARD LEPPERT is Morse Alumni Distinguished Teaching Professor of Comparative Studies in Discourse and Society, and Chair of the Department of Cultural Studies and Comparative Literature at the University of Minnesota. His work is concentrated on the relations of music and imagery to social and cultural construction, and his most recent books include *The Cultural Functions of Imagery* (1996) and *The Sight of Sound* (1993).

GEORGE LIPSITZ is Professor of Ethnic Studies at the University of California, San Diego. His publications include *The Possessive Investment in Whiteness* (1998), *Dangerous Crossroads* (1994), *Rainbow at Midnight* (1994), and *Time Passages* (1990).

RICHARD MIDDLETON taught from 1972 to 1997 at The Open University, and is now Professor of Music at the University of Newcastle-upon-Tyne. His principal research interests are in popular music. His books include *Pop Music and the Blues* (1972) and *Studying Popular Music* (1990), and he was co-founder of the journal *Popular Music*.

JOHN MOORE is Lecturer in Literary Studies at the University of Luton. His primary research interests are in American culture and science fiction.

PHILIP TAGG has worked as a composer, musician, teacher, and musicologist. He was co-founder of the International Association for the Study of Popular Music, and has published three books and over fifty articles, many of which deal with the semiotic analysis of popular music. He is currently Reader in Music at the University of Liverpool.

TIMOTHY D. TAYLOR is Assistant Professor of Music (Musicology/ Ethnomusicology) at Columbia University in New York City, and is the author of *Global Pop: World Music, World Markets* (Routledge, 1997).

BRIAN TORODE is a sociologist working at Trinity College Dublin. He has a special interest in analysing everyday narratives in ordinary conversation and in popular culture, and is currently completing a book on complaint calls to a consumer helpline.

SHEILA WHITELEY is Reader in Popular Music and Director of Media, Music, and Performing Arts Research at the University of Salford. She edited *Sexing the Groove: Popular Music and Gender* (Routledge, 1998), and among her other publications is *The Space Between the Notes: Progressive Rock and the Counterculture* (Routledge, 1991).

PETER WINKLER is Associate Professor and Director of Graduate Studies in Music at the State University of New York at Stony Brook. Trained as a composer, he has been teaching and writing about popular music since the 1970s. He writes both concert works and music for the theatre, and many of his pieces involve a synthesis of popular and classical styles.

Introduction: Locating the Popular Music Text

RICHARD MIDDLETON

Open any popular music paper and you will find interpretative comment on pop singers, records, and concerts. Tune in to any pop radio or TV programme and, again, opinion and evaluation frame the music. In a myriad less documented encounters, people of every kind and taste engage every day in dialogues about popular music's meanings and effects. And, as Simon Frith has pointed out (Frith 1996, chapter 1), academics—in their role as music consumers—are just as likely to be involved as anyone. Yet if we ask how far this involvement has fed through into the academics' *professional* work, the answer is surprising. Textual analysis has been a subsidiary strand in the expanding field of popular music studies; at the same time, much of the work has been marked by methodological hesitations which suggest deep-lying doubts about the viability of the enterprise itself. There are several reasons for this state of affairs, many of them to do with the particular histories of musical scholarship and of the way in which the study of popular culture has entered the academy. Underpinning all of them, however, is the simple issue—simple, but running deeply through the tissue of modern societies—of the interrelationship of elite and vernacular values. The threat of Pseud's Corner awaits anyone who dares to mention, say, 'aeolian harmonies' or 'pandiatonic clusters' in connection with a popular song; yet a street-conscious 'switch off your mind and boogie' is hardly more likely to succeed in closing the cultural rift. At the same time, the claims of 'the popular', as an ideological category, exert an inescapable pull on the analytical enterprise, outlawing any yearning for disinterested objectivity; a song, once identified as 'popular', cannot avoid having this effect (of course, there may be other claims made as well—of 'art', of 'politics', of 'entertainment', etc.).

In searching for answers to these dilemmas, it seems not immodest to suggest that the role of the journal *Popular Music*—founded in 1981—has been of some importance. Not that the problems have been solved; indeed, the proportion of articles published in the journal which have had an interpretative slant is smaller than one might expect, a fact which suggests that it has not been entirely immune from the effects of the difficulties just described. It is true as well that there has not been established a single core methodological trajectory which is available for evaluation. Yet the issues have been raised, a variety of approaches has been tried out—many of which can stand as models of their type—and hence some ground has been laid for an assessment of where textual analysis has got to, and where it might move next. The articles presented in this volume span the years (from 1982 to 1994) as well as many musical styles and analytic approaches. While they cannot pretend to represent a comprehensive picture of interpretative activity, certain commonalities emerge; the tripartite division of the contents reflects these, and the argument sketched in this Introduction takes them as its starting-point.[1] Prominent among questions that arise are those concerning the ontology of the popular music 'text': what exactly is this text? where is it located? what kinds of things does it do?

In considering these questions, it is useful to think back to the early history of popular music studies, the formation of which was to permanently mark the subsequent development of textually oriented work.

Much of the early musicology of pop (e.g. Mann 1963; Cooke 1968; Bowen 1970; Mellers 1973) drew on modes of descriptive and structural analysis, and of rather speculative hermeneutics, that were familiar from the existing traditions of the musicological discipline, as they had been applied to the classical repertories; the issue here, for many, was whether such modes were capable of grasping the pop texts as they were actually understood in the culture or whether, rather, they perhaps misrepresented them. During the same period, elsewhere in the networks of pop reception, a genre of criticism was evolving, much though not all by non-academics, in which the opposite problem can be identified. While a good deal of this writing (e.g. by Greil Marcus, Lester Bangs, Nik Cohn, Simon Frith[2]) does seem to capture aspects of contemporary vernacular response, it is often less successful at connecting these to precisely observed features of the music. In the first case, then, we find a formally constituted (some would say, reified) image of the 'text', only

---

[1] The selection was limited to articles which engage in some detail with specific texts. A fair number of other *Popular Music* articles contain material relevant to the subject of textual analysis; some (along with other works) are listed in the Select Bibliography at the end of the book.

[2] Books by such authors do not always communicate their success as contemporary critics as well as reading the original journalism does; but see Marcus 1977; Bangs 1990; Cohn 1970; Frith 1988.

weakly anchored in contemporary social and discursive settings; in the second, by contrast, discursive themes, mediated by educationally privileged 'fans', largely stand in for detailed study of sound-patterns. In a sense, though, it is not hard to feel that in both cases we are told more about the writers than about the musical practices of the popular culture.

Meanwhile, in the USA, popular music was also being discussed within the context of the scholarship of 'American music' (e.g. Chase 1966; Hamm 1979). For some time this had been more sympathetic to vernacular traditions than had European musicology. The American work was mostly historical rather than analytical—but one strand, focused on 'ethnic' musics and often oriented more towards ethnomusicology, would be important for the future; Charles Keil's *Urban Blues* (1966a/1991) pioneered themes and perspectives that have borne fruit in the more recent expansion of analytic interest in black music. At much the same time, in Britain, the first signs of approaches marked by concerns which would subsequently become associated with cultural studies—then just emerging as a distinct area of study—appeared (Laing 1969, 1971; Middleton 1972). The challenge to already existing musicology was patent.

For some time at least, though, ethnomusicologists and anthropologists did not follow Keil's pointer, largely ignoring popular musics of the Western societies. (In any case, textual analysis was not a strong feature of these disciplines.) At the same time, musicology—after the initial phase—marked time; it is not that there was a withdrawal from the field, more that the interest did not expand significantly, and, more important, that a tide of methodological self-doubt robbed the effort of the possibility of establishing a coherent core paradigm. But cultural studies, despite its sudden prominence, did not fill the gap. The dominant tendencies here—from the subcultural theory of the Birmingham School in the 1970s to the rush of Madonna exegesis in the late 1980s to the discussions of 'dance music' in the 1990s—have gravitated towards forms of 'consumptionism', which want to locate the textual moment, the moment of meaning production, overwhelmingly in acts of use, connected as a rule with the supposed resistances embodied in listeners' constructions of collective self-definition. The specificities of the sounds shrink (sometimes in embarrassment).

It is within this field of tensions—marked, always, by a problematizing of the textual—that textually oriented work on popular music has gone on, gradually accruing a range of working methods and a constitutive dialogue over theory, but with no dominant organizing paradigm.

What exactly is wrong with the old-style musicological pop text? There have been many critiques.[3] Usually the problems are seen as lying in the following areas:

(i) There is a tendency to use inappropriate or loaded terminology. Terms like 'pandiatonic clusters' applied to pop songs really do tend to position them alongside Stravinsky, even though it is not at all clear that anything comparable is going on there, while similarly a phrase such as 'the primitively repetitive tune', for example, is weighed down with evaluative baggage.

(ii) There is a skewed focus. Traditionally, musicology is good with pitch structures and harmony, much less good with rhythm, poor with timbre, and this hierarchy is arguably not congruent with that obtaining in most pop music.

(iii) 'Notational centricity' (as Philip Tagg calls it) tends to equate the music with a score. This leads to an overemphasis on features that can be notated easily (such as fixed pitches) at the expense of others which cannot (complex rhythmic detail, pitch nuance, sound qualities).

(iv) The most common aesthetic is one of abstractionism. Musical meaning is equated with an idealized image of the 'work', contextualized process turned into abstract product. This procedure is at its most extreme in formalist modes of analysis, which tend to reduce meaning to effects of structure, ignoring emotional and corporeal aspects.

(v) Listening is monologic. What the analyst hears is assumed to correlate with 'the music', and the possibility of variable aural readings is ignored.

In addressing these issues, the best 'new musicology' of pop has grasped the need to hear harmony in new ways, to develop new models for rhythmic analysis, to pay attention to nuances of timbre and pitch inflection, to grasp textures and forms in ways that relate to generic and social function, to escape from 'notational centricity'. There has also been a recognition that the methodological problems arise from deeper, conceptual contradictions within the traditional musicological paradigm—but these have been harder to deal with. To locate music's meaning in its objectively constituted sound-patterns, regardless of its cultural contexts, social and emotional effects, and the bodily movements which accompany and perhaps generate it, is in origin part of a broader Transcendentalizing tendency within post-Enlightenment bourgeois

³ e.g. Tagg 1982; Shepherd 1982; Middleton 1990, ch. 4; McClary and Walser 1990.

aesthetics. The trans-historical 'autonomy' of the work; the demand for 'disinterested' listening; the separation of a 'spiritual' from a lower, physical sphere of expression; the reification of the 'composition': all these fit together to form an ontology which would seem to quite exclude the secular life-processes of the pop song. To listen *that* way (as traditional analytic method implies we should) expropriates practice for 'art'. At the same time, for musicologists of pop, a justifiable anxiety to avoid collapsing the specificity of the musical into a vapid contextualist soup precludes a Year Zero radicalism; even in the more semiologically oriented work that developed in the 1980s, the pull of the traditional perspective, in certain modified aspects, can sometimes be felt, and the difficulty of isolating an object for discussion without falling into reification remained palpable. (The class, race, and gender correlatives of the traditional aesthetic—clear in the history—may be not unconnected too: one can hardly avoid noticing that virtually all the new musicologists of pop were male, white, and middle class.)

Frith (following Cook 1990) argues that 'musicology produces popular music for people who want to compose or play it' (1996: 267); in other words, that its text is constructed around the interests of production rather than listening. The issue of notation is often linked to this, since in practice it is difficult to 'produce' a musical text for such purposes without some sort of visual representation. In recent years, however, it has become clear that notation as such is not necessarily as big a problem as used to be thought— or at least that it is no more of a problem than *any* metalinguistic commentary on music (such as words). New forms of notation (sensitive transcription; sonic graphs) have been developed (see e.g. Brackett 1995); more generally, it has become clear that *how* notation is used within the analytical method is more important than any inherent properties it may possess. Similarly, on a broader front, it seems less fruitful to see the issue for musicology as an intrinsic fixation on producer interests than to couch it in terms of the question of *pertinence*: which 'text' is pertinent in a given situation, to given subjects (whose roles—as listeners, mediators, practitioners, or imaginary practitioners—will in any case usually overlap)? How can we find this out? What terms should we use to describe it?

This was one of the points of Keil's early ethnomusicology. In a 1966 article (Keil 1966*b*) he made an influential distinction between what he called 'embodied meaning' on the one hand, 'engendered feeling' on the other. The first—associated with Western classical music—focused attention on coherent syntactic structure; the second—exemplified by African-American styles—privileged the processual flow of moments, nuanced by rhythmic, pitch, and timbral inflections. The first, obviously, can be largely captured in conventional notation, the second, hardly at all—or with great difficulty and risk of misrepresentation. A few years later, in 1970, Andrew Chester (1990) came up with much the same distinction, under the terms 'extensional' and 'intensional development' respectively, and extended the intensional category to include, in large measure, contemporary rock music. While it is dangerous to apply such distinctions rigidly—probably all musics, in differing degrees, make use of (or can be heard in terms of) both modes of construction—all subsequent culturally sensitive musical analysis of pop has taken as axiomatic the need to be aware of their variable pertinence.

This is not always the case with the more recent excursions into pop analysis by American 'music theorists' (see e.g. Everett 1995; Headlam 1995; Forte 1995; Covach 1995; Covach 1998). Formed in a tradition characterized by a taken-for-granted formalism, this work rarely broaches the issue of pertinence, or demonstrates awareness of the danger of reification. Forte's book, a study of the 'classic' American popular ballad, exemplifies this. Forte applies a Schenkerian analytical method (the method that now dominates the formalistic analysis of tonal classical music), and it proves capable of revealing plenty of secrets (not surprising in this case, because this genre is still governed by many of the same harmonic and structural principles as the 'common practice' period of classical music). But he treats the music purely as scored objects; *performance* is hardly mentioned except to criticize singers for distorting what composers wrote, and discussion of *meaning* is largely confined to descriptions of his own untheorized feelings about the songs. The larger issues of method, as discussed above, are not broached until the final two pages of the book, and then Forte's response is a cheerfully confessed ignorance: 'At the present time there appears to be a distinct split between scholars who are interested in a music-analytical approach to the study of popular music and those who regard popular music as a sociological artifact . . . The issues are broad, cloudy and potentially significant . . . musicology cannot afford to neglect studies of popular music as music, for otherwise the sociological view . . . will prevail [—even though] . . . to show how incompetent I am to judge writings in this area, I readily acknowledge my inability to grasp . . . [examples of the "sociological view"]' (Forte 1995: 334, 335, 347).

The tradition to which Forte belongs is not represented in this book; indeed, some might regard it as embodying something of a reaction to the 'cultural musicology' which has emerged as the dominant species within popular music studies (and within *Popular Music*). If, as seems likely, a debate is in the offing, it is hard to assess the music theorists' chances of victory as high: without a grounding in a critique of its own assumptions, their approach is debarred from the self-reflexivity required for a properly theorized account of the relationship between analytical method and musical practice.

Notwithstanding these criticisms of traditional musicological currents, the alternative 'cultural studies' tendency in popular music studies is not without its limitations either, as remarked earlier. One factor here may be that for scholars trained in the social sciences, the most readily available approach to textual interpretation in the early period was a rather simplistic content analysis of lyrics (a more adequate approach to pop lyrics required the development of an awareness that they function not as verbal texts but as sung words, linguistically marked vocal sound-sequences mediated by musical conventions—and this is the principle that governs the varied methods applied to their analysis in Part 2 of this book).[4] Reacting against the manifest inadequacies of this approach, and at the same time nervous of the technicalities of musical analysis, many writers abandoned the textual as such. More important, though, was the dominating 'consumptionist' bias of early cultural studies, deriving both from the researchers' identification with the music's fans—the new category of 'youth'—and from their politically pressing desire to counter the received assumptions of the mass culture critics (both Leavisite and Marxist), for whom consumers were passive dupes dancing to the tune of all-powerful culture industry forces. The view that pop's meanings were to be found primarily in the uses to which it was put by its fans, and in the behavioural patterns within which it played such a vital role, spread more widely than the disciplinary core of cultural studies and became a foundational assumption in the sociology of the music (see Frith 1978, 1983).

The strongest form of this view was found in the 'subcultural theory' associated most of all with the Birmingham Centre for Contemporary Cultural Studies. Here the significance of a particular musical style was seen as being 'articulated' to the extramusical values and behavioural styles of a specific, class-related youth subculture, acquiring thereby the political potency required to make plausible the framework of cultural Marxism powering the overall approach. Critiques of subcultural theory have multiplied.[5] In the context of a concern with textual analysis, the most forceful point of criticism is, precisely, the tendency to neglect the text: interpretation of the music is often

---

[4] For both a critique of the content analysis of lyrics and broader discussions of how words work in songs, see Frith 1988, 1996, ch. 8.

[5] See Middleton 1990, ch. 5; McRobbie 1990; Clarke 1990. But notice that some key assumptions of subcultural theory, in modified forms, are still in use: see Thornton 1995; Shank 1994; Rose 1994.

scanty, vague, after-the-event, or taken direct from fans, and it is hard to avoid a sense that, in any 'resonance' between music and subcultural style, the music has been *made* to fit a pre-existing picture. The search for 'fit' is at its strongest in the early work (Hall and Jefferson 1976; Willis 1978); but, at this level of analysis (that is, of music within a specific cultural setting), music is so semantically porous that, as has been remarked, 'the difficulty with using such homologies is not that they cannot be produced. It is that they can always be produced' (Randel 1991: 320).[6]

The most influential Birmingham figure, it is now clear, is Dick Hebdige, and this is partly because he moved away from simple homologism. This is already obvious in *Subculture* (1979), where the assimilation of the post-structuralist variants of semiology associated with Kristeva and the later Barthes results in a new emphasis on *bricolage*, the polysemic 'play' of signifiers, and the productive power of 'signifying practice'. Yet the assumption that music and wider style fit together persists, and in a sense the stress on semiotic indeterminacy introduces a novel slant on the older cultural studies idea that meaning is made in the act of use. The musical interpretations, brilliant and persuasive as they are, result not so much from any engagement with the specifics of musical practice—the sounds are like *this*, not like *that*—as from a participant-observer's mediation of contemporary subcultural consensus: nowhere in *Subculture* is there sustained discussion of sounds. Yet the book's impact was profound, establishing a perspective whose main outlines continued to energize Hebdige's subsequent work and that of many others (e.g. Chambers 1985).

From within that lineage, the response to the reservations expressed here might run as follows: well, what exactly *is* the text here? Aren't the channels of dissemination, the institutions and social settings, the collective behavioural practices of musicians and fans, the associated visual styles, the surrounding media discourses, aren't these all parts of a *multiple text*—an interactive network of semantic and evaluative operations? This is fair comment: pop's mode of existence (dizzying chains of replication and intertextual relations; ubiquitous dissemination; production processes and reception contexts characterized by multi-media messages) does indeed render ideas of the bounded, originary text and of its single *auteur* outmoded. The fact that this argument would now be broadly accepted, across a whole range of differing analytical emphases, is one of the strongest contributions of the cultural

---

[6] The most rigorous attempt at a subcultural homology theory is Shepherd 1982.

studies tradition. Nevertheless, if participants in the music culture themselves attribute a disproportionate power and effect within this multiplicity to 'the music'—as they seem to do—one might think that commentators have an obligation to follow suit—or at least to try to explain why this is so.

The weakness of 'consumptionism' is its assumption (at the extreme) that listeners are completely free to use and interpret music as they wish—an assumption which, commonly, goes on to link freedom with 'resistance' (to the bland homogeneity attributed to the received meanings of commercial cultural provision). Such 'populism'—associated with writers like John Fiske —has been subject to considerable criticism. But there is a more beneficent legacy. At its strongest, this has contributed to the widespread realization that musical meaning cannot be detached from the discursive, social and institutional frameworks which surround, mediate, and (yes) produce it. This has pointed analytical work in several different (but complementary) directions. One is towards ethnography—and the first signs are appearing that this move may not (as often seems to be the case) imply a neglect of the textual. Björnberg and Stockfelt's study of music in a Danish holiday-resort pub (1996) situates closely observed details of the musical practice as an integral part of the whole thickly described collective cultural performance. Other writers have drawn on discourse theory in order to pursue the insight that the very categories within which our understandings of music move are associated with pre-existing, metasonorial discourses. At one level, discourses of aesthetic value, of political formation, of historical identity, of gender, sexuality, and the body, of class relationships, of locality, ethnicity, and nationality (etc.) function as interactive vectors producing fields of meaning within (and in relation to) which particular understandings of particular musical events operate. At another level—closer in—the specifically musical discourses (of genre, technique and technology, expressive and rhetorical modes, style history, lineages of creative influence, etc.) play an equally constitutive role, while linking the broader discourses situated at the first level to the world of sounds itself. It is no accident that the two most accomplished book-length analytical studies of the first half of the 1990s—Walser 1993, Brackett 1995—make productive use of these perspectives.

A third direction, again congruent with, but also in a sense overarching the first two, is represented by the increasing interest in theories of mediation.[7]

[7] The first writer to apply the category of mediation fruitfully to music was probably T. W. Adorno: see e.g. Adorno 1976, ch. 12. Yet ultimately, in his thought, the mediations circle back to a single foundational core— the dialectics of Reason, with their aesthetic dimension, the (Kantian) autonomy of art.

For Hennion—the most sophisticated proponent of such a theory—music out-side mediations simply does not exist. All musics, he argues, have recourse simultaneously to, and define themselves by, a range of technologies, texts, media, institutions, and public discourses; all mobilize and draw on specific intermediaries. Against conceptions of either 'texts' or 'social contexts' as fixed objects, he offers 'the view of music as a hardening mixture, a relationship which ties itself between humans while using material mediators' (Hennion 1997: 432). The musical worlds that we inhabit, then, are not clear sets, filled with autonomous entities which are foreign to each other and connected only via neutral 'links'; rather, they are half-way worlds, without clear bound-aries, filled with transient knots of variable meaning, practice, and status. Needless to say, such a perspective not only definitively destroys the basis for musicological formalism (not to mention, sociologism also), it also situates any interpretative act, including professional 'analysis', as just one among the mediations, a particular sort among many—and a peculiar sort too, for it not only coexists with all the rest but at the same time must take them into account in formulating its interpretation, and even commonly feeds back upon them, as a participant in an infinite spiral of multiplying mediations.

This spiral must be arrested at some particular point—the gaze fixed on *those* mediations not others, and the specific 'image' of the text that they produce—if the potential for an abstract relativism is to be avoided. It is easy to see, too, how the overall thrust of the approaches just outlined could result in a tendency to evacuate the specificity of the textual moment—that moment where the sounds actually register on the body (physical and cultural)—in favour of discursive and social data alone. There is also the danger inherent in all decriptivism—of whatever can be easily observed, recorded and verbalized —that it can be at the expense of dimensions which require to be uncovered and *made* to speak. Walser (1993) insists—rightly—that music is not only mediated by a web of interacting discursive fields, it also itself functions as a discourse. By this is meant not that music functions *like* (that is, in imitation of) verbal discourses, but that both music and language inhabit a larger set: 'the concept of discourse [may be used] to refer to any socially produced way of thinking or communicating'. Moreover, musical and extramusical discursive spheres are interlinked, for 'by approaching musical genres as discourses, it is possible to specify not only certain formal characteristics of genres but also a range of understandings shared among musicians and fans concern-ing the interpretation of those characteristics' (28–9). Further, the linkage means that not only are musical meanings (and hence also the structures of subjectivity associated with them) *constituted* in (extramusical) discourses, they are also *constitutive* of such discourses, and their subjectivity-effects. Work in psychoanalytic theory and in philosophy of communication make it feasible to suppose that both language and music originate in broader processes of semiosis. While this is not likely to reduce analysts' reliance on words, nor the difficulties this produces—even if it is possible to imagine gestural as well as graphic representations of sound-patterns—it is worth noting that in a sense the best commentary on music comes in the form of music itself: the ubiquitous phenomenon of covers, undoubtedly grasped by listeners as a species of 'interpretation', is merely the most striking exemplar of a widespread 'practical criticism' pursued through musicians' exploitation of stylistic intertextuality. Putting this simply: if music were not constituted as a discursive system, neither the Sex Pistol's cover of Frank Sinatra's 'My Way' nor Oasis's retexturing of the codes of sixties guitar-rock would work.

If music must be granted its own irreducible (though never pure) discursive moment, the correspondences, equivalences, and parallels that its sound-patterns suggest lie often not in the sphere of language but in that of gesture, somatic process, and tactile sensation. There is an anthropological lineage here, exemplified by John Blacking's 'if music begins . . . as a stirring of the body, we can recall the state in which it was conceived by getting into the body movement of the music' (1976: 111). To this have been added certain thematics from post-structuralism (Barthes, Kristeva, Foucault), and concerns with uncovering the codings of the encultured (gendered) body which have been pressed most strongly in feminism. From the last comes the important insight that, even if both music and language are rooted in body processes in some way, this 'body moment' is not *prior*, but always itself mediated by culturally, socially, and sexually variegated discourse (including musical and linguistic discourses). The 'confusion over whether music belongs with mind or with body'—a confusion deeply written into Western culture—which 'is intensified when the fundamental binary opposition of masculine/feminine is mapped onto it' (McClary 1991: 151), is thus false —but its effects have not disappeared from pop criticism, which often divides its attentions in this area into the 'groove' on the one hand (the music's danceability, associated with its 'bodily' power), discourses of sexuality and gender on the other (located in lyrics, singing style, and—especially in most video analysis—visual gesture and image). It is just as vital to conceive 'groove' more broadly (as the patterns through which somatic processes energize all rhythmic relationships in a performance, from backbeat through to vocal phrasing, from harmonic tensions through to performer kinetics) as it is to read the effects of the whole network of discursive mediations right through the entire musico-cultural event. Representation (of the body, of gender, of modalities of desire) and socio-musical action thus intersect; and this matrix, far from existing *outside* the details of the musical, as formalist analysis would prefer, then comes to inhabit—to a degree unrecognized in most culturally oriented interpretation—every last cranny of the text, where its work of *self*-(re)presentation (to musicians, to listeners) traces the possibilities of both identity formation and culturally meaningful socio-corporeal gesture.[8]

It is feminism too which has insisted most urgently on the inescapable *plurality* of meanings available for all pop songs, and in particular on the need to *excavate* the discursive architecture of the text in search of the ideological interests behind the natural-seeming assumptions which support dominant interpretations. At the extreme, 'reading against the grain' —so that, for example, 'romance' can appear as an aspect of female power, rock 'authenticity' as elitist purism, global-village hybridity as exploitation of the 'exotic'—offers a counter not only to simple forms of 'consumptionism' and homology theory but also to fashionable surface-fetishizing strands of postmodernism. Working in this perspective, the analyst becomes a participant in what is actually a much broader, continually active *politics* of representation. While a concern with this has come strongly to the fore in recent years, it has been an important constituent in interpretative work for some time, as the contents of Part 3 of this book indicate.

The story the analyst tells, though specific in its origins and tone, is one among many. From this point of view, it is not surprising that, to put it crudely, semiology has been tending to give way to discourse theory. The earlier focus (derived from semiology) on the quest for a rigorous, even exhaustive account of musical constituents is apparent in some of the chapters in Part 1. In recent years, however, the thrust has shifted to some extent to a concern (attributable to the influence of discourse theory) to fasten on the *pertinent features* (the definition of which will be subject to the influence of objectives that are in a broad sense politically coloured). While this does not lessen the obligation to be observant, to research the historical and cultural data, and to notice what others may miss (including the deep structures), the analyst on this view no longer appeals to some notion of a (scientifically) true account of

[8] Not much published work fulfils the programme outlined here, but see McClary 1991, ch. 7; Walser 1993, esp. ch. 4; Shepherd 1991, ch. 8; Bradby and Torode 1984 (repr. this volume). And for various aspects of the popular music/body relationship, see Middleton 1990, ch. 7; Frith 1996, ch. 6.

the music but to a sense of *collective complicity*: is this story plausible? The interpretation can function only as a form of *dialogue*.

Interestingly, if any emergent analytic paradigm may be represented as currently possessing the potential for dominance, it is, in my view, *dialogics*. Congruent with theories of discourse, mediation, and (post)modern ethnography, its recent prominence is nevertheless associated with a more specific influence, that of Mikhail Bakhtin. Bakhtin's materialist semiology posits— against structural formalisms and sociological and economic reductionisms alike—that meaning is always both socially and historically situated, and generically specific. Heteroglot networks of discursive conventions resulting from never-ending, historically contingent exchanges create a kind of giant intertextuality, operating both between utterances, texts, styles, genres, and social groups, and within individual examples of each. Any act of meaning production works through dialogue—echoes, traces, contrasts, responses—both with previous discursive moments and at the same time with addressees, real or imagined. Its signifying stream, therefore, is always multiply voiced. Bakhtin is radically decentring and anti-determinist yet also insistent that dialogic exchange is inextricably bound up in relationships of power. This semiology is grounded in a philosophical anthropology which sees human subjects themselves as produced through such processes: always incomplete, in process, polyvocal, each Self exists as a gift of Others.

Many writers are beginning to see pop songs in this light. Their meanings are produced through dialogue at many levels: within the textures, voices, structures, and style-alliances of the individual musical event; between producers and addressees; between text, style, and genre and other texts, styles, genres; between discourses, musical and other; between interpretations, mediators, and other involved social actors. Apparent univocality represents the attempt at hegemonic closure, but needs to give way, in interpretation, to recognition of impurity and contingency. Meaning, then, is always *at issue* but also *real* (not arbitrary)—it has material effects. And, always, it acknowledges (if only implicitly) the positivity of difference, the formative power of dialogue with what is absent, with the Other, in such a way that it provides both the means to problematize the boundaries of the 'popular' (external and internal), and to delineate their historical specificity.[9]

---

[9] For examples of work drawing explicitly on Bakhtin, see Middleton 1995; Walser 1993; Hirschkop 1989; Tomlinson 1991; Lipsitz 1990; Wheeler 1991. But many of the tendencies I describe here, even if not attributed explicitly to Bakhtin, can be found quite widely in writings of the 1990s; see e.g. Barbara Bradby's analysis of how the division of the female subject is structured into the textures of girl-group music (Bradby 1990) and Philip Tagg's discussion of the implicitly dialogic semiotic categories of 'genre synechdoche' and 'style indicator' (Tagg 1992).

Both theories of dialogics and theories of mediation say: the world as experienced by human beings is always multi-tracked and multi-mixed. Of course, this is more true today, in the world inhabited by contemporary pop songs, than ever before. Each of these types of theory needs the other. Dialogic analyses of texts, while in a sense insisting that the mediatory process is carried *into* the structure of the texts themselves, must constantly remind themselves of the many other layers of mediation which both produce the texts and organize their circulation, in historically and socially variable forms. For their part, theories of mediation too often end up with an 'art world', within which the specific forms of agency sedimented in musical events are methodologically secondary to the data of institutional and discursive relationships; while there are conceptual reasons why it is impossible, finally, to extract 'the sounds themselves' from the web of mediations, it is worthwhile (if only for heuristic purposes) to 'arrest' the flow, to freeze it temporarily *here*, in order to spotlight the radical *alterity* that belongs to any pattern of organized sounds—its irreducible 'this-ness'.

At the same time, mediation theories offer the promise of ways to close the most prominent remaining gap in the practice of textual analysis, namely, ways of properly incorporating the level of the political economy.[10] This gap hides multiple ironies. The debts to cultural Marxism in many of the dominant strands of popular music studies should, one might think, have prevented the opening of such a gap; yet the trajectory followed by Marxist theory in general in the 1970s actually tended to pull the work away from the heritage of economism towards theories of (often very) relative autonomy, separating cultural text from relations of production. Within popular music studies, this move can be explained in part, perhaps, as a response to the baleful example of Adornian determinism, which reduced popular music to 'social cement'. Yet Adorno it was (as remarked earlier) who was first to apply a mediation perspective in music sociology—even though, when confronted with pop, the method was quickly packed away. The two-sided reductionism characteristic of Adorno's work on popular music—formalism of the text, abstraction of the economy—should not, by way of reaction, blind us to the powerful role played by music industry forces in mediating musical meanings. If, for example, songs do often seem to have privileged interpretations—and are often

---

[10] For examples of work which use such theories to close this gap, see Hennion 1981; Born 1995. We can also find the inverse gap in studies of the music industry whose method neglects the level of the music—e.g. Chapple and Garofalo 1977—or which tend to reduce that level to an effect of a Marxist 'base' (e.g. Harker 1980).

made to appear monologic—it is unlikely that processes of production and dissemination have nothing to do with this. The apparently 'hyperreal' circulation of 'decentred' TV and video pop messages may, superficially, seem to offer support to 'postmodernist' suggestions that the 'sign economy' is now autonomous (Baudrillard 1988), but this interpretation is quickly dispelled by a glance at the financial bottom line; the routes these messages travel are real enough.

The neo-Gramscianism that provided the dominant (and most fruitful) strand in cultural Marxism in the 1980s may well be capable of the flexibility required to adapt where necessary to 'postmodernist' theorizing, while retaining a place for the political-economic moment.[11] But current deconstructions of large-scale explanatory theories suggest that Marxism (along with theories of the autonomy of art, and maybe the whole thematic of 'culture' too, with its stratifications and ethical posturings) may be most fruitfully understood as constituents of a still broader paradigm—that of Western 'modernity' itself. At one level this recontextualizes the issue of the relationship between cultural form and political economy; at another, it asks whether 'textualism' as such may not be just part of a now-faltering Enlightenment project to 'write the story of Man' (just as Marxism proposes His remaking). The evidence of the music suggests, to my mind, that, while greater modesty and flexibility in both political and hermeneutic claims are entirely in order, for analysts to make the further leap, into an embrace of 'meaninglessness' and the 'end of history' would be premature.

If this reading of the intellectual tendencies is anywhere close to the mark, it may suggest reasons why a clear retreat from 'modernist' frameworks in pop music analysis (see Hamm 1995) in favour of emphases on the micro-situation, malleability of interpretation, the irreducibility of difference, etc. has not so far led to attempts at a Derridean deconstructionist methodology in this field. By denying any necessary connection between semiosis and a 'real' world, such a methodology, it seems clear, would lead us back to a text-ualist prison mirroring, in strangely distorted form, the formalist dungeon which pop music analysis has worked in varied but persistent ways to escape.[12]

---

[11] For a neo-Gramscian approach to popular music studies, see Middleton 1990. Hebdige 1986 shows how the neo-Gramscian concept of 'articulation' has the potential to cope with the fragmentation of social formations and subjects described by postmodernists. For the sort of politics that might result—a 'Marxism without guarantees'—see Morley and Chen 1996.

[12] Sweeney-Turner 1994 calls for the development of such a methodology, and Sweeney-Turner 1995 attempts to exemplify it. Derrida himself recognizes that his critique of the Enlightenment cannot escape the embrace of its object.

It would thus negate what may come to be seen as the central thrust of that work: the attempt, in a range of nevertheless interlinked ways, to locate the texts as species of musically specific human activity, inextricably entangled in the secular life-processes of real people.

Telling this story about the development of popular music analysis has of course carried me beyond the role of simply introducing the contents of the book. The three parts of the book will each be preceded by a short preamble setting the constituent chapters in context in a more straightforward way. It seemed helpful to give this preface to the volume as a whole a broader function. While the chapters that follow are by no means fully representative of all the points and debates discussed above, and each has its own goals, which may often point in other directions as well, nevertheless the story told here can certainly be read out of them, and into them (and no doubt others can too). References enable readers to pursue ramifications, and poorly represented dimensions, for themselves; and of course, the ongoing course of the debates may be followed in the still-active pages of *Popular Music*.

References

Adorno, T. W. (1976). *Introduction to the Sociology of Music* (New York).

Bangs, L. (1990). *Psychotic Reactions and Carburretor Dung*, ed. G. Marcus (London).

Baudrillard, J. (1988). *Selected Writings*, ed. M. Poster (Cambridge).

Björnberg, A., and Stockfelt, O. (1996). '*Kristen Klatvask fra Vejle*: Danish pub music, mythscapes and "local camp"', *Popular Music*, 15/2: 131–47.

Blacking, J. (1976). *How Musical Is Man?* (London).

Born, G. (1995). *Rationalising Culture: IRCAM, Boulez and the Institutionalisation of the Musical Avant-Garde* (Berkeley and Los Angeles).

Bowen, M. (1970). 'Musical development in pop', in *Anatomy of Pop*, ed. T. Cash (London), 32–57.

Brackett, D. (1995). *Interpreting Popular Music* (Cambridge).

Bradby, B. (1990). 'Do-talk and don't talk: the division of the subject in girl-group music', in *On Record: Rock, Pop and the Written Word*, ed. S. Frith and A. Goodwin (New York), 341–68.

—— and Torode, B. (1984). 'Pity Peggy Sue', *Popular Music*, 4: 183–205; repr. in this volume.

Chambers, I. (1985). *Urban Rhythms: Pop Music and Popular Culture* (London).

Chapple, S., and Garofalo, R. (1977). *Rock 'n' Roll is Here to Pay: The History and Politics of the Music Industry* (Chicago).

Chase, G. (1966). *America's Music: From the Pilgrims to the Present* (New York).

Chester, A. (1990). 'Second thoughts on a rock aesthetic: The Band', in *On Record: Rock, Pop and the Written Word*, ed. S. Frith and A. Goodwin (New York), 315–19; first published 1970.

Clarke, G. (1990). 'Defending ski-jumpers: a critique of theories of youth subcultures', in *On Record: Rock, Pop and the Written Word*, ed. S. Frith and A. Goodwin (New York), 81–96.

Cohn, N. (1970). *Awopbopaloobop Alopbamboom: Pop from the Beginning* (London).

Cook, N. (1990). *Music, Imagination and Culture* (Oxford).

Cooke, D. (1968). 'The Lennon–McCartney songs', *The Listener*, 1 Feb.; repr. in *Vindications* (London, 1982), 196–200.

Covach, J. (1995). 'Stylistic competencies, musical satire, and "This is Spinal Tap"', in *Concert Music, Rock, and Jazz since 1945: Essays and Analytical Studies*, ed. E. W. Marvin and R. Hermann (Rochester, NY), 399–421.

—— (1999). 'Popular music, unpopular musicology', in *Rethinking Music*, ed. N. Cook and M. Everist (Oxford), 452–70.

Everett, W. (1995). 'The Beatles as composers: the genesis of *Abbey Road*, Side 2', in *Concert Music, Rock, and Jazz since 1945: Essays and Analytical Studies*, ed. E. W. Marvin and R. Hermann (Rochester, NY), 172–228.

Forte, A. (1995). *The American Popular Ballad of the Golden Era 1924–1950* (Princeton).

Frith, S. (1978). *The Sociology of Rock* (London).

—— (1983). *Sound Effects: Youth, Leisure and the Politics of Rock* (London).

—— (1988). 'Why do songs have words?', in *Music for Pleasure: Essays in the Sociology of Pop* (Cambridge), 105–28.

—— (1996). *Performing Rites: On the Value of Popular Music* (Oxford).

Hall, S., and Jefferson, T. (eds.) (1976). *Resistance through Rituals: Youth Sub-Cultures in Post-War Britain* (London).

Hamm, C. (1979). *Yesterdays: Popular Song in America* (New York).

—— (1995). 'Modernist narratives and popular music', in *Putting Popular Music in Its Place* (Cambridge), 1–40.

Harker, D. (1980). *One for the Money: Politics and Popular Song* (London).

Headlam, D. (1995). 'Does the song remain the same? Questions of authority and identification in the music of Led Zeppelin', in *Concert Music, Rock, and Jazz since 1945: Essays and Analytical Studies*, ed. E. W. Marvin and R. Hermann (Rochester, NY), 313–63.

Hebdige, D. (1979). *Subculture: The Meaning of Style* (London).

—— (1986). 'Postmodernism and "the other side"', *Journal of Communication Inquiry*, 10/2: 78–98.

Hennion, A. (1981). *Les Professioniels du disque* (Paris).

—— (1997). 'Baroque and rock: music, mediators and musical taste', *Poetics*, 24: 415–35.

Hirschkop, K. (1989). 'The classical and the popular: musical form and social context', in *Music and the Politics of Culture*, ed. C. Norris (London), 283–304.

Keil, C. (1966a/1991). *Urban Blues* (Chicago).

——— (1966b). 'Motion and feeling through music', *Journal of Aesthetics and Art Criticism*, 24: 337–49 (repr. in C. Keil and S. Feld, *Music Grooves*, Chicago 1994, 53–76).

Laing, D. (1969). *The Sound of Our Time* (London).

——— (1971). *Buddy Holly* (London).

Lipsitz, G. (1990). 'Against the wind: dialogic aspects of rock and roll', in *Time Passages: Collective Memory and American Popular Culture* (Minneapolis), 99–132.

McClary, S. (1991). *Feminine Endings: Music, Gender and Sexuality* (Minneapolis).

——— and Walser, R. (1990). 'Start making sense! Musicology wrestles with rock', in *On Record: Rock, Pop and the Written Word*, ed. S. Frith and A. Goodwin (London), 277–92.

McRobbie, A. (1990). 'Settling accounts with subcultures: a feminist critique', in *On Record: Rock, Pop and the Written Word*, ed. S. Frith and A. Goodwin (New York), 66–80.

Mann, W. (1963). 'What songs the Beatles sang . . .', *The Times*, 27 Dec.

Marcus, G. (1991). *Mystery Train: Images of America in Rock 'n' Roll Music*, 4th edn. (New York).

Mellers, W. (1973). *Twilight of the Gods: The Beatles in Retrospect* (London).

Middleton, R. (1972). *Pop Music and the Blues* (London).

——— (1990). *Studying Popular Music* (Milton Keynes).

——— (1995). 'Authorship, gender and the construction of meaning in the Eurythmics' hit recordings', *Cultural Studies*, 9/3: 465–85.

Morley, D., and Chen, K.-H. (eds.) (1996). *Stuart Hall: Critical Dialogues in Cultural Studies* (London).

Randel, D. M. (1991). 'Crossing over with Ruben Blades', *Journal of the American Musicological Society*, 44: 301–23.

Rose, T. (1994). *Black Noise: Rap Music and Black Culture in Contemporary America* (Hanover, NH).

Shank, B. (1994). *Dissonant Identities: The Rock 'n' Roll Scene in Austin, Texas* (Hanover, NH).

Shepherd, J. (1982). 'A theoretical model for the sociomusicological analysis of popular musics', *Popular Music*, 2: 145–77.

——— (1991). *Music as Social Text* (Cambridge).

Sweeney-Turner, S. (1994). 'Trivial pursuits? Taking popular music seriously', *Musical Times*, 135 (Apr.), 216–19.

——— (1995). 'Dictated by tradition? Queen's innuendo and the mercurial case of Farookh Bulsara', *Popular Musicology*, 2: 39–54.

Tagg, P. (1982). 'Analysing popular music: theory, method and practice', *Popular Music*, 2: 37–67; repr. in this volume.

—— (1992). 'Towards a sign typology of music', in *Studi e Testi: Secondo Convegno Europeo di Analisi Musicale*, ed. R. Dalmonte and M. Baroni (Trento), 369–78.

Thornton, S. (1995). *Club Cultures: Music, Media and Subcultural Capital* (Cambridge).

Tomlinson, G. (1991). 'Cultural dialogics and jazz: a white historian signifies', *Black Music Research Journal*, 11/2: 229–64.

Walser, R. (1993). *Running with the Devil: Power, Gender and Madness in Heavy Metal Music* (Hanover, NH).

Wheeler, E. (1991). ' "Most of my heroes don't appear on no stamps": the dialogics of rap music', *Black Music Research Journal*, 11/2: 193–216.

Willis, P. (1978). *Profane Culture* (London).

Part 1

Analysing the Music

To some degree the tripartite structure of the book is arbitrary. The relationship of words and music crops up as a topic in several essays in Part 1, as does the issue of 'representation'. Similar overlaps occur in Parts 2 and 3. Nevertheless, there is a *focus* on 'the music' in Part 1—even if, evidently, there is also a certain difficulty in separating it out. Overall the aim here is to illustrate ways in which the musicological legacy has been adapted, modified, supplemented, and even replaced in attempts by popular music analysts to produce a more satisfactory method.

All the writers take for granted the inadequacy of the 'old-style musico-logical pop text'. Nevertheless, several of them demonstrate how traditional methods can be refitted for productive use. For example, Peter Winkler draws on a range of relatively conventional approaches to analyse the musical lan-guage of several of Randy Newman's songs; but ethnomusicological methods also make an appearance, as do semiological ideas from Tagg and Laing, and Winkler's close readings of the song meanings are worked out in the context of a sensitivity to lyric content, theme, and performance style. (Interestingly, also, his diagnosis of the heterogeneity of Newman's musical language demon-strates, quite pragmatically, its *dialogic* quality: the songs, and by extension, all popular songs, are 'situated in a complex web of associations and connec-tions of various sorts with musical (as well as verbal and cultural) elements of widely diverse origins'.)

Similarly, Stan Hawkins lays out the harmonic and melodic components and the structural units of a song by Prince, in ways which are indebted to traditional analytical vocabularies; but the rigour of the segmentation process, not to mention the way the semantic level of the piece is seen as generated by the interaction of the components, owes more to semiological methods. Moreover, Hawkins is just as interested in the contribution made by studio production techniques to timbre and texture (and hence meaning), as he is in harmony.

The interest in semiology was typical of much writing in the 1980s, and a core reference point for this is the work of Philip Tagg. His 'Analysing pop-ular music' is a classic statement, drawing on and summarizing two larger, but less accessible studies (of the *Kojak* theme tune and Abba's 'Fernando', respectively). Tagg's approach has been influential more for its concepts than its detailed method: the latter demands a level of analytic application from which most researchers have excused themselves. Indeed, it is—again—the rigour of the method that stands out (and when Tagg has been criticized, it has often been for his alleged 'scientism'[1]). But if there is any sense in which this

---

[1] See e.g. Middleton 1990: 180–3, 233–7; Walser 1993: 38–9.

comprises a New Formalism—an idea which in any case would be qualified by the commitment to study of the 'extramusical fields of association'—it might arise from the weight given alongside this commitment to 'interobjective comparison': the play of codes *within* and *between* the style-categories making up the musical field as a whole.

The trajectory illustrated so far suggests a move from traditional musicology towards a variety of 'neo-structuralisms' capable of occupying the same ground. The essays by Richard Middleton and David Brackett amplify this picture, but at the same time broaden the front along which work was advancing. Middleton takes seriously the 'intramusical' level of meaning which formalists had privileged, but, in analyses of songs by Madonna and Bryan Adams, finds its reference in the operations of the human body. Thus 'gesture' takes centre-stage: the approach offers a theory of rhythm, though not one of the type so often forlornly called for by traditionalists—rather, a broadening of the vernacular concept of 'groove'. Methodologically, phenomenological reponse assumes a place alongside semiotic dissection; analysis becomes action as well as observation.

The analytic release of the body depends on a historicized understanding of its imprisonment under the 'structural listening' recommended for understanding the quasi-logocentric syntactic forms of Western classical music. From a different perspective, David Brackett also deconstructs this tradition, but in this case by drawing on Henry Louis Gates's theory of 'Signifyin(g)' in order to demonstrate black music's 'critical difference'. By attributing to the musical segments and features of James Brown's 'Superbad' the function of a kind of intertextual commenting, both on each other and on (black and white) cultural repertories, Brackett recasts self-referentiality within the text as a discursive strategy which is specific to an African-American tradition identified by Gates as always 'double-voiced' (Bakhtin again!).

As we start to see meaning emerging from the play of repetition and difference itself—signifiers always displacing signifieds—the move here is towards a post-structuralist position. This move becomes explicit in Sean Cubitt's study of Chuck Berry's 'Maybelline'. Drawing on Lacan, Kristeva, and the later Barthes, Cubitt focuses on the role of the listening subject in the construction of the song's meaning—and equally, of the song in the construction of subjectivity, both of which are seen as polysemic. While meanings are not inherent in the song's form, nor in the course traced by Chuck Berry's vocal—'both the object and the trajectory of desire'—these do provide the avenues through which the mechanisms of identification can be mobilized; yet finally this process turns upon a dialectic of representation and its absence: the song is 'radically incomplete', its meaning produced inter-subjectively, by listeners, within a fluid matrix of surrounding discourses.

It is in Cubitt's interpretation that one senses most forcibly, what is in play throughout the essays in Part 1, a pushing at the boundaries of 'the text'. His exploration of the relationship between sound and subjectivity, as this works at 'representation', points towards Part 3, just as his focusing of this on the operations of the singing voice carries us towards the concerns of Part 2.

References

Middleton, R. (1990). *Studying Popular Music* (Milton Keynes).
Walser, R. (1993). *Running with the Devil: Power, Gender and Madness in Heavy Metal Music* (Hanover, NH).

1

....

Randy Newman's Americana

PETER WINKLER

Introduction: 'I Think It's Going to Rain Today'

This essay is a study of the musical style of Randy Newman, one of the most intriguing singer-songwriters in the United States today. Since Newman's is hardly a household name, let me begin with a biographical note. Born in New Orleans in 1943, Randy Newman moved to Southern California at the age of five and has lived there ever since. While still a teenager he became staff songwriter for a small publishing company, and in 1966 achieved his first commercial success with a song recorded by Judy Collins, 'I Think It's Going to Rain Today'. He began recording for Warner Brothers/Reprise in 1968, and has released an album every two or three years since then. Except for one hit, 'Short People' (1977), his music has appealed to a relatively small but devoted following. Unlike many contemporary songwriters, Newman is classically trained, and is a skilled orchestrator who writes his own arrangements, as well as arrangements for other artists and occasional film scores.

Randy Newman's music has a distinctive and instantly recognizable sound, yet it deliberately draws elements from other musical styles, especially those evoking older American popular music. By investigating his music, then, I hope to address some more global questions about style in popular music: What are the musical qualities that define a style? Can elements from disparate styles be successfully blended? How do styles evoke particular moods and associations? And, perhaps most fundamentally, what does musical style have to do with musical meaning?

To answer such questions we need to look at a representative sample of Newman's songs, comparing them with each other and with a sample of the

This article was first presented in slightly different form at the second annual meeting of IASPM-USA, Las Vegas, Nevada, 12 May 1984.

music whose styles they evoke. Our investigation needs to consider such dimensions as harmonic and melodic structure, vocal style and instrumentation. The danger in such an approach is that of getting lost in a profusion of detail, of missing the forest for the trees. In an attempt to forestall such chaos, I will take a single song, 'I Think It's Going to Rain Today', as a starting point, with various observations and associations spiralling outward from this central point of reference.

Though the subject here is music, we must begin with a discussion of lyrics. Most studies of Randy Newman's songs (the best is Greil Marcus's essay in *Mystery Train* (Marcus 1982)) tend to focus on his brilliant, ironic lyrics and the meaning of the stories they tell. But though it is a mistake to assume that the meaning of his songs lies entirely in the lyrics, it would equally be a mistake to ignore them. In Newman's songs, as in any good popular song, the meaning involves the interaction of words and music.

Newman's lyrics tend to be simple in vocabulary, terse, and elliptical: what is left unsaid is often more important than what is said. And irony is his most characteristic mode. The words to 'I Think It's Going to Rain Today' begin with images of desolation, emptiness, absence:

> Broken windows and empty hallways
> Pale dead moon in a sky streaked with grey

The next two lines introduce striking discontinuities:

> Human kindness is overflowing
> And I think it's going to rain today

The fourth line is in keeping with the mood of the first two, though it shifts perspective as it introduces the 'I', the *persona*, of the song. But the third line is a puzzling break in the continuity of the verse: a moralizing generalization, almost a cliché, whose connection with the other three lines is not at first apparent. The empty landscape is populated in the second verse, though its inhabitants are just barely human:

> Scarecrows dressed in the latest styles
> With frozen smiles to chase love away
> Human kindness is overflowing
> And I think it's going to rain today

The third line is less enigmatic now, but it still stands in opposition to the images of the first two: these mannequins/fashion models are empty of 'human kindness'; they 'chase love away'. The last two lines are now understood as a refrain, though the tension between them is unresolved. The next stanza, musically a bridge section, begins with a single word, grammatically detached and repeated:

> Lonely
> Lonely
> Tin can at my feet
> Think I'll kick it down the street
> That's the way to treat a friend

The last three lines bring us a few steps closer to understanding the bitter, cynical world-view of the song: we can infer that the persona of the song feels that he, too, has been kicked down the street like a tin can.

> Bright before me, the signs implore me
> Help the needy and show them the way
> Human kindness is overflowing
> And I think it's going to rain today

The final verse finally gives a context to the enigmatic third line: the thought is prompted by the view of a sign, a charity appeal. By now we appreciate the deep irony of the third line: the persona of the song experiences no human kindness in his world, and feels no kindness towards others. He has been hurt, kicked around: presumably by a lover.

But the lover is never specifically mentioned or directly alluded to. Indeed, very little of the relationship is directly revealed in the song: the lover, the 'other', is conspicuous by her/his absence; the 'I' only appears in relation to inanimate objects: a remark about the weather, the act of kicking a can. Even the most direct expression of emotion is a detached adjective—'lonely', not 'I'm lonely'. The persona of this song (like many males in our society) has difficulty confronting his emotional life directly: we sense his hurt and pain indirectly, through his bleak view of the world around him. The closest we get to his tears is a remark about rain.

We have been able to discover something about the meaning and affect of the lyrics to this song by examining their internal workings—tensions, discontinuities, processes—and by relating these workings to the human situation the song depicts. As we turn now to the music, how much can we discover by observing the internal workings of the musical structure? Here are some preliminary observations about the music (shown in condensed form in Example 1.1) and its recorded sound (in Newman's two recordings of the song, on RS 6286 (1968) and RS 6459 (1971)):[1]

---

[1] All examples transcribed by Peter Winkler from recordings except for Examples 1.8*a*, 1.8*c*, 1.9*b*, 1.9*c*, 1.9*e*.

Ex 1.1. 'I Think It's Going to Rain Today' (condensed score: from *Live* 1971)

1. The harmony is diatonic, and, for the most part, triadic. The chord
   progression of the verses follows the principles of European common-
   practice functional tonality, except for the use of unresolved suspensions in the cadence (see Example 1.2). The harmonic language of the
   bridge section is radically different, combining diatonic elements in a
   non-functional way that destroys a sense of tonal hierarchy.

Ex 1.2. 'I Think It's Going to Rain Today': analysis of melody and bass-line of the verse

2. The melody is diatonic: the verse is almost entirely pentatonic (in A major) except for the fourth degree (D) in bar 2; the bridge uses the pentatonic scale of C major, a minor third higher. The melody of the verse describes an arch, beginning and ending on the tonic and reaching its apex in the third line ('Human kindness is overflowing').
3. Newman's singing voice is low, soft, with a raspy timbre to it. His pitch intonation is variable—not always perfectly in tune, and often sliding upwards or downwards within a single pitch. At times the inflection is almost like a groan (especially in the earlier recording). The vocal rhythm is loose, tends to lag after the beat, and is at times conversational.
4. The instrumentation in both recordings is limited to an acoustic piano, playing three- or four-part chords in open voicing which often involves parallel sixths in the upper parts. A string orchestra is added in the 1968 recording.

We can relate some of these observations to the meaning we discovered in the lyrics: Newman's vocal sound and inflections express the sad, bitter, withdrawn mood of the words, and the agitated, tonally disoriented music of the bridge lends an air of despair and anguish to the cry, 'lonely, lonely'. On the other hand, the music does not support the verbal discontinuity we found in the verse. On the contrary, the setting of 'human kindness is overflowing' is the keystone of the musical arch; the music tells us there is a continuity long before the words reveal it.

Is there also a meaning to the choice of harmonic language, of melodic style, of instrumentation? We can answer such questions only by broadening our frame of reference, saying, for example, that the harmony is 'hymn-like', the melodic style is 'like gospel music', the instrumentation is 'classical'. No successful popular song exists in isolation; it is situated in a complex web of associations and connections of various sorts with musical (as well as verbal and cultural) elements of widely diverse origins. The meaning of a particular musical element lies not so much in *what* it is as *where* it is—its particular location along a number of lines of association or differentiation.

To investigate systematically all the ways in which a particular piece of music connects with its musical and cultural environment is an endless task (though Philip Tagg's monumental *Kojak—50 Seconds of Television Music* (Tagg 1979) comes close). Our approach here is unsystematic and selective: we will examine just a few strands of musical connection in some detail, working outward from 'I Think It's Going to Rain Today' in a number of different directions.

Harmony: The Barbershop Connection

We can usually learn a lot about a harmonic style by observing its cadences. A cadence is a harmonic pattern that produces a sense of closure at the end of a phrase, and since it is so structurally significant, it tends to epitomize the harmonic processes generally at work within a style. Since cadences tend to be formulaic, and much the same from piece to piece within a given style, they also serve as useful stylistic indices.

Consider the cadence at the end of the verse of 'I Think It's Going to Rain Today' (Example 1.3(*a*)). The bass line moves to the tonic along the circle of fifths (VI–II–V–I)—a formula as old as tonality itself, and one which is especially characteristic of American popular music since the late nineteenth century. But we already noted that the suspensions in the upper harmonic voices are not treated according to harmonic common practice (Example 1.3(*b*) shows how the suspensions should be 'correctly' resolved). Indeed, rather than try to relate this cadence to traditional harmony, which posits triads built on

Ex 1.3. 'I Think It's Going to Rain Today'—the cadence in bars 7–9

(*a*) Abstract of the cadence
(*b*) 'Correct' resolution of suspensions
(*c*) Fifth-relations in the cadence

the interval of a third as the only stable structure, it makes more sense to see these chords as generated by the interval of a fourth or fifth (Example 1.3(*c*)).
'Thirdless harmony' (the term is Philip Tagg's) of this sort has become commonplace in European concert music since the beginning of this century, and has become increasingly common in jazz, pop, and rock since the 1960s. I agree with Tagg that it is impossible to 'attribute any specific affective significance to the use of thirdless harmony' in general (Tagg 1979: 139), but in particular cases such harmonies *can* have an affective impact. Here the thirdless cadence comes after six bars of functional, triadic harmony: at the half cadence (bar 4), for example, we hear a rich dominant ninth chord resolve in classical fashion to a tonic (decorated with an appoggiatura—the note B—that also resolves correctly). By contrast the cadence in bars 7–8 sounds bleak and austere. The usual structural force of a bass moving in fifths is undercut, because each new note in the bass has been anticipated by a note in an upper voice (the suspended fourth) in the preceding chord (see the broken lines in Example 1.3(*a*)). Thirdless harmony in general weakens traditional tonal hierarchies, and the use of suspended chords here supports the depressed, distanced, defeated effect of the line 'I think it's going to rain today'.

To take a circle-of-fifths cadence and fashion it into a repeating loop (or ostinato) is a time-honoured procedure in popular music, going back at least to the early years of this century.[2] Randy Newman's music is full of such devices, and a comparison of a group of representative repeated passages can yield further insight into his harmonic proclivities (see Example 1.4(*a–g*)).

Ex 1.4. The barbershop connection: ostinato repetitions of the barbershop progression in Newman

(*a*) 'Short people' (from *Little Criminals*, 1977)

---

[2] For a fuller discussion of the 'barbershop' paradigm and its structural importance in popular music, see Winkler 1978.

(b) 'Love Story' (from *Randy Newman*, 1968)

(c) 'Sail Away' (from *Sail Away*, 1972)

'Short People' is a good song to begin with: one of Newman's most popular recordings, it is built almost entirely out of several variants of this pattern. In its first appearance the pattern resembles the traditional 'barbershop harmony' formula (Example 1.4(i)), in which the bass line is harmonized with chromatically descending tritones, each tritone forming a dominant seventh chord. But in 'Short People' the tension of a chromatic descent in one voice from the fifth degree to the third (E to C♯) is undercut by the tonic pedal-point (A) in the other—how can there be tension in the chromatic motion toward a goal if that goal is present all along?

(*d*) 'Louisiana 1927' (from *Good Old Boys*, 1974)

What has hap-pen'd down here is the wind have changed

Clouds roll in from the North and it start to rain

Pno

Bass

(*e*) 'Jolly Coppers on Parade' (from *Little Criminals*)

They're com-in' down the street   They're com-in' right down the mid-dle

8ve basso

(*f*) 'Baltimore' (from *Little Criminals*)

Beat up lit-tle sea-gull   On a mar - ble stair

(g) 'Last Night I Had a Dream' (from *Sail Away*)

(h) 'Short People'

(i) The 'Barbershop' paradigm

I   V - of - V - of - V

For the sake of argument let us take the 'Short People' pattern as the norm, and consider the other passages in Example 1.4 as transformations of it. Though at least one of the three essential voices of the 'Short People' pattern is present in each of the other passages, it isn't always the same voice, and the range of transformation is quite wide. 'Sail Away' and 'Louisiana' (Examples 1.4(c), (d) and 1.5(c), (d)) elaborate the progression into complete four bar phrases, but there is actually more of the 'Short People' pattern in their voice-leading than in the passage from 'Love Story' (Examples 1.4(b), 1.5(b)). The voice-leading in 'Jolly Coppers' (1.4(e), 1.5(e)) employs the third-less harmonies we discussed earlier. The most striking transformations occur in the two songs in a minor key: in 'Baltimore' (Examples 1.4(f), 1.5(f)) we find the upper parts of the 'Short People' pattern given a new context by the bass, which reinterprets them in the key of the relative minor (E

Ex 1.5. Analysis of Ex 1.4 (all music transposed to C for comparison): the barbershop paradigm

(a) 'Short People' (b) 'Love Story' (c) 'Sail Away' (d) 'Louisiana 1927'

(e) 'Jolly Coppers' (f) 'Baltimore' (g) 'Last Night' (h) 'Short People'

minor: the pedal point is now the minor third (G), the chromatic descent is from D to B, the seventh to the fifth degree). In 'Last Night I Had a Dream' (Examples 1.4(g), 1.5(g)) the chromatically descending line is transferred to the bass. And we can connect the resulting new bass-line to another pattern in 'Short People' (Examples 1.4(h), 1.5(h)) which brings us full circle.

In observing Newman's characteristic uses of the repeated 'barbershop' pattern we can see the various ways in which he plays off the contrast between dynamic qualities (the fifth progression, the chromatic line, and the sense of harmonic motion that those elements generate) and static ones (the pedal-point, the repeating loop). The way in which he highlights one or another of these aspects often has expressive significance in a particular song: the insistent repetition and stubborn clinging to the pedal-point in 'Short People' underlines the dimwitted bigotry of the words; the 'you and me' passage in 'Love Story' evokes the clichés of the 1950s teen ballad; in 'Sail Away' (a song in which a slave trader tells Africans of the paradise awaiting them in America) the wistful, yearning quality of the strings' elaboration of the chromatic line counterpoints the gentle, hypnotic allure of the piano ostinato; in 'Baltimore' the insistent repeated pattern gives us the desperate feeling of being trapped on a treadmill; and the sinking bass-line of 'Last Night I Had a Dream', which never quite reaches its goal (the fifth degree), is ominous and disturbing.

Melody and Vocal Style: The Gospel-blues Connection

Anyone who is familiar with Anglo-American or Afro-American folksong will recognize the pentatonic scale and arch-like shape of the melody to 'I Think It's Going to Rain Today', for melodies of this type are common in both traditions. Example 1.6 compares the melody with a few typical examples: 'Barbara Ellen' (Child Ballad No. 84) from the secular repertory, 'Were You There When They Crucified My Lord?' and Sam Cooke's 'Jesus I'll Never Forget' from the gospel tradition. The slow tempo and hymn-like harmonies of Newman's song reinforce the gospel connotations, and place it in the genre of songs such as Jerome Kern's 'Old Man River' or Paul Simon's 'Bridge Over Troubled Water'. Newman's appropriation of these associations is entirely ironic: the gospel quality best fits the pious sentiments of such lines as 'Human kindness is overflowing' and 'Help the needy and show them the way', which are not to be taken at face value. The song is really an *anti*-hymn.

Ex 1.6. The melodic type of 'I Think It's Going to Rain Today'
(*a*) 'I Think It's Going to Rain Today'
(*b*) 'Barbara Ellen' (Child Ballad no. 86, as transcribed in Niles 1960)
(*c*) 'Were You There When They Crucified My Lord' (from Johnson 1966)
(*d*) 'Jesus I'll Never Forget' (as sung by Sam Cooke with the Soul Stirrers 1954)

Most of Randy Newman's melodies (every melody transcribed in Example 1.4, for instance) are pentatonic (see Example 1.5). This is hardly exceptional; pentatonic melodies are extremely common in popular music, for a number of practical reasons: they contain no half-steps or dissonant intervals, they are clearly centred around a triad, and they easily accommodate variable intonation—portamentos, blue notes, speech-like inflections, or just plain bad singing. This brings us to an important point: in popular music, questions about melodic structure cannot be separated from questions about vocal style. Consider Judy Collins's 1966 recording of 'I Think It's Going to Rain Today': her vocal timbre is clear; every note is precisely in tune, with little variation in pitch except a slight, controlled vibrato; though her rhythm is free it resembles more a classical musician's rubato than a jazz musician's compressions or expansions of the beat. Her style seems inappropriate. Aside from a certain dolefulness, the expression is rather deadpan. It doesn't do the song justice. The melody fares better in the hands of less technically skilled singers —Newman himself, or even Melanie Safka (in a 1974 recording)—singers who don't approach every note straight on, whose pitch intonation is highly variable, whose vocal qualities have a certain amount of 'dirt' (impurities such as raspiness or growliness) in them.

All of the melodic and stylistic elements we have just noted are characteristic of the blues, so it should be no surprise that many of Newman's songs evoke blues styles. Without getting too deeply embroiled in the ancient 'can a white boy sing the blues?' controversy, let us take a look at some samples of Newman's blues singing, and compare them with the styles of some other singers, both black and white. In Example 1.7 I have transcribed verses from Randy Newman's recordings of 'Lucinda' (1.7(a)) and 'Pretty Boy' (1.7(f)), Joe Cocker's version of 'Lucinda' (1.7(b)), Bob Dylan's 'Ballad of a Thin Man' (1.7(e)), Fats Domino's 'I'm in Love Again' (1.7(c)), and Ray Charles's 'Let's Go Get Stoned' (1.7(d)).

Using transcriptions to study vocal styles is problematic. The microtonal inflections and rhythmic subtleties of blues singing were never meant to be captured in traditional musical notation. The most a conscientious transcriber can hope for is a plausible correspondence between his notation and what is actually heard on a recording; there is no such thing as a completely accurate transcription. But, this *caveat* notwithstanding, a transcription can make a performance 'hold still' so that we can observe it—or some traces of it—in detail.

Ex 1.7. The blues connection: transcriptions of blues-styled vocals

(c) Fats Domino, 'I'm In Love Again'

Yes it's me and I'm in love____ a - gain_ Had no lov - in' since

you____ know when You know I love_ you Yes, I do__ and I'm

sav - in' all my love in jail_____ for you

(d) Ray Charles, 'Let's Go Get Stoned'

You know my_ ba - by_____ she won't let me in

I got a few_____ pen-nies____ I'm gon' buy my-self a bot-tle o' gin

An' then I'm gon' call my bud-dy__ On the tel-e - phone__ and say_

[Raelets:] Let's go get stoned!

The melodies in Example 1.7 were chosen because of their similarity of pitch structure: all are based on a characteristic blues motif moving between the tonic and various inflections of the third above. In Example 1.7(g) I have summarized the motion of each melody, using the analytic notation for blues melodies developed by Jeff Todd Titon in his *Early Downhome Blues* (see Titon 1977: 154–61).[3] Despite similar outlines, no two of these melodies move

---

[3] I hope the reader is not disoriented by the difference between the analytic notations used to summarize melodies in Example 1.6 and Example 1.7(g). Titon's system, used in 1.7(g), summarizes note-to-note connections by means of arrows, and is a useful way of seeing typical patterns of movement within a limited scale, and the total pitch-content of a particular passage. The notation in Example 1.6, which is based on Heinrich Schenker's theories, is useful for summarizing the overall contour and long-range pitch connections in a melody.

(*e*) Bob Dylan, 'Ballad Of A Thin Man' (first 8½ bars only)

You walk in to the room   With your pen-cil in your hand

You see some-bo-dy nak-ed and you   You say "who is that man?"   You tr(ha–ha)y so hard but you

Don't un-der-stand   Just what you'll_ say when you get___ home_   Be -

- cause some-thing is hap-pen-ing here.___ but you   don't know what it is___

Do you,   Mis - ter   Jones?___

(*f*) Randy Newman, 'Pretty Boy'

We got a tough guy here   We got a tough guy from the streets

Look just like that dan-cing wop   In those mo-vies that we've seen

His cute lit-tle chick-en shit boots on   His cute lit-tle chick-en shit hat

His cute lit-tle chick-en shit girl friends   rid-in' a long in back

(g) *Analysis of melodic motion (see Titon 1977 for analytical method)* Δ = *a blue 'note complex' variously inflected by microtones and glissandi*

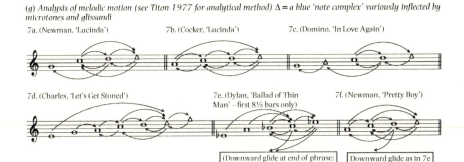

7a. (Newman, 'Lucinda')   7b. (Cocker, 'Lucinda')   7c. (Domino, 'In Love Again')

7d. (Charles, 'Let's Get Stoned')   7e. (Dylan, 'Ballad of Thin Man' – first 8½ bars only)   7f. (Newman, 'Pretty Boy')

(Downward glide at end of phrase; bottom note indistinct)   Downward glide as in 7e

from pitch to pitch in exactly the same way, and each employs one or more figures not found in the others.

All of the examples employ the characteristic 'blue' inflections of certain scale-degrees—most frequently the blue third—but in the case of the white singers this takes the form of undifferentiated glides between notes, or, especially in Dylan's case, a downward glide at the end of most phrases. The black singers tend to articulate their blues inflections into ornaments or melismas made of discrete pitches—see Fats Domino's ornamentation of the word 'love', for example, or Ray Charles singing 'got a few pennies'.

The examples show varying degrees of rhythmic freedom. Fats Domino's 'I'm in Love Again', sung at a moderately fast tempo to a dance beat, is the most metrical, with a majority of the principal stresses in each line occurring on the first or second beat of the bar. At the other extreme is Ray Charles, who *never* places a stress on the beat, and begins every phrase after beat one of the bar. Randy Newman's phrasing of 'Lucinda' resembles Ray Charles, while Joe Cocker is much more tied to the metre: most of his phrases place an accent squarely on beat one.

The transcriptions show complex subdivisions of the beat in most of the examples, but the notation can't reflect a fundamental difference in the way black and white singers play around with the beat: the difference between *polyrhythm* and *rubato*. In Ray Charles' singing, one can hear time-spans of varying length neatly subdivided into equal pulses whose periodicity is complexly related to the beat. The most striking example is the line 'I'm goin' buy myself a bottle o' gin', in which, as near as I can make out, a time-span of *seven* triplet-semiquavers (that is, a triplet-crotchet tied to a quaver) is divided into *six* equal pulses! Complex rhythm in the singing of Newman, Dylan, and Cocker, on the other hand, is more prose-like; it is a matter of tempo rubato, of accelerating and decelerating pulses, rather than precise articulation into polyrhythms.

These observations suggest that when white boys sing the blues, they do so by loosely approximating devices that, with black singers, are more precisely articulated and controlled. But aside from such questions of technique, what is the meaning of Newman's (and other white singers') appropriation of blues style?

Consider the bizarre story unfolded in the lyrics to 'Lucinda':

> We met one summer evening as the sun was goin' down
> She was lying on the beach in her graduation gown
> She was wrapped up in a blanket (I could tell she knew her way around)
> And as I lay down beside her, you know she never made a sound.
>
> On down the beach comes the beach-cleaning man
> Scooping up the papers and flattening down the sand
> 'Lucinda, Lucinda, Lucinda, we've got to run away
> That big white truck is closing in, and we'll get wounded if we stay'.
>
> Now Lucinda lies buried 'neath the California sand
> Put under by the beach-cleaning man.
> Lucinda, Lucinda, Lucinda, why'd you have to go?
> Well they sent her to high school, they sent her to low school,
> She just wouldn't go no further.

Blues lyrics are usually couched in the first person, and by convention the 'I' of the song is identified with the singer himself. This is not the case in 'Lucinda'—the first person is rather obtuse and passive. Lucinda is apparently paralysed with ennui, possibly even unconscious, but the narrator doesn't appear to notice this, nor does it occur to him to move Lucinda or stop the truck. He's nearly as immobile as Lucinda himself, and Newman's lazy, spacey blues phrasing captures the character perfectly. Writing of Newman's vocal style, Greil Marcus refers to:

> . . . his choice of a lazy, blurred sound, where words slide into each other, where syllables are not bitten off but just wear out and dissolve . . . It is as if Randy's real blues hero wasn't Howlin' Wolf, but Stepin Fetchit. (Marcus 1982: 116)

Joe Cocker, by contrast, approaches 'Lucinda' with his usual gritty, laboured soulfulness, determinedly hanging each phrase on the first beat of the bar. Nothing in his singing establishes any distance between himself and the character portrayed in the song. Did he even notice that the song was supposed to be funny?

In Bob Dylan's 'Ballad of a Thin Man' (Example 1.7(*e*)) we hear blues melodic and rhythmic inflection being used to express anger and derision. Dylan's scorn tumbles out in irregular, speech-like rhythms; the characteristic falling pitch-inflection with which he ends words and phrases feels like a sneer. But despite the sarcasm, we feel we are hearing Dylan *himself* in this song, expressing his (and his generation's) contempt for the straight world. (The song was reputedly inspired by Dylan's exchanges with a reporter from *Time* magazine, at the Newport Folk Festival in 1965.) Randy Newman's 'Pretty Boy' (Example 1.7(*f*)) also uses blues idioms to express scorn and contempt, but the anger is more veiled, more impersonal, and therefore more menacing. The ominous, low orchestration and Newman's icy, detached mockery create a chilling mood of foreboding. We never learn who is addressing the 'pretty boy' in this song—the leader of a street gang? A pimp running a seedy bordello? All we know is that his presence is alien and dangerous:

> Hope we're going to get the chance to show you 'round (*twice*)
> Talk tough to me, Pretty Boy
> Tell us all about the mean streets of home
> Talk tough to me

Randy Newman's songs, then, are founded on a sharp distinction between what Dave Laing has called the external level of communication (between performer and listener) and the internal level ('within the lyric of the song, between the protagonist of the lyric and its addressee'): 'Newman is like . . . an actor of the Brechtian school who is required to make a distance between her or himself and the character, rather than fusing with it. Most popular songs . . . do not have so unambiguous a gap between the external and internal levels of communication' (Laing 1985: 63). Many white singers are attracted to black blues and gospel styles because of the impression of authenticity, of heartfelt soulfulness that such styles can convey. Randy Newman seems to be appropriating black styles for precisely the opposite reason: to intensify a sense of alienation, to emphasize the gap between himself and the characters in his songs. He deliberately exploits the absurdity of a white, Jewish intellectual singing like a black from the deep South, mocking the conventions of 'white boy with the blues' even as he appropriates them. He is laughing at his own blackface act.

Evocation of Style: The Parlour Music Connection

When we speak of the hymn-like qualities of 'I Think It's Going to Rain Today', or the appropriation of blues elements in 'Lucinda' and 'Pretty Boy', we are talking about using a musical style as an expressive element in a song. Borrowing from other styles is a time-honoured tradition in popular music, but (aside from uses in musical theatre) the self-conscious choice of style as an element in the meaning of a song has only become a common practice since the 1960s—the Beatles' stylistic eclecticism being one of the early examples. Many pop artists of the seventies, eager to establish a sense of authenticity, would assemble a style out of disparate elements and then stick to it—for example, Bruce Springsteen's synthesis of the epic 'wall of sound' of early sixties pop, the raunchy attack of Southern soul bands, and the poetic aspirations of singer-songwriter lyrics. Less typical are stylistic chameleons like Billy Joel or Randy Newman, who adapt whatever style seems most appropriate to the meaning of a song. The danger in such eclecticism is that it can degenerate into mere stylistic pastiche (which sometimes happens in Billy Joel's case). Newman's distinctive approach and persistent irony usually help him avoid this pitfall. Aside from the blues and gospel allusions we have already seen, Newman often makes use of elements from Country music (e.g. 'Suzanne', 'My Old Kentucky Home (Turpentine and Dandelion Wine)', 'Rider in the Rain', and much of the *Good Old Boys* album). He is also adept at evoking the sound and world-weary mood of cabaret bands *circa* 1920 (e.g. 'Lonely at the Top' and his haunting arrangement of Lieber and Stoller's 'Is That All There Is?' for Peggy Lee). But perhaps most characteristic of all is his evocation of nineteenth-century parlour music.

By 'parlour music' I mean the entire spectrum of musical types that were played (usually on piano) and sung in American homes in the last century— classical favourites, hymns, sentimental ballads, minstrel show tunes, and, later on, ragtime and early Tin Pan Alley songs. Newman's sensitivity to such styles is well displayed in his score for the 1981 film version of Doctorow's novel, *Ragtime*. The musical atmosphere for the scene in which the black pianist Coalhouse Walker first visits the home in New Rochelle is perfect: first he establishes his 'legitimacy' by playing the Chopin A major prelude (Opus 28 No. 7), then moves into his own (Newman's) paraphrase of the piece (Example 1.8(*a*), (*b*)). Here we can see some of the sources of classical touches that pervade Newman's writing: his fondness for doubling the melody in sixths (which we also noticed in 'I Think It's Going to Rain Today'), his penchant for appoggiaturas and chromatic lower neighbours, his conservative harmonic sense and preference for clear, functional bass lines.

Ex 1.8. The parlour music connection: Newman, Chopin, etc. Boxed:App = appoggiatura; Boxed:N = chromatic lower neighbour

(a) Chopin, Prelude, Opus 28, No. 7

(b) Newman from *Ragtime*

(c) Henry Tucker, 'Sweet Genevieve' (1890) transposed (from Jackson 1976)

Ex 1.9. Comparison of verses of (*a*) Newman's 'Marie' and (*b*) Stephen Foster's 'The Voices that are Gone'

(*c*) Scott Joplin 'Solace', beginning of first strain

All of these elements, of course, are also found in the parlour songs of nineteenth-century America, which adapted the European classical tradition to domestic use (see Example 1.8(*c*)). Newman's song 'Marie' (Example 1.9(*a*)) makes particularly effective use of this genre. Its nostalgic atmosphere is established by harmonic and melodic means not too different from those of Stephen Foster; a comparison of Foster's 'The Voices that Are Gone' with 'Marie' is particularly enlightening (Example 1.9(*a*), (*b*)). Both songs use chromatic alterations sparingly and in analogous places: a diminished seventh chord supporting a melodic sixth in the first phrase, and a secondary dominant in the third phrase. In a predominantly diatonic context like this, merely emphasizing the unstable degrees of the scale—the seventh and fourth degrees—in the melody can be extremely poignant. 'Marie' begins with the seventh degree in the melody, supported by a very unstable harmony (dominant seventh in third inversion) and in the second phrase the melodic climax is the fourth degree, which also receives unstable support. Foster's style doesn't permit quite so unsettled a beginning, but his second phrase poignantly emphasizes both the seventh and fourth degrees. (A closer parallel to 'Marie' is the opening phrase of Scott Joplin's 'Solace', see Example 1.9(*c*)). The choruses of the two songs are strikingly parallel: a harmonic reduction shows nearly identical voice-leading (Example 1.9(*d*), (*e*)), though the rhythmic points at which the voices move vary.

The lyrics to 'Marie' play on the idealized, sentimental view of women and of love that characterize the work of Foster and other nineteenth-century songwriters:

> You looked like a princess the night we met
> With your hair piled up high—I will never forget
> I'm drunk right now, baby, but I've got to be
> Or I never could tell you what you mean to me
> > I loved you the first time I saw you
> > And I always will love you, Marie (*twice*)
>
> You're the song the trees sing when the wind blows
> You're a flower, you're a river, you're a rainbow
> Sometimes I'm crazy, but I guess you know
> I'm weak and I'm lazy, and I've hurt you so
> And I don't listen to a word you say
> When you're in trouble, I just turn away
> > But I love you, and I loved you the first time I saw you
> > And I always will love you, Marie (*twice*)

Ex. 1.9 *cont.*

(*d*) The choruses of 'Marie' and (*e*) 'Voices That Are Gone'

Marie is set on a pedestal—she is compared to a princess, a flower, a river, a rainbow—but we learn nothing about who she *really* is. The man who sings this song seems more involved with his own feelings of guilt and unworthiness than he is with Marie as a person. Yet he says he loves her and probably does: on one level this is a heart-felt love song. But on another level it is an ironic commentary on the strange meanings the word love can assume.

The Hollywood Connection: Prairie Pandiatonicism, Uncle Alfred, and the Question of Taste

I have left until last a detailed consideration of the bridge to 'I Think It's Going to Rain Today' (see Example 1.1). The extended non-functional tonal language of this section is not part of the technique of most musicians, and it is not surprising that many of the cover versions of this song either rewrite this section or leave it out entirely. Writing of this sort—sometimes called pandiatonicism—employs diatonic, tonal-sounding melodic and harmonic elements, but systematically destroys any sense of tonal hierarchy or harmonic functionality by juxtaposing elements from opposing triads (for example, in bar 1 of the bridge, C major is suggested in the bass clef while G major is implied in the treble clef). Dynamic tonal progressions are thus collapsed into a single sonority, neutralizing tonal hierarchies and holding all the pitches of the diatonic scale in suspension, so that no element predominates. This can be thought of as a further extension of the thirdless harmony that we noted in the cadence of the verse. But the circle-of-fifths bass-line in that cadence still kept it within the realm of functional tonality: here bass-line and melody alike have been cut free from tonal functions. The rhythm and contour of bars 1–4 of the bridge recall the opening idea of the verse, but it is like an 'exploded view' of that idea, tonally disoriented, as though the gravity had been shut off and the music were floating in free fall. This agitated, restless, disoriented music says all the things that the persona of the song is unable to express, other than by repeating the single word, 'lonely'.

The roots of this pandiatonicism are in the music of Stravinsky and other composers active in Paris in the early twentieth century. Through the medium of Paris composition teacher Nadia Boulanger and her American students such as Aaron Copland and Virgil Thomson, this technique became one of the cornerstones of the populist style in American concert music of the 1920s and 1930s. But a more direct source of Newman's pandiatonicism is probably his family ties to the movie industry. Alfred Newman, his uncle, is the composer of scores for over 250 films, and was head of the music department of Twentieth-Century Fox for many years. Two other uncles, Lionel and Emil Newman, are also involved in film music, and Randy himself has scored two recent productions: *Ragtime* (1980) and *The Natural* (1984). Hollywood composers are typically well-trained in the western European tradition—Arnold Schönberg was one of Alfred Newman's teachers—and they typically make use of a wide range of styles and genres, drawing from classical as well as popular traditions, to evoke particular associations and moods. In this sense, Randy Newman was thinking like a film composer long before he actually began scoring films. Greil Marcus puts it well:

> The movie music side of Newman's songs grows out of a tradition so well absorbed by generations of film fans that by now it seems completely American, regardless of its classy European antecedents . . . He uses the familiarity of the music to set us in the moods and situations the music automatically calls up; we respond in predictable ways to the music, and as we do, Newman's words and his singing pull us in other directions, or shift the story just enough to make it new. (Marcus 1982: 116–17)

As Marcus notes, it is often the striking contrast between the voice and the words on one hand, and the musical setting on the other, that gives Newman's songs their power. His own film music, as heard on soundtrack albums, is always well-crafted and at times quite lovely (for example, the title music for *Ragtime*, a haunting slow waltz (!)), but, like most film music, it can also be rather commonplace and one-dimensional. Heard in context as a part of the film, however, the music functions perfectly, deftly underlining the emotional tone of the scenes. In his own songs Newman's music is more effective because he has control of the entire work of art, and since his songs are miniature stories, this extends beyond music, words, and singing to include characterization, scene-setting, and plot line. The unsavoury, morally despicable characters frequently portrayed in his songs are made more real to us through the music, which reveals the continuity between their inner world and our own. In 'Suzanne' (1970) we hear a rapist crooning to his intended victim: the music reveals his seductiveness (the relaxed country beat and lyrical steel guitar fills) as well as his menace (the creepy, dissonant organ harmonies). It is almost as if we could hear the music that runs through his head as he waits for Suzanne in the shadows. In 'Sail Away' the slave-ship owner's image of America is coloured with glowing orchestration that makes it seem like a true vision of the promised land. And the bridge to 'I Think It's Going to Rain', whose style is particularly close to the Coplandesque manner often used in Hollywood to portray the wide open spaces of the American prairie, is just right for the mood of emptiness, desolation, and disorientation portrayed in the text.

The subtlety and appropriateness of Newman's Hollywoodisms can better be appreciated if we consider a counter-example: a performance by Joe

Cocker of 'I Think It's Going to Rain Today' (1975). Curiously enough, this arrangement uses the bridge as Newman wrote it, though it is played fortissimo, grandioso by strings doubled by brass and piano, while Joe Cocker bawls 'Lonely! Lonely!' as though he were Charlton Heston suffering the wrath of God. The arrangement as a whole (by Jim Price and Peggy Sandvig) is an interesting grab-bag of Americana. It begins with a violin section playing a newly-composed, pentatonic melody over the chord changes of Newman's verse, which ends with a Broadway-ish modulation up a whole step. Cocker sings the first two verses against a moderate rock beat with interjections from lead guitar and the string section. The irregular rhythm at the cadence of the verse (bars 8–9) is smoothed out and modified to end on a suspended dominant chord which is the occasion for drum fills and upward flourishes in the strings and lead guitar. At the end of the Cecil B. DeMille version of the bridge, a soulful gospel trio (modelled after Ray Charles' Raelets) is added. They kick the tempo back into high gear, singing against a funky bass a verse I haven't heard elsewhere (and suspect is not Newman's work):

> Mornin' Sun risin' on an empty avenue
> No surprise memorizin' faces I once knew

Cocker re-enters for the final verse, which, after a slower reprise of the final couplet, leads to a coda which must be heard to be believed (Example 1.10(*a*)). A solo horn intones a motive from the added theme that began the track, answered by strings playing very progressive-sounding altered chords. A solo violin sweetly intones a Steven Fosterish pentatonic phrase which is answered by an exultant 'yeah, yeah, yeah, yeah' from the gospel group. This call and response is repeated with even greater fervour, and the track ends with the full orchestra playing a grandiose fanfare that modulates down a step at the last possible moment.

This little extravaganza is an assemblage evoking a variety of American traditions: rock 'n' roll, gospel music, nineteenth-century popular song, Hollywood—the same ingredients we have found in Newman's own recordings. But, to put it as kindly as possible, the recipe isn't working here. Why does it fail? There are several problems, one being simple lack of technical competence. The writing for strings and horns is primitive, with mechanical, muddy-sounding doubling of parts. The newly-composed tune that serves as a prelude is a good demonstration of how cramped and limited a pentatonic melody can sound if it lacks a sense of direction, and the alteration between major and minor third (also heard in the coda, Example 1.10*a*, bars 1, 2)

Ex 1.10. (a) The coda to Joe Cocker's version of 'I Think It's Going to Rain Today' (arranged by Jim Price and Peggy Sandvig); (b) Newman's string arrangement for verses 2 and 3 of 'I Think It's Going to Rain Today'

would perhaps have been thought a hip, bluesy touch in Paul Whiteman's day. But, more fundamentally, one wonders what the point of this arrangement is: what do the rock beat, the hosannas, and the fanfares contribute to the meaning of this song? I can only guess that the intention is to put the song in a more positive light and give it a Hollywood happy ending, turning the bitter irony of Newman's last verse into a hymn to human brotherhood. The appropriateness of this reinterpretation is dubious, but we have yet to mention the most fundamental problem with the arrangement: it doesn't know when to stop. It lacks Randy Newman's secret ingredient: economy.

Newman's economy (one is tempted to say minimalism, but that would be simply a trendy, *avant-garde* interest in repetitive musical processes; the kind of simplicity Newman practices is in an older tradition that includes figures as disparate as Beethoven, Webern, and Count Basie) can be seen in all aspects of his work: his laconic, terse lyrics whose impact often lies in what is left unsaid; his simple, pentatonic melodies; the clarity of his harmonic writing, with its impeccable voice-leading; and the style of his arrangements. His own arrangement of 'I Think It's Going to Rain' (1968) begins with solo piano for the first verse, then uses a string orchestra (*not* doubled by piano!) for the remainder of the song. The setting of the bridge is a literal transcription of the original piano part (see Example 1.1); and the second and third verses are supported by a string part whose subtle counterpoint enriches the harmonies with suspensions and passing tones without destroying its basic diatonic character (Example 1.10(*b*)). While one couldn't exactly call the setting simple, it is understated and free of the usual clichés of pop string arrangements, and it adds a touch of sweetness and melancholy to the bleak atmosphere of the song. In a word, the arrangement is tasteful. Good taste is not always appropriate in popular music, and especially when he deals with such matters as bigotry or sexual perversion (to mention two of his favourite topics) Newman's lyrics can be exuberantly tasteless. But the music itself always manages to avoid triteness or banality, even when Newman is working with deliberately commonplace materials.

Conclusions: Newman's Americana

I hope that the reader has not been unduly disoriented by the rather scatter-shot approach of this essay. In an attempt to present a comprehensive picture of Randy Newman's musical style I have made abrupt jumps from song to song, and from comparison to comparison. I have employed a variety of analytical approaches without taking the time to outline theoretical justifications for those approaches. The hope is that the consistency of Newman's style itself provides the thread of continuity that ties together all of these observations, and that the analytical ends justify the theoretical means. I may have given the misleading impression that Newman's style is fixed and unchanging. In fact, there have been significant changes: the 'prairie pan-diatonicism' discussed earlier, for example, dropped out of his songs (but not his film scores) after 1968. And in his most recent work he uses synthesizers frequently, and his harmonic language more often uses the sorts of modal progressions found in mainstream rock.[4] But from his earliest music to his most recent, one can always detect a distinct, individual musical voice.

Let me return one last time to Newman's lyrics. Their subject matter, as we have seen, is the darker side of American life: the decay of our cities, the collapse of the family, bigotry, chauvinism, perversion, etc. One might wonder how such songs could appeal to any but the most hardened cynic. But two crucial factors keep Newman's songs from falling into a *National Lampoon*-like attitude of total nihilism. For one thing, no matter how depraved Newman's characters are, they are portrayed without condescension, and often with outright affection—the songs seem to ask, 'are you and I really any better?' And for all its use of allusion, the music never degenerates into mere stylistic parody. The musical traditions Randy Newman evokes are always treated with loving respect, and the music often betrays a sensuousness and romanticism that rarely surfaces in the lyrics. Though his view of American society is bleak and pessimistic, Newman's music is an affirmation and celebration of the richness and variety of American musical life.

References

Chopin, F. *Preludes, Op. 28*.
Foster, S. (1974). *Songs of Stephen Foster* (New York).
Jackson, R. (ed.) (1976). *Favourite Songs of Nineteenth-Century America* (New York).
Johnson, J. W., and Johnson, J. Rosamond (1956). *The Book of American Negro Spirituals* (New York).
Laing, D. (1985). *One-Chord Wonders: Power and Meaning in Punk Rock* (Milton Keynes).

[4] For more on the difference between the harmonic language of rock and older popular styles, see Winkler 1984.

Marcus, G. (1982). *Mystery Train—Images of America in Rock 'n' Roll Music* (revised edn.) (New York).

Newman, R. (1975). *Words and Music by Randy Newman* (New York).

Niles, J. J. (1960). *The Ballad Book of John Jacob Niles* (New York).

Tagg, P. (1979). *Kojak: 50 Seconds of Television Music* (Gothenburg).

Titon, J. T. (1977). *Early Downhome Blues, A Musical and Cultural Analysis* (Urbana).

Winkler, P. (1978). 'Toward a theory of popular harmony', *In Theory Only*, 4: 2.

—— (1984). 'The harmonic language of rock' (abstract, without musical examples), *Sonneck Society Newsletter*, Vol X. (Boulder).

Discography

Charles, R. (1966). 'Let's Go Get Stoned', ABC 1080; reissued on ABCS-590X, *A Man and His Soul* and elsewhere.

Cocker, J. (1975). 'Lucinda' and 'I Think It's Going to Rain Today', from *Jamaica Say You will*, A&M SP 4529.

Collins, J. (1966). 'I Think It's Going to Rain Today', From *In My Life*, Elektra EKS 7320.

Cooke, S. (1954). 'Jesus I'll Never Forget', from *The Gospel Soul of Sam Cooke with the Soul Stirrers*, Speciality 2116.

Domino, F. (1956). 'I'm in Love Again', Imperial 5386. Numerous reissues.

Dylan, B. (1965). 'Ballad of a Thin Man', from *Highway 61 Revisited*, Columbia CS 9189.

Lee, P. (1969). 'Is That All There Is?' (Jerry Lieber and Mike Stoller), Capitol 2602.

Melanie (Safka). (1974). 'I Think It's Going to Rain Today', from *Madrugada*, Neighborhood NRS 48001.

Newman, R. (1968). *Randy Newman*, Reprise RS 6286.

—— (1970). *12 Songs*, Reprise RS 6373.

—— (1971). *Live*, Reprise 6459.

—— (1972). *Sail Away*, Reprise MS2064.

—— (1974). *Good Old Boys*, Reprise MS2193.

—— (1977). *Little Criminals*, Warner Bros. BSK 3079.

—— (1979). *Born Again*, Warner Bros. RS 3346.

—— (1980). Music for *Ragtime*, Elektra 565.

—— (1983). *Trouble in Paradise*, Warner Bros I-23744.

—— (1984). Music for *The Natural*, Warner Bros 1-25116.

—— (1987). *¡Three Amigos!* (soundtrack), Warner Bros 2558-1.

2

....

Prince: Harmonic Analysis of 'Anna Stesia'

STAN HAWKINS

Musically, it (*Lovesexy*) is probably the most complex and unconventional body of work he (Prince) has ever produced. The dense undergrowth of twists and disjunctures to which even the most structured songs are subjected brings to mind once again the extended jam rehearsal technique Prince has always favoured. (Hill 1989: 210)

'Anna Stesia', off the album *Lovesexy* (1988), offers up a wealth of innovative and thought-provoking harmonic ideas for analysis. My purpose is to explore the harmonic thread running through the musical fabric of this song, with a view to exposing a number of techniques that govern and control it. Through a series of analytical procedures it is my intention to examine the intrinsic harmonic qualities of the song, and to assess the effects these have on its meaning.

As with all Prince's output, stark dualities exist between simplicity and complexity of gesture within almost every conceivable parameter. In 'Anna Stesia', Prince pleads, 'praise me, ravish me', portraying himself as a 'rapacious subject of desire and fey object of bliss' (Reynolds 1990: 50). 'In an escalation of his personal theology to a crusading intensity, refined lust and a love of the Lord are lavishly celebrated as synonymous' (Hill 1989: 210).

Against this backdrop, to what extent does the harmony reflect the ideological sentiments of the song, and to what extent is it indeed possible to analyse the harmonic 'nuts and bolts' of, what may at first, deceptively, appear, a straightforward structure?

As a starting-point to my analysis, I have devised a semiotic, transcript table (see Table 2.1) to identify the principal musical components directly

I would like to thank Lynne Sharma (University College Salford—music librarian) and John Gill (Mekons).

Table 2.1

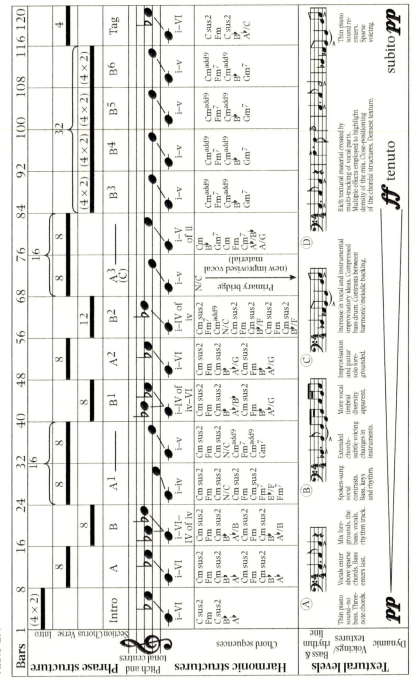

pertinent to the harmonic structure of 'Anna Stesia'. This facilitates an instant overview of the song in its entirety, and functions to classify and locate the numerous component characteristics and interrelationships directly affecting the harmonic structure at any given point.

With reference to Table 2.1, the 'phrase' structure indicated below the bar numbers is representative of the formal, skeletal framework of the song. It is the fusion and organization of these phrases in a specific order that fastens and shapes 'Anna Stesia' into its 'complex' binary form.[1] The duration of these phrases mainly comprises eight-bar units, a conventional length in most songs. Significantly, however, a break in the symmetrical shape occurs towards the centre of the song, with the emergence of a twelve-bar phrase at bar 56, which includes a four-bar chorus hook and an eight-bar 'primary bridge'. At this point the vocal part becomes distinctly more excitable and improvisational, whilst superimposed over the main chord sequence. This passage might also be viewed as a C section due to the departure from the eight-bar phrase structure, although, however, the harmonic material does not undergo any noticeable changes. In relation to the rest of the song, this alteration in the structural layout serves to enhance the tension within the music, heighten the emphasis on the lyrics, and break the rigidity of a tightly controlled, repetitive symmetrical form. In representing the climactic point of the song, an extended thirty-two bar chorus (B^3, B^4, B^5, B^6), bars 84–116, signals a number of salient harmonic (as well as numerous other musical and lyrical) changes, which receive closer attention later on in this essay. The song concludes with a four-bar tag, based on the introductory material.

Moving on to the next section of the Table, it becomes evident that the song is self-contained within a common song format, the complex binary form:

intro– A B A^1 B^1 A^2 B^2 –primary bridge (A^3)– B^3 B^4 B^5 B^6 – tag

Generally, the A sections comprise the verse, whilst the B sections represent the choruses.[2] These alternating phrases function as units, linking all the patterns of harmonic events together. It is noteworthy that the verse A^3 (bars 68–84), which functions as a primary bridge, introduces new ideas in an electric guitar solo passage, whilst the chorus section—B^3 B^4, B^5,

---

[1] Binary form is one of the most common structures found in popular music song, and is usually determined by structural and stylistic content. As a rule it follows a straightforward A B scheme, with each section being repeated. 'Complex binary' form includes numerous extensions of sections or elaborations of the simpler format, which in the case of 'Anna Stesia' is exemplified by the primary bridge solo section, bars 68–74, and the repeated B section chorus from bar 84–116. Note that the verse (A) in this song functions predominantly as an introduction to the chorus (B).

[2] Digits to the top right of each letter denote the variations within the original phrases.

B⁶—involves eight repetitions of a chord sequence, in which jam-style, free-improvisational ideas occur.

Contrasting levels of musical and harmonic interest are skilfully regulated by the subtle variations within each phrase. It is the change of harmonic content from one phrase to the next that becomes the basis for further analytical attention.

The principal pitch and tone centres derived from the harmonic and melodic material throughout the song, are identified in the next section of the Table. These comprise the most influential harmonic reference points, serving to gravitate the music towards the specific root centres within each phrase.

In scrutinizing Table 2.1, it becomes evident that the pitch C, in its movement to the pitches A♭, B♭, F, and G at the end of phrases, occupies a foremost position in the song. With regard to their harmonic functions, each of these pitches is designated by traditional roman numeral nomenclature.

Classification of every chord, as it occurs within its progression, becomes one of the main areas for examination within Table 2.1. It should be noted that C minor derived chords (Cm^{sus2}, Cm, and Cm^{add9}) occupy all the starting positions in every sequence. The functioning and positioning of these tonic chords, in harmonic terms, warrants further analysis at a later stage. A scan reveals some five chords inherent within the structure (excluding the tonic variants and inversions), which might seem fairly normal in quantity for a pop song. However, in the economy of these chords lies a sophisticated harmonic formation. Perhaps, most significantly, in demonstrating the economical employment and choice of chords in 'Anna Stesia', this section additionally identifies the resulting subtleties of texture and colour in the harmony.

Four predominant bass and rhythmic motifs are identified in the following section of Table 2.1.[3] These ideas play a leading role in driving the harmonic line and other musical material. Whilst contributing to the rhythmic feel of the music, these thematic cells constitute an integral part of the harmony by reinforcing the root pitches and scales of the home key. In addition, they function as punctuation points in binding the dotted, funk-rhythm with the contrasting 'straight feel' of the kit line.

Table 2.1 concludes with a brief, written description of the extra-harmonic musical events within each phrase. Following this, a crescendo hairpin symbol

---

[3] Note the interrelationships between these motifs: the d) riff cell actually comprises a fusion of cells a) and c).

registers the general level of dynamic intensity throughout the song. More-over, this also relates to the gradual increase in musical activity, from the sparse material in the beginning to the fuller and more energetic final chorus section (B^3 to B^6) at the end. Dissection of the song into these relevant sections is meant to provide a restatement of the harmonic structure, and in addition, to prompt a more detailed investigation of the harmonic properties of the musical text.

Chords

The consistent recurrence of C minor-type chords (Cm^{sus2}, Cm, C^{add9}) in tonic position throughout 'Anna Stesia' has already been illustrated in Table 2.1. The unique and harmonically neutral quality of the C^{sus2} chord can be attributed to a number of factors, including the absence of a major or minor third, its frequent dotted harmonic rhythm, and its timbral treatment (a thin, almost feeble, electric piano sound). Continuous employment of the minor third pitch, E♭, in the vocal part, significantly affects the quality of the C^{sus2} chord by enhancing its minor-modal flavour. This, therefore, warrants a more precise description of the chord as Cm^{sus2}, rather than C^{sus2} (see Example 2.1). Apart from the introduction and tag, bars 116–20, the C^{sus2} never surfaces without the pitch E♭ forming an integral part of its structure.

Movement from the C minor chords at the beginning of phrases to the chords A♭, B♭, Fm, and Gm at the end, contributes to the song's distinctly modal flavouring. With the continuous movement back to the ubiquitous Cm^{sus2} chord at the beginning of phrases, any traditional resolutions at the end of phrases never takes place.[4] The avoidance of any clichéd or predictable cadences establishes an element of unresolved tension and harmonic uncertainty; this simultaneously serves to enhance the mood of the lyrics.

Ex 2.1. Cm^{sus2} or C^{sus2}

[4] Such resolutions are characteristic of much traditional diatonic harmony. The absence of such devices in this song further supports the original and unconventional manipulation of harmony by Prince.

Through a process of cyclical repetition, created by the continuous return to the tonic chord on the first beat of each cellular sequence, it is significant that the cadence V⁷–I never occurs.[5] The almost extreme extent to which circular sequential patterns become a harmonic metaphor for the restless nature of the lyrics is epitomized in the final thirty-two-bar chorus sequence.

The harmonic structure of 'Anna Stesia' compactly fits into an original modal framework. This use of modality, in contrast to diatonic harmony, is by no means unique in pop and rock music (the Aeolian mode, for example, has been identified as a prevalent feature by musicologist Alf Björnberg[6]), but the specific ways in which modality is manipulated and organized within 'Anna Stesia' assume central importance in this analysis. As with most modality, the harmonic features of 'Anna Stesia', on first hearing, seem to occupy a transitional space between tonality and modality. The subdominant F minor chord, prominent throughout, and always clasped in between the tonic chord, Cm^{sus2}, temporarily suggests a diatonic minor tonality.

Until such time that the B♭ major chord (VII of C Aeolian) has firmly established itself as an intrinsic feature of the harmony, tonal or modal ambiguity remains an issue very much in the foreground. It is the continual recurrence of the B♭ and A♭ major chords that ultimately dispel any diatonic possibilities. Although at a stretch, B♭ major and A♭ major chords might qualify as secondary dominants and subdominants, respectively, of the relative major, E♭ major.

Given that the C minor-based chords form the central axis around which the other chords revolve, and, that there is a noticeable absence of a dominant seventh chord (with the raised leading tone, in this case a B natural), the case for modality is strengthened. Furthermore, the inclusion of principal chords constructed on the seventh degree (B♭ major), the sixth degree (A♭ major), and the fourth degree (F minor), in direct association with the scale source of C D E♭ F G A♭ B♭—from which most of the melodic material is derived—clearly enforces the C Aeolian mode. All things considered, with the exception of A dominant seventh (A⁷), the chords that occur in the song all, undoubtedly, belong to this mode (see Example 2.2).

Prince's subtle and masterly control of harmony is further exemplified by the detail in his chordal voicings and positionings. The transformation of the

---

[5] Note that V⁷–I implies the dominant seventh, with raised leading note. The V⁷m^{add9}, which occurs in the gospel chorus (bars 84–116) is actually non-diatonic in its feel. This is a result of the absence of the leading note.

[6] Björnberg (1989) links various chord sequences, such as I–♭III–IV and I–IV–♭VII with blues minor pentatonic scales in various branches of popular music.

Ex 2.2. Modal chords in 'Anna Stesia'

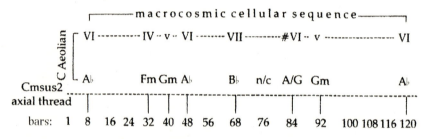

Figure 2.1 Macrocosmic cellular sequence

C minor chords, for example, from Cm^{sus2} in the beginning to Cm^{add9} in the gospel chorus section (bars 84–116), by the inclusion of a minor third with the superimposed minor ninth interval,[7] greatly alters the entire harmonic feel of the song. The transition from a suspended chord (Cm^{sus2}) to a triadic structure with the added ninth (Cm^{add9}), symbolizes a definite arrival point within both the musical and ideological meaning of the song.

Viewed from another perspective, the harmonic layout of 'Anna Stesia' includes a number of significant chordal shifts at various 'non-diatonic' cadence points throughout the song (see Table 2.1). These function as temporary excursions away from the home modal centre of C Aeolian, providing a release from the harmonic tension of the central tonic chord. Moreover, the cadential chord changes could be perceived as part of a larger macrocosmic sequence, held together by the Cm^{sus2} axial thread. The macrocosmic sequence, as illustrated in Figure 2.1, consists of the progression, VI–IV–v–VI–VII–♯VI–v–VI in C Aeolian. With the single exception of the chord A^7 (♯VI),[8] all the chords are directly related to the home mode. Within the

---

[7] The superimposed minor 9th interval constitutes the same note as the suspended 2nd, pitch D. In other words, the chord, Cm^{add9}, is altered simply by the addition of one pitch.

[8] Note that A^7 occurs in third inversion, A/G. This enhances its role as a passing, pivot-type chord, with the bass note (G) resolving to the C (perfect fifth) on the next chord (Cm^{add9}).

c.s.A = Cm(sus2) – Fm – Cm(sus2) (b. 1–68)

c.s.A1 = c.s.A + B♭ – A♭

c.s.A2 = c.s.A + B♭ – A♭/B♭

c.s.A3 = c.s.A + Cm^{add9} – Fm7 – Cm^{add9} – Gm7

c.s.A4 = c.s.A + B♭ – A♭/G

c.s.A5 = c.s.A + B♭/F

c.s.B = Cm + B♭ + Gm7 + Cm + Fm + Cm(7) + A♭/B♭ + A/G (b. 68–84)
— c.s.A —

c.s.C = Cm(^{add9}) + Fm(7) + Cm(^{add9}) + B♭ + Gm7 (b. 84–20)
— c.s.A —

Figure 2.2 Extensional transformation of c.s.A.

duration of one minim, bar 84, the A^7 chord suggests a modulatory departure from C Aeolian modality. Not only does this chord serve to heighten the
tension at this climactic moment in the song, but it also prompts the resolution to the newly voiced tonic chord, Cm^{add9}, in the following gospel chorus
passage. The macrocosmic cellular sequence, therefore, holds the key to the
broader plan of harmonic events in 'Anna Stesia'.

Up to now, we have observed how 'Anna Stesia' comprises a formation of
chordal cells which are linked into larger units. The particular order of these
sequences reveals the harmonic structure of the song. Each sequence carries a specific code relating to the harmony. In further analysing the harmonic growth of the song, it is possible to trace the evolution of most of the
chordal ideas through the scrutiny of one, single progression—Cm+Fm+Cm
—which is referred to as cellular sequence A (c.s.A) in Figure 2.2. This
sequence, which embraces the tonic and subdominant chords, undergoes a
number of extensional transformations during the course of the song. The
subtle variations in harmonic shades of each chord strand, therefore, stem
from the principal sequence, c.s.A. Within this relatively simple framework,
the sequences, c.s.A, c.s.B, and c.s.C serve to create a multi-faceted circuit
of harmonic patterns.

Studio Work

Responding to the aesthetics of the mix is crucial to the analysis of the
structure of any song realized in a recording studio. The harmonic analysis
of 'Anna Stesia' could hardly be complete without at least acknowledging
the role of studio production from a compositional perspective; there is an

inextricable link between the musical and recording parameters. The overall structure of the song, whilst being held together by numerous factors, is controlled and generated primarily by studio devices and processes.

With respect to the broader vertical density of the musical structure, the harmony might, then, be considered as a product of the mix. This conclusion is borne out of the common knowledge that Prince creatively uses his own studio, the famous Paisley Park, as an integral compositional tool. The expert blending of ideas within 'Anna Stesia' embraces a wide spectrum of sophisticated and highly discretionary recording techniques, which greatly influence and intensify the harmonic treatment. Through his complete command of the studio, Prince manages to create a three-dimensional image, which constantly transforms, changing colour and position within an audio space. Although it is not possible, or indeed that relevant, to pinpoint precisely the exact studio procedures and processes employed, it is likely, however, that the song incorporates a number of the following techniques.

The creative use of signal processing is greatly enhanced by equalization, which serves to locate and place each instrument in its own unique band of frequencies. A gradual overlap of frequency bands is then employed to fill up the entire audio spectrum. In 'Anna Stesia', this serves to increase the 'apparent' loudness without actually altering the overall volume. The aural separation of individual sounds has a significant effect on the harmony by enhancing specific key pitches at particular moments. An example of this is the coupling of the synth bass with the brightly eq'd (equalized) kick drum, especially towards the climactic part of the song. This results in an overlapping of frequency bands stretching the bass pitches into the mid-range. It has a direct bearing on the tonic notes occurring in the bass, which purposely serve to reinforce the root notes of the harmony.

The harmonizer or pitch shifter (a digital effects-unit present in any modern studio) is used with feedback to shift the pitch and expand the frequency range occupied by the voice. As well as increasing the volume by consuming a broader range of frequencies, this also serves to transpose solo lines at any desired pitch above, below or equal with the original. Octave pitch shift results in intervallic transpositional treatment of backing vocals, as is evident in the gospel chorus. This increases the effectiveness of the harmonies by broadening and expanding the apparent range of frequencies and densities occupied by the voice, thus creating a distinctive texture. The harmonizer is utilized to manipulate sound in such a way that the lead vocals, for example, can be distinctly separated from the backing vocals. It is likely that in the first chorus, bars 16–24, this device has been used to shift the pitch up an interval of a fifth. The vocal lead line, mainly centred around the E♭ pitch, is supplemented by a dynamically softer line exactly a fifth above throughout this chorus. Harmonically, this added pitch influences both the voicing and structure of the chords, so that, rather than the Cm^{sus2}–Fm–Cm^{sus2} progression occurring here, to be more exact, we hear Cm^{7sus2}–Fm^{7add11}–Cm^{7sus2}. This substantiates the subtleties of the mix and the effect it has on the harmonic flavour.

The success of the mix in 'Anna Stesia' is largely dependent on the analogue compressor which is used to emphasize a multitude of musical qualities in the song. Aspects such as breathing and unsung vocal sounds, bass and kit lines, brass stabs, guitar solo, and keyboard riffs are all compressed. This eliminates the natural dynamics, greatly enhancing the loudness and clarity of the track.

Prince often records his vocal and instrumental tracks twice or more on separate tracks creating very slight delays and discrepancies in time. The entire balance, control, reinforcement, and manipulation of sound through the mixer is a determining factor in shaping the harmonic structure. The sheer density of the polyphonic texture and the use of multi-tracking within the final chorus section suggests that Prince has purposely saved up all his forces for this moment.

Stereophony also assists in sculpturing the sound by enhancing the textural and timbral contrasts through panning processes. The use of differing amounts of reverb and positional information, for example, on the lead brass stabs creates a very hard sound, whilst the other keyboards are eq'd in a slightly more mellow and soft fashion. Further reverbs are employed, with very short decay times (nothing more than 1.5–2.0″ RT.60[9]) in the lead vocals and a number of underlying keyboard lines. This provides a sense of depth and, in conjunction with the musical and lyrical connotations, suggests a constantly moving object by foregrounding, backgrounding, and generally illuminating the sound.

The main piano line, which transports the central harmonic message (c.s.A), is modulated in a way to simulate tape flutter, softening the overall sound, and introducing more harmonics into the overall texture. This piano

---

[9] 'RT' means 'reverberation time'. 'RT60' is the time that sound takes to decay by 60 decibels from its peak amplitude. In concert halls, for example, typical RT60 times are from 1.5 to 3 seconds.

Ex 2.3. Prolongation of chord A♭/C

part functions as a dominant textural and harmonic centre, embodying all the vocals, keyboards, and guitar tracks; it introduces and concludes the piece, as well as running all the way through; it symbolizes the common point, the locus, which integrates all of the harmonic parts.

Meaning

Having examined the harmonic, structural, and procedural devices in detail, it is worth turning to the effects these have on the verbal text. The diverse range of emotions and meanings evoked by the lyrics, clearly work in close proximity with the contrasting levels of musical colour and intensity. Thematic collages of craving, searching, despairing, suffering, realization, and fulfilment, represent the expressive shadings endemic in the song. The main melodic ideas, which serve to complement the harmonic structure, are always simple and yet poignant, depicting a natural, naive beauty. They never detract from the clarity and meaning of the text.

Anna Stesia . . . has the loveliest tune, a low, swaying paen to the painless state that its punning title alludes to, decorated with zig-zagging guitar . . . (Hill 1989: 212)

Prince's play with the ambiguous, unrelenting, central sequence (c.s.A) for the first half of the song, is symbolic of his continuous craving for the girl, Anna Stesia. With every repetition of this sequence, the tension and passion of the music heightens as he searches for a solution. The Cm^{sus2} chord stands as a single, harmonic metaphor for the unsettled nature of the song up to its climactic resolution to Cm^{add9} in bar 84. Symbolically, the C^{sus2}, which subtlely converts to Cm^{sus2}, triggers off the song with the thin-sounding electric piano introduction (and concludes it with the same idea, with the exception of the last chord, A♭/C, which actually gives a sense of resolution through the prolongation of the bass note, C, in the mix—see Example 2.3). Underpinning and accompanying the melancholic lyrics in the vocal line of the opening question of the song—'have you ever been so lonely that U felt U were the only one in this world?'—the harmonic ideas from the introduction are continually repeated at a constant low dynamic level.

Moving towards the first chorus, 'Anna Stesia come 2 me, talk 2 me, ravish me, liberate my mind', the repetitions of harmonic ideas and lyrical themes start emerging as a central structural idiom. On first hearing, the repetition of progressions, sequences, and ideas might quite likely appear simple and bland. However, closer scrutiny of this song—as in the case of a large portion of pop songs—reveals that 'the total meaning of straightforward patterns of reiteration and recapitulation can often be more than their deceptive simplicity suggests' (Tagg 1982: 59). The musical portrayal of the image of desire for Anna Stesia is to be found in the main chorus hook, which is revisited and, as a result, reinforced by the continuous c.s.A sequence (Cm^{sus2}–Fm–Cm^{sus2}).

As the song progresses, the lyrical focus shifts from the carnal to the theological, a controversial thematic feature of Prince's output. Dave Hill explains this as Prince's 'apparent implication that overt, unburdened sexual expression and Christianity can accommodate each other . . .' (Hill 1989: 166). His pleading in the final verse (A^3), 'Save me Jesus, I've been a fool, How could I forget that You are the rule. You are my God, I am Your child . . .', signifies a departure from a sung to a more excitable, spoken text in the vocal track, during which the harmonic line almost vanishes (bars 68–76). This respite serves to enhance the text, while simultaneously providing a temporary platform for harmonic retrospection and anticipation.

The lyrics of the final verse, 'We're just a play in your masterplan, Now my Lord I understand' are nourished by the impending sense of harmonic change. This is finally achieved by the unexpected A^7 chord, which functions as a pivotal link. At this point the song experiences its moment of catharsis on all levels as it moves to its final point of destination, the gospel refrain. The resolution, via the A^7 chord, to the new, modified tonic chord of Cm^{add9}, serves as a concluding cadence, in which all the energy built up during the song is ecstatically unleashed. This chorus embraces a multitude of significant factors relating to the aesthetics of the song. Through the various repetitions of the newly transformed chord progression (c.s.C), Prince has summoned up all his forces to proclaim his 'non-conformist faith' (Hill 1989: 212). And in direct association with the allegorical connotations of the lyrics in the ultimate chorus, 'Love is God—God is Love—Girls and boys—love God above', the music and lyrics reach an unparalleled point of unification. Rather than ending on this note of elation, the four-bar tag then enters, serving as a gentle reminder of how this journey originally started.

An Afterthought

The selective procedures and assumptions of this article cannot be justified as an objective survey of the musical content of 'Anna Stesia'. They result more from the interaction between personal dimensions of musicological, analytical, and stylistic thought. My aim has not been to stake out the entire territory of the musical content, but to present methods by which *some* of the harmonic procedures can be identified. An underlying theme in my preoccupation with harmonic analysis in contemporary pop music is how it should be done—that it should involve an investigation related to social causes and programmatic effects is unquestionable. For this task, I believe that analysis has to instigate a codification of data resulting from processes of detailed listening, and, to this end, an awareness of our mental image of music as a living object is, in my opinion, the most critical factor.

References

Björnberg, A. (1989). 'On Aeolian harmony in contemporary popular music', IASPM-Nordic Branch Working Papers, DK 1 (Gothenburg).

Cutler, C. (1984). 'Technology, politics and contemporary music: necessity and choice in musical forms', *Popular Music*, 4: 279–300.

Hill, D. (1989). *Prince—A Pop Life* (London).

Kramer, J. D. (1988). *The Time of Music* (New York).

Middleton, R. (1990). *Studying Popular Music* (Milton Keynes).

Reynolds, S. (1990). *Blissed Out. The Raptures of Rock* (London).

Tagg, P. (1982). 'Analysing popular music—theory, method and practice', *Popular Music*, 2: 37–67, repr. in this volume.

—— (1979). *Kojak—50 Seconds of Television Music. Towards the Analysis of Affect in Popular Music* (Gothenburg).

Discography

Prince, 'Anna Stesia', *Lovesexy*. Paisley Park Records, 25720-1 (1988).

3

.....

Analysing Popular Music:
Theory, Method, and Practice

PHILIP TAGG

Popular Music Analysis—Why?

One of the initial problems for any new field of study is the attitude of incredulity it meets. The serious study of popular music is no exception to this
rule. It is often confronted with an attitude of bemused suspicion implying
that there is something weird about taking 'fun' seriously or finding 'fun' in
'serious things'. Such attitudes are of considerable interest when discussing
the aims and methods of popular music analysis and serve as an excellent
introduction to this essay.

In announcing the first International Conference on Popular Music
Research, held at Amsterdam in June 1981, *The Times Diary* printed the head-
line 'Going Dutch—The Donnish Disciples of Pop' (*The Times*, 16 June 1981).
Judging from the generous use of inverted commas, *sics* and 'would-you-
believe-it' turns of phrase, the *Times* diarist was comically baffled by the idea
of people getting together for some serious discussions about a phenomenon
which the average Westerner's brain probably spends around twenty-five per
cent of its lifetime registering, monitoring, and decoding. It should be added
that *The Times* was just as incredulous about ' "A Yearbook of Popular
Music" (sic)' (their *sic*), in which this 'serious' study of 'fun' first appeared.

In announcing the same conference on popular music research, the *New
Musical Express* (20 June 1981, p. 63) was so witty and snappy that the excerpt
can be quoted in full.

Meanwhile, over in Amsterdam this weekend, high foreheads from the four corners
of the earth (Sid and Doris Bonkers) will meet for the first International Conference
on Popular Music at the University of Amsterdam. In between the cheese and wine
parties, serious young men and women with goatee beards and glasses will discuss

such vitally important issues as 'God, Morality and Meaning in the Recent Songs of Bob Dylan'.[1] Should be a barrel of laughs . . .

This wonderfully imaginative piece of poetry is itself a great barrel of laughs to anyone present at the conference with its zero (0 per cent) wine and cheese parties, one (0.8 per cent) goatee beard, and a dozen (10 per cent) bespectacled participants. (As 'Sid Bonkers', I do admit to having worn contact lenses.) Talks were given by active rock musicians, by an ex-*NME* and *Rolling Stone* journalist, by radio people, and by Paul Oliver, who may have worn glasses but who, even if maliciously imagined with a goatee beard, horns, and a trident, has probably done more to increase respect, understanding, and enthusiasm for the music of black Americans than the *NME* is ever likely to.

This convergence of opinion between such unlikely bedfellows as *The Times* and the *NME* about the imagined incongruity of popular music as an area for serious study implies one of two things. Either popular music is so worthless that it should not be taken seriously (unlikely, since pop journalists obviously rely on the existence of popular music for their livelihood) or academics are so hopeless—absent-mindedly mumbling long Latin words under their mortarboards in ivory towers—that the prospect of them trying to deal with anything as important as popular music is just absurd. However, *The Times* and *NME* are not alone in questioning the ability of traditional scholarship to deal with popular music. Here they join forces with no mean number of intellectual musicians and musically interested academics.

Bearing in mind the ubiquity of music in industrialized capitalist society, its importance at both national and transnational levels (see Varis 1975; Chapple and Garofalo 1977; Frith 1978; *Fonogrammen i kulturpolitiken* 1979) and the share of popular music in all this, the incredible thing is not that academics should start taking the subject seriously but that they have taken such a time getting round to it. Until recently, publicly funded musicology has passively ignored the sociocultural challenge of trying to inform the record-buying, Muzak-registering, TV-watching, and video-consuming public 'why and how who'—from the private sector—'is communicating what to them'—in the public sector—'and with what effect' (apologies to C. S. Peirce). Even now it does very little.

Nevertheless, to view the academic world as being full of static and eternal ivory tower stereotypes is to reveal an ahistorical and strangely defeatist

---

[1] No such talk was on the conference programme! Actually it is the title of Wilfrid Mellers's article in *Popular Music 1* (1981: 143–57).

acceptance of the schizophrenic status quo in capitalist society. It implies atomization, compartmentalization, and polarization of the affective and the cognitive, of private and public, individual and collective, implicit and explicit, entertaining and worrying, fun and serious, etc. This 'never-the-twain-shall-meet' syndrome is totally untenable in the field of popular music (or the arts in general). One does not need to be a don to understand that there are objective developments in nineteenth- and twentieth-century music history which demand that changes be made, not least in academic circles.

These developments can be summarized as follows: (1) a vast increase in the share music takes in the money and time budgets of citizens in the industrialized world; (2) shifts in class structure leading to the advent of socioculturally definable groups, such as young people in student or unemployment limbo between childhood and adulthood, and their need for collective identity; (3) technological advances leading to the development of recording techniques capable (for the first time in history) of accurately storing and allowing for mass distribution of non-written musics; (4) transistorization, micro-electronics, and all that such advances mean to the mass dissemination of music; (5) the development of new musical functions in the audio-visual media (for example, films, TV, video, advertising); (6) the 'non-communication' crisis in modern Western art music and the stagnation of official music in historical moulds; (7) the development of a loud, permanent, mechanical lo-fi soundscape (see Schafer 1974, 1977) and its 'reflection' (see Riethmüller 1976) in electrified music with regular pulse (see Bradley 1980); (8) the general acceptance of certain Euro- and Afro-American genres as constituting a *lingua franca* of musical expression in a large number of contexts within industrialized society; (9) the gradual, historically inevitable replacement of intellectuals schooled solely in the art music tradition by others exposed to the same tradition but at the same time brought up on Presley, the Beatles, and the Stones.

To those of us who during the fifties and sixties played both Scarlatti and soul, did palaeography and Palestrina crosswords as well as working in steelworks, and who walked across quads on our way to the 'Palais' or the pop club, the serious study of popular music is not a matter of intellectuals turning hip or of mods and rockers going academic. It is a question of (*a*) getting together two equally important parts of experience, the intellectual and emotional, inside our own heads and (*b*) being able as music teachers to face pupils whose musical outlook has been crippled by those who present 'serious music' as if it could never be 'fun' and 'fun music' as though it could never have any serious implications.

Thus the need for the serious study of popular music is obvious, while the case for making it a laughing matter, although understandable (it *can* be hilarious at times), is basically reactionary and will be dispensed with for the rest of this essay. This is because the aim of what follows is to present a musicological model for tackling problems of popular music content analysis. It is hoped that this might be of some use to music teachers, musicians, and others looking for a contribution towards the understanding of 'why and how does who communicate what to whom and with what effect'.

Musicology and Popular Music Research

Studying popular music is an interdisciplinary matter. Musicology still lags behind other disciplines in the field, especially sociology. The musicologist is thus at a simultaneous disadvantage and advantage. The advantage is that he can draw on sociological research to give his analysis proper perspective. Indeed, it should be stated at the outset that no analysis of musical discourse can be considered complete without consideration of social, psychological, visual, gestural, ritual, technical, historical, economic, and linguistic aspects relevant to the genre, function, style, (re-)performance situation, and listening attitude connected with the sound event being studied. The disadvantage is that musicological 'content analysis' in the field of popular music is still an underdeveloped area and something of a missing link (see Schuler 1978).

Musical Analysis and the Communication Process

Let us assume music to be that form of interhuman communication in which individually experienceable affective states and processes are conceived and transmitted as humanly organized non-verbal sound structures to those capable of decoding their message in the form of adequate affective and associative response (see Tagg 1981*b*). Let us also assume that music, as can be seen in its modes of 'performance' and reception, most frequently requires by its very nature a *group* of individuals to communicate either among themselves or with another group; thus most music (and dance) has an intrinsically collective character not shared by the visual and verbal arts. This should mean that music is capable of transmitting the affective identities, attitudes, and behavioural patterns of socially definable groups, a phenomenon observed in studies of subcultures and used by North American radio to determine advertising markets (see Karshner 1971).

Now, although we have considerable insight into socioeconomic, subcultural, and psycho-social mechanisms influencing the 'emitter' (by means of biographies, etc.) and 'receiver' of certain types of popular music, we have very little explicit information about the nature of the 'channel', the music itself. We know little about its 'signifiers' and 'signifieds', about the relations the music establishes between emitter and receiver, about how a musical message actually relates to the set of affective and associative concepts presumably shared by emitter and receiver, and how it interacts with their respective cultural, social, and natural environments. In other words, reverting to the question 'why and how does who say what to whom and with what effect?', we could say that sociology answers the questions 'who', 'to whom' and, with some help from psychology, 'with what effect' and possibly parts of 'why', but when it comes to the rest of 'why', not to mention the questions 'what' and 'how', we are left in the lurch—unless musicologists are prepared to tackle the problem (see Wedin 1972: 128).

Popular Music, Notation, and Musical Formalism

There is no room here to start defining 'popular music' but in order to clarify the argument I shall establish an axiomatic triangle consisting of 'folk', 'art', and 'popular' musics. Each of these three is distinguishable from both of the others according to the criteria presented in Figure 3.1. The argument is that popular music cannot be analysed using only the traditional tools of musicology. This is because popular music, unlike art music, is (1) conceived for mass distribution to large and often socioculturally heterogeneous groups of listeners, (2) stored and distributed in non-written form, (3) only possible in an industrial monetary economy where it becomes a commodity, and (4) in capitalist societies, subject to the laws of 'free' enterprise, according to which it should ideally sell as much as possible of as little as possible to as many as possible. Consideration of these distinguishing marks implies that it is impossible to 'evaluate' popular music along some sort of Platonic ideal scale of aesthetic values and, more practically, that notation should not be the analyst's main source material. The reason for this is that while notation may be a viable starting point for much art music analysis, in that it was the only form of storage for over a millennium, popular music, not least in its Afro-American guises, is neither conceived nor designed to be stored or distributed as notation, a large number of important parameters of musical expression being either difficult or impossible to encode in traditional notation (see Tagg 1979: 28–31). This is however not the only problem.

Characteristic		Folk music	Art music	Popular music
Produced and transmitted by	primarily professionals		X	X
	primarily amateurs	X		
Mass distribution	usual			X
	unusual	X	X	
Main mode of storage and distribution	oral transmission	X		
	musical notation		X	
	recorded sound			X
Type of society in which the category of music mostly occurs	nomadic or agrarian	X		
	agrarian and industrial		X	
	industrial			X
Main twentieth-century mode of financing production and distribution of the music	independent of monetary economy	X		
	public funding		X	
	'free' enterprise			X
Theory and aesthetics	uncommon	X		X
	common		X	
Composer/author	anonymous	X		
	non-anonymous		X	X

Figure 3.1 Folk music, art music, popular music: an axiomatic triangle. (This model is an abbreviated version of a lengthy discussion in Tagg 1979: 20–7.)

Allowing for certain exceptions, traditional music analysis can be characterized as formalist and/or phenomenalist. One of its great difficulties (criticized in connection with the analysis of art music in Rösing 1977) is relating musical discourse to the remainder of human existence in any way, the description of emotive aspects in music either occurring sporadically or being avoided altogether. Perhaps these difficulties are in part attributable to such factors as (1) a kind of exclusivist guild mentality amongst musicians resulting in the inability and/or lack of will to associate items of musical expression with extramusical phenomena; (2) a time-honoured adherence to notation as the only viable form of storing music; (3) a culture-centric fixation on certain 'notatable' parameters of musical expression (mostly processual aspects such as 'form', thematic construction, etc.), which are particularly important to the Western art music tradition. This carries with it a nonchalance towards other parameters not easily expressed in traditional notation (mostly 'immediate' aspects such as sound, timbre, electromusical treatment, ornamentation, etc.), which are relatively unimportant—or ignored—in the analysis of art music but extremely important in popular music (see Rösing 1981).

Affect Theory and Hermeneutics

Despite the overwhelming dominance of the formalist tradition in university departments of musicology, such non-referential thinking should nevertheless as seen as a cultural and historical parenthesis, bordered on the one side by the baroque Theory of Affects and on the other by the hermeneutics of music (see Zoltai 1970: 137–215). Obviously, the normative aesthetic straitjacket of Affect Theory, a sort of combination of feudal absolutist thought and rationalist curiosity, and its apparent tendency to regard itself as universally applicable, render it unsuitable for application to the study of popular music, with its multitude of 'languages', ranging from film music in the late romantic symphonic style to punk and from middle-of-the-road pop to the Webernesque sonorities of murder music in TV thrillers. Musical hermeneutics, as a subjectivist, interpretative approach, is often violently and sometimes justifiably criticized and indeed it can from time to time degenerate into exegetic guesswork and intuitively acrobatic 'reading between the lines'. (Good examples of this are to be found in Cohn 1970: 54–5, Melzer 1970: 104, 153, and Mellers 1973: 117–18.) Nevertheless, hermeneutics can, if applied with slightly greater discretion and in combination with other musicological sub-disciplines, especially the sociology and semiology of music, make an important contribution to the analysis of popular music. In short: a rejection of hermeneutics will result in sterile formalism while its unbridled application can degenerate into unscientific guesswork.

The Semiology and Sociology of Music

The transfer of structuralist and semiotic methods, derived from linguistics, to the realm of music seemed to offer considerable possibilities for the understanding of musical messages (see Bernstein 1976). However, several musicologists of semiotic bent (Lerdahl and Jackendoff 1977; Keiler 1978; Stoïanova 1978) have pointed to the obvious but overlooked fact that models constructed to explain the structure of semantic, denotative, and cognitive verbal language cannot be transplanted wholesale to the epistemology of music with its associative and affective character (see Shepherd 1977). Unfortunately, a great deal of linguistic formalism has crept into the semiology of music, the extra-generic question of relationships between musical signifier and signified and between the musical object under analysis and society being either regarded with intradisciplinary scepticism as intellectually suspect or as subordinate to congeneric relations inside the musical object itself (see, for example, Nattiez 1974: 72–3). However, instead of establishing such opposition between extra-generic (emic, referential, hermeneutic, multidisciplinary) and congeneric (etic, non-referential, formalist, uni-disciplinary) approaches, it seems wiser to treat these two lines of reasoning as complementary rather than contra-dictory. In this way it will be possible to establish relations (extragenerically) between given items of musical code and their respective fields of extramu-sical association and (congenerically) between these various individual parts of the musical code as processual structures.

The empirical sociology of music, apart from having acted as a sorely needed alarm clock, rousing musicologists from their culture-centric and ethnocentric slumbers, and notifying them of musical habits amongst the population at large, can also provide valuable information about the functions, uses, and (with the help of psychology) the effects of the genre, performance or mu-sical object under analysis. In this way, results from perceptual investigation and other data about musical habits can be used for cross-checking ana-lytical conclusions and for putting the whole analysis in its sociological and psychological perspectives.

It is clear that a holistic approach to the analysis of popular music is the only viable one if one wishes to reach a full understanding of all factors inter-acting with the conception, transmission, and reception of the object of study. Now although such an approach obviously requires multidisciplinary knowledge on a scale no individual researcher can ever hope to embrace, there are nevertheless *degrees* of inter- and intradisciplinary outlook, not to mention the possibilities afforded by interdisciplinary teamwork. An inter-esting approach in this context is that of Asaf'ev's *Intonation Theory* (see Asaf'ev 1976), which embraces all levels of musical expression and perception, from onomatopoeic signals to complex form structures, without placing them on either overt or covert scales of aesthetic value judgement. Intonation theory also tries to put musical analysis into historical, cultural, social, and psycho-logical perspective and seems to be a viable alternative to both congeneric formalism and unbridled hermeneutic exegesis, at least as practised in the realm of art music by Asaf'ev himself (1976: 51 ff.) and, in connection with folk music, by Maróthy (1974). Intonation theory has also been applied to the study of popular music by Mühe (1968) and Zak (1979). However, the terminology of intonation theory seems to lack stringency, *intonation* itself being given a diversity of new meanings by Asaf'ev in addition to those it already possesses (see Ling 1978*a*). It seems wise to adopt the generally holistic and dynamically non-idealist approach of intonation theory in popular music analysis, less wise to adopt its terminology, at least in the West where it is still little known.

There are also a number of other important publications within nonformalist musicology which combine semiological, sociological, psychological, and hermeneutic approaches, thereby offering ideas which might be useful in the analysis of popular music. Apart from pioneer work carried out in pre-war Germany (see Rösing 1981, n. 11) and by Francès (1958), I should mention in this context publications by Karbušicky (1973), Rösing (1977), Ling (1978*b*), and Tarasti (1978). However, in none of these publications are the analytical models applied to popular music; this still remains an extremely difficult area, as Rösing (1981) points out in his critique of several West German attempts at tackling the problem. The difficulties are also clearly epitomized by the surprising dearth of analytical methods developed in the Anglo-Saxon world.

In an interesting analysis of a fourteen-minute LP track by an East German rock group, Peter Wicke (1978) puts forward convincing arguments for treating popular music with new, non-formalist analytical methods. Wicke's analysis poses questions arising from an approach similar to that used here. Therefore, in an effort to fill some epistemological gaps I shall proceed to attempt the establishment of a theoretical basis for popular music analysis.

An Analytical Model for Popular Music

The conceptual and methodological tools for popular music analysis presented here are based on some results of current research (Tagg 1979, 1980, 1981*a*, *b*). The most important parts of this analytical model are (1) a checklist of parameters of musical expression, (2) the establishment of musemes (minimal units of expression) and museme compounds by means of interobjective comparison, (3) the establishment of figure/ground (melody/accompaniment) relationships, (4) the transformational analysis of melodic phrases, (5) the establishment of patterns of musical process and their relative congruence with eventual patterns of extramusical process, and (6) the falsification of conclusions by means of hypothetical substitution. These points will be explained and some of them exemplified in the rest of this article. I shall draw examples mainly from my work on the title-theme of the *Kojak* TV series (see Tagg 1979) and on Abba's hit recording 'Fernando' (see Tagg 1981*a*). First, however, this analytical process should be put into the context of a scientific paradigm. The discussion that follows should be read in conjunction with Figure 3.2. A reading down the centre of this diagram, following the bold lines, takes one through the process of analysis. Down the sides, joined by thinner lines, are the extramusical factors which feed into the processes of production of the music and, at the level of ideology, must also be taken into account by the analyst. First, however, let us concentrate on the hermeneutic/semiological level, reading down Figure 3.2 as far as the moment of 'verbalization'.

Methodological Paradigm for Popular Music Analysis

It should be clear that popular music is regarded as a sociocultural field of study (SCFS). It should also be clear from Figure 3.2 that there is an access problem involving the selection of analysis object (hereinafter 'AO') and analytical method. Choice of method is determined by the researcher's 'mentality' —his or her world view, ideology, set of values, objective possibilities, etc., influenced in their turn by the researcher's and the discipline's objective position in a cultural, historical, and social context. From the previous discussion it should be clear that the analysis of popular music is regarded here as an important contribution to musicology and to cultural studies in general. This opinion is based on the general view of modern music history presented above (see p. 73).

The choice of AO is determined to a large extent by practical methodological considerations. At the present stage of enquiry this means two things. Firstly, it seems wise to select an AO which is conceived for and received by large, socioculturally heterogeneous groups of listeners rather than music used by more exclusive, homogeneous groups, simply because it is more logical to study what is *generally* communicable before trying to understand particularities. Secondly, because, as we have seen, congeneric formalism has ruled the musicological roost for some time and because the development of new types of extrageneric analysis is a difficult matter, demanding some caution, it is best that AOs with relatively clear extramusical fields of association (hereinafter 'EMFA') be singled out at this stage.

The final choice to be made before actual analysis begins is which stage(s) in the musical communication process to study. Reasons for discarding

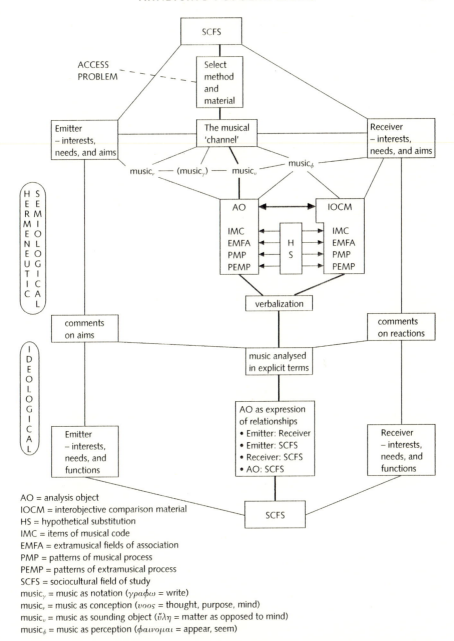

AO = analysis object
IOCM = interobjective comparison material
HS = hypothetical substitution
IMC = items of musical code
EMFA = extramusical fields of association
PMP = patterns of musical process
PEMP = patterns of extramusical process
SCFS = sociocultural field of study
music$_y$ = music as notation (γραφω = write)
music$_r$ = music as conception (νοος = thought, purpose, mind)
music$_v$ = music as sounding object (ὕλη = matter as opposed to mind)
music$_\phi$ = music as perception (φαινομαι = appear, seem)

Figure 3.2 Methodological paradigm for analysis of affect in popular music. (Thanks to Sven Andersson, Institute for the Theory of Science, Gothenburg University, for help in constructing this model.)

music as notation (music$_y$) have already been presented. Music as perceived by listeners (music$_\phi$) and as conceived by the composer and/or musician before actual performance (music$_v$) are on the other hand both highly relevant to the study of popular music, since their relations to each other, to the sounding object (music$_u$) and to the general sociocultural field of study are all vital parts of the perspective into which any conclusions from the analysis of other stages in the musical communication process must be placed. Nevertheless, however important these aspects may be (and they *are* vital), they can only be mentioned in passing here, being referred to as the 'ideological' part of the paradigm which follows the hermeneutic-semiological stage.

Thus, choosing the sounding object (music$_v$) as our starting point, we can now discuss actual analytical method.

Hermeneutic–Semiological Method

The first methodological tool is a *checklist of parameters of musical expression*. Having discussed general aspects of the communication process and any forms of simultaneous extramusical expression connected with the AO, it is a good idea to make some sort of transcript of the music$_v$, taking into consideration a multitude of musical factors. In drastically abridged form (from Tagg 1979: 68–70), the checklist includes:

1. *Aspects of time*: duration of AO and relation of this to any other simultaneous forms of communication; duration of sections within the AO; pulse, tempo, metre, periodicity; rhythmic texture and motifs.
2. *Melodic aspects*: register; pitch range; rhythmic motifs; tonal vocabulary; contour; timbre.
3. *Orchestrational aspects*: type and number of voices, instruments, parts; technical aspects of performance; timbre; phrasing; accentuation.
4. *Aspects of tonality and texture*: tonal centre and type of tonality (if any); harmonic idiom; harmonic rhythm; type of harmonic change; chordal alteration; relationships between voices, parts, instruments; compositional texture and method.
5. *Dynamic aspects*: levels of sound strength; accentuation; audibility of parts.
6. *Acoustical aspects*: characteristics of (re-)performance 'venue'; degree of reverberation; distance between sound source and listener; simultaneous 'extraneous' sound.
7. *Electromusical and mechanical aspects*: panning, filtering, compressing, phasing, distortion, delay, mixing, etc.; muting, pizzicato, tongue flutter, etc. (see 3, above).

This list does not need to be applied slavishly. It is merely a way of checking that no important parameter of musical expression is overlooked in analysis and can be of help in determining the processual structure of the AO. This is because some parameters will be absent, while others will be either constant during the complete AO (if they are constant during other pieces as well, such a set of AOs will constitute a style—see Fabbri 1982) or they will be variable, this constituting both the immediate and processual interest of the AO, not only as a piece in itself but also in relation to other music. The checklist can also contribute to an accurate description of *musemes*. These are minimal units of expression in any given musical style (not the same definition as in Seeger 1977) and can be established by the analytical procedure of *interobjective comparison* (hereinafter IOC).

The inherently 'alogogenic' character of musical discourse is the main reason for using IOC. The musicologist's eternal dilemma is the need to use words about a non-verbal, non-denotative art. This apparent difficulty can be turned into an advantage if at this stage of analysis one discards words as a metalanguage for music and replaces them with other music. This means using the reverse side of a phrase coined in a poem by Sonnevi (1975): 'music cannot be explained away—it can't even be contradicted unless you use completely new music'.[2] Thus using IOC means describing music by means of other music; it means comparing the AO with other music in a relevant style and with similar functions. It works in the following way.

If an analytical approach which establishes consistency of response to the same AO played to a number of different respondents is called *intersubjective*, then an *interobjective* approach would be that which can establish consistency of sound events between two or more pieces of music. Establishing similarities between an AO and other 'pieces of music' can be done by the researcher himself, referring to the 'check list'. The scope of the *interobjective comparison material* (IOCM) can, however, be widened considerably by asking other people to do the same.

This process establishes a bank of IOCM which, to give some examples, can amount to around 350 pieces in the case of the *Kojak* title theme and about 130 in Abba's 'Fernando'.

[2] The Swedish original is somewhat more poetic than the translation:
> Musiken
> kan inte bortförklaras
> Det går inte ens
> att säga emot,
> annat än
> med helt ny musik

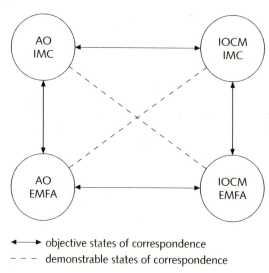

- ◄───► objective states of correspondence
- ─ ─ ─ demonstrable states of correspondence

Figure 3.3 Hermeneutic correspondence by means of interobjective comparison

The next step is to search the IOCM for musical elements (items of musical code: IMC) which are also to be found in the AO. These elements are often extremely short (musemes), or else consist of general sonorities or of overall expressional constants. Particular musemes, 'motifs' and general sonorities in both the AO and the IOCM which correspond must then be related to extra-musical forms of expression. Such relationships can be established if pieces in the IOCM share any common denominators of extramusical association in the form of visual or verbal meaning. If they do, then the objective correspondences established between the items of musical code in the analysis object (AO/IMC) and those in the IOCM (IOCM/IMC), and between the musical code of the IOCM (IOCM/IMC) and its extramusical fields of association (IOCM/EMFA), lead to the conclusion that there is a demonstrable state of correspondence between the items of musical code in the analysis object (AO/IMC) and the extramusical fields of association connected to the inter-objective comparison material (IOCM/EMFA)—also of course, between IOCM/IMC and AO/EMFA (see Figure 3.3).

There are obvious pitfalls in this method of determining musical 'meaning'. Just as no one would presume the same morpheme to mean the same thing in two different languages (for instance, French and English [wiː]), so it would be absurd to presume that, say, a B♭13 chord will 'mean' the same in nineteenth-century operetta (Example 3.1) and in bebop (Example 3.2).

Ex 3.1.

Ex 3.2.

The same kind of confusion might also result in describing 'What Shall We Do with a Drunken Sailor' as sad, and 'He was Despisèd' from the *Messiah* as happy, just because minor is supposed to be sad and major happy—as though the specificities of musical language were not the most important operative factors.

To overcome such difficulties, IOCM should be restricted to musical genres, functions, and styles relevant to the AO. Thus, in dealing with punk rock, IOCM would need to be confined to pop and rock from the sixties and after, whereas the IOCM used in connection with middle-of-the-road pop, film music, etc. can be far larger, due to the eclectic nature of such musics and the heterogeneity of their audiences.

Having extracted the IMC of the AO (thirteen main musemes for *Kojak*, ten for 'Fernando'), their affectual meaning in associative verbal form should be corroborated or falsified. Since it is impossible or totally impractical to construct psychological test models isolating the effects of one museme in any listening situation, it is suggested that hypotheses of musematic 'meaning' be tested by means of a technique well known from such practices as 'majoring', 'minoring', 'rocking up', 'jazzing up' and applied by Bengtsson (1973: 221 ff.) to illustrate theories on musical processes. This technique is called *hypothetical substitution* and is best explained by example.

The Swedish national anthem ('Du Gamla, du Fria'), together with most patriotic songs and hymns (whatever their musical origins[3]), can be assumed

---

[3] The Swedish national anthem took its tune from an old folksong with 'naughty' lyrics.

Ex 3.3. Swedish national anthem

Du gam - la, du fri - a, du fjäll - hög - a Nord

to be of a traditionally solemn and positively dignified yet confident character. Furthermore, it can be assumed that there is great intermusematic similarity between most national anthems. To test these assumptions, it is necessary to alter the various parameters of musical expression one by one, in order to pinpoint what part of the music actually carries the solemn-dignified-confident affect. Using the first melodic phrase (Example 3.3) as a starting point, *hypothetical substitution* (HS) can falsify the theory that (*a*) the melodic contour, (*b*) the melodic relationship of the initial upbeat-downbeat[4] and (*c*) the key and the intervallic relationship of the melody to the tonic are instrumental in the transmission of the assumed affective meaning.

In all three cases (Example 3.4*a*, *b*, *c*) the original melody has been changed. The drastically altered HS of Example 3.4*a* bears nonetheless a striking resemblance to the 'Marseillaise' and could have been made to sound like 'The Stars and Stripes for Ever', 'God Save the Queen' or the 'Internationale'. The second HS (3.4*b*) shows the first interval as a rising major sixth from fifth to major third, the most characteristic leap in the Soviet national anthem, while the third HS (3.4*c*) sounds like a mixture of musemes from such labour movement rousers as 'Bandiera Rossa' and 'Venceremos'. It also resembles the 'release' of the 'Revolutionary Funeral March', Beethoven's setting of Schiller's 'Ode to Joy' and a triumphant chorus from Handel's *Judas Maccabeus*, not to mention the 'send her victorious' phrase from 'God Save the Queen'.

It is, however, possible to corroborate assumptions about solemnity, dignity and confidence by changing the phrasing (Example 3.4*d*), the tempo (3.4*e*), the lyrics (3.4*f*), and the time signature (3.4*g*).

By changing the phrasing to staccato, the melody loses much of its dignity, becoming more like a Perez Prado cha-cha (Example 3.4*d*).[5] By increasing

---

[4] This seems to contradict Maróthy (1974: 224–7, 241 ff.) The initial interval (the *initium* 'intonation' of plainchant, for example) should not be confused with Asaf'ev's various usages of 'intonation'. Asaf'ev calls this type of initial interval *vvodniy ton* (= introductory tone).

[5] See Prado's 'Patricia', RCA Victor 47-7245, no. 1 on the Hot 100, 1958. See also Tommy Dorsey's *Tea for Two Cha-Cha*, Decca 30704, no. 7 on the Hot 100, 1958.

Ex 3.4.

(a) altered melodic contour

Du gam - la, du fri - a, du   fjäll - hög - a Nord

(b) altered upbeat

Du gam - la, du fri - a, du   fjäll - hög - a Nord

(c) altered key

Du gam - la, du fri - a, du   fjäll - hög - a Nord

(d) altered phrasing

Du gam - la, du fri - a, du   fjäll - hög - a Nord

(e) altered tempo

Du gam - la, du fri - a, du   fjäll - hög - a Nord

(f) altered lyrics

On route six - ty six I'll be   get - ting my kicks

(g) altered metre

Du gam - la, du   fri - a, du   fjäll - hög - a   Nord

the pulse rate to an allegro of 130 or more, dignity, solemnity, and confidence become a bit rushed; by lowering it to an adagio pulse of forty-two, the confidence turns into something dirge-like (3.4e). Solemnity seems also to be destroyed by the substitution of 'undignified' lyrics, resulting in something more like blasphemous versions of hymns (3.4f), and also by retaining the original tempo while stating the tune in triple metre, thus warranting a waltz accompaniment (3.4*g*).

It would also have been possible to alter the dynamics to, say, pianissimo, to give the harmonies the sharpened or flattened added notes characteristic of chords in bebop, to put the melody through a fuzz box, harmonizer or ring modulator, into the minor key or, say, some gapped Balkan folk mode. The original melody could also have been played at an altered pitch on bassoon, piccolo, celesta, synthesizer, hurdy-gurdy, bagpipes or steel guitar; it could have been accompanied by a rock band, crumhorn consort or by offbeat hand claps. There is an infinite number of HSs which can corroborate or falsify correspondences between conclusions about musematic meaning (AO/IMC —IOCM/EMFA). However, from the examples presented here it is at least clear that the last four parameters of musical expression (Example 3.4*d*, *e*, *f*, *g*) are more important determinants of the affective properties of dignity, solemnity and confidence than the first three (Example 3.4*a*, *b*, *c*), although change in melodic contour was far easier to detect in notation than these more important factors.

Having established extramusical 'meaning' at the micro level, one should proceed to the explanation of the ways musemes are combined, simultaneously and successively. Unlike verbal language, where complexities of affective association can generally only be expressed through a combination of denotation and connotation, music can express such complexities through simultaneously heard sets of musemes. Several separately analysable musemes are combined to form what the listener experiences as an integral sound entity. Such 'museme stacks' can be seen as a vertical cross-section through an imaginary score. Subjectively they seem to have no duration, never exceeding the limits of 'present time' experience in music; objectively this means they are never longer than the length of a musical phrase, which may be roughly defined as the duration of a normal inhalation plus exhalation (see Wellek 1963: 109). In popular music, museme stacks can often be found to correspond to the concept of 'sound', one of whose characteristics is a hierarchy of dualisms consisting, firstly, of the main relationship between melody and accompaniment (which may be interpreted as a relationship between figure and ground, individual(s) and environment), and, secondly, subsidiary relationships between bass (plus drums) and other accompanying parts. The relative importance of simultaneous musemes and their combined affectual message, shown as a theoretical model in Figure 3.4, can be

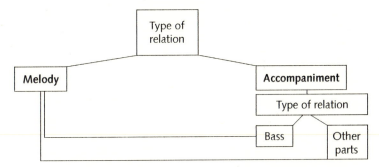

Figure 3.4 Model for analysis of museme stacks

Melody	Type of relation	Accompaniment		
		Bass	Type of relation	Other parts
a call to action and attention, strong, individual movement up and outwards, virile, energetic and heroic, leading to undulating swaying, calm, and confidence, something individual, male, martial, and heroic	stands out against, is heard above, is stronger than, is engaged in dialogue with	energy, excitement, desultory unrest, male aggressivity, threat of subcultural environment in large North American city	is part of, rumbles below, is heard through	general, constant, bustling activity, agitated, pleasant, vibrant, luminous, modern, urban American, sometimes jerky, unresting, exciting

Figure 3.5 Analysis of museme stack in the *Kojak* theme, bars 5–8

exemplified by the affectual paradigm of the first melodic phrase in the *Kojak* theme (Figure 3.5).

There is no room here to account in detail for stages of musematic analysis leading to the associative words found in Figure 3.5 (see Tagg 1979: 102–47). The example is included merely to make more concrete a little of this otherwise theoretical presentation.

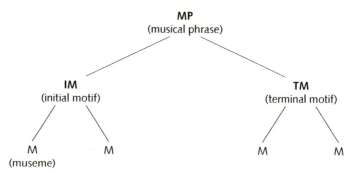

Figure 3.6 'Deep structure' of melodic phrases

Having established correspondence between on the one hand 'static' items
of musical expression (musemes and museme stacks) in the AO and, on the
other hand, the EMFAs of the IOCM—which leads to conclusions about the
relationship between these items as signifiers and signifieds—it is also necessary to determine the *processual* meaning of the AO. Thanks to the melody
—accompaniment dualism of much popular music (see Mühe 1968: 53, 67;
Maróthy 1974: 22; Tagg 1979: 123–4, 142–7), in which there are rarely
more than two parts with melodic material, the remaining voices either
executing riffs or sustaining notes or chords, the way to determine the relative syntactic importance of individual musemes along the 'horizontal' time
axis is reasonably simple. It is in fact possible to construct a model according
to which any melodic phrase can be generated according to the transformational norms to which the AO belongs (see Figure 3.6). This does not imply
that there are any hard and fast rules about the way in which melodic phrases
are actually generated. The model is a purely theoretical conception, which
helps us find out the syntactical meaning of melodic phrases. A generative
analysis of the first fully stated melodic phrase from the *Kojak* theme (Figure
3.7) should make this clearer. Starting from the original pitch idea shown
in Figure 3.7, an infinite number of transformations are possible. Two of these,
simply using different sequences of musemes, are suggested in Examples 3.5
and 3.6. These examples are both melodic nonsense; neither the mere sum,
nor the haphazard permutation of musemes can constitute the syntactical
meaning of melodic phrases. Instead it is their specific type of contiguity, their
type of overlap-elision according to the 'law of good continuation' (Meyer 1956)
and that of 'implication' (Narmour 1977), that give specific meaning to the
phrase. This can be seen in a comparison of the original melodic phrase of

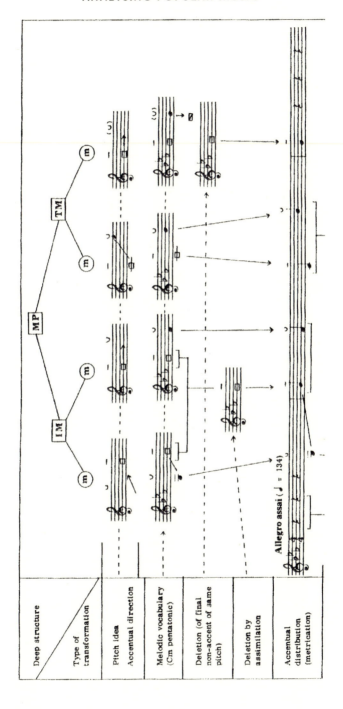

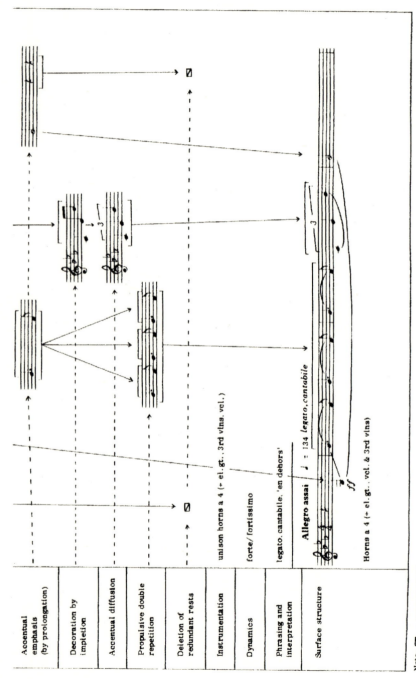

Figure 3.7 Generative analysis of melodic line in first full melodic phrase of the *Kojak* theme

Ex 3.5.

Ex 3.6.

Ex 3.7.

Ex 3.8.

the *Kojak* theme (Example 3.7) and a HS in which the middle museme, together with its transformation by propulsive double repetition, has been replaced while all other elements have been retained (Example 3.8).

In this way it is possible to distinguish between the affectual syntax of the original version and that of the HS. The differences can be verbalized as follows. Example 3.7: (bar 1) a strong, virile call to attention and action upwards and outwards/(bar 2) undulates, sways calm, and confident, gaining momentum to lead into/(bars 3 and 4) something strong, broad, individual, male, martial, heroic, and definite. Example 3.8: (bar 1) a strong, virile call to attention and action upwards and outwards/(bar 2) redescends smoothly to/(bar 3) something strong, broad, individual, male, martial, and heroic which grows in height and intensity, driving forward to/(bar 4) a confident point of rest. In short: although these two melodic phrases contain exactly the same musical material, the order in which the material is presented and the way in which its constituent parts are elided into each other are both instrumental in determining the difference in affectual meaning.

Climbing further up the structural hierarchy from the microcosm of musemes, through melodic phrases, we arrive at the point where larger patterns of musical process (PMP) should be examined. This area is generally regarded as the private hunting ground of traditional formalist musicology with its sophisticated conceptual apparatus of thematic germination, mutation, and development. However, as Chester (1970) has suggested, there are clear differences between the 'extensional' type of musical discourse to be found in the heyday of sonata form and the 'intensional' blocks through which much popular music (not least rock) is structured in a much more immediate way.

Nevertheless, this does not mean that patterns of musical process are a simple matter in popular music analysis (see Wicke 1978; Tagg 1979). Although block shifts (simultaneous changes in several parameters of musical expression) are reasonably clear in joins between verse and chorus, A and B sections, etc., the total meaning of straightforward patterns of reiteration and recapitulation can often be more than their deceptive simplicity suggests. (For discussion of some of the processes involved, see Tagg 1979: 217–29.) The situation becomes even more complex when there is incongruence between musical processes and extramusical processes (PEMP: visual images or words, for instance) in the same AO. Only a depth analysis of simultaneity, staggering or incongruence of change and return in both musical and extramusical processes within the AO can actually reveal the true nature of the musical discourse. The sort of problem involved here is probably best explained by an example.

In Abba's 'Fernando',[6] patterns of musical and extramusical process seem reasonably clear. The song has two parts: instrumental plus verse (V), and chorus (C). The order of events is V V C V C C. By means of musematic analysis the verse can be said to conjure up a postcard picture of a young European woman alone against a backcloth of a plateau in the high Andes. Periodicity, vocal delivery, lack of bass and drums, and other musical aspects say that she is sincere, worried, involved in a long-ago-and-far-away environment. The words of the verse underline this mood: she has taken part, together with her 'Fernando', in a vaguely-referred-to freedom fight. The music of the chorus can be said to represent here-and-now in pleasant, modern, comfortable, leisurely surroundings; the young European woman is pleasantly nostalgic. The words are congruently nostalgic and totally devoid of concrete references (guns, bugle calls, Rio Grande, etc.) mentioned in the verse. Everything in the analysis seems relatively simple so far, and judging from the words of the chorus, this could be quite a 'progressive' song.

---

[6] Epic EPC 4036, no. 1 in the UK, 1976. Also on LP *Abba's Greatest Hits*, Epic EPC 69218, fifty-one weeks in British LP charts. As a single in the USA (Atlantic 45-3346) sixteen weeks in the 'Hot 100'. For a thorough analysis of 'Fernando', see Tagg 1981a.

There was something in the air that night, the stars were bright, Fernando,
They were shining there for you and me, for liberty, Fernando,
Though we never thought that we could lose, there's no regrets:
If I had to do the same again, I would, my friend, Fernando.

Ex 3.9. Abba, 'Fernando'

There was some-thing in the air that night, the stars___ were bright,

Ex 3.10.

(a) Bach, *Matthäus Passion* (1729), 'Ich will bei meinem Jesu wachten'

(b) Gluck, *Orfeo e Euridice* (1774), 'Che farò senza Euridice?'

Adagio

he - ar my___ pray-er so___ sad___ and___ sigh - ing

(c) The Righteous Brothers, 'You've Lost That Loving Feeling', Philles 124

You ne - ver close your eyes___ a - ny more when you kiss my lips___

The only trouble is that the musical element corresponding to this nostalgia
and longing to return to the exotic environment (Ex. 3.9) is a highly ambiguous museme, for not only is its falling tritone (marked *x*) a stereotype of
'longing' (for IOCM see Exx. 3.10*a*, *b*, *c*) but also a typical pre-cadential sign of
the imminent relaxation of tension (see Exx. 3.11*a*, *b*). A depth analysis of the
patterns of musical process in 'Fernando' reveals that when the ambiguous
museme occurs at the start of the chorus it has a clearly longing character
(Ex. 3.9), since it cannot be pre-cadential when it not only initiates the phrase
but also the whole section. However, when it recurs at the end of the chorus,
it still admittedly starts the melodic phrase but it is at the same time in a
typically pre-cadential position of announcing relaxation of tension and

Ex 3.11.

(a) Njurling and Dahlqvist. 'Skepp som mötas i natten' (1924). In *Svensk Schlager*. ed. E. G. Sundelöf (Stockholm 1968)

(b) Alf Prøysen. 'Lilla vackra Anna' (n.d.). In *Visesangboka*, ed. O. Leren and L. Damstad (Oslo, 1971)

Ex 3.12. Abba, 'Fernando'

[Start second half of chorus (something new)]

Though we ne - ver thought that we could lose,___ there's no re - grets___

If I had to do the /same a - gain, I would,___ my friend, Fer-nan - do.
[return of the familiar (relief)]

therefore no real longing. This is because it occurs towards the end of a much longer but equally well-entrenched musical process, that of a familiar VI–II–V–I circle-of-fifths finish (Ex. 3.12). This means that, whereas the words say 'If I had to go back and fight for freedom in Latin America, I would', the music expresses the affective attitude 'I may be longing for something here at home but I'm really quite content with things as they are.'

Difficulties in interpreting patterns of musical process can also be found further up the processual hierarchy in the same song. Ostensibly, three main processes are to be found. The first and third move from the sincere-worrying-and-involvement-about-fighting-for-freedom-in-the-sierras sphere to the world of here-and-now-at-home in pleasant, comfortable surroundings, reminiscing with relief (that is, V → C); the second process moves in the opposite direction (C → V). However, not only are there more shifts from verse to chorus than vice versa, there is also an overall process *from* 'more "Andes" (verse) and less "soft disco" (chorus)' (the first half of the song) *to* 'less "Andes" and more "soft disco"' (the second half). A processual HS reversing this order of events leads to a totally different statement of emotional involvement in musical terms.

At this point in the analytical model we are poised on the brink of 'ideological critique', the next and final step in the methodological paradigm presented earlier (see Figure 3.2).

Ideological Critique

This part of the study is strictly speaking outside the jurisdiction of the type of 'textual analysis' sketched above. However, it seems important, if only in passing and by way of summary, to pose a few questions arising out of the sort of musematic analysis illustrated there. These questions also put the analytical model into a broader perspective.

The results of the detailed musematic analyses of both *Kojak* and 'Fernando' (Tagg 1979, 1981a) showed that this mainstream popular music was able to carry messages which, at a preconscious, affective, and associative level of thought, were able to relate types of personality, environments, and events to emotional attitudes, implicit evaluations, and patterns of affective response. In the case of *Kojak*, for example, the music was found to reinforce a basically monocentric view of the world and to emphasize affectively the fallacy that the negative experience of a hostile urban environment can be overcome solely by means of an individualist attitude of strength and go-it-alone heroism. In 'Fernando', a similar sort of monocentricity prevails, but the threat and worry epitomized by oppression, hunger, and rebellion under neo-colonialism are warded off by the adoption of a tourist attitude (most strikingly expressed in the spatial panning, which has 'ethnic' quena flutes in the stereo wings and the West European vocalist up centre front—a HS reversing these positions could have been interesting!) and by nostalgic reminiscences heard against a familiar 'home' accompaniment of 'soft disco' (these elements gaining a repressive, *Angst*-dispelling upper hand).

Obvious questions arising from such results are of the following type. How do 'emitter' and 'receiver' relate to the attitudes and implicit ideologies which seem to be encoded in the analysed 'channel'? Starting with the 'emitter' we might ask how, as far as the 'emitter' is concerned, the conception and composition of these affectively encoded attitudes are influenced by the circulation of capital in the popular culture industry. Does this connect with the demand for quick turnover and the creation of 'product' capable of eliciting immediate audience reaction leading to such turnover? If so, how aware is the 'emitter' of these pressures? Is there any conscious or unconscious self-censorship at this stage? It seems probable, for example, that the production of much film music, including titles and signature tunes, is influenced by a need to follow well-entrenched stereotypes of affective code, in terms of both musematic structures and the implicit attitudes conveyed by such structures when connected in a stereotypic fashion to extramusical phenomena (see Tagg 1980). Can such tendencies really be seen as a sort of evil conspiracy and as the reflection of a conscious ideological position on the part of the 'emitter'? Is it not more likely that they should be attributed to the objective social and cultural position of the 'emitter' in relation to the music business, the 'receiver' and society in general?

Turning to the receiving end of the communication process, we might ask how the musical statement of implicit attitudes prevalent in society at large affects those listening to such culturally eclectic and heterogeneously distributed types of music as title tunes and middle-of-the-road pop. Are the attitudes and behaviour patterns implied in such music as *Kojak* and 'Fernando' actually capable of reinforcing the attitudes and behaviour patterns implied by prevailing social tendencies of monocentricity, privatization, and idealist individualism; or are these messages merely received at a distance as entertaining reflections of an outdated mode of relating to current reality? Obviously, reception of such 'consensus music' (Hamm 1981) will vary considerably between different cultures, subcultures, classes, and groups. Thus, whereas parts of the 'fourth audience' (ibid.) may well be able to identify with the affective attitudes towards love, family, society, and nature (on 'nature' in music, see Rebscher 1976; Rösing 1977; Tagg 1982) presented in such TV music as *Kojak* or in such middle-of-the-road pop as 'Fernando', it is clear that many will be unable to identify. This raises yet another question: how does the latter type of listener relate to prevailing ideologies and attitudes both in music and in society at large?

Analysing Subcultural Music Codes in Industrialized Society

The way in which 'counter-cultures' and subcultures express their own stand, profile, and group identity in extramusical terms has been documented in numerous studies (see the work of the Centre for Contemporary Cultural Studies at the University of Birmingham). However, the *musical* coding of such identities and attitudes is an underdeveloped field of study. There are admittedly numerous accounts of trends within Afro-American music, but few of these deal with the actual musical code of the counter-culture or subculture in question. This could be because no real theory yet exists which explains how the *prevailing* attitudes, patterns of behaviour, and ideology of late capitalism are encoded in the musical *mainstream* of popular musics such as signature tunes, Musak, advertising music, middle-of-the-road pop, and rock, etc. In fact it appears that the study of popular music has, with very few exceptions (such as Mühe 1968; Czerny and Hoffman 1968; Hamm 1979, 1981, 1982; Gravesen 1980; Helms 1981), shown a remarkable bias towards tributaries or offshoots, while strangely ignoring the mainstream itself.

It is difficult to refrain from speculating about possible reasons for such bias. Perhaps there is a tendency among intellectual musicians or musically interested academics to be critical towards the stereotypic encoding of mainstream attitudes and ideas in our society. If so, it seems natural that such researchers will be more likely to identify with musics 'contradicting' this mainstream and thus be motivated to explain the 'contradicting' position they themselves assume rather than the 'contradicted' which they leave shrouded in mystery, an inaccessible, unidentified enemy. But it is hard to understand how the popular music researcher will ever be able to explain his 'music in opposition' (or even how 'music in opposition' will be able to develop a valid strategy) if the ideologies encoded in the musical mainstream are not to be touched.

This was put tersely by William Brooks at Keele University during a seminar on Afro-American music in 1978. He expressed the opinion that it is no use trying to find out why Chuck Berry is so great if you do not know why Perry Como is so successful. How, one wonders, can the true values of Sonnevi's 'contradicting musical exception' (see p. 83 above) be realized if the face of the 'prevailing musical norm' is never demasked.

Analytical methods developed along the lines of the model presented here may perhaps contribute to this demasking operation. Whether or not they might then be applicable to subcultural musical codes, such as Tyneside workers' song, reggae or punk, is another question. The problems would be numerous and can be generalized as follows. (1) Detailed genre definitions will need to be made (for a possible method, see Fabbri 1982). (2) Acceptable style criteria will need to be established on the basis of the musical traits accepted and rejected by musicians and listeners belonging to the subculture. (3) The subcultural musical code will probably need to be considered as a potential carrier of *particular socialized* relationships between members of the musical subculture and the musical mainstream—this presumably reflecting comparable extramusical relationships—rather than as carrier of quasi-universalized attitudes and relationships towards an apparently wider and vaguer set of *general, individualized* experience (see Wicke and Mayer 1982). Such considerations seem to imply that the model presented in this article will require some alteration before being applied to the analysis of subcultural popular musics.

Popular Music Analysis—Its Uses

As usual in theoretical presentations like this, more questions seem to get asked than answers given. However, results from the depth studies of title music and middle-of-the-road pop carried out so far suggest that the sort of hermeneutic–semiological analysis presented here can provide some insight and act as a basis for understanding '*what* is being communicated' and '*how*'.

Now it is true that my analytical model has been distilled from detailed, almost microscopic studies of individual pieces of popular music. Such microscopic investigation was carried out in order to test thoroughly the scientific viability of certain hypotheses and intuitive analytical practices. It resulted in pieces of writing (300 pages for a one-minute title theme, sixty pages for four minutes of pop!) far too cumbersome to be used as models for normal teaching situations. However, this does not mean that the basic techniques problematized and tested in this way are unusable in normal circumstances, not least because the need to test and develop these models evolved from the practical problems of teaching popular music history at a teachers' training college, where there was certainly no time to spend more than a few minutes talking about single pieces of music.

The methods of interobjective comparison, of establishing correspondence between the IOCM and its EMFA and then between the musical code of the analysis object (AO/IMC) and the extramusical fields of association connected with the interobjective comparison material (IOCM/EMFA) (see Figure 3.3) can be carried out by anyone willing to exercise their synaesthetic and associative capacities as well as their intellect. Any musician can carry out simple HS (hypothetical substitutions) and, with a tape recorder, tape, a razor blade, and a reasonable ear, anyone can even manage to reassemble a processual HS. Anyone with a bit of imagination can sing bits of tune in the wrong order, or substitute new continuations, and thereby discover what actually makes the music say what it says.

In other words the analysis of popular music should in no way be considered a job reserved for 'experts' (although I will admit that describing its mechanisms may require some specialist knowledge). The sort of analytic model presented here should rather be seen as an effort to underpin cognitively that form of affective and implicit human communication which occupies parts of the average Westerner's brain during one quarter of his waking life. (Can any other form of communication rival this, quantitatively?) Analysing popular music should also be seen as something which counteracts 'split brain' tendencies, resists the sort of mental apartheid advocated by the newspapers quoted at the start of this article and breaks the schizophrenic taboos prohibiting contact between verbal and non-verbal, explicit and implicit, public and private, collective and individual, work and leisure. Analysing popular music takes the 'fun' seriously and is itself both a serious business *and* a lot of fun.

References

Asaf'ev, B. (1976). *Die musikalische Form als Prozess* (Berlin).

Bengtsson, I. (1973). *Musikvetenskap—en översikt* (Lund).

Bernstein, L. (1976). *The Unanswered Question* (Cambridge, Mass.).

Bradley, D. (1980). 'The cultural study of music', stencilled paper from the Centre for Contemporary Cultural Studies, no. 61 (Birmingham).

Chapple, S., and Garofalo, R. (1977). *Rock 'n' Roll is Here to Pay: The History and Politics of the Music Industry* (Chicago).

Chester, A. (1970). 'For a rock aesthetic', *New Left Review*, 59: 82–6.

Cohn, N. (1970). *Awopbopaloobop Alopbamboom* (London).

Czerny, P., and Hoffman, H. P. (1968). *Der Schlager* (Berlin).

Fabbri, F. (1982). 'A theory of musical genres: two applications', in *Popular Music Perspectives*, ed. P. Tagg and D. Horn (Gothenburg and Exeter), 52–81.

Fonogrammen i kulturpolitiken (1979). Rapport från Kulturrådet, 1979: 1 (Stockholm).

Francès, R. (1958). *La Perception de la musique* (Paris).

Frith, S. (1978). *The Sociology of Rock* (London).

Gravesen, F. (1980). ' "Party-musik"—introduktion til en genre', in *Nordisk musik och musikvetenskap under 70-talet*, ed. A. Carlsson and J. Ling (Gothenburg), 261–76.

Hamm, C. (1979). *Yesterdays—Popular Song in America* (New York).

—— (1981). 'The fourth audience', *Popular Music*, 1: 123–42 (Cambridge).

—— (1982). 'Some thoughts on the measurement of popularity in music', in *Popular Music Perspectives*, ed. P. Tagg and D. Horn (Gothenburg and Exeter), 3–15.

Helms, S. (1981). *Musik in der Werbung* (Wiesbaden).

Karbušicky, V. (1973). 'Das "Verstehen der Musik" in der soziologisch-ästhetischen Empire', in *Musik und Verstehen*, ed. P. Faltin and H.-P. Reinecke (Cologne), 121–47.

Karshner, R. (1971). *The Music Machine* (Los Angeles).

Keiler, A. (1978). 'Bernstein's *The Unanswered Question* and the problem of musical competence', *Musical Quarterly*, 64/2: 195–222.

Lerdahl, F., and Jackendoff, R. (1977). 'Toward a formal theory of tonal music', *Journal of Music Theory*, 1977/1: 111–71.

Ling, J. (1978a). 'Assafjevs Intonationsteori—ett försök till analys', stencilled paper from Gothenburg University Musicology Department (Gothenburg).

—— (1978b). 'Hjort Anders's "12th Night March"—stylistical and ideological change', *Antropologiska Studier*, 25/26: 122–39.

Maróthy, J. (1974). *Music and the Bourgeois, Music and the Proletarian* (Budapest).

Mellers, W. (1973). *Twilight of the Gods—The Beatles in Retrospect* (London).

Melzer, R. (1970). *The Aesthetics of Rock* (New York).

Meyer, L. B. (1956). *Emotion and Meaning in Music* (Chicago).

Mühe, H. (1968). 'Zur Intonation des deutschen Schlagers', unpublished dissertation, Karl-Marx-Universität (Leipzig).

Narmour, E. (1977). *Beyond Schenkerism—The Need for Alternatives in Music Analysis* (Chicago).

Nattiez, J.-J. (1974). 'Sur la relation entre sociologie et sémiologie musicales', *International Review of the Aesthetics and Sociology of Music*, 5/1: 61–75.

Rebscher, G. (1976). *Natur in der Musik* (Wiesbaden).

Riethmüller, A. (1976). 'Die Musik als Abbild der Realität—zur dialektischen Wiederspieglungstheorie in der Ästhetik', *Beihäfte zum Arkiv für Musikwissenschaft*, 15 (Wiesbaden).

Rösing, H. (1977). *Musikalische Stilisierung akustischer Vorbilder in der Tonmalerei* (Munich and Salzburg).

—— (1981). 'Die Bedeutung musikalischer Ausducksmodelle für das Musikverständnis', *Zeitschrift für Musikpädagogik*, 16: 258–64.

Schafer, R. (1974). *The New Soundscape* (Vienna).

—— (1977). *The Tuning of the World* (New York).

Schuler, M. (1978). 'Rockmusik und Kunstmusik der Vergangenheit: ein analytischer Versuch', *Archiv für Musikwissenschaft*, 35/2: 135–50.

Seeger, C. (1977). *Studies in Musicology 1935–1975* (Berkeley), especially 'On the moods of a musical logic', pp. 64–88.

Shepherd, J. (1977). 'Media, social process and music', 'The "meaning" of music' and 'The musical coding of ideologies', in Shepherd *et al.*, *Whose Music? A Sociology of Musical Languages* (London), 7–124.

Stoïanova, I. (1978). *Geste—Texte—Musique* (Paris).

Tagg, P. (1979). *Kojak—50 Seconds of Television Music* (Gothenburg).

—— (1981*a*). 'Fernando the flute', stencilled paper from Gothenburg University Musicology Department, no. 8106 (Gothenburg).

—— (1981*b*). 'On the specificity of musical communication', stencilled paper from Gothenburg University Musicology Department, no. 8115 (Gothenburg).

—— (1982). 'Natur som musíkalisk stereotyp', in *Naturresurser i Kultursociologisk belysning*, ed. Frängsmyr and Swedin (Stockholm).

—— (ed.) (1980). 'Film music, mood music and popular music research', stencilled paper from Gothenburg University Musicology Department, no. 8002 (Gothenburg).

Tarasti, E. (1978). *Myth and Music—A Semiotic Approach to the Aesthetics of Music* (Helsinki).

Varis, T. (1975). *The Impact of Transnational Corporations on Communication*, Tampere Peace Research Institute Reports, no. 10 (Tampere).

Wedin, L. (1972). 'Multidimensional scaling of emotional expression in music', *Svensk Tidskrift för Musikforskning*, 54: 115–31.

Wellek, A. (1963). *Musikpsychologie und Musikästhetik* (Frankfurt am Main).

Wicke, P. (1978). ' "Licht in das Dunkel"—Popmusik in der Analyse', *Beiträge zur Musikwissenschaft*, 1978/1: 3–15.

Wicke, P., and Mayer, G. (1982). 'Rock music as a phenomenon of progressive mass culture', in *Popular Music Perspectives*, ed. P. Tagg and D. Horn (Gothenburg and Exeter), 223–31.

Zak, V. (1979). *O melodike massovoy pesni* [On the melodies of the popular song] (Moscow).

Zoltai, D. (1970). *Ethos und Affekt* (Budapest).

4

#####

Popular Music Analysis and Musicology: Bridging the Gap

RICHARD MIDDLETON

Since their beginnings, popular music studies have conducted an implicit (sometimes explicit) dialogue with musicology. To be sure, the musicological side of this conversation has more often than not been marked by insult, incomprehension or silence; and popular music scholars for their part have tended to concentrate on musicology's deficiencies. But musicology is changing (more about this later); at the same time, recent work on popular music suggests a new confidence, manifesting itself in part in a willingness to engage with and adapt mainstream methods.[1] I believe each needs the other.

Within the sphere of analysis, the main problem felt to attach to mainstream methods has been the tendency to formalism. In contrast, popular music analysis has insisted (rightly, I think) on the priority of *meaning*. Much of the best work has been semiotic or interpretative (Laing, Tagg, Bradby, Grossberg) or has pursued theories of social and cultural homology (Hebdige, Shepherd). However imposing this body of work, though, there is a suspicion that sometimes insufficient attention has been paid to the sounds themselves —to the intramusical structures of what I call the 'primary' level of signification (Middleton 1990: 220). Somehow, we need to find ways of bringing the patterns created in the sounds themselves back into the foreground, without as a consequence retreating into an inappropriate formalism. And if we can do this, we may well find that we are contributing to an advance in *general* musical analysis. (I will come back to the important question of how music labelled 'popular' and musics labelled in other ways are positioned within the general analytical enterprise.)

---

[1] Despite differences in approach, recent work by Van der Merwe (1989), Moore (1993), Brackett (1992), Hawkins (1992), and Walser (1992) exemplifies this point.

Theory

My proposal is directed towards a search for a theory of gesture. This I understand as possessing affective and cognitive as well as kinetic aspects—by which I mean simply that how we feel and how we understand musical sounds is organized through processual shapes which seem to be analogous to physical gestures (see Coker 1972). Such a broadened notion of gesture does not deny that in some sense a theory of gesture would be also a theory of rhythm; but a satisfactory theory of rhythm is one of the things musicology does not possess, and if it did, it would necessarily encompass far more musical parameters than just the obviously rhythmic. For a basis, therefore, we need to look outside musicology, to anthropology and cultural theory—for example, to Lévi-Strauss's theory of 'correspondences' between musical and somatic structures, to Blacking's idea that musical processes are linked to somatic states and rhythms, to Barthes' proposal that they trace the operation of 'figures of the body' or 'somathemes'.[2]

One musicologist who has explored similar territory is the Hungarian, János Maróthy, in an important study on 'the musical infinite' (Maróthy and Batári n.d.). Maróthy defines rhythm as 'a repetition of any element, whereby heterogeneity can be made coherent'; its periodicities 'reveal the identity hidden in difference' (ibid. 19, 52). In this broad sense, rhythm, for Maróthy, is the basic principle of all reality, traversing not only physiological processes and sense modes (the structure of light and sound waves, for example) but the entire spectrum of matter/energy, from the processes of micro-physics to those of cosmic interrelationships. Bio-communication, including music, occupies one part of this spectrum, and for humans, argues Maróthy, 'rhythmic sension' snatches us out of particularity, 'switching the individual into the circuit of universality' (ibid. 32).

Drawing on all these perspectives, I would propose that musical 'gesture' should refer here to the 'performance'—that is, the 'furnishing' of the communicative field with self-validating 'performatives'—of somatic processes through structurally analogous musical processes. The analytic objective is to develop methods of identifying and categorizing the structures concerned.

There is an obvious danger in this kind of approach of falling into an essentialist assumption that music is a pre-cultural feature of species behaviour.

[2] For more detailed discussion of the theories of Lévi-Strauss, Blacking, and Barthes, and references, see Middleton 1990, chapters 6 and 7. Despite many differences, these theories all see meaning in music as *embodied* rather than *signified*.

My own feeling is that musical gestures—deep structures or principles which give unity to a music culture—are underlaid with still deeper generating 'gestures': kinetic patterns, cognitive maps, affective movements. But these are probably specific to a culture too: people seem to learn to emote, to order experience, even to move their bodies, through locally acquired conventions. Modern genetic theory insists that the question of whether 'nature' or 'nurture' has priority is in principle not susceptible of resolution; this is because it is impossible to find, or to conceive of finding, even the smallest, the most embryonic bit of human nature which is not already nurtured. Human nature is always already encultured (see Jones 1991). But this need not rule out the proposition that culturally specific gestures are rooted in human biology—and hence, widening out, in the greater bio- (and metabio-) sphere. Sustenance from what is concretely given, mediation by the variables of the cultural environment: these are the complementary sides of a properly materialist theory. Thus the gestures we are concerned with always take musical (rather than some other) form; while never autonomous (always pregnant with 'correspondences'), they maintain a systemic integrity: 'musical space is nothing but an imaginary and ideal spot for the evolution of human gestures' (Maróthy and Batári n.d.: 106).

This applies to all music. But looking round our present musical culture, popular songs seem to provide a good place for experimental attempts at analysis to start—simply because, as common-sense interpretation tells us, 'movement' is usually so important here. More clearly than in, say, classical symphony or chamber music, this music is unquestionably rooted in the structures, inner processes, and operational patterns of the secular human body. Even with pieces not intended for dancing, listeners usually find themselves *moving*, really or in imagination. And certainly rhythm is a key—but, as I have already implied, not solely in the strict sense of the term. There are vital roles too for the rhythms governing phraseology; chord and textural change; patterns of accent and intensity, of vocal 'breathing', vibrato and sustain; not to mention the micro-rhythms responsible for the inner life of sounds themselves, and the quasi-'spatial' rhythms organizing the hierarchies of relative pitch strength and tonal tension, both in melodic contour and in harmonic sequences. Maróthy and Batári (n.d.) have eloquently described the permeation of the whole spectrum of musical parameters (and beyond) by rhythmic principles. The physical spectrum of periodicity zones (lungs—heart—feet—fingers—speech organs—vocal cords—ear drum—ultra-sound perception—electro-chemical neural circuits—eye (light waves)) is mapped (or partly so) by the musical spectrum covered by the frequency zones of rhythm (in the strict sense) and pitch, which together cover the distance from pulsations occupying several seconds each, up to a frequency of approximately 20,000 pulsations per second. This gives a theoretical basis to the idea that 'gesture' occupies a spectrum, with relationships to obvious corporeal movements at one end and neural pulsations at the other. Not only beat and metre, then, but also the micro-physics of intonation, sound-articulation, and timbral adjustment: both are parts of the rhythmic ensemble. Moreover, the bottom end of the spectrum can be extended, as the longer periodicities of affective and cognitive movements come into play; the manœuvres, traverses, outpourings, and reflexes associated with corporeal activities, we might say, are transferred to a mental and emotional setting, where their scale can be expanded, to generate the patterns of phrase-relationships, pitch-contours, harmonic rhythms, and so on. All the components and periodicities overlap, combine, complement, and at times contradict each other in a complex gestural totality. And just as physical bodies (including parts of our own) can resonate with frequencies in the pitch zone, so they can with the lower frequencies found in the rhythm zone. 'The producer of sound can make us dance to his tune by forcing his activity upon us' (Maróthy and Batári n.d.: 98), and when we 'find ourselves moving' in this way, there is no more call for moral criticism of the supposedly 'mechanical' quality of the response than when a loudspeaker 'feeds back' a particular pitch. Boosting the volume can force zonal crossover, as when very loud performance makes us 'feel' a pitch rather than hearing it in the normal way; our skin resonates with it, as with a rhythm.

The textural location of this complex gestural totality is what Allan Moore has called the 'sound-box' (Moore 1993); it is within the four-dimensional space-time of this imaginary cuboid that the gestural intersections take place. Modern recording technique has hugely increased the variety of possible configurations, and the sense of specific physical place that can be created has enormous potential effects on the power and types of gestural resonance which listeners feel. In European music history, the nearest analogy is perhaps performances in church, theatre, and courtly chamber before the rise of the massed symphony orchestra, with its uni-directional relationship to the audience, changed our way of listening. But electronically mediated mixing can greatly magnify the 'staging' possibilities found in pre-classical ritual, drama, and dance. In modern popular songs, the listener seems to be related to the sound-box not only—often, perhaps, not mainly—through a perspective, derived from a single, objective point of view, but through a feeling of being inserted into the mix, a process which produces gestural identification and resonance. The first offers blended textural space for assimilation, or mastery, by the detached listener-subject; in the second, it is the subject, a gestural subject, who is assimilated into the textural space, as a participating actor.

Method

The detachment to which traditional analysis often pretends becomes diffi-cult if the experience of somatic movement is the guide to analytic decisions. One research method would be hypothetico-deductive, generating models— 'action-models'—of song-types, whose characteristics could then be tested for their applicability in particular cases: aspects of real songs would be more or less matched to the models by means of 'participant listening'. One would have to work out quasi-objective sets of 'rules' governing gestural force, direc-tion, and shape in, for example, melodic contours. Pitch direction and distance, interval quality, and tonal rhythm and function are all factors—though they interact, and may well not reinforce each other. Similar factors apply to harmonic sequences, though the presence of polyphony now (different voices, perhaps moving different distances in different directions) compli-cates matters. But in applying such models to particular instances, subject-ive decisions concerning 'pertinence' cannot be avoided; which gestures are in play, or are predominant, at any given moment? (On pertinence, see Middleton 1990: 173 ff.) We could, and should, test the validity of the deci-sions by comparing them with those made by other participants in the music. And indeed, it may be easier to develop a language for such inter-subjective comparison when it is gestural as well as, or more than, verbal. Dancers know if they are feeling the music the same way—though that simple starting-point would need considerable refinement. On this level, the analyst is no more privileged than any other participant because he or she is totally reliant on 'implicit theory': the unconscious schemas guiding one's phenomenology of subjective response. But an advantage of the method being sketched here is that in principle the analyst can double as 'informant' from within the culture—laying out the gestures through participation—and as 'critical outsider', cross-checking the information against schemas drawing on a wider body of musical data. The role of the 'scholar-fan' becomes vital.

Not only the choice of which gestures are in operation will vary; so too will the *level* at which the textural map is read. Each level, from the inner vibrations of sounds, and the shortest of rhythmic values, through to phrases, verses, and choruses, corresponds to a different span of gesture, and hence to a different somatic location: foot, pelvis, nodding head, breathe in/breathe out, excitement growing/then released, proposition/reiteration, etc. And the nerves are pulsating, the muscles vibrating, the feet moving, *within* the longer spans of action: the more slowly gyrating pelvis, the patterns of inhalation and exhalation, the charge and discharge of emotion, and so on. There is, then, a hierarchical 'tree' relating the spectrum of structural levels in the music with the spectrum of somatic equivalents. Some ethnomusicologists have remarked on the 'polycentric' nature of much African music, with dance-movement of various body areas being associated with different components in the rhythmic texture (see for example Kubik *et al.* 1989: 148). We can surely extend this to much popular music—especially that influenced by Afro-American styles—and, more speculatively, to cover affective and cognitive moves as well as kinetic ones.

A basic starting-point to the gestural modelling of song-types is the notion of rhythmic 'groove'. Different configurations of note placing, articulation and accent from the various components of the percussion kit, at specific tempi, play a large part in defining styles. But very quickly this takes on more extended textural aspects; the gestural shape varies according to type of bass-line and placing and articulation of notes from other instruments: guitars, keyboards, horns. These interactions produce a gestural centre or 'given', around which many popular songs orientate themselves, and listeners are intimately familiar with the different 'grooves' associated with, say, rock ballad, reggae, funk, and so on. These 'groove tracks' can best be modelled in visual or kinetic forms as the analyst's body responds to (resonates with) the sound-gestures. Around this centre operate varied types of phrase-relationship, of melodic intonation and of chord-sequence (not to mention the micro-gestures associated with many individual sounds). On the level of phrase-relationships, we can distinguish between units that are open or closed; antiphonal, complementary or iterative; musematic (that is, two or three-note, self-contained segments) or discursive (longer structures, more analogous to verbal phrases). Examples of common types of melodic intonation are descending, arch-shape, shouted or chanted, circling and what I call 'narrative' (this is the kind that seems to be telling a story—pulling us through a 'what will happen next?' note-string). Characteristic chord-sequences include chord-alternations and three- or four-chord riffs (of many types), circle of fifth sequences and twelve-bar blues patterns. In all these cases, it is the exploration of tonal space that is important, along with the effects of movement, relative distance, and tension that this produces. (For more detailed discussion of all these types, see Middleton 1990, chapter 6.)

If musical gestures lie semiotically beyond the linguistic domain (as Lévi-Strauss, Blacking, and Barthes in their different ways all imply), the search for a verbal analogue of their meaning is a forlorn one (even if unavoidable). Two-dimensional graphics (while also not problem-free) are often helpful. It is not difficult to represent a chord-alternation—because switches of tonal tension are involved; and a strong backbeat can be marked visually in an obvious way. It is harder to depict something like a twelve-bar blues chord-sequence—even though any sympathetic listener will feel the gesture involved: to do, somehow, with a particular intersection of structurings of time on the one hand, tonal space on the other. But so often one feels the need for more dimensions. There may be a future for moving real-time three-dimensional images. Many ethnomusicologists now film as well as record performance; certainly in much African music, for instance, body movement can help reveal musical structure. Perhaps this example should be pursued, and expanded, in popular song analysis, using freely created 3-D images as well as film of performance, dance, and other participative activity.

This is not possible here. In discussing a couple of examples, I will just try to bring out what strike me as the basic gestural features, using two-dimensional diagrams and a few words.[3] First, Madonna's 'Where's the Party?' I am confining myself to the verse, and chorus (that is, omitting the bridge) (see Figure 4.1). Here we would certainly have to represent:

(1) the 'groove'. In typical disco fashion, this is founded on a heavy regular beat—that is, on the feet. But predominantly strong-beat bass is complemented by backbeat snare drum (sways of body?), strung on a sixteen-to-the-bar cymbal chatter (felt as a sort of muscular vibration?). And notice how the bass joins in this semiquaver figuration in the choruses, adding to the feeling of spasmic excitement. In the verses, the ongoing rhythmic groove is articulated by the guitar-keyboard riff (one to each phrase—see Example 4.1), its accentual 'hit-point' marking an (upper-body jerk?) punctuation. The riff—basically on-beat—is offered by the bass in more syncopated variants (Example 4.2), and Madonna's vocal (double-tracked—which muddies the

---

[3] It will be obvious that not only are the analyses here less full than would be desirable but also the methodology is less than fully adequate, in terms of what is proposed earlier. I can only claim limitations of space and time in mitigation.

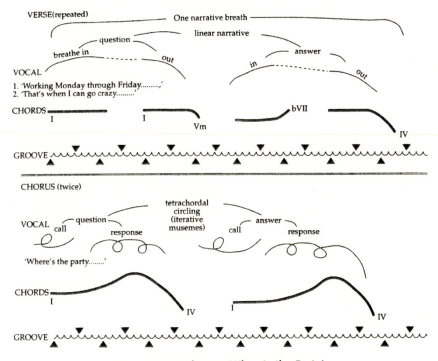

Figure 4.1 Madonna: 'Where's the Party'

Ex 4.1.

Ex 4.2.

on-beat clarity) sometimes pulls away from the strict metrical divisions. These are examples of what Maróthy calls 'noise': the tendency in all rhythmic phenomena towards systemic unity (abstract mathematical order) is subverted by the attractions of 'difference' (the disorder of concrete reality); and the effect of this is to widen the field of gestural reference.

(2) the shapes of the repeating chord-sequences used in both verse and chorus. Both are really filled-out I–IV moves, and the subdominant trajectory produces a relaxation (because we are moving flatwards on the circle of fifths), so overall the harmonic gesture is one of comfort. However, this is tempered by a slight ambiguity over which pitch is the tonic. The internal structure of the sequence differs between verse and chorus, modifying the tensional shape. The move to Vm in the verse 'ought' to increase tension but it does not seem to, perhaps because the dominant chord is minor, perhaps because of harmonic rhythm and phrase-structure: coming at the end of the two-bar phrase, it takes on a quasi-cadential resolving quality. The harmonic sequence (one falling fourth answered by another, I–Vm by ♭VII–IV) supports the question-answer formulation of the vocal. In the chorus, by contrast, squashing the I–IV move up from 4 bars to 2 increases the energy level, and the repetition is relentlessly iterative. The move, upwards through IIm and Vm, increases the tension, which then drops back with the fall to the subdominant.

(3) the various combinations of question/answer, call/response, inhale/exhale found in the vocal phraseology which is laid over the chord sequences. Notice here the contrast between the basically 'narrative' shapes in the verse —the internal 'rhyming' simulates a conversational account—and the compact, tetrachordal 'circling' shapes, organized into repeating call-and-response patterns, in the chorus. This contrast, between linear narrative and dance-ritual, is a common one.

(4) the micro-gestures of individual sounds. A few examples from Madonna's lead vocal: the tremulous vibrato on 'fun' (nervous anticipation?); the rasp on *'party'* (anticipation sensually fulfilled?); the slide up to pitch on *'Friday'* and the structurally equivalent *'crazy'*—these coincide with the 'hit-point' of the accompanying riff (see Example 4.1), forming the tensional climax of the gesture, and assisting the conversational structuring of the vocal narrative (each phrase answered by the keyboard response: 'oh yeah'; 'uh uh').[4]

(5) the texture. The fact that the frequent dissonances between the vocal and the chords are not heard as such demonstrates the extent to which the

---

[4] Of course, lyrics almost always have other functions than the purely gestural—a point which is neglected throughout this essay. Furthermore, not only would their denotations and connotations have to be taken into account in a full analysis, their contribution to gestural process itself—through prosodic features and through sound-quality features such as consonant attack and vowel-modulation—is often more important than may be apparent here.

texture here is gesturally layered. Although there is not much horizontal spread within the 'sound-box', the mix has quite a bit of depth, with bass and snare drum heavily foregrounded, vocals behind (and above) them, and harmony further back again. The predominantly sharp timbres, with lots of high frequencies transmitting high energy levels, contribute to the clarity.

Even in this apparently simple song, then, the variety of gestural spans (from semiquaver up to four-bar unit) and the complexity of the combinations, demand a genuinely polycentric somatic response from the participant listener.

Of course, Madonna's record is a dance-song and, it might be argued, you would expect lots of kinetic energy here. Let us look now at a ballad—Bryan Adams' '(Everything I Do) I Do It for You' (see Figure 4.2).

Perhaps the most striking feature here is the pervasive arch-shaped vocal intonations, typical of the ballad genre—and indeed of the entire bourgeois song tradition, from at least the Renaissance period. Gesturally, this intonation suggests a bodily and psychological reaching out, an assertion of energy and control, but always in the knowledge that this will be followed by a gathering in, a return to the safety of the Self's own little world. All the phrases in the main section of the song follow this pattern, though the first (A) starts with a descent, not an ascent, an initial drawing in or invitation to the listener: and this is emphasized in the first appearance of A by a tonic pedal under the chords shown in the diagram, establishing at the outset a bedrock quality of 'home'. The arch principle operates hierarchically. In the third phrase (B) (A having been repeated) both the harmonic centre of the melody and its overall tessitura rise, compared with A, falling again in the fourth phrase. Then in the bridge, the rising sequence carries the voice up to its highest point in the song. From there it descends again through the reprise of the main AABC section—though the relaxation effect of this is delayed and intensified, first, by the interruption provided by the guitar solo (this substitutes for the A phrases), second, by variants in the vocal line which introduce some higher pitches than the first time round, and third, by a lengthening of C (it is actually elided with a varied version of A). Over the span of the whole song, then, there is a (slightly undulating) large-scale arch. (For completeness, I should add that the initial chorus (AABC) comes twice, and in the second the tessitura is lifted slightly by melodic variants (see Figure 4.2); at the same time, textural thickening and rhythmic enlivening —the percussion kit enters here—increase the energy level and so also contribute to pushing this section somewhat up the overall arch structure.)

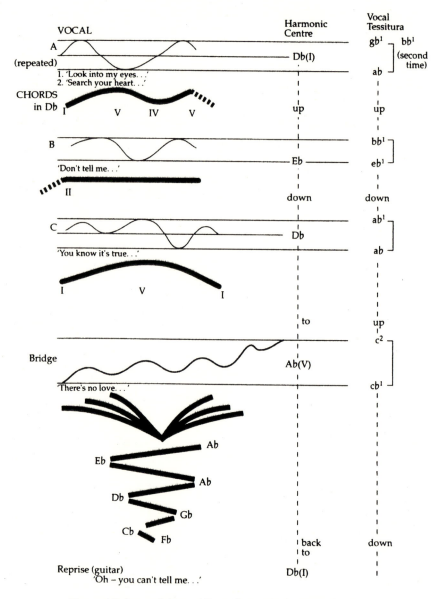

Figure 4.2 Bryan Adams: '(Everything I Do) I Do It for You'

This large-scale arch form is underpinned by the harmony. In A and C the chords move away from the tonic—so that they can return there subsequently. This kind of out-and-back circling round the primary triads has roots in hymns but also in a myriad of popular genres, going back, for example, to the *passamezzo* formulae of the sixteenth century. In B the harmony is pushed up to II—a minor triad, lying a good way from I both in terms of distance on the harmonic series and of pitch-consonance relationships—screwing up the tension (the nerves tense). In the bridge, the chords move through a circle of descending fourths—or, as it actually sounds, a circle of rising fifths. Gesturally, the effect of this is interesting. The rise in pitch and the sharp-ward move increase tension, but the lack of leading notes, and the feeling of a succession of plagal (IV–I) cadences, seems to soften this, producing a more receptive, lump-in-the-throat kind of tension. I feel this as a gradual opening-of-the-arms invitation and appeal. And the repetition inherent in the sequential technique—this is the most iterative part of the song— generalizes this: one feels the whole audience joining in this gesture, as against the I–You individualism constructed before and after this.

The subdominant chord and the IV–I progression play a big part in this song. Though only a suggestion in the first part, this importance picks up from the bridge onwards. The guitar solo substitutes a repeated IV–I oscilla- tion for the harmonies of A, and in the full-length version of the song this pattern recurs in an extra quasi-improvised section following the final cadence. The gestural equivalent of the plagal progression seems to me to be something like a 'benediction', the arms opening and descending to reassure, absolve, bless; this is not just because of the 'Amen' associations, but arises from the centrality of the tonic pitch in both chords—there is a relatively low level of tensional difference—and from the fact that usually so many constituent notes of IV resolve downwards to I ($\hat{6}$ to $\hat{5}$, $\hat{4}$ to $\hat{3}$). Over the whole song, the role of the plagal effect is to modify the otherwise strong I–V–I tendency which Schenkerians[5] could easily find in the *Ursatz* (see the 'harmonic centre' column on Figure 4.2; Schenkerians could easily locate a $\hat{3}$–$\hat{2}$–$\hat{1}$ *Urlinie* as well—but this is not surprising in a genre with deep roots in European bourgeois tradition). A hint of Gospel ecstasy tempers bal- lad desire and aspiration. The most explicit focus for this desire is Bryan Adams' voice. Husky, limited in high frequencies (i.e. lacking energy and confidence,

---

[5] For Schenker's theory, which sees all good music as based on an underlying I–V–I harmonic progression, see Middleton 1990: 192–5.

requiring assistance), rich in dissonant 'noise', this places us in the (imagined) world of concrete reality; disturbing ordered structure, its disordered quality, its incompleteness, demands listener participation, invites embrace. It is right in the centre of the mix, above the bass and drum-kit. Piano and synthesizer are slightly to the left, guitars slightly to the right, but there is not much spread—they are all blended in towards the centre—and there is even less depth: instead there's rather a 'wall-of-sound' effect, but the use of heavy reverb means that this comes out at the listener, enveloping her, rather than inviting her in (as in the Madonna record).

Surmounting bass and drums, Adams, so to speak, 'rides' the groove. This is of classic rock ballad type. It is vital to get the tempo right for this, so that the combination of strong on-beat, emphasized by bass fills around it, and moderate (hi-hat) backbeat produces the required sways and dips of the body (shoulders, hips, flexing of the knees?). Throughout, unschematized fragments from bass, guitars, and piano of eight-to-the-bar and sixteen-to-the-bar 'fills' (with off-beat accent) offer possibilities of more complex, flexible movements —almost like individualized variants of a generalized eroticism. These fills, a rhythmic equivalent to the concreteness of the vocal timbre, are the other side of the more abstract, 'collectivizing' effect of the basic beat (audience swaying together). Nevertheless, in general, this latter effect defines more than any other quality the specificity of the rock variant of the ballad genre's personalized gestures.

Gesture and Connotation

Nothing in my argument so far should be taken as implying that, in the analysis of popular music—still less music as a whole—*only* the sphere of gesture matters. In both the pieces I have discussed, for example, connotations are important too. The girlish but provocatively knowing sound of Madonna's voice calls up all kinds of associations, certainly in the male mind, standing in a long-established intertextual tradition (represented, for instance, by Marilyn Monroe); and the genre itself, disco, gives rise to many connotations. Bryan Adams' voice-type, together with piano and (synthesized) string backing, immediately signals 'sentiment', 'romance', 'confession'; and the 'Amen' fourths suggest a hymnic sincerity. But often the fields of gesture and connotation (primary and secondary meaning, as I have called them elsewhere) are actually correlated, through the action of what some semiologists have termed a 'semantic gesture': a unifying, generating principle, traversing semiotic levels (somatic; referential) and tied to deep cultural functions (see Mukarovsky 1977; Middleton 1990: 224). For example, the bourgeois 'arch' relates on one level to a gestural agenda, as we have seen: the personal mastery of the body; the individualization of emotion; the expansive-but-controlled, rationally-timed symmetries of the Self as 'little home'. But on another level it also relates to an expansive field of connotations: boundless ambition, directed at mastering external reality, making history and so on, but limited, ultimately, by the assumptions of 'empirical individualism' ('I know, and possess, that which I can see'); the result, through 'contracts' between individuals (individual phrases?) representing the 'greater home' of bourgeois culture. (On 'arch' structures and bourgeois culture, see Maróthy 1974.) Similarly, it might be possible to find the roots of both the nervous excitement modelled in the rhythms of 'Where's the Party?' and the suggestions of hedonism conjured up by Madonna's voice and by the connotations of disco culture in certain key developments in late capitalist consumerism, which begin to write the bourgeois individual out of the script in favour of *homo communalis desiderens*: 'we know, and want, that which we enjoy'.

Popular and Classical

I see no reason why the mode of analysis proposed here could not be applied to music other than popular songs.[6] The musicological time may be right. Joseph Kerman, in his important book on musicology (1985), constantly circles round the limitations of formalistic analytic methods, tying them to their historical roots: the development of musicology itself, of idealist aesthetics—with its notion of the 'autonomous' work—and of the 'canon' of 'classical' masterworks, which all began in the early nineteenth century. These developments gave rise to a preferred mode of listening, closely linked with formalistic analysis, and based on the proposition that understanding is directly proportional to the ability to grasp cognitively all the details of a work's underlying structure and their interrelationships. Subotnik (1988) and Cook (1990), among others, have clarified the specific historical location of this 'structural listening'. It is applicable, they argue, purely to the 'common-practice canon' of Western art music, from Corelli to Mahler—and may be not entirely appropriate even there.

---

[6] I have concentrated here on the Western musical field. The extent to which the argument applies elsewhere is a larger question which should certainly be pursued.

The deconstruction, within musicology itself, of 'structural listening', together with the ideology of structural autonomy which is linked with it, brings into sharp focus the historical and cultural limits within which they have validity. To the extent that structural analysis triumphed alongside the musical category of autonomous art with which it was historically connected, we can also say that to historicize structural analysis casts light on the split of the musical field into 'popular' and 'classical' sides. It has been common-place—and is so still—to defend the distinction between the two by exposing popular music to examination by structural analysis and finding it wanting. This historical model has, since the early nineteenth century, tended to reserve 'mind' for art music, 'body' for popular; 'argument' and 'visceral pleasures' have been separated in line with a quasi-sociological distinction of categories. But if the relevance of structural analysis is now being revealed as distinctly partial, it is tempting to wonder if the last 200 years have been, in one sense, something of a diversion, the popular/classical split a side-effect of the gigantic, if glorious, failure of post-Enlightenment bourgeois thought. This would have implications not just for analytic methodology but for music his-toriography as well, for it raises the possibility that the differences setting apart twentieth-century popular songs from the lineages of European music are less than commonly thought.

Before being superseded in the late eighteenth century, the dominant European music theory, explaining compositional technique and expressive effect alike, was that of mimesis. There is a certain congruence between aspects of this theory and aspects of a theory of gesture (though there are also dif-ferences). The system of musical 'figures' developed by Baroque theorists and composers, as a means of 'imitating' emotions, actions, character-types, and so on, was symptomatic of a pervasive relationship between music and classical rhetoric, for the figures were modelled on oratorical figures of speech and structural devices, and in both cases the aim was the arousal and direction of the audience's passions.[7] While many of the musical figures were to do with word-painting or devices of musical logic (repetition, sequence, etc.), others were more obviously 'gestural': *exclamatio* and *interrogatio*, for example. Moreover, both Cartesian science and the older theory of humours emphasized the emotions' physiological roots. One theorist, Heinichen, drew on the rhetorical concept of *loci topici*—rationalized categories of topics which could give rise to concrete musical figures in the composer's mind—and

---

[7] The *New Grove* article on 'rhetoric' is a good starting-place for this topic.

these might perhaps be compared to deep somatic gestures. It is true that the theory of figures and the whole rhetorical tradition on which it was based are overwhelmingly weighted towards considerations of verbal syntax and meanings. But oratorical performance is intimately concerned with the moulding of verbal intonations in time and pitch-space, and here rational and affective meanings, and their musico-gestural delivery by the vocal body —with the assistance of the physiological body—are fused. Wilson Coker's book, *Music and Meaning* (1972), persuasively shows how in musical syntax the equivalents of logical devices or cognitive shapes have physiological links.

Mimetic theories gradually faded, as notions of music's structural autonomy came to the fore. Or perhaps it would be truer to say that they were ideologically written out—for I think it is perfectly possible to do a gestural analysis of many nineteenth-century pieces. Take Beethoven, high priest of the autonomists—the initial presentation of the first subject of the first movement of the fifth symphony ('da-da-da-dah'). How easy it would be to describe this passage in terms of the gestural references of its dramatically undulating pitch shapes, its variability of motion, from cascades of notes to lengthy pauses, its variety of harmonic rhythm and its use of accent. Agawu (1991) in his semiotic study of Classical music (Haydn, Mozart, Beethoven) describes its principle of operation not in the formalist terms generally used but in terms of an interplay between two semiotic levels, one intramusical (but organized as rhetorical structure), the other extramusical (organized through conventionalized 'topics', each associated with familiar musical figures, manners, and textures). This is not too far distant from my gesture/connotation pairing, and 'What emerges is a fluidly defined sense of movement, often most accessible through rhythm' (Agawu 1991: 130).

Even in the twentieth century, when at first sight formalism seems to reign supreme, we find a 'poor relation' situated in Central and Eastern Europe, which we may represent by the figures of Ernst Kurth—who based his analytic theory on the 'energies' manifested by tensional processes—and Boris Asaf'ev, whose 'intonational theory' saw music as a product of the dynamic interrelationships of sounds, conceived as models of socio-historical relationships (Kurth 1991; Asaf'ev 1977). The work of both men can be felt to lie behind the work of Maróthy, mentioned earlier. In Western Europe, Cook (1990) at times comes close to a gestural theory; and several recent writings apply methods derived from rhetorical analysis (for example, Greene 1992).

The rehabilitation of a more kinetically oriented mode of analysis does not mean, I must repeat, that other modes are always irrelevant. To return to the opening of Beethoven's fifth symphony for a moment: as well as functioning gesturally, this passage obviously carries a range of connotations (fate, heroism, and all that); and at the same time it stands at the beginning of a large-scale musical argument, which will not be completed until the very end of the final movement, and which for its full assimilation certainly does demand the techniques of structural listening. What I would suggest is that these three areas —gesture, connotation, argument—operate in different repertories in diverse ratios and interrelationships; and analysis needs to reflect that. Within musicology, gestural analysis is the poor relation. For historical and cultural reasons, popular songs offer ideal material for starting to put that neglect to rights.

References

Agawu, K. (1991). *Playing with Signs* (Princeton).

Asaf'ev, B. V. (1977). *Musical Form as a Process*, trans. J. R. Tull (Ann Arbor).

Brackett, D. (1992). 'James Brown's "Superbad" and the double-voiced utterance', *Popular Music*, 11/3: 309–24.

Coker, W. (1972). *Music and Meaning* (New York).

Cook, N. (1990). *Music, Imagination and Culture* (Oxford).

Greene, R. (1992). 'A musico-rhetorical outline of Holst's "Egdon Heath" ', *Music and Letters*, 73/2 (May), 244–67.

Hawkins, S. (1992). 'Towards new analytical methodologies in popular music', *Popular Music*, 11/3: 325–36.

Jones, S. (1991). BBC Reith Lectures, *Independent*, 14 November, 21 November, 28 November, 5 December, 12 December, 19 December.

Kerman, J. (1985). *Musicology* (London).

Kubik, G. *et al.* (1989). 'African Arts', in *Encyclopedia Britannica*, i. 134–80.

Kurth, E. (1991). *Selected Writings*, ed. and trans. L. A. Rothfarb (Cambridge).

Maróthy, J. (1974). *Music and the Bourgeois, Music and the Proletarian* (Budapest).

—— and Batári, M. (n.d.). *An Essay on the Musical Infinite*, typescript translation by the authors of *Apeiron Musikon: A Zenei Végtelen* (Budapest, 1986).

Middleton, R. (1990). *Studying Popular Music* (Milton Keynes).

Moore, A. (1993). *Rock: The Primary Text* (Buckingham).

Mukarovsky, J. (1977). *Structure, Sign and Function* (Cambridge, Mass.).

Subotnik, R. R. (1988). 'Toward a deconstruction of structural listening: a critique of Schoenberg, Adorno and Stravinsky', in *Explorations in Music, The Arts and Ideas. Essays in Honor of Leonard B. Meyer*, ed. E. Narmour and R. A. Solie (Philadelphia).

Van der Merwe, P. (1989). *Origins of the Popular Style* (Oxford).

Walser, R. (1992). 'Eruptions: heavy metal appropriations of classical virtuosity', *Popular Music*, 11/3: 263–308.

Discography

Bryan Adams, '(Everything I Do) I Do It for You'. A & M, AMCD 789 (1991).

Madonna, 'Where's the Party?', *True Blue*. WEA, WX54 925442-1 (1986).

5

·····

James Brown's 'Superbad' and the Double-Voiced Utterance

DAVID BRACKETT

JB was proof that black people were different. Rhythmically and tonally blacks had to be from somewhere else. Proof that Africa was really over there for those of us who had never seen it—it was in that voice. (Thulani Davis, quoted Guralnick 1986: 242–3)[1]

If there is any black man who symbolizes the vast differences between black and white cultural and aesthetic values, Soul Brother No. 1 (along with Ray Charles) is that man. (David Levering Lewis, quoted Guralnick 1986: 240)[2]

Brown has never been a critics' favorite principally because of the apparent monotony of so many of his post-1965 recordings. But attacking him for being repetitive is like attacking Africans for being overly fond of drumming. Where the European listener may hear monotonous beating, the African distinguishes subtle polyrhythmic interplay, tonal distinctions among the various drums, the virtuosity of the master drummer, and so on. Similarly, Brown sounds to some European ears like so much harsh shrieking. (Palmer 1980: 141)

During the 1960s James Brown single handedly demonstrated the possibilities for artistic and economic freedom that black music could provide if one constantly struggled against its limitations . . . He was driven by an enormous ambition and unrelenting ego, making him a living symbol of black self-determination . . . Motown may have been the sound of young America, but Brown was clearly the king of black America. (George 1988: 98–9)

As the quotations at the beginning of this essay indicate, many members of James Brown's audience equate him with the concept of difference. This

An earlier version of this paper was presented at the IASPM conference in Berlin, Germany, 15–20 July 1991. I wish to thank the many people who offered their thoughtful suggestions and remarks on that occasion.

[1] Guralnick identifies Davis as a *Village Voice* reporter and the context given is 'writing of growing up . . . black and female'.

[2] Guralnick describes Lewis as a 'young black historian' writing 'in 1986'. Lewis is the author of *King: a Biography*, *When Harlem Was in Vogue*, and co-author of *Harlem Renaissance: Art of Black America*.

difference is usually linked to various oppositions: black to white, African to European, abnormal to normal. The recurrent and persistent manner in which these oppositions are invoked suggests that James Brown's music might present acute difficulties for those who would write about it without a careful re-examination of critical terminology. This essay presents a musical and textual analysis of James Brown's 1970 recording 'Superbad' in the context of previous critical discourses surrounding James Brown and his music.[3]

A quick glance at the lyrics (Example 5.1) introduces us to a discursive universe far removed from the poetry of Western art song, the urbane witticisms of Tin Pan Alley, and the folksy, anecdotal narrative of country-western music. The linguistic differences embodied in 'Superbad' reflect one of the often observed differences between African-American and Euro-American culture on the whole: the role and use of language, specifically in rhetorical styles and performances. As in the matter of general culture, these differences are far-ranging and difficult to summarize; there are also, unsurprisingly, many points of intersection between what linguists refer to as Black English (BE) and Standard English (SE). Some of the differences may be summarized as follows: emphasis on the *sound* of the words (BE) rather than on their meaning (SE); speech as a performance or a game (BE) rather than an act of information giving (SE); patterns of expression without clear distinctions between performer and audience (BE) as against patterns of expression with clear distinctions between performer and audience (SE); conversations which are consciously stylized (BE) as against conversations which are unplanned, spontaneous (SE); performance as a process (BE) rather than performance as a thing (SE) (see Abrahams 1976: 8–9).

Building upon these differences and extending them to the field of literature, Henry Louis Gates, jun. has identified the term 'Signifyin(g)' as the black rhetorical 'trope of tropes', a term which subsumes the many varieties of black rhetorical strategies—that is, African-American linguistic difference as it manifests itself in speech, and in oral and written narratives. Gates describes

---

[3] Previous analyses of 'Superbad' include Olly Wilson's (1974) examination of the polyrhythmic structure and its relationship to West African rhythmic procedure and the current author's dissertation (Brackett 1991: 85–147), a considerably more detailed study of the parameters explored in the present essay, as well as of the parameters of timbre, rhythm, phrasing, and form. The issue of a potentially essentialist notion of the use of terms such as 'Afro-American' and 'Euro-American' is addressed by Tagg (1989). While Tagg provides an important corrective to overly facile, reductive equations between ethnicity and music as well as the tendency of white writers to romanticize the idea of 'blackness', the term 'African-American music' retains its validity through historically determinate enunciations. In other words, it is contingent upon *who* uses the term in *what* context.

Ex 5.1. Lyrics of 'Superbad'. Source: 'Superbad' (King K1127). 'Superbad' was recorded on 30 June 1970 and released in a shorter version (King 45-6329) in October 1970.

'Superbad'

Introduction:	1	Watch me, Watch me
	2	I got it, Watch me, I got it, Yay
A1:	3	I got something that makes me want to shout
	4	I got somethat that tells me what it's all about.
	5	Huh! I got soul and I'm superbad
	6	I got soul and I'm superbad.
A2:	7	Now I got a mood that tells me what to do
	8	Sometimes it feels, Hah!
	9	Now I got a mood that tells me what to do
	10	Sometimes I feel so nice, I want to try myself [a few?].
	11	I got soul and I'm superbad, Huh!
A3:	12	I love, I love to do my thing, ah
	13	And I, And I don't need no one else.
	14	Sometimes I feel so nice, Good God!
	15	I jump back, I wanna kiss myself
	16	I got soul—huh!—And I'm superbad
	17	Hey! Said I'm superbad—Bridge, come on!
B1:	18	Up and down, and round and round
	19	Up and down, all around.
	20	Right on people, let it all hang out
	21	If you don't brothers and sisters
	22	Then you won't know, what it's all about
	23	Give me, give me, etc.
A4:	24	(sax solo) Unh! Come on!
	25	I got that something that makes me want to shout
	26	I got that thing, tells me what it's all about.
	27	I got soul, and I'm superbad.
	28	I got the move, that tells me what to do
	29	sometimes I feel so nice, said I wanna [try myself a few].
	30	I, I, etc.
	31	I got soul, and I'm superbad. Bridge! With me!
B2:	32	Up and down and all around.
	33	Right on people, let it all hang out,
	34	If you don't brothers and sisters
	35	then you won't know, what it's all about.
	36	give me, give me, etc.
A5:	37	(sax solo) unh, come on, come on, Robert, etc.
	38	Good God! Up and down and all around.
	39	Right on people, ayy; let it all hang out.
	40	If you don't brothers and sisters
	41	then you won't know what it's all about.
	42	said give me, give me, etc.
	43	Right on people, let it all hang out,
	44	Don't know, what it's all about.

45 I'm Superbad, I'm Superbad.
46 Early in the morning, about noon,
47 right on brother, make it soon.
48 In the evening, I get my groove,
49 got the soul, got to move.
50 I've got it, I've got it!
51 Said I'm superbad.
52 Do your thing Robert (sax solo) Superbad.
53 Fellas, I need some power, [yeah], soul power.
54 Gimme, gimme, etc.

the difference between the black linguistic sign 'Signification' (which he denotes in upper case) and the standard English sign 'signification' (which he denotes with lower case) as the difference between paradigmatic and syntagmatic relations (Gates 1988: 46–8). The emphasis on paradigmatic relations means that speakers (or writers) 'draw on . . . figurative substitutions' that 'tend to be humorous, or function to name a person or a situation in a telling manner' (ibid. 49). The text of 'Superbad' embodies the difference between these uses of the term 'Signification' as well as between what the sociolinguist Roger D. Abrahams terms Black English and Standard English: in 'Superbad' we find an extreme emphasis on the materiality of the signifier, an almost complete lack of emphasis on narrative and on syntagmatic or chain-like continuity. So much of what others have described as free association and non-sequiturs results from this emphasis on sound.[4]

Another highly important aspect of Signification that figures prominently in the text of 'Superbad' is what Gates terms 'intertextuality'. This type of intertextuality stresses the creative use in oral narration of 'formulaic phrases' rather than the creation of novel content. The emphasis, then, in these narratives—often referred to as 'toasts'—is on reusing and recombining stock phrases in an original way from one context to another rather than creating phrases that are strikingly original in themselves. Similarly, evaluations of performers depend not so much upon the ability of the narrator 'to dream up new characters or events' but rather 'to group together two lines that end in words that . . . bear a phonetic similarity to each other' (Gates 1988: 60–1). The concept of intertextuality provides a key to understanding the text of 'Superbad'. Beginning with the title word, 'Superbad', formulaic

---

[4] Guralnick makes the following observation: 'by the time that "(When you Touch Me) I Can't Stand Myself" and "There Was a Time" came out as a double-sided hit in the winter of '67–'68, lyrics had reduced themselves to free association, melody has virtually disappeared' (Guralnick 1986: 242). Cliff White adds: 'I like his style . . . enjoying the inevitable non-sequiturs once he's made the initial point' (White 1987).

phrases of BE slang permeate the song: 'what it's all about', 'I got soul', 'I love to do my thing', 'jump back', 'Right on people', 'let it all hang out', 'brothers and sisters', and 'I need some soul power'. The importance of the ability to end lines with two words that sound alike is certainly evident; at times this seems to be the primary motivation for certain lines of the text. The first two verses, comprising lines 3–6 and 7–10, have an a-a-b-b rhyme scheme; this changes to an a-b-c-b pattern in the third verse, lines 12–15, presumably to increase the emphasis on the striking phrase, 'I jump back, I wanna kiss myself', in line 15.[5] This parallels a tendency that Gates has detected in the 'Signifying Monkey' poems in which 'disturbances in the rhyming schemes often occur to include a particularly vivid or startling combination of signifiers' (ibid. 61).

Another factor contributing to the proliferation of meanings is the importance of *delivery*; that is, the manner of delivery profoundly affects the semantic content. Nowhere is this more apparent than in the title itself, particularly the 'bad' part of it. This exemplifies what Gates has observed as one of the primary qualities of black discourse, what he terms (after Bakhtin) the 'double-voiced' utterance, the manner in which a word can partake simultaneously of both black and white discursive worlds (ibid. 50–1).[6] These semantic shifts occur primarily through changing inflection. The semantic reversal of the term 'bad' may also be due to the glorification of the outlaw or badman in the black community, perhaps because the badman/hustler figure refuses to be defined by the dominant culture.[7] In general, Gates sees this disruption of 'the signifier . . . displacing its signified' as 'an intentional act of will' most notably present in the term 'Signification' itself (Gates

---

[5] Interestingly, Iain Chambers chose to precede his discussion of developments in African-American music in the late 1960s with this line (Chambers 1985: 142).

[6] The dual meaning of 'Signification' is another striking example of this phenomenon. Abrahams adds: 'Perhaps the most dynamic and most inverse of all the performance-centered word categories are those slang terms with high affect in Standard English parlance, used in senses which are sometimes diametrically opposed to their accustomed meanings . . . The meaning of the utterance, "Man, you bad", depends almost entirely on the inflection of the voice' (Abrahams 1976: 21). For Mikhail Bakhtin's classic discussion of the 'double-voiced (or dialogic) utterance', see Bakhtin (1978).

[7] A great quantity of literature exists on the heroic figure of the 'badman' in African-American discourse. Abrahams identifies the figure of the 'badman' as one of the two primary categories of heroes in the toasts, the other being the 'trickster', which is exemplified by the namesake of the 'Signifying Monkey' toast (Abrahams 1970). For an account of how the 'badman' archetype might be manifested in the persona of recent African-American musicians and their music, see Greil Marcus's portrait of Sly Stone (Marcus 1982: 75–111). Charles Keil cautions against attaching negative value judgements to these archetypes: 'If we are ever to understand what urban Negro culture is all about, we had best view entertainers and hustlers as culture heroes—integral parts of the whole—rather than as deviants or shadow figures' (Keil 1966: 20). For an investigation which traces the discourse of the badman as African-American hero, see Levine (1977: 407–40).

1988: 51). In this context, the act of titling a song, 'Superbad' appears as a celebration of black difference, as a refusal to be defined by white culture.

Performance/Environment

As mentioned earlier, Abrahams details two characteristics of Black English that have far-reaching implications for the analysis of 'Superbad': speech as performance and the loss of distinction between audience and performer (Abrahams 1976: 8–9). Before exploring these implications directly, I would like to raise another factor in the *production* of the performance environment that bears on the interpretation of 'Superbad'.

One Marxist critique of mass entertainment maintains that in a capitalist society, a work of art masks its ideology by effacing the means of its production; in other words, hiding the means of production serves to 'naturalize' the text. The Brechtian notion of 'distanciation' argues that conscious reference to the means of producing art will expose the ideology behind it (see Heath 1974). 'Superbad' has both everything to do with this concept and nothing: on the one hand, this particular recording effaces the signs of its own production, overdubbing audience sound to simulate a live recording.[8] This contrasts with the way studio recordings typically efface the signs of their production by seeking to minimize the effect of human performance: individual mistakes can be re-recorded, weak voices bolstered, 'thin' accompaniments 'sweetened' by additional instruments. 'Superbad', though effacing signs of its original studio production, emphasizes the recording as a *performance*: Brown instructs his 'audience' to 'watch' him; he exhorts the members of his band by name and engages in a call and response with them at the end of the song. Brown's vocals and the sax solos appear improvised; rather than presenting a safe, sanitized product, 'Superbad' calls attention to its rough edges. While these effects possibly engender 'distanciation' from the mainstream pop audience, they serve as an invitation for involvement with another—and Brown's principal—audience. The crowd noise positions the listener at a live

---

[8] The information on 'Superbad' derives from the lengthy discography found in Brown's autobiography, *The Godfather of Soul* (Brown 1986: 269–326). The discography in *Godfather of Soul* notes that the crowd noise on this particular recording, released on the album *Superbad*, was added after the initial studio recording. This was obviously an important effect for Brown and his recording company and one they employed on numerous recordings beginning in 1964. This may well have been a response to the extraordinary success of his 1962 recording, *Live at the Apollo*, released in 1963, a recording cited by virtually every account of James Brown and 1960s soul music as enormously influential. See Peter Guralnick's reverential account (Guralnick 1986: 233–8) and Brown's recollection (Brown 1986: 133–44).

performance; the words 'watch me, watch me' invite the audience to scrutinize the performer; the identification of parts of the song (as when Brown calls out 'bridge' in lines 17 and 31) gives an effect of immediacy, as though the course of the song were being decided spontaneously; this identification also directs attention toward the artifice of the song's structure.

There exists another level of relationship between 'Superbad' and the African-American community: the manner in which the song, musically and lyrically, evokes the late 1960s movement known as 'Black Nationalism'. In the late 1960s, Brown became known as 'Soul Brother No. 1', due to his influence in the black community and the release of such 'message' songs as 'Papa's got a Brand New Bag', 'Don't be a Drop Out', 'Say it Loud—I'm Black and I'm Proud', and 'Soul Power'. Brown agreed to televise his Boston concert the evening after Martin Luther King, jun.'s assassination on 4 April 1968, a decision that helped avert race riots in that city (George 1988: 102–3). Many of the lyrics index slogans popular in the sixties 'black power' movement: 'right on, brother', 'let it all hang out', 'brothers and sisters' and, particularly evident in the closing call and response section, 'I need some power—soul power'. The manner of saxophone playing in the solo sections evokes styles of jazz players such as John Coltrane, Pharoah Sanders, and Albert Ayler, all players identified to some extent with the Black Nationalism movement.[9]

Intertextuality and Fragmentation

There are two main ways in which Brown enacts the 'Signifyin(g)' practice of repetition and difference in musical terms in 'Superbad'. The first case may be termed an intertextual referentiality: Brown, in the course of a performance, invokes other musical referents—in the form of songs, gestures, modes of performance, dances—lying outside the text of that particular performance. The various allusions to Black Nationalism in the lyrics and saxophone solo are two of the ways Brown 'Signifies' or comments on other texts in 'Superbad'. The second form of Signifyin(g) that plays an important role in creating variety in this song is the repetition with variation of small musical cells: bits of text, a syllable, or a type of scream.[10] Example 5.2 displays five such cells,

[9] Frank Kofsky goes to considerable lengths to demonstrate the presence of social content in jazz, specifically linking the black avant-garde jazz musicians of the late 1960s with the Black Nationalist movement of that period (Kofsky 1970). For more on the historical formations of social content in African-American music, see Jones (1963).

[10] Abrahams indicates that 'frequent injected sounds and exclamations [are] also used to intensify and further the action' in toasts (Abrahams 1970: 93).

Ex 5.2. Cells *a–e*

Cell *a*

lettered *a* through *e*. These cells create a 'Signifyin(g)' commentary when they are repeated and varied in parallel parts of sections: for instance, cell *b* (which contains the words 'I got soul') tends to occur towards the latter part of the A section of the piece, shown in lines 6, 11, and 16 in Example 5.1. Another kind of Signifyin(g) occurs when a cell becomes detached from its initial place in the formal structure. Cell *d*, which consists of rhythmic manipulation of the word 'gimme', exemplifies this procedure: it appears first towards the end of the B1 section (the names and numbers of sections are shown in Example 5.1), it appears a second time in a similar position toward

Ex 5.2. (*cont.*):

Cell *b*

the end of the second B section, but its third appearance occurs during the long sax solo in the A5 section. Cell *d4* appears in the third B section closely parallel to its position in sections B1 and B2; however, it is varied by being extended for twenty bars.

Cell *d* also exemplifies another way in which Brown comments on aspects of his own performance: cell *d*, by anticipating the downbeat in its first three occurrences, creates expectations that Brown 'disappoints' on the fourth occurrence. Gates, in his discussion of the musical uses of Signifyin(g), states that 'this form of disappointment creates a dialogue between what the listener expects and what the artist plays' (Gates 1988: 123). The cells *b*, *c*, and *d* also tend to emphasize the downbeat so that these types of accents become the expected norm against which repetitions that do not follow this accentual pattern can be felt as exceptions. Other utterances that might be considered 'marginal' from a Eurocentric viewpoint, including a variety of grunts and groans, also occur on the latter part of beat four: the 'hunh's', transcribed in cell *b5* and in cell *d3*, are examples of this phenomenon. In fact, these Signifyin(g) relationships came to my attention when I concentrated on phenomena that I had originally assumed to be marginal: the various 'extemporaneous' exhortations that occur during the sax solos; the vast variety of grunts and groans; and the other fragmented phrases illustrated

Cell *c*

Ex 5.2. (*cont.*):

Cell *d*

Cell *e*

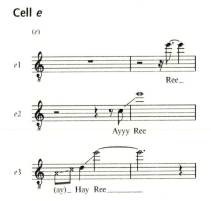

in Example 5.2. This is precisely the part of the piece in which a great deal of what is most characteristic about it emerges: the repetition of fragments with discrete variations that alternately create expectations and thwart them; and, the self-referentiality and the self-conscious allusions to the act of performance.

The screams that constitute cells *a* and *e* deserve further comment, for close analysis of them also contradicts commonplace assumptions. Rather than being gestures without pitch, more or less extemporaneously added to spice up the musical flow, both cells evidence specific characteristics both with regards to pitch and to their formal placement. Specifically, cell *a* focuses on the pitch D, while cell *e* focuses on the pitch E. Cells *a* and *e* tend to occur in tandem at the end of the B sections. At the very end of the song, the last two statements of cell *a* occur at the end of section B3 and frame within them the final statements of both cell *d* and cell *e*. This illustrates how cells can be recombined to create 'new' musical ideas, similar to the way in which the stock phrases of the 'toast' are reused and recombined.

Careful examination of the cells also reveals that the tessitura of the voice plays an important role in the formation of Brown's vocal timbre, described as 'one of the harshest in rhythm and blues' (Palmer 1980: 139). Brown takes care to choose the key of a song so that it places his voice in the uppermost portion of his range. In his songs, one rarely finds instances of pitches lower than G below middle C, the pitch which forms the lower vocal boundary of 'Superbad'. In fact, songs that centre around the pitch D are exceedingly common in Brown's output; a far from exhaustive list of songs with a tonal centre of D includes such stylistic antecedents of 'Superbad' as 'Cold Sweat', 'There Was a Time' and 'Mother Popcorn', to take only songs released as singles during the 1967–70 period. Brown exploits this consistency of tessitura by recycling many vocal cells at identical pitch levels from song to song, thereby implementing another variant of the first form of 'intertextuality' mentioned earlier. 'There Was a Time' provides a case in point: the line, 'there was a [dance, day, time]', is virtually identical in contour and pitch level to figure *b* (containing the words 'I've got soul') in 'Superbad'.[11] Other passages in 'Superbad' closely resemble the pitch content of cell *b*, among them, the phrase 'I've got something' that begins line 3; and the phrase 'all around' that occurs many times in section B. That Brown emphasizes the words 'I've got soul' in this fashion is entirely in keeping with the song's celebration of African-American culture. A later demonstration of Brown's awareness of the sonic advantageousness of the key of D can be found in the song 'Doing It to Death' (1973); although the song begins in F, Brown requests that the band change keys to D about two-thirds of the way through, exclaiming 'in order for me to get down, it's got to be in D'. After Brown repeats his request several times, the band complies and switches keys from F to D![12]

Harmonic Stasis or Harmonic Signifyin(g)?

Let us turn to Robert Palmer for a description of the changes in Brown's music circa 1964:

> Brown would sing a semi-improvised, *loosely* organized melody that *wandered* while the band riffed rhythmically on a single chord, the horns tersely punctuating Brown's declamatory phrases. With no chord changes and precious little melodic variety to sustain listener interest, *rhythm became everything*. Brown and his musicians and arrangers began to treat every instrument and voice in the group as if each were a drum. (Palmer 1980: 140) (emphasis added)

Later in the same article, Palmer accuses critics who would dismiss Brown as monotonous of applying irrelevant criteria. I would suggest that Palmer's own description repeats this critical move but in a much more subtle guise. Close inspection reveals very few songs with 'no chord changes'; it also reveals songs that possess a great deal of 'melodic variety' if the concept of 'melody'

---

[11] These figures also derive from a common pool of vocal gestures found in blues and gospel music (see Titon 1977: 157–69).

[12] 'Doing It to Death' (the title is another instance of the humorous paradigmatic substitutions typical of Signifyin[g]) was originally released and credited to Brown's backing band, 'Fred Wesley and the JBs'. Despite this, there can be little doubt as to the identity of the lead vocalist. The alliteration of the title provides a further connection to Brown's preference for 'D-ness'.

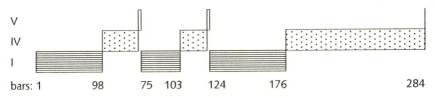

Figure 5.1 Harmonic proportions in 'Superbad'

is based on subtle nuances and variations of melodic cells rather than on the European ideal of a sustained (preferably legato) melodic line. Much has been written about the absence of harmonic motion in James Brown's music. Although harmonically static ostinati occurred in his music from 1964 on, complete songs consisting of long ostinati only began appearing in 1967 with songs such as 'Cold Sweat', 'There Was a Time' and 'Mother Popcorn'; however, most of these songs *do* feature harmonic shifts and more than one ostinato, thereby avoiding complete harmonic stasis. Songs heralded as innovative for their concentration on rhythm in the 1964–5 period such as 'Out of Sight', 'Papa's Got a Brand New Bag' and 'I Got You (I Feel Good)', are actually based on I–IV–V blues progressions. 'Superbad', despite long passages in which the bass ostinato focuses on a single pitch, does contain harmonic movement—indeed, harmonic movement that may be understood as an extended I–IV–V harmonic progression. Figure 5.1 displays the relative amount of time spent in each harmonic area. This use of the I–IV–V progression amounts to a Signifyin(g) commentary upon the use of this progression in Euro-American music, an instance of a 'double-voiced utterance' in yet another parameter. In Western art music, the IV (subdominant) harmony usually serves as an intermediate step between the structurally more important I (tonic) and V (dominant) harmonies; instead, in 'Superbad', harmonic weight shifts toward the subdominant, while the tonic is emphasized somewhat less and only brief allusions are made to the dominant. The concluding section lasts 108 bars and centres around the subdominant pitch, G. This has the effect of eclipsing D—the putative tonic—as the tonal focus. The final shift to the dominant on A for the concluding beat of the song comes as an abrupt jolt and effectively proscribes a sense of tonal closure. Thus the most common harmonic progression in the common practice period of Western art music is present in 'Superbad' but is presented in an extremely subtle fashion. This places the harmonic context of the song in a position similar to the linguistic context: it belongs to, while it simultaneously comments upon, the mainstream Euro-American discourse.

For the sake of this exercise, I have limited the discussion to three parameters—lyrics, melody, and harmony. I do not mean to undermine the importance of other elements, such as rhythm, phrasing, timbre, larger questions of form, and the interaction of these elements.[13] Rather, my intention is to show, within a fairly limited space, how a cultural/linguistic practice such as 'Signifyin(g)' might be brought to bear in a fairly thorough manner in the three parameters discussed here.

James Brown remains an enigmatic figure shrouded in controversy; in the last few years his legal difficulties have made him a frequent subject of caricature and derision. This can be interpreted as symptomatic of the manner in which the dominant culture, through the mass media, can defuse the threat of a man whose music once formed a vigorous challenge to the prevailing aesthetic. Brown affirms a system of alternative values both in lyrics— through the explicit references to Black power slogans, African-American street language and values—and in music—through the explicit invocations of specific African-American practices and a perhaps unconscious reference to West African music. His music exemplifies what Charles Keil termed the 'appropriation-revitalization' process: the manner in which each form of African-American pop music has become 'more African in its essentials' in response to the previous style's 'appropriation' into Euro-American pop music (Keil 1966: 43).[14] In fact, Brown's post-1965 music is central to many of the stylistic shifts in African-American music since then. 'Funk' music, as Brown's post-1965 music is usually labelled, became widely influential in the late 1960s, first through Sly Stone's importation of funk elements into his hybrid

---

[13] See note 4 above for previous discussions of these parameters.

[14] This brief presentation of Keil's 'appropriation-revitalization' process may appear profoundly undialectical in its portrayal of a monolithic one-way march in African-American music towards West Africa. Keil himself admits to exceptions to this theory: writing in the mid-1960s, he recognized the Motown-Tamla sound (and particularly the singing of Diana Ross) as music that spoke more to the emergent black middle class and to sectors of the white middle class than music that represented some sort of in-group solidarity among African-Americans. At the same time, we can recognize the increased popularity during this period—in addition to James Brown—of the 'Stax' artists and Aretha Franklin in support of the 'appropriation-revitalization' process (see Nelson George's characterization of the same opposition—Motown/James Brown—in the prefatory remarks). Olly Wilson, in his discussion of the relationship between James Brown's late sixties music and West African music, corroborates and extends Keil's theory, stressing that the process is rooted in similar *conceptual* approaches and is therefore potentially infinite (Wilson 1974: 19–20). In light of this, it might be more accurate to say that each successive form of African-American pop music has revealed new aspects of the African-American musical/cultural tradition to the mass public. Arguments for the dialectical nature of 'progress' in African-American music can be found in the 1980s in the persistence, alongside of hip-hop, of such 'retronuevo' artists as Anita Baker. This trend is currently institutionalized in the 'Quiet Storm' radio format (see George 1988: 186–8).

of 'psychedelic' music, and later through its wider dissemination in the music of such 1970s bands as the Ohio Players, Kool and the Gang, KC and the Sunshine Band, and Funkadelic. Disco, in the late 1970s, simplified many of the rhythmic complexities of funk but still retained an obvious debt to Brown, as he was only too happy to point out in his 1979 release, 'The Original Disco Man'. Rap represents the latest manifestation of the appropriation-revitalization process, bringing 'material that was exclusively the province of the black oral tradition and race-record tradition' (Gates, quoted in Pareles 1990) into the cultural mainstream. Moreover, rap owes multiple debts to James Brown, primarily in its use of ostinati; rap further elevates the ostinato to a position of importance through the use of 'sampling', whereby fragments of previous recordings overlap or are superimposed onto the basic rhythm track, or are even used as the basis for the rhythm track. This forms an obvious instance of the Signifyin(g) practice identified by Gates as 'intertextuality', as many pre-recorded snippets are combined heterogeneously. These samples often form an even further primary link with Brown's music in that the samples for many rap songs are frequently taken from Brown's late 1960s–early 1970s recordings.

Olly Wilson's statement—that 'Africanness consists of the way of doing something, not simply something that is done' (Wilson 1974: 20)—and Henry Louis Gates, jun. observation—that 'the black tradition emphasizes refiguration, or repetition and difference, or troping, underscoring the foregrounding of the chain of signifiers, rather than the mimetic representation of a novel content' (Gates 1988: 79)—echo what many other writers have observed: Brown's lyrics matter not so much for what he says as for how he says it; his music matters not so much for the pitches it uses as for how those pitches are inflected. At the same time we must remain sensitive to whatever role elements such as pitch might play and not dismiss them entirely. What I have gone to some trouble to demonstrate here is that connections exist between the musical processes and the linguistic processes. Building on Wilson's and Gates's work, I have attempted to explicate further the process by which Brown varies small musical cells through repetition and recombination and through variation of pitch, rhythm, and timbre.

A few words of methodological caution are in order at this point. In discovering connections between linguistic, cultural, and musical processes, one runs the danger of finding overtly pat homologies. And 'the difficulty with using such homologies is not that they cannot be produced. It is that they can always be produced' (Randel 1991; cf. Middleton 1990: 150). What is important here is not the homologies that have been produced; it is that social/cultural differences noted in other domains—linguistics, literature —might influence a music analysis so as to suggest a relationship between the musical object and the historical moment in which it appeared. Analytical methodologies carry with them implicit or explicit value judgements; merely importing techniques from art music can yield information of only limited relevance to the study of popular music. Since these value judgements are embedded in the analytical techniques, the results may be interpreted as revealing deficiencies in the music rather than failures in the techniques; or, the musical object may be distorted to overemphasize parameters that fit the analytical methodology but are unimportant to the reception or perception of the piece.[15] Attempting to reorient an analysis through a concept such as 'Signifyin(g)' may help to reveal the way in which values—signalled by the use of terms such as 'melody', 'harmony', and 'musical interest'—are embedded in the discourse surrounding the music of James Brown.[16] The value of the 'appropriation-revitalization' concept is that it identifies some aspects of the diachronic *process* which constitutes African-American music at a given historical moment.

The more I analysed and thought about James Brown's music, particularly 'Superbad', the more I found that I could not avoid discussing the 'critical difference' between African-American and Euro-American music and culture —that this text compelled me to confront this issue.[17] If soul is, in Charles Keil's words, 'the ability to communicate something of the [African-American] experience' (Keil 1966: 43), we must interpret a line like 'I've got soul and I'm Superbad' as the singer's affirmation of that experience. Both in what it expresses and in how it expresses it, 'Superbad' results in a musical and lyrical celebration of that very 'experiential' difference.

[15] A large literature exists on the need to develop alternative analytical methodologies for music outside the Western art music canon, particularly for African-American music. Recent summaries of the issues involved may be found in Brackett (1991: 20–41), McClary and Walser (1990) and Middleton (1990: 103–26). Discussions concerning the relevance of analysis—and the 'structural' listening that it encourages—to the contextual contingencies of perception may be found in Cook (1990).

[16] Simon Frith (1990) has discussed how value judgements manifest themselves in the discourses surrounding 'folk', 'popular', and 'art' musics. In many respects the similarities—revolving around oppositions such as authenticity vs. 'selling out'—are more striking than the differences.

[17] Henry Louis Gates, jun. has substituted race for sex in Barbara Johnson's 'provocative assessment of the interpretation of sexuality and textuality which she terms, The Critical Difference' (Gates 1989: 207); Barbara Johnson adds her own explanation of the term, an explanation which illustrates the potentially contradictory nature of the term: 'It is not simply a question of literature's ability to say or not to say the truth of sexuality. For from the moment literature begins to try to set things straight on that score, literature itself becomes inextricable from the sexuality it seeks to comprehend' (Johnson 1980: 13).

References

Abrahams, R. D. (1970). *Deep Down in the Jungle: Negro Narrative Folklore from the Streets of Philadelphia* (Chicago).

—— (1976). *Talking Black* (Rowley, Mass.).

Bakhtin, M. (1978). 'Discourse typology in prose', in *Readings in Russian Poetics: Formalist and Structuralist Views*, ed. L. Matejka and K. Pomorska (Cambridge, Mass.), 176–96.

Brackett, D. (1991). 'Three studies in the analysis of popular music', DMA dissertation, Cornell University.

Brown, J. (1986). *The Godfather of Soul* (with Bruce Tucker) (New York).

Chambers, I. (1985). *Urban Rhythms: Pop Music and Popular Culture* (New York).

Cook, N. (1990). *Music, Imagination and Culture* (Oxford and New York).

Frith, S. (1990). 'What is good music?', *Canadian Music Review*, 10: 92–102.

Gates, H. L., jun. (1988). *The Signifying Monkey: A Theory of African-American Literary Criticism* (New York).

—— (1989). *Figures in Black: Words, Signs, and the 'Racial' Self* (New York).

George, N. (1988). *The Death of Rhythm and Blues* (New York).

Guralnick, P. (1986). *Sweet Soul Music: Rhythm and Blues and the Southern Dream of Freedom* (New York).

Heath, Stephen. (1974). 'Lessons from Brecht', *Screen*, 15: 103–28.

Johnson, B. (1980). *The Critical Difference: Essays in the Contemporary Rhetoric of Reading* (Baltimore and London).

Jones, L. (1963). *Blues People: The Negro Experience in White America and the Music that Developed from It* (New York).

Keil, C. (1966). *Urban Blues* (Chicago and London).

Kofsky, F. (1970). *Black Nationalism and the Revolution in Jazz* (New York).

Levine, L. W. (1977). *Black Culture and Black Consciousness: Afro-American Folk Thought from Slavery to Freedom* (Oxford and New York).

Marcus, G. (1982). *Mystery Train: Images of America in Rock 'n' Roll Music*, rev. edn. (New York).

McClary, S., and Walser, R. (1990). 'Start making sense! Musicology wrestles with rock', in *On Record: Rock, Pop, and the Written Word*, ed. S. Frith and A. Goodwin (London), 277–92.

Middleton. R. (1990). *Studying Popular Music* (Philadelphia).

Palmer, R. (1980). 'James Brown', in *The Rolling Stone Illustrated History of Rock and Roll*, ed. J. Miller (New York), 136–42.

Pareles, J. (1990). 'Rap: slick, violent, nasty and, maybe, hopeful', *New York Times*, sec. 4, 17 June 1990.

Randel, D. M. (1991). 'Crossing over with Ruben Blades', *Journal of the American Musicological Society*, 44: 301–23.

Tagg, P. (1989). 'Open letter: Black music, Afro-American music, and European music', *Popular Music*, 8: 285–98.

Titon, J. T. (1977). *Early Downhome Blues: A Musical and Cultural Analysis* (Urbana, Ill.).

White, C. (1987). Liner notes for *James Brown, the Second CD of JB: Cold Sweat and Other Soul Classics*, Polydor 831 700-2.

Wilson, O. (1974). 'The significance of the relationship between Afro-American music and West African music', *The Black Perspective in Music*, 2 (Spring), 3–22.

Discography

Note. Many of the songs listed below have been reissued on the two following recordings (hereafter referred to as Brown 1985 and Brown 1987):

Brown, J. (1985). *James Brown, the CD of JB: Sex Machine and Other Soul Classics*, Polydor 825 714-2.

Brown, J. (1987). *James Brown, the Second CD of JB: Cold Sweat and Other Soul Classics*, Polydor 831 700-2.

'Cold Sweat', King 45-6110 (July 1967), reissued on Brown 1987.

'Doing it to Death', People PE-621 (Apr. 1973), credited to Fred Wesley & the JBs, reissued on Brown 1985.

'Don't be a Drop Out', King 45-6056 (Oct. 1966).

I Got You (I Feel Good)', King 45-6015 (Nov. 1965).

Live at the Apollo, King K826 (Jan. 1963).

'Mother Popcorn', King 45-6245 (June 1969), reissued on Brown 1985.

'The Original Disco Man', Polydor PD-2034 (Oct. 1979).

'Out of Sight', Smash S-1919 (July 1964), reissued on Brown 1985.

'Papa's got a Brand New Bag', King 45-5999 (July 1965), reissued on Brown 1985.

'Say it Loud—I'm Black and I'm Proud', King 45-6187 (Aug. 1968), reissued on Brown 1987.

'Soul Power', King 45-6368 (Feb. 1971), reissued on Brown 1985.

'Superbad', original 45 r.p.m. version released in Oct. 1970 as King 45-6329, reissued on Brown 1985. The extended version was released on *Superbad*, King K1127 (Jan. 1971).

'There was a Time', King 45-6144 (Dec. 1967), reissued on *Live at the Apollo, Volume 2*, Polydor 823-001 (1986).

6

'Maybellene': Meaning and the Listening Subject

SEAN CUBITT

There appeared in the summer of 1982 a song written and performed by three German structuralists, a song characterized by the simplicity—to the point of banality—of its musical structure and instrumentation. Intended as a critical intervention in the production of ordinariness in popular music, 'Da Da Da' reached number one in the British charts, and Trio's appearance on the British TV show, *Top of the Pops*, was no more threatening than that of Captain Sensible or any other novelty act: welcome to the whacky world of deconstructive minimalism. Clearly the intended meanings of the song were not always the ones it evoked for the listener. Recordings have a way of taking on a life of their own in their meetings with the public; in Voloshinov's phrase, the production of meaning is intersubjective, involving artists, promotional campaigns, disc jockeys, and the audience. This article addresses particularly the role of the listening subject in the construction of a song's meanings.

Richard Middleton's Open University work on popular music (Middleton 1981) crystallized for me a group of concerns around the analysis of music, specifically his use of generative-transformational grammar as the basis for musicological analysis. Transformational grammars offer a wealth of analytic tools and an admirably clear means of explicating musical structures to the musically illiterate (among whom I count myself), but they have traditionally tended to rest on the *a priori* subject capable of generating meaningful utterances. I began to become interested in the different, but complementary, application of semiotics to popular music.

I would like to thank my colleagues on the Open University *Popular Culture* summer school of 1982 for their help and discussion, especially Susan Boyd-Bowman, Anthony Easthope, Dave Laing, Debbie Phillips, and Paddy Scannell. My thanks also to David Connearn for help with the manuscript and to Richard Middleton for help, encouragement, and patience.

Semiotics rests on the thesis—which derives from the work of the Swiss linguist Ferdinand de Saussure—that language is not an effect of meanings intended by speaking subjects, but rather that meaning is itself a product of the rule-governed structure of language. The natural languages, and every other sign-system which functions like a language, produce meanings; these then provide the materials from which are constructed the contents of consciousness. In its classical, structuralist form, semiotics insists that the conscious subject is an effect of language. More recent developments have concentrated on the conflict between and within discourses—groups of utterances sharing additional rules over and above those required to produce meaningful utterances, as verse requires metre or detective stories a plot with a denouement. Allied to the psychoanalytic discovery that individuals do not become social beings simply or without difficulty, this concentration has produced a central concern with the problem of the subject. It now appears that consciousness is neither won nor maintained without difficulty; that the subject is at root decentred, unstill, discontinuous; and that there is a polysemy of the subject just as there is a multiplicity of meanings in any text, be it linguistic, gestural, cinematic or musical. It is this dual problematic— the production of meaning and of the listening subject—in musical communications that this essay confronts.

The popular song undoubtedly has meaning for us. However cynical the artifice of a hit record's industrial genesis, the emotions it evokes are undoubtedly real: real tears, real excitement, real relaxation, virtually measurable physiological reactions. I want to suggest some ways in which a semiotic approach might be of help in developing an understanding of at least some areas of the process of producing these felt meanings, particularly the use of the singing voice. This kind of attention seems especially valid for the kinds of music that have evolved from the meeting of black and white traditions in twentieth-century popular music. The tensions between savage oppression and equally savage freedoms of violence and sexuality, between a yearning for wealth, contentment, and decency and the desperate lust for honky-tonk angels, liquor, and the endless highway; the risk, the danger, the threat of successive waves of ragtime, jazz, and rock 'n' roll: these speak directly to the experience of being alive in our times. The singers who populate our fantasies, the songs we can't get out of our heads, have meanings that reach into our most intimate sense of ourselves. As a start, I would like to draw some parallels between songs and another ancient art, the art of the storyteller.

As well as sharing many of its social functions, songs seem to possess in their melodic structures some of the traits of narrative, except that musical functions replace the events of the diegesis. (It should be noted that the analysis of narratives differentiates between the diegesis—the linear arrangement of events to be told about—and the narration—the way in which these events are ordered and the mode of their telling.) Like narrative, melody promises a dual enjoyment, a pleasure in order and a pleasure in its disruption. Melody must disrupt the perfection of the tonic just as any good story has to begin with a departure, a mystery or some similar intervention into the 'normal' state of affairs; and, like the narrative, in its departure from the norm, melody must contain a promise to return to the narrative closure of restored order. The tonic functions like a good marriage at the end of a realist novel: having dealt with the thrill of loss and trouble, it can only guarantee our pleasure by confining it within the reassuring closure of the restored tonic, just as the narrative restores it in the harmonious form of the heterosexual couple. But, without the initial troubling, there would be no pleasure. Unmoved, unchanging, the subject becomes bored, as is the effect of some of John Cage's pieces, and is lost to the communicative intent of the music. But without the promise of narrative closure, the feeling that this troubling will be resolved, the subject hears 'just a lot of noise'. The expected pleasures are not produced, only a bafflement that most people reserve for their working hours, not their leisure.

Chuck Berry's 'Maybellene', originally recorded in May 1955, exemplifies some of these traits. The song begins with a brief blues lick on the guitar, which slides straight into the basic rhythmic pattern of the song, on the tonic chord. Berry's vocal goes straight into the first chorus, an up-tempo blues addressed to Maybellene herself. This chorus will be repeated four more times, grounding the story of the verses in the erotic melodrama of the chorus. This was Berry's first Chess release, the first of his sagas of the eroticized automobile, and, in spite of the repetitiveness of the musical structure, the tension between the guitar and Willy Dixon's churning bass, added to the almost cinematic car-chase lyric, maintains a dynamic so strong that the song fades out over a still unresolved guitar break. The last verse ends with Berry's V-8 Ford catching Maybellene's Coup-de-Ville on top of the hill: both the music and the vocal push confirm the erotic undertow to the story, the catch and the climax indistinguishably intertwined. Yet there is the further tension between the mono-directional narrative lyric and the repetition of the chorus. On the one hand 'You just started back doing the things you used to do' takes on a new meaning at the end of the song; on the other the drama is itself resolved only temporarily. The only way to confirm possession of the woman is to repeat the process again and again, to play the record again, the singer caught in the trap of his own possessiveness. There is an anxious pessimism underlying the otherwise assured, even arrogant, sexuality of the song. Instead of finding reassurance in the repeated verse/chorus structure, it is as if that nagging question 'Why can't you be true' returns as jealously as the eagle to Prometheus' liver, and with as much to say about the nature of being human.

The fade-out at the end of the song raises several interesting questions. This is one of the earliest fade-outs I have found, and it would be interesting to know whether it had an earlier history. Is it simply a production device, to contain the jam session that might just develop here? Was Berry just unwilling to close the song as a completed entity—as he was later to close Johnny B. Goode; a refusal of restored harmony? Or is it, as seems to be the case with the Beatles' 'Hey Jude', a conscious evocation of infinite replicability? As Aristotle pointed out, 'A whole is that which has a beginning, a middle and an end' (Aristotle 1965: 6), but we have in this case an aesthetic object which is not whole, not complete in itself, and therefore not aesthetic in Aristotelian terms.

The central tenet of almost any aesthetics is that the aesthetic object should contain in itself all the means to its appreciation. It is as if 'Maybellene' abdicates that responsibility, referring not inward, to the mythologizing repetition of the refrain, but through the fade-out to the activity of the auditor, with whom lies the only available fulfilment: to give it another spin, to put another coin in the juke-box. It is an obsessive music, mythologizing its pain, making it not so much permanent as always repeatable. The fade-out pledges that the performance of the pain has an existence beyond the recording, both as the potentially infinite repetition of plays on the record-player or radio, and as the aural disappearance of the performers over the auditory horizon. This refusal of completion refers us, not back into the song, as is the case with the classic aesthetic object, but outwards to the ways in which the song is heard.

This raises in turn the problem of the mechanism by which we engage in the listening process, in so far as it is an emotional and intellectual experience. Narrative forms depend heavily on the process of identification. We require a position in the reading of a novel or the viewing of a film to provide a point of access into the narrative sequence—a perspective from which the narrative becomes comprehensible. In a detective story, for example, we tend to take up the position of the detective, knowing no more than he or she does, trusting them not to lie to us. In the uncritical reading which most examples of the genre invite, we are prompted to identify with the detective, and it is only from that point of view that the story becomes comprehensible. Without identification, the narrative dissolves into noise, as sometimes occurs with radio plays when the voices of two or more characters are too similar. That kind of confusion debars us from the truth of the narrative: we need to identify with the detective to get to the truth, or with the hero to discover the emotional authenticity of an action story. We have to identify with Chuck Berry in order to grasp the power of 'Maybellene'.

The foregrounding of the vocal in most productions of pop songs operates, with the emphasis on singers in filmed performances and fan magazines, in such a way as to focus attention on the vocal line in the song. Not only do lyrics position the listener through the frequent use of second-person address —'I love *you*'—and the equally intimate recounting of personal experience; but the singing voice is itself intimate. Firstly, there is the profound ambiguity of the word 'I', which allows the listener to become the 'I' of the song, just as the singer has become the 'I' of the songwriter. Secondly, singing is a very personal act: think how vulnerable we feel about singing in front of others, how much emotional effort it requires. The voice is directly of the body, of its warm and vital interior, and our voices identify us as surely as our physical presence. An early rock 'n' roll film, Frank Tashlin's *The Girl Can't Help It* (1957), makes great play of this. Jayne Mansfield exhibits a horrible lack of singing talent throughout the film until, at the very end, she sings; but when she sings, she sings for Tom Ewell, her husband-to-be. In the heavily censored sexual code of Hollywood in the 1950s, singing stands for the offer of Mansfield's body. This is the same intimacy as that offered in Sheena Easton's recent recording of 'For Your Eyes Only', the theme song to the James Bond film of the same name. The song plays on the ambiguity of the word 'you' in order to invite the listener into identifying with the privileged, implicitly male possessor of the woman's body. The offer of the voice promises the intimacy of being the only man allowed a sexual gaze. That promise, and the social and sexual positioning of singer and subject, is effected as much in the act of singing as in the lyric.

It is the voice which typically, if not in every case, provides the level of the song which engages our desire most directly, and leads it through the troublings and resolutions of the melody and lyrics. It is also, typically, the most prominent identity in the song: though the instrumentation may change, and the melody lead in unexpected directions, the voice is a constant, a personality—or rather its signifier, since it represents a personality for us. The voice evokes desire through its promise of intimacy, maintains its hold by the way in which it is always recognizable, and thus provides the central means by which our attention is held and our emotions involved in the vagaries of the tune. In our example of Chuck Berry's 'Maybellene', it is the blackness of the voice, the rounded vowels and elided consonants of his St Louis, Mo. accent, the play between vocal timbres drawn alternately from chest and throat, that define the Chuck-Berry-ness of the singer as an identity, and these along with the stretched vowels twisted into diphthongs, the urgency and 'attack' of the lines, evoke an empathetic sense of excitement underwritten by the dum-DAT dum-DAT rhythm and Johnny Johnson's boogie piano. The dynamic of the voice, its movement from phoneme to phoneme, from note to note, makes Berry both the object and the trajectory of desire, a paradox to be investigated below. The energy with which Berry sings is energy for us, and the nature of that energy is desire, his and ours following the same winding route.

It is from this position of engaged desire that the narrative of the song becomes accessible, comprehensible, interesting. Watch any group of dancers at any disco or party and they will be singing along with the vocal line. The voice allows us to participate in the song even more closely than the participation of dancing to the beat (the difference between dancing *to* and singing *with*). We can appropriate the performance individually, and, through vocal identification, become the singer and produce the song as our own. This is particularly clear in the ways in which indecipherable lyrics are adapted to provide auditors with something to sing, whether or not it matches the original lyric: the semantic content of the lyric takes second place to the essential vocal role in identification.

Interestingly enough it is the less 'perfect' voices that seem to succeed the most in recent years, the broken tones that seem to guarantee the emotive and erotic side of the auditory experience. An approximation to the classic blackness of the great blues singers has its appeal still, from Eric Burdon and Mick Jagger to Patti Smith and Joe Strummer. This has a great deal to do with an ideology of black music which holds that jazz and blues, reggae, funk, high-life, and Tamla are more spontaneous and therefore more authentic musical forms. The representation of authenticity is crucial to popular song, as even a cursory glance through the music press will prove. It is an essential part of the ideology that surrounds, particularly, those singers with a claim to greatness from Bessie Smith to Bruce Springsteen, whether that claim be measured in critical accolades or sustained selling power. The ideology of authenticity describes an emotional commitment in which the listener can participate, a commitment traced in the very personal timbre, pitch and, in Barthes' phrase, 'grain' of the voice; that voice which promises a physicality that goes beyond what is available to the trained voice. Though Molly Bloom may have fallen for Blazes Boylan's fine tenor, the sensuality involved in a performance by Pavarotti has a very different effect from that of Chuck Berry.

Like a close-up screen image of a favourite star, the grainy, lived-in voice of the popular singer, especially when amplified, promises—indeed in some senses actually is—a physical intimacy. But in the case of recorded songs, that presence is illusory. The voice is the site of a paradoxically simultaneous promise and denial of intimacy. In this it is rather like the close-up: from our proper position in the cinema, the close-up admits us to the personal space surrounding the star, but if we get too close to the screen we discover that the image is impossibly big, and if we approach closer still it becomes apparent that this is not a face but a pattern of light in two dimensions. Like a close-up, an amplified and recorded voice marks an absence. It is a re-presentation, a signifier, the grounds of whose existence is the absence of the thing represented.

The recorded performance is a *revenant*, a representation of something which is already past (if indeed, with modern technology, it ever took place as a single event). The presence of the recording overlays the absence of the artist, an effect which lies at the core of that glamour which pop music and its stars share with film and its stars. Glamour is a function of a relationship with the viewer/auditor in which the audience is allowed a freedom of access to the star which everyday life denies: freedom to stare, to be a voyeur in the cinema, and in a musical context to repeat performances over and over, to give that intimate moment of singing an intensity of attention rarely possible in the social world. This attention and its attendant pleasures are only possible because of the gap between performance and recording, representation and reality, signifier and signified. There is an impassable gap between Chess LP-1514D and that May day in 1955 when Chuck Berry laid down his first single release. The song itself seems to play upon this through the use of the past tense in the verses, counterpointed against the insistent presentness of the music and rhythm: the song is scarcely nostalgic or reflective. The refrain returns to the present tense: the pain is always present, its solution in the narrative always past. (One might contrast in this respect the much more unambiguously joyful present tense in another automobile song, 'You Can't Catch Me'.) The condition of its existence for us, as representation, is the absolute loss of any 'original' event: 'Maybellene' is its reproductions. A song is a play of musical and, crucially, vocal signifiers. Its success depends on how far it can engage our desire in that play. A great performance engages us so profoundly that, as in a dream, we can experience things that in waking life we have not experienced and perhaps could not or would not allow ourselves to experience.

Even on stage, the performance is only possible because of the distance between audience and performers, and the latter do not even hear themselves as the audience do, relying on their monitors, not the PA. Any attempt to break through that boundary, to invade the stage, ends in policing action or the end of the show. For this is not a person on stage, but a performance image, not an individual but the bearer of the voice, gesture, costume. We don't go to have a chat with Charles Edward Berry, son of Henry and Martha, fifty-three this year; we go to find the performance image and the singing voice working together to produce the point in the discursive structure of the event in which desire can enter the play of signifiers. Even the most flagrantly erotic of spectacles is still a discourse, one of whose rules is that whatever desires are aroused cannot be satisfied within the context of the performance. No performance can be finally satisfying, for the object of our desire is always absent. What is presented to us is a direction in which desire can travel: its goal is always somewhere else.

Stephen Heath (1981: 176) has an interesting observation of '. . . a London sex-shop close to the offices of *Screen*, a notice advertising "Films now showing: silent £1, sound £1.50"'. The soundtrack—presumably of vociferous orgasms—comes more expensive because it is proof of the woman's pleasure and therefore of the validity of the spectator's voyeuristic pleasure. Because it is in many ways a more intimate sense, hearing is more persuasive, more realistic. Yet perhaps for that very reason, sound is taken for granted far more. It is far easier to ignore an aural than a visual stimulus, to reduce extraneous sound, including music, to the background of, say, a conversation. Perhaps this is a protective device to prevent sensory overload, for there is no way we can close our ears as we close our eyes. Music can become part of an aural continuum, a flow scarcely registered except when it is interrupted, yet which is actively sought, for example in the act of turning on a radio. Listening to the flow of songs on Radio One, for example, engages us in a pleasure which operates at a level other than that of conscious attention. It is as if a song in this listening situation addresses an absent subject, or more accurately an absence in the subject, a lack of attention. Yet even as such, the song has its effects, a truth long since appreciated and employed by the Musak Corporation. More attentive listening—as when a favourite tune crops up among the general flow—provides a more acute pleasure. In either case interruption is experienced as a quite violent frustration, or even a momentary bewilderment (an effect deployed in the game of Musical Chairs).

Yet though sound has this function of underwriting and producing pleasure, there is, as Heath points out, no word parallel to 'voyeurism' covering pleasure in listening. There is particularly a pleasure in hearing the human voice, so strong that people can hallucinate the presence of voices in solitary confinement or religious ecstasy. In the case of jazz and popular music there is scarcely need to emphasize the role of eroticism in performance, rhythms, and lyrics, but we are almost without a vocabulary to express how singing means for us. What needs to be theorized is how Berry's voice can draw such a powerful reaction from me even when the banality of some of his material debars me from another kind of pleasure. The connection is undoubtedly erotic—a voice is so much a function of a body, of the interior of a body—yet the desire evoked is not for the body of the singer. In a preliminary way we might say that the voice has two closely interrelated ways of working, which the remainder of this article will look at in an exploratory way. The voice has firstly a diegetic function, to carry the 'narrative' structure of the melody; and secondly an erotic function, to provide a point of identification through which to engage and mobilize the subject's desire. The two analytic categories combine in the voice's work in signifying the unobtainable presence of another, the singer.

The question of diegesis is in some ways the most difficult. In what way do musical sounds and structures have meaning (and here I am even begging the question of what is a musical sound)? By analogy with the study of narratives I would say that the singing voice 'speaks', that it operates like a language. Like language, the musical discourse of the song is a rule-governed structure of notes and syllables and their relations in time: these are the song's signifiers, the material agitation of the air by which music communicates. To avoid the danger of presenting songs as referential, I'll use the word 'effects' to denote the mental verso of this material recto, the signifieds or semantic effects of the song's signification. Since it is not referential, we cannot say that the song has meaning, but rather that it means, that it produces meaning. It is in the senses in which it acts like language that we can say that the song speaks, and when it speaks it speaks to and means for us who listen.

This production of meaning is then the effects of the song. I assume that, as in language, there is an isomorphic relation between signifiers and effects, and that therefore a complete study of effects would demand a musicology which I am ill-equipped to deliver, a grammar of musical signifiers by which could be understood the sequence and structure of effects. In terms of voice, such a grammar would have somehow to describe the overtones that characterize the individuality of the voice, dialectal variants in pronunciation, the niceties of bending notes and the mysteries of timing. In doing so it would have to avoid the justification of dislikes and the rationalization of enthusiasms: it would have to be above the mere discussion of tastes.

Taste would in fact be a central object of analysis of the semantic level. We need to understand that while the structure of signifiers constrains the structure of effects—most clearly by their duration—yet although the two systems are formally isomorphic, they are substantially quite autonomous. Again by analogy with language, the elements of musical structure are arbitrary, in that there is no reason why, say, middle C should 'mean' some particular effect. The rules governing musical expression are conventional, not necessary, and are therefore subject to historical change. To illustrate this point: the *Oxford English Dictionary* gives two illuminating early uses of the word 'diatonic': Burney's 1774 *History of Music* which states that 'In modern music the Genera are but two: Diatonic and Chromatic'; and Ramboul writing in 1848 (that significant date) of 'Diatonic, the natural scale'. Would this suggest that between the Wilkes riots and the June revolution, what has been modern had become natural? Even if we place this change earlier, in the period between Palestrina and Bach perhaps, doesn't this suggest that the diatonic scale served to naturalize new kinds of emotional response in a form whose rise to dominance occurred precisely in the period of the bourgeoisie's triumphant rise to cultural hegemony? Does it still serve to naturalize novel—and hence potentially subversive—emotional traumas? Or does the deployment of new elements such as modal, atonal, and electronic techniques in twentieth-century popular music represent a refusal of the naturalization achieved by more middle-of-the-road performances? In any case, the conventions of any one epoch still constrain us to certain modes of listening, and no one will try jiving to Walter von der Vogelweide's medieval

'Palestinalied'. Constrain, but not determine: there is still a gap between signifier and effects, the gap which makes individual response possible. The signifier has a material existence as a physical agitation of the air and ear and concomitant psycho-chemical reactions in the brain. The effects, on the other hand, are an experience, a movement of emotions, an evocation of ideas. What is the substance of these feelings and thoughts?

I would suggest that as diegesis, songs speak to or address us by organizing a particular stretch of time into a conscious experience, and an experience of consciousness. In so far as the musical conventions involved are familiar to the listener, in so far as they make the song re-cognizable, the song creates the conditions within which the listener can be a conscious subject: I listen, therefore I am. Consciousness is present, in short, as an effect of musical language. Music partakes of what is referred to in contemporary semiotics as the Symbolic: the domain of language and every other signifying system which pre-exists the subject and is presented to him or her as a completed whole by a social order which, inasmuch as it too has meaning for the subject, also partakes of the Symbolic. The act of speaking, social activity, common sense and consciousness itself are products of the Symbolic, within which alone we can become truly human. This is not to deny either the genetic predisposition to consciousness in the human race or the difficulties and contradictions which arise in the process of acquiring a place in the Symbolic domain: it is rather to emphasize that the diegetic function of singing acts to reproduce and confirm our conception of who we are and of our place in the order of things. The diegetic construction of melody enunciates for us our common-sense expectations of the world: that a song will be melodic, that it will resolve at the end, that our emotions are natural and familiar. To this extent the diegesis is the ideological function of the song, constructing for the listener a subject-position from which, as much formal difficulty as possible having been removed, the emotional life of the subject can be contained within the limits of the song. This is the formal prerequisite for the enunciation of more specific ideological themes in the performance and the lyrics.

Perhaps the clearest ways of showing this is to look at moments in the history of the popular song when dominant ideological beliefs have been subverted. A central theme in our notion of the world is the second-class status of women, and it has frequently been observed that pop music is male-dominated (e.g. Frith and McRobbie 1979; Taylor and Laing 1979). As far as women enter the field of the popular song it has been as objects of male sexuality or as its victims, constructed in either case *for* a male sexuality. Even in those rare cases when a female sexuality transgresses the norms of the nuclear couple, as in the performance styles of Janis Joplin or Billie Holiday, such sexuality is contained within a patriarchal code. This code (which we might call the code of *A Star is Torn*, after Australian Robyn Archer's one-woman show on the biographies of singers from Bessie Smith to Janis Joplin) takes the expression of a sexuality different from and threatening to the couple and the family, and contains and recuperates it through punishment —archetypically by self-immolation through drink and drugs. Those that contradict even that code face the absolute silence that surrounded Dusty Springfield when her lesbianism became public, or the silence that surrounds a group like the Raincoats. It is as if the patriarchal code of vocal performance is so determining that its transgression can only produce monsters. This is particularly the case with the Raincoats, who use highly unusual rhythms, melodies, and harmonies, and who mix their voices down to the same level as the instruments. Their songs can ellicit a very genuine sense of having been insulted in some listeners. Apart from the discomfort—and thus ideological disruption—brought about by their unfamiliar music, the absence of a lead vocal is here a key factor. There is no single voice to address the listener, no single position for him or her to occupy vis-à-vis the song, and therefore no re-cognition. The process of production of the subject through the song's diegesis is disrupted: the emotional effects can be startling.

The insult, the disorientation, and the new kind of pleasure available from the Raincoats is indubitably involved with their refusal of the centred and centring role of the lead vocal in providing a guarantee of the listener's place in the song. But this is also an explicit refusal of a sex role prepared in the code of the pop song for the female vocalist. This subversion belongs to a particular moment of feminism, and it is a reaction to an equally specific moment in the history of the organization of sexuality. There is nothing essential, natural or universal about the construction of gender or of the nuclear family. There exists a well-documented history of the family (for two quite different approaches to the historicizing of the family, see Stone 1977 and Coward 1983): as current concerns of Margaret Thatcher's Conservative Party demonstrate, it is an institution in crisis in contemporary Britain.

The same is even more true of the construction of sexuality among the teenage market for popular song. This is an age group in the throes of puberty, whose experience of sexual roles is often painful and ambiguous, whose sexuality is often perceived as a threat to social order and whose accept-ance of the institutions of sexuality, the family, and the nuclear couple, can by no means be taken for granted. If puberty is not only the final phase of socialization, but also the moment at which the erotic configuration of the individual gells, then the centrality of the representation of sex and its institutions in the popular song can be understood as the key to the success and failure of particular songs. Both in the individual listening event and on the scale of the mass market, to succeed a song must match a particular need, a particular configuration of the elements of sexuality. It must appear at the right time and provide a musical and lyrical structure that will invite the kind of play of desire that a person or a sector of the population can identify with. Songs are produced in particular social contexts, but they are consumed in them too. The sexual paranoias of sixties Detroit may find a home in Wigan fifteen or twenty years later (Kimberley 1982; Cosgrove 1982).

The circulation of music as sound-texts must always be understood in relation to its circulation as images for consumption through marketing, sleeve design, interviews, fanzines, and so forth. Stars and even whole styles are sexualized in their extra-musical constructions, and this secondary circulation of musical signifiers undoubtedly affects the sexual construction of meaning in the listening situation. (Some excellent work, to which these comments are indebted, has been done on the circulation of stars as signs in the film industry: see Dyer 1979; Cook 1982; Ellis 1982.) A detailed typology of musical texts would have to articulate relations between these two modes of circulation. It would also have to cope with differences between media (radio, record, concert, TV, video . . .), degrees of intensity of listening, the cultural construction of particular instruments, effects, and melodic figures as signifiers of, for example, the Orient, the electronic age, fairgrounds, and circuses; and so on. Whatever is intrinsic to the music in and of itself is only part of the construction of its effects. The meaning for us, the effects, are to do with the social construction and production of meaning. That is to say that a pure musicology of formal properties is as incapable of producing a typology of songs as is a pure psychoanalysis. An analysis of all elements of the listening situation is required, including an historical contextualization.

My central point here is that this important concern of pop songs with sexuality reflects the dominant role of masculinity as the norm from which femininity is an aberration. Songs operate to position the listener by mobilizing socially encoded masculinity and femininity, qualities immediately available in the subject's recognition of the singer's voice. Each of these positionings is carried out by non-musical means as well as by the music itself; but that only confirms that the listening situation, overdetermined as it is by the constitution of the individual listener, is also a deeply social practice. But it is equally essential to remember that the site of this practice is in the experience of the subject who listens, and whose position is guaranteed by the lead vocal.

In this experience, even though it be no more than one of the mere passing of time, there is signification. And any act of signification, any Symbolic action, must also be ideological. And any ideological function must in turn depend upon the construction of a subject of that ideology. Thus the *sine qua non* of the diegetic and ideological function of the song is the production of the subject and its position. Since representation is the only means at the song's disposal, its task is to represent the conscious subject or ego to itself, and it will do so typically in the mirror of the amplified, independent, and perfected identity posited in the singing voice. The position of the lead vocal in the song engages consciousness, the ego, as the central and centring truth of the subject. It is in this mode of address that the ego is constructed for itself, in and for the ideology of the song. 'Maybellene' backs up this function with a lead guitar break, played by Berry, which troubles by interruption only to reconfirm by repetition the centrality of the ego. On stage the characteristic Berry hops and shuffles provide a continuum which underwrites this singleness of purpose.

Obviously this construction is not determining in any absolute sense. It does not account for degrees of engagement in the listening process, which must be at least partly determined by relations to other songs, other discourses, other activities. But its address does determine what is to be the optimum position for the listener to occupy for optimum effects. In order to listen, the listening subject must be constructed as an ego, whose position is spoken by the diegesis of the lead vocal. But this should not be taken to mean that the ego is all that is engaged in the act of listening. Precisely because it is conscious and enjoys a prestige belonging to unique and irreducible experience, the ego tends to preoccupy analysis. Yet its role is in one way subordinate: the ego is spoken by the song, it is passive. We have to look elsewhere for the active component: 'In the unconscious, excluded from the system of the ego, the subject speaks' (Lacan 1978: 77, my translation). The productive enterprise of listening, the active engagement in the listening process, participation in the production and therefore in the productivity of the song, occurs in the unconscious. Here our second, erotic function of identification operates not as an effect of which the song is the cause, but as an active involvement, pleasurable or not, in the process of signification.

'Maybellene' speaks an ideology of sexual jealousy, of pursuit and capture. Perhaps its greatest novelty is in the eroticization of the motor car, a process already well under way in the marketing of consumer durables at the end of the period of post-war austerity, but compounded with a representation of black sexuality to introduce an element of threat. Later car anthems like 'You Can't Catch Me', or 'Jaguar and Thunderbird' use the automobile as an icon of freedom: 'Maybellene' concentrates on a representation of power in sexuality that reproduces the subject in a patriarchal ideology of masculinity. This alone would account for the popularity of the song: an address that confirms in a novel way central themes in the American ideology. For me its greatness lies in the way in which the internal 'contradictions' of the song —contradictions between past and present, presence and absence, St Louis vocals and Chicago backbeat, sexual power and sexual jealousy—create a space in which the obverse of the dominant ideology can be mobilized: where the subject can speak (or sing) another theme, that speaks of discomfort with the order of the world, of self-doubt and the difficulty of playing out the role appointed for masculinity in our society.

The amplified voice is an ideal form, an image like a mirror image. It is like us yet bigger, more perfect, almost godlike; like Socrates' daemon, it is more coherent and more fully in control of its identity than we often feel ourselves to be. Its function in identification derives from the mirror phase, a metaphor developed by Jaques Lacan (1966: 89 ff.) to describe the stage at which an infant first becomes aware of her- or himself as an individual. The child sees in the mirror an image which it knows to be itself, yet which possesses a coherence which it has yet to sense of itself. Two things are happening: the child interiorizes this ideal form as a self-image to which it will constantly aspire; but it also experiences for the first time an identification with another, an experience at the root of all subsequent identifications and empathy. Thus, in the process of becoming aware of its individuality, the child also becomes aware of itself as an object, initially and classically as an object of desire.

The amplified voice commands an awareness of difference and of identity, of another greater than oneself yet like oneself, both admirable and available: all the conditions of identification are present. In that we can identify with it, this voice can allow us to partake of emotions that were not available in ordinary life. The ideal image of ourselves that it offers is the site of a complex organization of our relations with the world, the connection between our inner being and the exterior world. In that it is like us, it engages a primary narcissistic desire—the narcissism of the infant child—and in that it is unlike us, it involves the mirror phase, the earliest appreciation of the separateness of self from the world and its dialectical relationship with it. By appealing to such primitive emotional configurations, the song slips in under the censoring eyes of our social conscience, to allow pleasures that otherwise we would deny ourselves: pleasures of rebellion, of philandering, of identification with the opposite sex. These are, as Meredith describes it, sentimental pleasures, in that they allow us 'to enjoy without incurring responsibility for the thing enjoyed'. In identification, melody invokes and assuages primary anxieties about relations between self and the world.

But melody is also a process of signification, and as such produces the subject as effect of language, as consciousness. The subject's place in language is marked by the word 'I': in songs, by the lead vocal. But this in turn refers us to the Lacanian category of alienation: the division of the subject between its presence to itself and its presence in signification. The subject is represented in language only by the fact that representation relies on the absence of the thing represented. The subject's presence in the song is in fact an absence, a lack. Its activity in listening is pursuing this felt lack with all the energy of its desires along the stream of signifiers in search of an impossible completion. Nowhere is this clearer than in the dialectic of desire and possession in 'Maybellene', in its final inability to complete the desire of the subject in the desire of the other, who constantly 'starts back doing the things you used to do'. The dialectic started twenty-nine years ago is still pursued today.

It is in this gap between signification and the subject that Lacan situates the unconscious. For Lacan the unconscious is not a place in the brain, or a zoo for monsters from the id. He describes it as an edge, the meeting point between the Symbolic and the subject, the trace left behind by the operation of language in constructing the subject. There is for Lacan an excess in any signification, language which escapes the subject, something which is always beyond the conscious mind. Identification with the vocal line creates that exclusion. Wherever there is representation, the object represented is absent, lacking. That lack is precisely the object of desire, that which desire pursues along the stream of signs. Where the conscious mind perceives presence —the presence of the song as a chain of signifiers, the presence of the ego to itself in the song's address—the unconscious moves towards the absence constitutive of the song as sign. Desire comes into being with language: the instinctive needs we share with the animals only become human desire with the acquisition of language. It is as an effect of language that desire is most truly human. Yet desire is radically unable to coincide with whatever there is in play in the field of consciousness because consciousness, the ego, is founded in representation, where nothing signifies that is not a lack.

If work alters the physical state of the real world to fit our desires, signifying practices occupy the space between desire and the social world where work takes place. Yet what we find or make is not what, finally, we desire: if it was, we would stop desiring, signifying, and working. The real object of desire flees before us like Maybellene's Cadillac. Listening is the pursuit of that impossible reality along the trace of the singing voice. There is a deal of play between the conscious enjoyment of presence and the activity of the unconscious about absence, a play that underlies the pleasure of listening. The simultaneous presence and absence of the singer foreshadows the split in the subject itself, the fundamental gap between language and being and the function of desire to seek constantly to suture that breach. The power of music is to represent that vital dialectic to and for the subject, to offer both a model of the resolution of that constant to and fro—drive a car, possess your woman; most of all, be a man—and simultaneously to propose the impossibility of satisfaction, the irreducible lack that denies us any finality in life, but makes us the suffering and struggling beings that we are. The yearning and pain in Berry's voice emerge from the gap between the people we are constructed as in the whole discursive field that makes up a culture and the people we feel ourselves to be, a gap of excess and dissatisfaction which allows us the possibility of change, both personal and historical.

As 'Maybellene' fades out over the second guitar break, two things are affirmed. Firstly, the fade-out is a recording studio device which announces that this is a recording, and is therefore more or less infinitely repeatable. And secondly it asserts that the song is radically incomplete. As it spirals down to the silence of the last grooves, it sends us outwards from itself to seek the completion of the song elsewhere. The melody does not even offer the fictional resolution of the restored tonic. It does not, in Coleridge's famous phrase, 'contain in itself the reason why it is so and not otherwise'. The great interest of the popular song for me is the way in which it confounds the Aristotelian aesthetics of the object, and with it the Cartesian notion of the subject: whole, autonomous, independent, closed. It demands instead a materialist aesthetic, where any single utterance is meaningful only in the context of the other discourses that surround it and the multiplicity of subjects imbricated in its production, both as artists and as listeners. It insists that the listening subject is radically split, unstill, unsure, and ever-changing. It urges that this open, decentred subject is involved erotically, in the widest sense of the term, through signification with every other subject on the planet.

It is in that intersubjective production of meaning, the activity of listening, that the song is reproduced by the listening subject, never the same twice. I would go so far as to say that it is never the same even once: the first meeting of two forces—song and psyche—contains already a germ of the memory of their meeting, knowledge that the performance is always already in the past, the promise of repetition. We hear both representation (presence) and its object (absence) and in their interplay we are already engaged in a difference which must permit that which it seeks to contain: that excess and openness which grounds us in the dialectic of desire. No straight textual analysis will capture that play which most attracts us to the popular song. To quote the liner notes to that most enigmatic of LPs, Captain Beefheart's *Trout Mask Replica*, 'Owing to the condition of the players and the environment of the recording, certain portions are inaudible, thus we can only guess at the real meaning.' Truth flies from us like the impossible reality of fulfilled desire.

References

Aristotle (1965). 'On the art of poetry', in *Classical Literary Criticism*, ed. and trans. T. S. Dorsch (Harmondsworth), 31–75.

Berry, C. (1955). 'Maybellene', Chess 1604 (Chicago), reissued on *Chuck Berry's Golden Decade*, Chess 6641 018.

Cook, P. (1982). 'Stars and politics', in *Star Signs* (London), 23–32.

Cosgrove, S. (1982). 'Long after tonight is all over', *Collusion*, 2: 38–41.

Coward, R. (1983). *Patriarchal Precedents* (London).

Dyer, R. (1979). *Stars* (London).

Ellis, J. (1982). 'Star/industry/image', conference paper for British Film Institute 'Star Signs' weekend school.

Frith, S., and McRobbie, A. (1979). 'Rock and sexuality', *Screen Education*, 29: 3–19.

Heath, S. (1981). *Questions of Cinema* (London).

Kimberley, N. (1982). 'Paranoid sex in sixties soul', *Collusion*, 2: 9–11.

Lacan, J. (1966). 'Position de l'inconscient', in *Ecrits II*, 2nd edn. (Paris), 193–217.

—— (1978). *Le Seminaire, Livre II: Le moi dans la théorie de Freud et dans la technique de la psychanalyse* (Paris).

Middleton, R. (1981). 'Reading' Popular Music, Unit 16 of Popular Culture, Open University course U203 (Milton Keynes).

Stone, L. (1977). The Family, Sex and Marriage in England 1500–1800 (Harmondsworth).

Taylor, J., and Laing, D. (1979). 'Disco-pleasure-discourse: on "rock and sexuality"', Screen Education, 31: 43–8.

Part 2

Words and Music

In many of the essays in Part 1, when lyrics are drawn into the analysis, it is largely as guides to thematic content; they help indicate the semantic field of the song. Sometimes, however, they are seen as helping to demarcate song structure. And for David Brackett, the lyrics of 'Superbad' are part of a general play of signifiers, an aspect of the overall 'musical' process. This divergence maps out the field of possibilities for the relationship of words and music in pop—with 'linguistic content' at one extreme, 'musical sound' at the other. From a different angle, the axis can be seen as running from the idea—so popular in the sixties—of lyrics as 'poetry' to the argument that actually listeners pay no particular attention to words at all. There is some research evidence in favour of the latter proposition (see Frith 1988: 119–20)—but hardly sufficient to rule out what seems intuitively probable, that practice is variable. Similarly, an emphasis on 'poetic' qualities begs the question of what 'poetry' might be when words are sung and accompanied by other sounds; and again a range of relationships and possibilities seems most likely. At issue always, though, when song lyrics are considered, would seem to be the questions *who* it is that is speaking, and *to whom?*

Even if crude 'content analysis'—a method that grounds verbal meaning directly through a realist aesthetic—has been long discredited, this does not rule out the possibility of connections between lyrics and 'real life'—or even autobiography. Timothy Taylor's discussion of Chuck Berry's 'Johnny B. Goode' (and related songs) finds just such an autobiographical connection—but the interesting point is that the 'author' (writer and singer) of this story is a mythologized rather than the real Chuck Berry; moreover, the themes of the story connect deep into broader myths of American culture. Further, the precise form they take is shaped by the negotiations going on in the musical style between aspects of hillbilly and blues legacies. And then this whole process relates (right down to details of diction and rhythm) to career strategies: to the way a little-known African-American musician might *aim* a record, intended for a mixed but largely white adolescent audience, in the mid-1950s.

Taylor—listening to Berry's subsequent versions of 'Johnny B. Goode', and to other songs in the 'Johnny' series—finds a move from clear ideological message towards a more 'aestheticized' object, in which qualities of the sounds themselves are indulged. Umberto Fiori, in his essay, is also interested in 'aesthetics'—both in the issue of aesthetic quality in pop and in a genre (progressive rock) which is usually seen as claiming such quality. As in 'Johnny B. Goode', too, the aesthetic strategy of the song at issue here—Peter Gabriel's 'I Have the Touch'—is identified as dependent in some sense on the authorial 'I'. Again, however, this 'I' is a (here multi-valent) construction; and the song, far from claiming either poetic transcendence or the completeness of the traditional aesthetic object, draws on verbal commonplace and reveals, through the details of the musical setting, a range of paradox, irony, and ambivalence: a Bakhtinian 'polyphony' of meanings. While he wants to insist on the integrity of the pop record (it 'sticks together'), Fiori, like Sean Cubitt, takes the 'completeness' of the vocal persona, which acts as guarantee for this integrity, to be a fiction, its 'presence' an unredeemable promise.

In exploring a song in a less obviously 'aesthetic' genre—Bruce Springsteen's 'The River'—and one that on the face of it is much more of a narrative than is 'I Have the Touch', Dai Griffiths nevertheless also finds multiple layers of meaning. And here it is not just a matter of identifying parallels between lyric and music (as in Taylor's essay) or interactions between words and vocal performance (as in Fiori's) but also taking account of the several, overlapping and sometimes contradictory, structural schemes at work in the song. Griffiths lays them out in neo-structuralist detail; but more important, he shows how the relationships work on our sense of time and feeling, so that the intersections of the variable periodicities and tones of rhyme, tense, scansion, melodic shape, chord progressions, and verse structure enable a five-minute song to make us feel the emotional drama of a whole life.

In their essay on 'Peggy Sue' by Buddy Holly, Barbara Bradby and Brian Torode also segment the verbal and musical phrases in neo-structuralist detail (though the emphasis on the interaction of competing musico-verbal discourses within the song, working at the process of constructing subjectivity, carries the interpretation towards a post-structuralist postion). They too are interested in narrative (multi-voiced though it is in this song). However, if the thrust of the previous three chapters has been towards emphasizing how lyrics are transformed in performance, here the focus, if not a reversal, is on the power of verbal images and rhythms to direct the course of the entire musical process. For Bradby and Torode, linguistic discourses and musical, especially rhythmic, discourses, far from originating in different semiotic spheres, are thoroughly intertwined in the same basic processes of social identification. Pop songs, in enacting such processes in symbolic terms, re-present to us the 'solutions' through which our culture organizes itself (such as those that structure adolescent sexual learning). And here we are moving, clearly, into the sphere of interests which is the particular concern of Part 3 of this book.

7
.....
His Name was in Lights: Chuck Berry's 'Johnny B. Goode'

TIMOTHY D. TAYLOR

Introduction

Chuck Berry recorded 'Johnny B. Goode' in December 1957 and it has since become one of his best-known songs. The reasons for its lasting popularity are varied, and one of the goals of this essay is to elucidate and discuss them. But the main purpose is to raise 'Johnny B. Goode' as an example of the choices and problems Berry faced in his career as an African-American musician in the 1950s and 60s and the ways he dealt with them in this tune.

In short, he made compromises, but these changed over time. To appeal to a white audience Berry made certain career moves early on—the decision to play 'white' hillbilly music is the most important—but later in his career he attempted to court a broader white audience. Two recorded versions of 'Johnny B. Goode' point out those changes, and I will consider them, the original one for Chess, and another, nine years later, for Mercury.

To discuss the song's popularity and longevity I will examine the many meanings evoked by the lyrics, which include three powerful myths Berry taps into, myths that are not specifically African-American or white, but that all Americans can share. Despite Berry's courting of a broad audience with the material of his lyrics, some elements of an African-American identity remain, as do some distinctly African-American traces in the music. The African-American aspects of Berry's music, while not always on the surface, none the less helped contribute to the improvement of race relations in America.

I would like to thank Richard Crawford, James Manheim and Robert Walser for helpful comments on drafts of this paper.

The Story Told and the Story Not Quite Told in the Lyrics

Since I will be discussing the lyrics of 'Johnny B. Goode' at length, I will first quote them below (transcribed from the original Chess recording, re-released in 1984 on *The Great Twenty Eight* MCA CHD-92500).

verse 1   Deep down in Lou'siana close to New Orleans
Way back up in the woods among the evergreens
There stood a log cabin made of earth and wood
Where lived a country boy named Johnny B. Goode
Who never ever learned to read or write so well
But he could play a guitar just like a ringin' a bell.

chorus 1   Go, Johnny, go, *etc.*
Johnny B. Goode.

verse 2   He used to carry his guitar in a gunny sack
Would sit beneath the tree by the railroad track
Engineer could see him sittin' in the shade
Strummin' with the rhythm that the drivers made
The people passin' by they would stop and say
'Oh my but that little country boy could play.'

chorus 2   Go, Johnny, go, *etc.*
Johnny B. Goode.

verse 3   His mother told him, 'Someday you will be a man
And you will be the leader of a big old band;
Many people comin' from miles around
To hear you play your music when the sun go down.
Maybe someday your name will be in lights
Sayin' "Johnny B. Goode tonight." '

chorus 3   Go, Johnny, go, *etc.*
Johnny B. Goode.

To begin my discussion of these lyrics I turn to the cultural critic John Fiske, who writes that television programmes must be polysemic in order to be popular, and those multiplicities of possible meanings must be negotiable, or appropriable by the viewers (Fiske 1987: 267). In other words, many resonances, meanings, must be activated in order for a diverse range of people to respond. This is necessarily true of all forms of popular culture; otherwise they are not popular. 'Johnny B. Goode' is popular and polysemic, and the many potential meanings contribute to its continuing popularity. These meanings are achieved, in this text and others, by the use of puns and *double entendre* in the lyrics,[1] and so I will discuss the lyrics of 'Johnny B. Goode' in depth.

Berry's title, hinting at several meanings, activates two explicit ones and implies another. The pun on Johnny's name causes some: he is a good musician, and it is his name as well. Another meaning could be in African-American dialect: 'Johnny be [is] good'. Finally, the title contains a couple of autobiographical elements: Berry was born on Goode Street in St Louis.[2] And Berry's great-grandfather was John Johnson, a slave who lived for a time in a log cabin in Ohio after becoming free.

Acknowledging that 'Johnny B. Goode' is partly autobiographical, Berry writes in his autobiography that he was inspired by his first visit to New Orleans, a city with which he had long been infatuated because of his love of Muddy Waters' 'Going Down in Louisiana, Way Down Behind the Sun', and his father's stories of the city. Berry himself is Johnny, although at first he intended this song to be about Johnnie Johnson, a pianist with whom he collaborated sporadically for many years and from whom he may have learned his best licks. Despite that original plan, 'Johnny B. Goode' quickly became a song which told Berry's story.

The subsequent Johnny songs confirm their autobiographical nature, which Berry continues in songs which are obscure compared to this first Johnny song. 'Bye Bye Johnny' (1960) picks up where 'Johnny B. Goode' left off: Johnny is now heading out for California to make movies. 'Bye Bye Johnny' starts *in media res*, which makes it clear that it is a continuation of 'Johnny B. Goode', which provides the listener with background information.[3]

> *verse 1* She drew out all her money at the Southern Trust
> And put her little boy aboard a Greyhound Bus
> Leavin' Lou'siana for the golden west
> Down came her tears from her happiness.
> Her own little son named Johnny B. Goode
> Was going to make some motion pictures out in Hollywood.

Berry thus continues the rags-to-riches myth-making from the first song (which I shall discuss later) and again Johnny's humble early existence is noted, since

---

[1] George Lipsitz (1990: 111) writes that one of the continuations of African or African-American traditions into popular culture is word-play, an important feature of much of Berry's music. 'You know, poetry is my blood flow' says Berry in *Hail! Hail! Rock 'n' Roll* (1987).

[2] Richard Crawford points out that there may also be a pun on George Gershwin's 'Lady be Good'.

[3] Transcribed from the original recording, released on *The Great Twenty Eight*, MCA CHD-92500.

it takes all of Johnny's mother's money to put him on a bus; he does not have a car like the people driving by and hearing him in 'Johnny B. Goode'. The story also sustains the autobiographical nature of the Johnny songs, since Berry himself went to California (Culver City, not Hollywood) to make a film, *Rock, Rock, Rock*, released in 1956. Two years later, Berry made a movie entitled *Go, Johnny, Go*, about a rock musician named Johnny Melody whom Alan Freed (playing himself) was promoting to become a star.

The third Johnny song is 'Go Go Go' (1961) which portrays Johnny/Chuck as a star, looking back on his achievements with some humour:[4]

> *verse 4* Backed up by a jazz band, layin' on the wood
> Mixin' Ahmad Jamal in my 'Johnny B. Goode'.
> Sneakin' Erroll Garner in my 'Sweet Sixteen'
> Now they tell me Stan Kenton's cuttin' 'Maybellene'.

Two more songs, 'Tulane' (1969) and 'Have Mercy Judge' (1969) also tell of Johnny/Chuck's exploits, this time of trouble with the law, continuing the explicitly autobiographical nature of the Johnny songs. Berry, however, says that 'Tulane' is about a different Johnny (Salvo 1972: 42). Because these depart from the themes of Johnny/Chuck's music and musical development, I will not discuss them further.

An autobiographical element originating in 'Johnny B. Goode' is the rags-to-riches story, which Berry's mother predicted for him. Berry writes that she

constantly proclaimed she knew I would become lucky in my life and urged me on to get an education (which I fumbled around with until I was grown) to aid me in maintaining that fortune that I would likely come into. (Berry 1988: 155)

A powerful reason for the lasting success of 'Johnny B. Goode' is that Berry's lyrics effectively and succinctly tap into three compelling American myths: genius, the notion that talent will prevail, and one I have already discussed, the American dream of financial success.[5] I want to consider these myths in some depth, beginning with the idea of genius.

---

[4] Transcribed from *Chuck Berry: More Rock 'n' Roll Rarities from the Golden Era of Chess Records*, Chess 9190.

[5] Howard A. DeWitt (1985) writes that there have been more covers of 'Johnny B. Goode' than any other Chuck Berry tune except for 'Memphis Tennessee'. And there are some versions which were released after he compiled his list, such as one by Judas Priest, among others. Berry himself writes, 'For a long while, "Memphis" was the song covered most by other groups, until the sleeper, "Johnny B. Goode", caught on to take precedence' (Berry 1988: 161). There are currently forty-nine versions commercially available, including those by Berry himself.

Not only is Johnny a musician, but his talent is natural, untrained. Johnny is such a good guitarist that he can even pick up rhythms from passing cars.[6] He 'never, ever learned to read or write so well', but playing the guitar was for him as easy as ringing a bell.

Tied to the idea of genius is Johnny's climb to success, which he achieves because of his gift. In order to emphasize Johnny's ascent, Berry carefully and deliberately humbles Johnny's background; Berry writes in his auto-biography that it was his intention to write a rags-to-riches story, and some of the words he uses are extremely effective and telling in this way.

For example, from the start we know that Johnny grew up in the country, by Berry's using the words 'deep down'. Johnny's home was a log cabin in the woods, a cabin 'made of earth and wood'. The word 'earth' carries connotations. 'Dirt' might have worked as well, but by using 'earth' Berry enhances the idea that Johnny's talent is natural, perhaps even divine; for 'earth' I would argue, is a trope, a momentary swerve in the discourse, evoking poetic or even biblical associations.

The word 'earth' also generalizes outward, making universal Johnny's talent and appeal. Johnny is neither black nor white, but everyone (every male, anyway); Johnny, with such a common name, is everyman. Berry purposely made the listeners' identification with Johnny possible by altering him, away from the singular, autobiographical and toward the general. Berry writes

My first thought was to make [Johnny's] life follow as my own had come along, but I thought it would seem biased to white fans to say 'colored boy' and changed it to 'country boy'. (Berry 1988: 157)

Berry also said in a 1972 interview that the reason he changed 'colored' to 'country' is so that it would be played on the radio (Salvo 1972: 42).

A shift away from autobiography also occurs since Berry's upbringing was neither rural nor poor; his was a solid working-class family. Such a portrayal of one's background is a common autobiographical device, however: by lowering one's early life, the heights eventually attained appear higher.[7]

---

[6] The French jazz critic, Hugues Panassié, contributes to the mythologizing of the African-American musician's 'natural' talent when he tells a strikingly similar anecdote about Louis Armstrong, who, he says, picked up a rhythm and melody from a passing horse and carriage while walking with Panassié in Paris (Panassié 1971: 24). Berry's reference, of course, could equally be to train rhythms.

[7] The rags-to-riches myth is the strongest one in evidence in this song, and it is for this reason that it was borrowed for the 1985 hit movie *Back to the Future*. The plot follows predictable lines. The main character, Marty McFly, because of his ingenuity and talent, realizes the rags-to-riches myth, and enriches his parents, just as Chuck Berry was able to do for his parents. Marty identified with Johnny (or Berry) in that song in the movie, and the few minutes when he sings 'Johnny B. Goode' in *Back to the Future* are a microcosm of the entire film.

The second myth, the idea that talent cannot be suppressed, is subtler. The chorus of 'Johnny B. Goode' contains a double meaning. 'Go, Johnny, go!' sounds at first like an encouragement to Johnny/Chuck to play a guitar solo. Berry, however, intends this to be in the imperative. He writes in his auto-biography that if you have talent you must prove yourself, and asks 'will the name and the light . . . come to you? No! You have to "Go!"' (Berry 1988: 158).

Berry's idea that genius will prevail is only partly borne out by his own career, and there is some irony in that. Johnny 'never, ever learned to read or write so well', but solely by virtue of his talent he comes out of nowhere and makes a huge career for himself. Berry on the other hand spent nearly a decade playing minor gigs in clubs around St Louis and was rejected by several record companies before being signed by Leonard Chess of Chess Records in 1955. And Berry experienced many setbacks in his career, some because of his race. In obscuring Johnny's race, Berry made his hypothetical career far smoother than Berry's own.

'Johnny B. Goode' carries strong racial overtones. I have talked about the alteration from 'colored' to 'country', but many cultural or racial clues remain. For example, the lyrics are filled with rural African-American imagery, such as gunny sacks and railroad tracks.

Except for a possible meaning of the title which I already discussed, little evidence of African-American dialect remains. Further examples are 'sun go down' and 'a ringin' a bell'. Berry could have disclosed his race with his dic-tion as he does in other songs, but since 'Johnny B. Goode' is aimed at a broad audience his diction is extremely clear, i.e. intended to appeal to the white audience. He writes about his varying of diction in his autobiography:

The songs of Muddy Waters impelled me to deliver the down-home blues in the lan-guage they came from, Negro dialect. When I played hillbilly songs, I stressed my diction so that is was harder and whiter. All in all it was my intention to hold both the black and the white clientele by voicing the different kinds of songs in their cus-tomary tongues. (Berry 1988: 91)

In his autobiography Berry often characterizes hillbilly music as white and the blues as black, and admits that his use of hillbilly music was part of his bid for achieving popularity with a broad audience ('Anglopinionated' is his word to describe music that will appeal to whites). Berry's use of such music marks a tension between the African-American identity he was attempting to assert in 'Johnny B. Goode' and other songs, and the white music with which he was making his statement. I will talk more about this conflict in the last section of this essay.

An interesting aspect of the lyrics of 'Johnny B. Goode' is their structure, which is a Faulknerian *tour de force* of cadential denial. The first stanza (six lines) is all one sentence; it works by employing 'there', 'where', 'who', and 'but' as conjunctions in lines 3 through 6 (see verse 1 above). The second stanza is less clear; the published sheet music may well be correct in making a sentence out of the first four lines and one out of the last two lines; this certainly seems correct for the third stanza. What all this means is that Berry's long sentences contribute to the tension, the forward motion of 'Johnny B. Goode'. Berry's voice, ensemble, and music all create an atmosphere of great excitement, and the lyrics which rarely come to a fully stop add to that impression.

Retention and Subversion in the Music

The music of 'Johnny B. Goode' bears many resemblances to the blues. Berry's tune is the familiar speeded-up twelve bar blues which he used so frequently, with some small variations. The opening guitar lick and entrance of the rest of the band follow the chord progression considered to be within the normal bounds for that form in the rhythm and blues tradition: I–IV–I–V–IV–I. The rest of the verses and choruses all use the more common twelve-bar I–IV–I–V–I pattern, except for the two instrumental choruses before the last verse: here the chord progressions are the same except that the opening four bars on the tonic are replaced by a foray to IV for a bar, then back to I.

But this is not to say that 'Johnny B. Goode' is a blues because it has the blues chord progression, but that the differences between 'Johnny B. Goode' and a traditional blues do not occur at a formal level. While keeping the harmonic progressions of the blues essentially intact, Berry varies other blues conventions, which I will consider below.

Berry's use of the twelve-bar blues form is significant because of its heritage, its association with so many previous African-American performers, some of whom Berry idolized as models. Berry's employment of the form makes an important link with past African-American music, and the way he uses the twelve-bar blues is similarly significant because the continuity is maintained. As an African-American inheritance, the form is a sign of the African-American condition, a sign of covert protest against white domination. George

Lipsitz, arguing from a Bakhtinian dialogic standpoint, says that African-Americans' retention of traditional forms were a way of preserving collective memory about a place where they were free, and that this retention also serves as a protection against white hegemony (Lipsitz 1990: 111). Even though Berry altered the blues form and conventions, that repository of meanings remains; in borrowing the form Berry borrowed the ideology as well.

A deviation from the traditional blues is that Berry's stanzas are twice as long (i.e. six lines listead of three), for Berry speeds up not only the tempo but the delivery as well, and eliminates all melismas (except a small one on 'name') which are a common feature of a blues. Other blues conventions remain unchanged. Jeff Todd Titon (1977) writes that the typical line in a blues lyric tends to consist of two sub-phrases, with a break or a rest in between, while the third line often does not have the rest. The expanded stanzas of 'Johnny B. Goode' do just this: there are breaks between lines one and two, and then between three and four, but not between five and six.

Melodically, 'Johnny B. Goode' behaves typically for a Berry song. It occupies a more limited range than many blues songs but within its range of a perfect fifth Berry's song is like a blues, with the bending of the third degree. The melodic contour also falls into Titon's categories of melodic contours for the blues as one of the most common: start on the highest note, end on the lowest note. (This is Titon's 'Specific Contour Case IA', which he discusses on pp. 162–5.)

And the melody has features of many oral musics: formulaic repetitions of melodic fragments. Titon's typical blues line, with its division into sub-phrases, is accurate for 'Johnny B. Goode', in which the first part of each phrase is an antecedent to the second part. While Berry's a, c, and e sections vary somewhat (the opening portions of each phrase), the, b, d, and f parts (closing portions) are similar (see Example 7.1).

Such variation on a, c, and e parts with different, but related, b, d, and f sections is a common feature of the blues. Berry's tune, however, is constrained by tempo which prohibits extensive ornamentation or melismas, and is varied less than a blues would be. Titon discusses this formulaic phenomenon at length, saying that in any one stanza, 'phrases b, d, and f are usually identical, or nearly so; and that phrases a and c are very close', while phrase e is most likely to be independent of the other phrases (Titon 1977: 166).

In 'Johnny B. Goode' however, the a and e parts are related; c is the independent one, with the introduction of D♭s. Example 7.1 is a transcription

Ex 7.1. 'Johnny B. Goode', verse 1

of the melody in which the similarities and differences just discussed are visible. Berry thus maintains many of the structural and melodic features of the blues (after compensating for the changes caused by his up-tempo rendition) while adding a few twists of his own.

Berry's tune differs from traditional blues more in its text than in its form, in its turning of the blues from a reflective form into a narrative one. 'Johnny B. Goode' tells a story; Berry's propensity for telling stories with his music is another of Lipsitz's (1990) characteristics of African and African-American culture. Alfons Dauer writes that the blues 'reflects events or situations, it does not use narrative means: the Blues is a presentation—not a narration' (Dauer 1979: 10). David Evans makes the same point, characterizing the blues as lyric, distinct from narrative songs (Evans 1982: 27). Since early rock and roll is usually thought to be a hybrid between the blues and hillbilly music, it is important to ask if hillbilly music tells stories. Some songs do, some do not; it is not easy to generalize. At any rate it is clear that Berry did not follow the reflexive convention of the blues.

Berry uses a catchy rhythmic figure in the opening bluesy guitar lick of 'Johnny B. Goode', sort of an 'inverted hemiola': groups of three quavers in a duple metre instead of groups of two or four (a hemiola is a group of two when three are expected, and occurs usually in triple metre).[8] This recurring figure provides the strongest musical analogy to the words in this song.

---

[8] Berry says in *Hail! Hail! Rock 'n' Roll* that he borrowed the opening lick from guitarist Carl Hogan's music, and goes on to acknowledge T-Bone Walker, as well as Charlie Christian as his great guitar influences. Guitarist Rick Vito (1984) notes that this lick is similar to other openings of Berry songs: 'Carol', 'Little Queenie', and 'Roll Over Beethoven' are examples he offers.

Ex 7.2. 'Johnny B. Goode', guitar rhythmic gestures

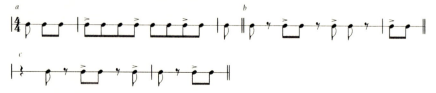

Berry uses it frequently in different ways, and the resulting fabric of rhythms in 'Johnny B. Goode' is complex. This figure occurs first at the opening of the song, so there is no mistaking its importance. Also, Berry's 'Let it Rock', recorded in July 1959, is essentially the same tune, and this figure is missing, since it is not important for the message Berry is making in that tune (an ambiguous song about a railroad worker who panics because of an out of control train). For ease of discussion I shall label this rhythmic figure 'inverse hemiola'.[9] Some of the permutations of this inverse hemiola appear in Example 7.2. The first is the opening guitar figure, a Berry trademark, which I have labelled as 7.2*a*; the others are variations of this rhythm that Berry uses in his guitar solos in the choruses; 7.2*b* is also from the introduction; and 7.2*c* is from the instrumental chorus preceding the last verse. The accents indicate the groupings of three.

Akin to this figure and its variations is the backbeat (accented second and fourth beats), another salient feature of Berry's music. And that backbeat (and almost any pop music backbeat) has ideological implications, since it is a deliberate thwarting of western European musical conventions, where 'natural' accents tend to fall on the odd-numbered beats in duple metre. John Shepherd (1987) writes that the backbeat in popular music is a sign of the marginalized in western European and American culture attempting to win back cultural space which had been previously occupied by the dominant culture.

I think he is right. An unvarying 4/4 metre, with nearly constant quavers is homologous to the socio-politico-cultural status quo, which in Berry's time was white. His music often subverts this hegemonic norm. The backbeat in 'Johnny B. Goode' constantly upsets the first and third beat accents normally

---

[9] 'Inverse hemiola' is my term; there is no accepted label for this figure. A similar figure occurs in ragtime and is called 'secondary rag', which John Hasse (1985) writes was so common that it became a cliché after 1906. Hasse links this and other ragtime rhythmic figures to African music's additive rhythms. I would say that this figure in ragtime represents, like Chuck Berry's use of it, an assertion of Otherness, an attempt, to borrow John Shepherd's (1987) words, to win back cultural space.

Ex 7.3. 'Johnny B. Goode', guitar rhythm of final two bars

found in 4/4. And the inverse hemiola does likewise. This polarity is never resolved, for at the end of the song we hear—unusually in 'Johnny B. Goode' —accents on beats one and three in the penultimate bar, then the inverse hemiola in the final bar, not, I think, to show that Berry's (and, by extension, all African-Americans') disenfranchised view prevails, but to maintain the rhythmic/ideological tension to the end, unresolved.

The backbeat and inverse hemiola have further political implications because they are homologous to the many oppositions in the song: white and black, country and city, old and young and, finally, poverty and wealth, the rags-to-riches story.[10] These tensions are less strong in 'Bye Bye Johnny', which makes use of a subdued backbeat but no groupings of quavers other than the usual groupings of two, and are absent altogether in 'Go Go Go'. The oppositions thus dissipate over the span of the three songs, as does Berry's tripartite tale itself: 'Go Go Go', unlike the earlier two songs, fades away.

At this point a digression is necessary, for such claims for ideological meanings need to be supported theoretically. Steven Connor, like Bruce Tucker (1989), writes that rock music is a postmodernist phenomenon because it is an attempt by the disenfranchised to 'articulate alternative or plural cultural identities, of groups belonging to the margins of national or dominant cultures' (Connor 1989: 186). George Lipsitz (1990) makes a similar point, as does Jean-François Lyotard, who writes in *The Postmodern Condition* that, in the most general terms, postmodernism is 'incredulity toward metanarratives' (Lyotard 1984: p. xiv), or, for my purposes, incredulity to points of view held by the dominant culture. My reading of the backbeat, then, is one of the ways that African-American musicians mapped out their own music and their own space.

Musical and ideological discussions such as this rely heavily on constructing homologies between perceived social, cultural, and political attitudes and musical events; sometimes the connections are difficult to make, and even more difficult to verify. Claiming that Berry's backbeat or 'inverse hemiola'

---

[10] Bruce Tucker (1989) noticed many of these oppositions in other Berry songs, and many are equally applicable here.

have political implications means that other musicians' uses of these devices are also political, and that is a complicated issue; musical devices which were originally political or ideological can be aestheticized, and their meanings changed or erased.

The backbeat is a good example. Because of Berry and other early rock musicians, the backbeat became a feature of the rock and roll style, and as such could be borrowed by other musicians and made to mean other things, if anything. Elvis Presley, for instance, could use the backbeat and instead of signifying African-Americans striving to create their own subculture, it is usually taken to indicate an assertion of male sexuality.

Deciding specific musical meanings is difficult. Susanne K. Langer (1979) writes of music as an unconsummated symbol; music means, but just what it means we can never know. She is right in that we cannot know the meaning, but what she does not say is that her position allows that music can have a multiplicity of meanings. George Lipsitz writes of the same problem in popular culture: 'It is impossible to say whether any one combination of sounds . . . innately expresses one unified political position' (Lipsitz 1990: 13).

I am thus deliberately shying away from assigning a more specific meaning to Berry's backbeat in 'Johnny B. Goode'; if it had a specific meaning, it would not be reused by so many other musicians, black and white. It is more productive to view the backbeat in the terms outlined by Fredric Jameson in 'Reification and utopia in mass culture' (1979). Jameson forwards a relevant analysis of *Jaws*, in which he argues that one of the reasons the film was so powerful is that the shark could be viewed as a symbol for all kinds of tensions, depending on which meaning the individual viewer mapped onto the shark.

Finally, the work of John Fiske (1989) is useful in this context as well, and he echoes Jameson's idea. Fiske argues that consumers of popular culture can form numerous alliances, sometimes dependent on age, gender, race, religion or whatever. In other words, one person can receive popular culture in different ways, depending on how they identify with the product. Fiske's model works in the other direction, too: producers of popular culture can use the same device—such as a backbeat—to fight against the various aspects of dominant culture. For Berry, it was whites; for Elvis, it was the dominant culture's suppression of the sexual; for an African-American woman rock musician like Tracy Chapman it is the dominant culture in general and male hegemony in particular.

Two Recordings, and their Ideological Implications

Berry recorded 'Johnny B. Goode' more than once, so a comparison of his recordings is revealing. The two most interesting are the original Chess version and the Mercury version recorded in 1966, which is essentially a cover by Berry of his own tune. Like so many covers by white artists of tunes by African-American artists, Berry's later rendering of 'Johnny B. Goode' is sanitized, the rough edges smoothed off. None of the Mercury tunes, incidentally, made any *Billboard* chart, probably because the fans whom Berry and Mercury thought that they were aiming at were more interested in the British Invasion than Berry reruns.

A major difference in these two recordings is the amount of reverb used. The first recording features a stripped down, ready for action ensemble consisting of Berry on guitar and vocals, Lafayette Leake on piano, Willie Dixon on bass, and Fred Below on drums. The lack of reverb highlights the extraordinary clarity of the ensemble; it sounds as if the listeners are right there with Berry and the other musicians. In the later version, the ensemble is augmented, and the reverb turns the listeners into voyeurs, detached from the visceral directness of the first version.

This last point is important. In the original version the listeners are close to the musicians; in the Mercury version they are much further away. In a sense, Berry's first version of 'Johnny B. Goode' is functional, the ideological message clear. He is telling a tale with a moral and political message, and everything about his performance contributes to this: his voice quality, the rhythms used, the backbeat, the use of an African-American form and the clarity of all of these devices.

In the later version for Mercury, one of the six major recording companies, this functional aspect is less noticeable. The ideological aspects of the lyrics and music are undermined by the various ways Berry has souped up the music and recording. 'Johnny B. Goode' has been aestheticized—it is now an aesthetic object whose social meanings have been suppressed by the distance between the producers and the receivers, and Berry's distance between relative poverty and affluence.[11] His switch from a small independent record label to a much larger one is partly responsible for this change.

---

[11] Berry's versions of 'Johnny B. Goode' after the one for Mercury vary. His version recorded live in London returns the backbeat but not the inverse hemiola. The version in *Hail! Hail! Rock 'n' Roll* has the backbeat, but the inverse hemiola is less prominent than in the first version.

His earlier statement which had clear political implications was co-opted by the dominant culture, represented by the major label.[12]

This argument is derived from Pierre Bourdieu's writing about aesthetic distanciation in *Distinction: A Social Critique of the Judgement of Taste* (1984). His main point in the first chapter is that a person's freedom or distance from economic necessity plays a direct role in his or her aesthetic taste. People with low educational capital (as he calls it, relating this state with economic class, somewhat problematically) have tastes that tend to be functional, and those with higher educational capital have tastes which are more aesthetic. That is, poor people view objects, and art, as functional objects, while wealthier people are more capable of aestheticizing that object: its use is less relevant to them because of their relative economic freedom.

I am probably using Bourdieu's ideas differently than he intended, since he was concerned with consumers of culture, not producers. But John Fiske (1989) has convincingly problematized the notion of mass culture and consumers: he argues that everyone makes their own meanings out of popular culture, and they do this so consistently that to characterize them as consumers ignores the fact that they produce their own meanings. Fiske goes so far as to label popular cultural texts 'producerly': for Fiske, such a text is one from which the receiver can produce their own meanings, and he intends his idea to apply to most popular culture texts. The upshot of all this is that the placement of consumers and producers of popular culture at opposite poles is too simple a model, and so to use Bourdieu's ideas as I do here acknowledges the blurred distinction between consumer and producer.

Berry himself experienced a distancing from economic necessity between the recordings of these two versions of 'Johnny B. Goode'. Although he was a major star by the time of his switch to Mercury in 1966, the change in labels was prompted by a huge fee of $150,000. After that Berry was freer to experiment with music as an aesthetic, formal entity, not a functional one expressing political ideas, and so in the Mercury version we hear changes.

There is little written evidence for Berry's aestheticization. But I think the changes made in the Mercury version of 'Johnny B. Goode' argue for this point of view: Berry's incorporation of a Latin rhythm and the increased complexity of the bass part show his increased interest in music as sound, rather than music as a way of conveying meanings.

[12] George Lipsitz makes a similar point about Elvis Presley's move to RCA from Sun in 1955: he says that RCA 'smoothed off the rough edges of his style for mass distribution' (Lipsitz 1990: 124).

Ex 7.4. 'Johnny B. Goode', Mercury version, bass part

Other differences between these two recordings abound. In the original Chess version of 'Johnny B. Goode', Berry's voice is high, but not emotively so. He is not struggling in that register, and his voice conveys energy, excitement. Contrast that with the recording for Mercury. The later recording sounds all right when heard by itself, but played next to the earlier version, the Mercury recording sounds like a parody. Berry's voice is thinner, more nasal—he almost whines.

And this Mercury version *is* a parody in a way, although not an intentional one. Berry used an expanded ensemble which, compared to the earlier one, sounds vague, fluffy. And he beefed up the bass part, which now outlines a dominant seventh with quavers, instead of a triad with crotchets. Also, this bass part has a new, more complex rhythm, a Latin rhythm which Berry was experimenting with around this time (see Example 7.4). I include this example not because it is musically important—it is not. But it is an example of Berry's aestheticizing of this tune, which is simpler, more direct, and more convincing in the first version.

Although these two versions of 'Johnny B. Goode' are extremely different, they do have Chuck Berry in common. While some of the changes are easily attributable to him (such as the bass guitar's Latin rhythm), others, like the reverb, might not be. Berry admits in his autobiography that he knew little about producing a record,[13] and perhaps some of the differences between the two recordings were added by the production staff who are uncredited on the album.

Still, I cannot ignore the possibility that Berry might have deliberately rounded off the rough edges of the tune in order to appeal to a mass audience. Throughout his career, Berry tried to give his audience what he thought they wanted to hear, and that meant occasionally sanitizing his music so that objectionable or subversive elements were obscured or even omitted. His changing of 'colored boy' to 'country boy' is an example in 'Johnny B. Goode'. Perhaps, to come back to Bourdieu, as Berry became more successful

---

[13] Berry said in an interview with Patrick William Salvo that he was involved with all aspects of production: 'As far as producing, let me tell you for the last time that since the very start, when I first signed with Chess, I have been in total creative control' (Salvo 1972: 23).

economically he found it less necessary to write and perform his music in a way which made his ideological message clear.

Now, I realize that this sounds like a condemnation, but I do not mean it to be; nor do I mean that Berry sold out. Berry, like all artists from the marginalized, faced a difficult choice in his career: ghettoization or integration into the mainstream. In other words, he could remain faithful to his African-American musical heritage and so probably never transcend his economic class, or he could escape that class and appeal to a mass audience by tapping into apolitical experiences common to blacks and whites: school, cars, and love, as he said in *Hail! Hail! Rock 'n' Roll* (1987). This is the question Berry asked himself:

> Why can't I do as Pat Boone does and play good music for the white people and sell as well there as I could in the neighborhood? And that's what I shot for. (*Hail! Hail! Rock 'n' Roll* 1987)

The dominant culture's posing of choices to the marginalized—ghettoization or integration—is one of its greatest achievements. It effectively removes clearly attractive options for marginalized artists and replaces them with various forms of betrayal: betraying your community in order to make it big, or betraying the American Dream in order to remain in your community.

Writers with Marxian inclinations offer a solution to this structure of cultural hegemony. Jacques Attali argues in *Noise: The Political Economy of Music* (1985) that the capitalist mode of production and distribution of music can only be broken if people start to make their own music for their own reasons, and if they want to sell it, to do that themselves. He cites an example relevant to this discussion: free jazz, produced by African-American musicians who were finding that their music was being monetarily censored by some American record companies. These musicians organized, and eventually attempted to make and market their own recordings, splitting an equal share of the total earnings.

This sort of self-organization and distribution is the kind of solution to the exploitation of African-Americans by the dominant cultural music industry that Harold Cruse demands in *The Crisis of the Negro Intellectual*, published in 1967. Cruse writes:

> No social movement of a protest nature in Harlem can be successful or have any positive meaning unless it is at one and the same time a *political, economic and cultural movement*. (Cruse 1967: 86)

If Berry had formed his own record company or established his own method of distribution, he probably would not have had access to a mass audience and so enjoyed less of a career, but, on the other hand, his covers of his own tunes for Mercury would not be so limp when compared to his earlier, more ideologically-charged work for Chess. Nonetheless, Berry managed to communicate his African-American viewpoint in 'Johnny B. Goode' and many other songs, and his widespread popularity helped to break down racial barriers in America. The sanitized covers, by Berry himself and others, cannot obscure the sheer exuberance and directness of his earliest and best songs.

References

Attali, J. (1985). *Noise: The Political Economy of Music* (Minneapolis).

Berry, C. (1988). *Chuck Berry: The Autobiography* (New York).

Bourdieu, P. (1984). *Distinction: A Social Critique of the Judgement of Taste* (Cambridge, Mass.).

Connor, S. (1989). *Postmodernist Culture: An Introduction to Theories of the Contemporary* (Oxford).

Cruse, H. (1967). *The Crisis of the Negro Intellectual* (New York).

Dauer, A. (1979). 'Towards a typology of the vocal blues idiom', *Jazzforschung*, 11: 9–92.

DeWitt, H. (1985). *Chuck Berry: Rock 'n' Roll Music*, 2nd edn. (Ann Arbor).

Evans, D. (1982). *Big Road Blues: Tradition and Creativity in the Folk Blues* (Berkeley).

Fiske, John (1987). 'British cultural studies and television', in *Channels of Discourse*, ed. Robert C. Allen (Chapel Hill, NC).

—— (1989). *Understanding Popular Culture* (Boston).

Hasse, J. (1985). 'Ragtime: from the top', in *Ragtime: Its History, Composers, and Music*, ed. John Edward Hasse (New York).

Jameson, F. (1979). 'Reification and utopia in mass culture', *Social Text*, 11 (Winter), 130–48.

Langer, S. (1979). *Philosophy in a New Key: A Study in the Symbolism of Reason, Rite, and Art*, 3rd edn. (Cambridge, Mass.).

Lipsitz, G. (1990). *Time Passages: Collective Memory and American Popular Culture* (Minneapolis).

Lyotard, J.-F. (1984). *The Postmodern Condition: A Report on Knowledge* (Minneapolis).

Panassié, H. (1971). *Louis Armstrong* (New York).

Salvo, P. W. (1972). 'A conversation with Chuck Berry', *Rolling Stone*, 42 (23 Nov.).

Shepherd, J. (1987). 'Music and male hegemony', in *Music and Society: The Politics of Composition, Performance and Reception*, ed. Richard Leppert and Susan McClary (Cambridge).

Titon, J. T. (1977). *Early Downhome Blues: A Musical and Cultural Analysis* (Urbana, Ill.).

Tucker, B. (1989). ' "Tell Tchaikovsky the news": postmodernism, popular culture, and the emergence of rock 'n' roll', *Black Music Research Journal*, 9 (Fall), 271–95.

Vito, R. (1984). 'The Chuck Berry style: A modern rocker pays tribute to the master', *Guitar Player* (June), 72–5.

Discography

[1967]. *Chuck Berry's Golden Hits*. Mercury SR 61103.

1972. *The Chuck Berry London Sessions*. Chess CH 60020.

1984. 'Bye Bye Johnny'. *The Great Twenty Eight*. MCA CHD-92500.

1984. *The Great Twenty Eight*. MCA CHD-92500.

1984. 'Let it Rock'. *The Great Twenty Eight*. MCA CHD-92500.

1986. 'Go Go Go'. *Chuck Berry: More Rock 'n' Roll Rarities from the Golden Era of Chess Records*. Chess 9190.

Filmography

Hail! Hail! Rock 'n' Roll. 1987. Universal Studios. Directed by Taylor Hackford.

8

.....

Listening to Peter Gabriel's 'I Have the Touch'

UMBERTO FIORI

The very existence of popular music research in its various aspects can be considered, with its investment of attention, as a general value judgement on the music's potentialities. Moreover, we should not forget that a serious interest in popular music research would probably not have been possible without the emergence of more ambitious musical products testifying to a need for emancipation. Even so, perhaps because of a bitter awareness of its own roots in the same cultural and political processes, popular music research has somehow more and more tended to ignore 'quality' products in the field, whether because of their decline since the 1970s, or for the sake of some 'scientific' suspension of value judgement.

We must admit that notions of *progress, experimentation, avant-garde*, and the like, which once gave a solid foundation to those 'quality' products, and which are indebted to various extramusical ideologies, find themselves today in a deep state of crisis—not only in the field of art, as everyone knows. Is that a reason to conclude that—deprived of its eschatological connotations—'quality' has gone bankrupt and that finally, as in the glamorous, glossolalic prelude to *Indiana Jones and the Temple of Doom*, 'Anything Goes'?

Comfortable and liberating as it may seem, such a conclusion could not prevent the problem of value judgement re-emerging sooner or later. I offer here a contribution to consideration of that problem, starting from a personal aesthetic experience focused on the use of voice and words in a song by Peter Gabriel, 'I Have the Touch', which is included in his solo album, *IV*. For obvious reasons, the following discussion presupposes the reader's familiarity with the original text, that is, the recording. Paper does not sing.

'I Have the Touch'

The time I like is the rush hour,
'cos I like the rush.
The pushing of the people
I like it all so much.
Such a mass of motion
do not know where it goes:
I move with the movement and . . .
I have the touch.

I'm waiting for ignition, I'm
looking for a spark.
Any chance collision and I
light up in the dark.
There you stand before me,
all that fur and all that hair:
oooh . . . do I dare . . .
I have the touch.

Wanting contact   I'm
wanting contact   with you.
Shake those hands! Shake those hands!
Give me the thing I understand,
shake those hands! Shake those hands!
Shake hands,
shake hands.

Any social occasion
it's: hello, how do you do?
All those introductions,
I never miss my cue.
So before a question,
so before a doubt
my hand moves out and . . .
I have the touch.

Wanting contact . . .

Pull my chin, stroke my hair,
scratch my nose, hug my knees,
try drink, food, cigarettes,
tension will not ease.
I tap my fingers, fold my arms,
breathe in deep, cross my legs,

shrug my shoulders, stretch my back—
but nothing seems to please:
I need contact,
I need contact,
Nothing seems to please,
I need contact.

It's not hard to recognize, in 'I Have the Touch', a rather typical rock song pattern: the experience of everyday life is sung in the first person, statements are very straightforwardly formulated, argumentation is totally implicit, as if in a conversation with someone sharing the speaker's opinions. We can say, in this sense, that we are dealing—from the lyrics' point of view, at least—with a *classic* rock song, in the tradition of, say, '(I Can't Get No) Satisfaction'.

Traditionally, though—in 'Satisfaction' as in more recent examples—the experience of the individual in a mass society is described in its most frustrating aspects, and, not rarely, there is a clear and explicit social criticism.

The urban crowd, the mass—a pure negativity—had to be ritually re-created in a sublimated version at concerts, where it could assume the transfigured form of a community—the 'rock community'. Among the values constituting, in that context, the community's 'authentic', 'alternative' essence, so as to make one more crowded situation 'special', were—homologous to the values of the music—immediacy, spontaneity, non-verbal communication, so-called 'body language', and the like. Gabriel, through a very delicate and rich form of irony, seems to reveal something that was understood but at the same time hidden in that ideology: the metropolitan crowd of common men, thronging in subways and elevators, along sidewalks or in public buildings, relies—no less than 'alternative' tribes and subcultures—on instinctuality, immediacy, on subtle bodily communication. Isn't it common sense to say that 'you can understand people by their handshake'? An extreme sense of surrender to such commonplaces is here the symptom of a certain distancing.

So before a question
so before a doubt
my hand moves out and
I have the touch.

This is not to say that this song is just a rhetorical, ideological counterpart or a parody of traditional rock ideologies. The experience of the press, the feeling of a loss of self, full of anguish and pleasure, the sense of diffuse intimacy, of forced promiscuity, show all their dynamic ambiguity here. Just as with other songs in the same album (I'm thinking, especially, of 'The Rhythm of the Heat', inspired by Jung's experience of tribal rites in Africa), the sense of protection, of comfort, of regression, which is characteristic of the individual when he finds himself wrapped up by a mass of people, the pleasure coming from the reduction of faculties to a minimum of sensorial attention, to convention, to courtesy, to rituality, is offered in 'I Have the Touch', together with its dark side. Still it's not *this plus that*: the complex process of rejection-surrender, the dialectics between individual and crowd, between 'authentic' relationships and formalized, objectified sociality, and so on, are played with (or, if you prefer, *encoded*) through a very simple vocal strategy.

The lyrics are—superficially—transparent. Their language is more than ordinary—it sounds here and there like *quotations*: quotations from *anybody's speech*. As often happens in rock and pop songs, the voice injects emotion into the shreds of everyday words, commonplaces, ordinary experience. In particular, there's a point in the eight-line verse (four-line, in the sleeve transcription) where it has to climb up to the highest note in the melody; there, musical pathos is at its peak; vocal emission, betraying some effort, charges with a strange hysteria the words in the seventh, penultimate line: 'I move with the movement' (first verse), 'my hand moves out' (third verse), and 'do I dare' (second verse; by the way, this is a formula whose multiple levels of sense are also exploited in T. S. Eliot's 'Prufrock').

It's not hard to notice that the vocal emphasis falls where a situational knot exposed in the verse promises to be unravelled, and the voice that says 'I' must tell us of his pragmatic response. But: what knot? Was there something tragic?

A typical, dynamic disproportion works here between the enunciative tone the words would imply by themselves, and the way they are sung. This sort of arbitrary climax, of apparently unmotivated tension and effort, leads to an effect of multi-levelled sense (for example in 'do I dare') which can only be reinforced by the fact that it is followed by a disphoric conclusion, where the slackening of tension in vocal emission together with the descent of the melody suggests that presence of a fatalistic sense of surrender in the title line, 'I have the touch'.

Similar dialectics can be observed in the refrain, where the neutral, technical, impersonal sense of the line 'wanting contact' is obviously alluding to some more substantial, more 'human' need for communication, a need for contact which is in fact over-satisfied within the crowd or in public relations, and at the same time eluded, made abstract by its mere immediacy and indefinite repetition.

The 'message' is clear, and probably it even sounds too obvious when it's analytically decomposed and 'clarified', showing its bones: the concrete dimension of the song makes a living process out of what could seem—in my very rough description—a rigid conceptual pattern; it *consumes* conceptuality, we could say, through a particular combination of enunciative, melodic, verbal, and vocal dynamics.

The tension between an 'intimate' and a 'technical' sense of the line 'wanting contact' operates through a very simple and effective differentiation within Gabriel's vocal. While 'wanting contact' is sung by a full, doubled voice, scanning the syllables upon each note, 'I am' and 'with you' are almost whispered by a single voice, very close to the microphone:

(I am) wanting contact (with you)

I would insult my reader's intelligence if I insisted on the meaning of this. I just want to observe that the refrain's obsessive password, 'shake those hands' (which inevitably reminds me of the 'clap your hands' rock and pop formula), seems to reproduce the verse's disphoric ending in the refrain.

This summary analysis may give a reasonable example—I hope—of how rich, multiple sense can be produced within rock music by specific means, that is, by exploiting some of the possibilities which are open to the art of the recorded voice. After the age of content analysis, after that of the literary interpretation of rock and pop songs, the specificity of rock aesthetics has been not only remarked upon but deeply clarified in recent years (see the work of Frith, Laing, Middleton, Shepherd, and Tagg). Naturally, since the emphasis had previously been on the 'message' or on traditionally conceived 'poetic' qualities, most of the new perspectives felt the need to insist on the purely musical dimension of the word within rock and pop music, considering lyrics as a pretext for vocal epiphanies, manifestations of the singer's personality, or symptoms of cultural identity.

Such interpretations, liberating rock lyrics from literary responsibilities, are generally shared and encouraged by the artists. Gabriel, in particular, gave support to this position during an ITV interview just before the final cut of the record featuring 'I Have the Touch', declaring that lyrics come last in his creative work and that in any case they are substantially subordinated to the dimension of the naked voice and to the music.

During the same interview one could listen to a provisional version of 'I Have the Touch', containing a rather interesting variant in the refrain:

> I am
> only
> only
> wanting contact
> with you.

In the final version, that 'only'—which can also be heard in a live recording —was to be rejected together with the short musical phrase 'containing' it. A relatively long absence of the voice took the place of that minimal bridge. Why?

One answer could be that, because of its position and its repetition, the adverb risked becoming unreasonably prominent within the refrain, suffocating the rest of the words. But when I listened to the provisional version, knowing the final one, I immediately gave to myself a—for me—more substantial explanation of a rejection I enthusiastically agreed with: the whole dynamic, ambiguous irony in the refrain and in the whole song is somehow made unpleasantly explicit by that 'only'. The whole sense becomes slackly allusive, winking at the listener to *suggest* the presence of some additional or contradictory meaning, instead of leaving him free to discover it. The song becomes more *eloquent*; even its musical sense (if ever we can isolate it from the rest) is changed by the introduction of such a little, unimportant word.

Starting from our minimal clue and its variant, we could come to some conclusions. One is that the obstinate rock myth of 'spontaneity' should be revised—not only with regard to pop-oriented products but more widely, at least when we are dealing with recorded material. Secondly, another myth, that of rock and pop as 'oral poetry', seems to be contradicted by our example. The two variants we just considered are not interchangeable; one is *better*, and the author has sanctioned this view by rejecting what at first had come, 'spontaneously', to his mind.

In this sense, the role of improvisation in popular music (and I would not consider relevant here any differentiation of genres) doesn't seem much different from that of similar practices within 'serious', written poetry and music. In both cases, a series of preliminary sketches leads to a final version, to the *work*, which, by reason of a creative choice, is more 'absolute' (*concretely* absolute, in its recorded dimension) than the variants that were rejected. Gottfried Benn's *glass-blower* is at work in the recording studio: the amorphous, white-hot block slowly becomes a shape; a delicate but resolute stroke cuts it off from the pipe and from the blower's body when the moment is right. Someone says: *now*. Someone says: *this*. The choice can often be a collective choice, the result of compromise and arrangement; but what is chosen is the *final cut*. Isn't exteriorization, objectification, in this sort of *sound writing*, very similar to that of ordinary writing and printing?

A third conclusion is more specifically to do with the role of words. Here we have Gabriel himself—as others do—admitting, in the interview I've been referring to, that no really good piece of rock music is allowed to have shoddy lyrics; one should always write a text the best way he can; but our clue—his practice—says that the role of words is much less general than that. As Antoine Hennion (1984) argues, 'In the world of pop music, it is pretty meaningless to say of a lyric that it is good: it is only one piece of the jigsaw puzzle and must be judged not on its own merits but on the way it fits in with the other pieces, both distinct from them and at the same time completely dependent on them'.

Hennion is not the only one to propose a notion of jigsaw puzzle or *bricolage* as characteristic of popular song's creative practices. If that implies an opposition to some more organic creation, it seems very hard to me to establish a reasonable borderline between the two, and much harder to recognize in *bricolage* a specificity of popular song, especially when one thinks of opera and even of contemporary poetry.

Hennion indicates an exception to patchwork techniques and *bricolage* in what he calls '*chanson à texte*', the work of 'artistic' singer-songwriters, where, for reasons of poetic ambition—he says—there is more integration of formulae and images. But when we speak of 'artistic' singer-songwriters, what kind of integration are we referring to? Is it a more 'literary' integration? Does that mean that the more 'artistic' a song is the less specifically popular it is? And, moreover: isn't some kind of integration working in straight popular song as well? What makes the pieces of the puzzle stick together, when artistic integration is lacking?

'What's going on when we listen to rock'—Frith has observed—'is a response to a perceived person; our pleasure in the music can't easily be separated from what it means to "like" someone' (1982: 152). Words would be, therefore, mainly a vehicle for someone's personality, and that's what they stick to. 'Song words, in short'—Frith argues elsewhere—'work as *speech* and *speech acts*, as structures of sound that are direct signs of emotions and mark of a character . . .' (Frith 1988: 120)

The notion of *speech acts* seems to me to apply brilliantly to rock and pop aesthetics of the word. I am more doubtful about the notion of 'direct signs' as it is proposed here. In what sense can we say that these signs are *direct?* If it is true that rock songs have much in common with theatre plays and drama (Frith, again), why should they escape the nature of fiction, that is of *mediation?*

Only a very naive audience would take a *play* of speech acts for *real* speech acts, just as early movie spectators stepped aside in front of a train coming from the screen in their direction. I'm not sure that rock and pop audiences are of this kind, although technical, structural, historical, and ideological factors do unceasingly push rock and pop fiction towards 'real life', towards some empirical notion of authenticity.

Despite typical, strong effects of an immediate presence of the body, signs in rock—no matter how 'direct' and symptomatic—must in fact share the divided nature of any sign; their perception cannot be reduced to ordinary perception, to global, inarticulated perception like that of smells or of flavours.

It's true that 'what's going on when we listen to rock is a response to a perceived person'; but the person we perceive is the result of artistic artifice; only previous acts of selection can make our perception simple and clear; and when we listen to a song like 'I Have the Touch', we find that the person we perceive tends to become the field to be crossed by a dissemination of speakers. Who's *really* speaking?

Speech acts are not only simulated, as they are in poetry, literature, theatre, or in a film: here we have a subtle play involving a multiplicity of (individual, collective) sources of speech, including Gabriel both as the author and as the body whose 'real' presence is testified to by the voice. It's more than a person we are perceiving and responding to here, it's a (*paradigmatic*) process of speech.

Polyphony of language (as investigated, for example, by Michail Bakhtin) is nothing new to 'serious' traditions of poetry and literature of our time: 'He Do the Police in Different Voices' was the original title of Eliot's *Waste Land.* Popular song seems in various ways to be assimilating some of the deep, anthropological roots of this, rather than just superficial stylistic symptoms, and to be elaborating word polyphonies in its own specific context.

Whereas an *absence* of the poet's body was crucial to a whole historical phase of western poetry of this period, its *presence* in popular song is the somehow reassuring guarantee that all ambiguity and division, all speech acts, all speakers, the whole puzzle, are to be referred in the end to one root, to one human being. In this sense, when performed, rock and pop lyrics tend to assume the quality of an oath, of a witness, made to their audience. Through its concrete and at the same time symbolic function as *origin* of speech (*os-oris*, mouth, according to a suggestive etymology proposed by Zumthor), the voice, automatically opposing itself to the aristocratic '*deshumanizaciòn del arte*' as conceived by Ortega Y Gasset, seems crucial in a process of re-humanization of art which forms popular music's labour of Sysiphus.

In the song we just considered, such re-humanization has lost much of its ideological 'magic'. Aiming at authenticity, it shows the price to be payed not only to fiction (a variously simulated 'presence' of the voice in the recording) but to social un-authenticity, to commonplace, to 'communication'. The immediate, deep truth of which the voice would be a direct sign or symptom is offered as a rainbow's end, a substantially extramusical goal, the promise that a song can perform but never keep.

What seems very important to me is that differentiation from rock and pop clichés never takes the form, here, of a wall-to-wall, programmatic opposition, a global 'alternative' to the stereotypical. Rock and pop patterns, commonplaces and procedures are not simply rejected: they are taken to a point where they, as it were, reveal themselves. In this 'quality' song, quality is not given *a priori*, from without; it's not the obvious, obligatory reward for a multiplication of chords, greater skill, a richer vocabulary, increased 'creativity'. Gabriel draws his quality less from abundance than from a process of *intensification* and *economy*.

References

Frith, S. (1982). 'The sociology of rock: notes from Britain', in *Popular Music Perspectives*, ed. P. Tagg and D. Horn (Göteborg and Exeter), 142–54.
—— (1988). 'Why do songs have words?', in *Music for Pleasure: Essays in the Sociology of Pop* (Cambridge), 105–28.
Hennion, A. (1984). 'The production of success: an anti-musicology of the pop song', *Popular Music*, 3: 159–93.

Discography

Gabriel, P. (1982). *IV*, Charisma PG4.
—— (1983). *Peter Gabriel Plays Live*, Charisma PGDL 1.

9

Three Tributaries of 'The River'

DAI GRIFFITHS

'The River'

I come from down in the valley where mister, when you're young
They bring you up to do like your daddy done
Me and Mary we met in high school when she was just seventeen
We'd drive out of this valley down to where the fields were green

We'd go down to the river and into the river we'd dive
Oh down to the river we'd ride

Then I got Mary pregnant and, man, that was all she wrote
And for my nineteenth birthday I got a union card and a wedding coat
We went down to the courthouse and the judge put it all to rest
No wedding day smiles, no walk down the aisle, no flowers, no wedding dress

That night we went down to the river and into the river we'd dive
Oh down to the river we did ride

I got a job working construction for the Johnstown Company
But lately there ain't been much work on account of the economy
Now all them things that seemed so important, well, mister they vanished right
    into the air
Now I just act like I don't remember, Mary acts like she don't care

But I remember us riding in my brother's car, her body tan and wet down at
    the reservoir
All night on them banks I'd lie awake, and pull her close just to feel each breath
    she'd take
Now those memories come back to haunt me, they haunt me like a curse
Is a dream a lie if it don't come true, or is it something worse

That sends me down to the river though I know the river is dry
That sends me down to the river tonight

Down to the river, my baby and I
Oh down to the river we ride

(Bruce Springsteen, 1980)

Naturally, in appealing to so many consumers, pop music admits of little formal complexity. Whatever a song's concern, it occurs stringently within the demotic constraints of verse, chorus, middle eight, and their like. So often is the familiar blast of Bob Dylan's harmonica an end in itself that he is able to contradict this expectation by withholding the true final verse. Describing Handel's practice within the formal convention of recitative and aria in eighteenth-century opera seria, Winton Dean observed: 'His care for dramatic values led him to modify the formal scheme to express not only states of mind but character in action; and here most of all the stiffness of the convention enabled him to bring off all manner of surprises' (Dean 1969: 171). In Bruce Springsteen's song 'The River', an established structure suffers rupture:

harmonica—verse—chorus
verse—chorus
harmonica—verse—*verse*—chorus—chorus—voices al fin

so that, just when the singer has said, 'Now I just act like I don't remember', he is dragged by the music into confessing, 'But', hang on, 'I remember . . .' So what's his problem? What's so haunting about these memories that they should afflict him 'like a curse'?

Although the song builds steadily through its four verses, the second comes as something of a shock:

Then I got Mary pregnant

'and', immediately:

man, that was all she wrote.

So bleak, that 'that was all she wrote', that was all there was to say; but also, from the music, '*man*', the bitch, 'that was *all* she wrote'. 'Pregnant', loaded, tumid, has had its fullness denied. Pop music is full of babies, but very few need food and clothes: 'Take Good Care of My Baby' is not a note for the nanny but the song of a spurned and spineless lover. When at last it reaches the end-result of its inveterate love-making this is often idealized, a child in early Joni Mitchell, a family in the fifties' musical or, hedging bets, a son or boy. At the end of 'The River' the singer rather pointedly echoes 'pregnant' with 'my baby and I', and although it may be simply another term of affection for Mary—the power of cliché—we can't really tell, and ought to allow the ambiguity.

Even so, it is around Mary that the song turns, ubiquitous despite being off-centre of attraction. She is the only female in the song, set off by a surprisingly large bevy of males. The narrator is incontestably so, getting her pregnant and, although engrossed in bar conversation with another man, it is nevertheless 'mister' and 'man'. Not woman, not lady: resonance is one thing, but in song it is most crucially a question of filling in the all-too real time of performance. In the song I, mister, and man far outweigh Mary and she, turning mundane observation into the larger import of the valley's being a man's world. Other men are daddy, the judge (surely a white-haired elder, and note the balance of 'man, that was all she wrote' and 'judge put it all to rest'), John of Johnstown (not Santa Barbara, not Helena, certainly not Maryland), and the enigmatic brother (Springsteen?) in whose car they ride, but who remains a mystery: 'I remember us riding in my brother's car' might imply his darkly watching over the last verse. These characters and ambiguities recur in 'Highway Patrolman', the chorus of which runs:

> Me and Frankie laughing and drinking,
> Nothing feels better than blood on blood,
> Taking turns dancing with Marie
> As the band played 'Night of the Johnstown Flood'.

By then she is a folk-like Marie; here still the Catholic, virginal Mary. A virgin Mary: she is 'just seventeen' and rhymes with 'green'. She's green because she's just seventeen, and neither has evidently taken precautions. William Empson in the chapter on Marvell in *Some Versions of Pastoral* drew attention to the pun of 'a green thought in a green shade' in 'The Garden' (Empson 1935: 119). Springsteen's rhyme resounds in diverse ways: a personal attribute projected onto an environment (Dylan's 'Idiot Wind/Blowing like a circle around my skull/From the Grand Coulee Dam to the Capitol'), the clash of number and adjective (Wimsatt 1954: 153–66), but especially the juxtaposition of pastoral with one of pop music's favourite pastimes, the lecherous observation and coveting of inexperienced and under-aged girls:

> You come on like a dream,
> Peaches and cream,
> Lips like strawberry wine,
> You're sixteen, you're beautiful, and you're mine.

Would you allow your daughter anywhere near lipsmacking Johnny Burnette? Such unease is pointed up by Springsteen's contrasting 'just seventeen', just like that, at the end of a line, and the lowest note so far, with:

> And for my nineteenth birthday I got a union card and a wedding coat

where the age is both celebrated—although birth and union in the context of a shotgun wedding is indeed ironic—and safely tucked into the line, the number less striking. 'Just seventeen', for all its poignancy, has a finger pointed towards it.

Male and female, young and old: this opposition is present from the start in the rhyme of 'young' and 'daddy done', young and male old. Antagonisms are expanded in the second verse into the rhymes of 'she wrote'/'coat' and 'judge put it all to rest'/'dress'. This turns on the detail that where he has a wedding coat she, in the four hammer-blows that conclude the second verse, has 'no wedding dress'. Here too:

No wedding day smiles, no walk down the aisle, no flowers, no wedding dress

having driven 'out of this valley down to where the fields were green', where another kind of fertility is manifest; back in the valley there are 'no flowers', a sterile environment in which nothing is able to grow. Commenting on Deuteronomy Tony Tanner observed:

It is possible to identify a recurring opposition or alternation of realms in the novel of adultery for which 'the city' and 'the field' provide generic equivalents. This simple distinction suggests that there is an area that is inside society and one that is outside, where the socially displaced individual or couple can attempt to find or practice a greater freedom. (Tanner 1979: 23)

'No wedding dress': indeed Mary is always seen *déshabillée*:

> But I remember us riding in my brother's car,
> Her body tan and wet down at the reservoir,
> At night on them banks I'd lie awake
> And pull her close just to feel each breath she'd take.

Nuptial bliss perhaps, but beware: there is more than a touch of the voyeur, and these memories are soon accursed.

With the haunting memories song and singer are spent; we are reminded that when asked his own favourite recordings Bob Dylan replied with the question, 'Song or performance?', and while it is possible so to engage the verbal fecundities of song qua poem, there is nevertheless a considerable absence of *raison d'être*, that a song, and more especially its performance, projects the space, the imagined time of poem, into the real time stuffed and sellotaped by music theory as the bulky packet of rhythm. There are several time schemes

—melody, harmony, rhythm, text, interpretation—and worse, they all proceed simultaneously, like all the cars at the start of a Grand Prix, so that there
is a danger for analysis that by breaking down a whole into constituent parts
it destroys the very unity which song strains and affects to establish. We shall
begin then with the single most pertinent and incontestable feature of the
temporal aspect in 'The River', within which all its multifarious shades exist
and beyond which the song must take its place in the larger demands of
everyday life: it lasts for four minutes fifty-nine seconds.

So far it has been taken for granted that the song has a rhyme scheme—
aabb—and this was then interpreted. Taken as read, it is not so easy to take
as heard, and here the relation of rhyme and meaning becomes, because
challenged, crucial.

Before that, is there a way in which the rhyme scheme is supported and
brought out in the music? Most overtly, in the rate of harmonic change, the
song's harmonic rhythm. By this is meant simply that lines ending in 'a' rhymes
are differentiated from 'b'-rhyming lines, in that the latter contain a chord
held for two bars while the former, and the chorus, maintain a regular rate of
change, one chord per bar. So, lines one and two change harmony four times:

> I come from down in the valley where, mister, when you're young
> *   *   *   *
> They bring you up to do like your daddy done
> *   * *   *

but lines three and four change only three times:

> Me and Mary, we met in High School when she was just seventeen
> *   *   *
> We'd drive out of this valley down to where the fields were green
> *   *   *

It is quite important that the held chord occurs at the beginning, rather than
at the end, of the 'b'-rhyming lines: a song—say, 'Blowin' in the Wind'—with
elongated line endings implies less likelihood of verbal action at that point
('Before he can see the sky', rum tee tum tee, 'How many . . . ?'). Here the extra
bar on the first chord creates a void, alluring, poignantly empty for verses one
and two, but in three and four loquaciously full. Tempting the voice too, falling
down a note, as on 'High School', so pre-empting the next, delayed chord.

The main claim for the last paragraph resides in the rhyme itself, but against
it works the single most important factor, the voice, its tone and its melody.
According with Barthes' 'Grain of the Voice' (Barthes 1977: 179–89), it would
be mistaken to disregard this and to discuss the song in terms of, say, the tenor

Ex 9.1.

Ex 9.2.

repertory. This is a song by and for Bruce Springsteen. So, when he reaches 'haunt me' in the final verse, he strains to the top of his range, where it goes all fuzzy and off the mark; but still it registers as a shift from a third to a fifth over a major chord, if not in such language. We allow and welcome such expression; however, we should not leave it at that: after all, its effect is over in a jot and ought to take its place within the expressive structure of the song as a whole. Otherwise you end up in one of the banes of pop music: that incurably romantic, magic-of-the-moment listening, where people screw up their faces to look 'emotional' when the time comes.

The rhyme scheme is aabb: across it the melodic structure cuts chiastically, ABBA. Here 'A' is a low group, ranging in pitch from E to A, and 'B' its complement, B back up to E an octave higher. Example 9.1 is included to illustrate this, but better by far to hear the record, and perhaps envisage this graphically:

Melody	Rhyme
A	a
B	a
B	b
A	b

The chorus melody (Example 9.2) then plays around the keystone, or inversional balance point—the pitch area of A/B.

The notion of balance is most useful: when the voice eventually strains above the octave, at 'back to haunt me', E–F sharp–G, it is inverting the familiar cadential figure, like 'something worse', G–F sharp–E; such is the combined power of register shift and inversion (Lewin 1968). This circular structure can be extended into harmony, x, y, z, as Example 9.1 has it. The first line, x, is set off as a closed group in which melody returns to its low starting-point, although its harmony moves from E minor, through G and D major, to land on C major. The second line begins harmonically like the first, E minor to G major, but stays there, playing around its plagal, C major, and back to G. This second line is thus called x–y. The third line has a retrograde of the second, hence y–x, C to G major, ending on E minor. The last line is mostly concerned with the new chord of A minor, plagal of E, but ends with G major and its plagal, C. This cadential line is then z.

Although it cuts across the rhyme scheme, this harmonic structure more closely follows the sense, the emotional content of the song. The verses thus turn on their respective y's: x sets the scene, y is a point of despair, z its aftermath. In these z's are contained telling moments: directed inwardly, poignant, but bitter towards Mary. This offers a reading for the song as a whole, in which rhyme and meaning are in structured opposition.

However much this may seem more than sufficient, there remains, as ever, the sense that it goes no further than description, whereas a song truly engages time. Edward Cone once wrote that the only literary analogue 'rich enough and complex enough to come near serving as a model' for song is *Ulysses* (Cone 1974: 37). Clearly then we have a long way to go. What I aim for is that words and music be constantly interacted, intertwined, interpreted, so that the potential richness of song form may emerge. Is there some idea which goes beyond content, beyond form? Is there some higher unity and if so, will it undermine the observations so far? According to what follows, 'The River' is not so much an overheard bar conversation as a session with a shrink.

First, note that most felicitous of pop music's devices, the naturalistic colloquialism which belies and distorts its background scansion. Dylan's phrasing plays structure against expression; he gets in there, acting out the phrase, though almost always ending in the formal comfort of rhyme. Effects vary; in 'True Love Tends to Forget' there's a comic congruity:

I'm getting wea——ry   (yawn)
                    Looking in my baby's eyes
When she's near——me
                    She's so hard to recognize
                    But I fin'lly realize
                                        There's no room for regret
                    True Love (?)
                    True Love (repeat/remind)
                    True Love (finally realize) Tends to forget.

Springsteen will play off 'latin' and 'rock 'n' roll' rhythms—threes and twos, divisive and additive—in a manner formally very distantly reminiscent of Gerard Manley Hopkins and sprung rhythm, thematically conjuring up the Italian American mixture of Leone, Coppola, or Scorsese. An earlier song, 'Thunder Road', contains this couplet, in which each syllable except those numbered occupies one beat:

> You can hide (3) 'neath your covers and (2) study your pain (4)
> Make crosses for your lovers throw (3) ro-(2)-ses in the rain.

Being slow, 'The River' has plenty of holes for the voice to fill, and as the song progresses the speaker grows more and more voluble. The syllable count to begin with is 7–6–6–5, at the courthouse 7–8–10–7; the next two joined verses run:

9–7–8–9–10–11–10–7–13–12–9–11–9–6–10–6

so that he's most garrulous at the rhyme of 'brother's car' and 'reservoir'. Notice the two sixes at the end of the list, giving perhaps a cadential air to these lines, where memory is followed by analogy:

> Now these memories come back to haunt me,
> They haunt me like a curse,
> Is a dream a lie if it don't come true,
> Or is it something worse . . . ?

and this seems to contain the crux of the song, the difference between, on the one hand being able to differentiate between memories, dream, and lie, all of which seem hideously true, and sheer fantasy on the other, curse and something worse, which would seem to contain, yet crucially to exclude, the quotidian realities of memory and dream, mendacity and veracity. One way in which language is able to convey this, apart from coming right out and saying it as there, is the means of smudged time offered by the past conditional, 'would'. In 'The River' this is explicitly so in the difference between the choruses of verses one and two where, first:

> We'd go down to the river
> and into the river we'd dive (we dive)
> down to the river we'd ride.

but second:

> That night we went down to the river
> and into the river we'd dive
> down to the river we did ride.

Embittered by returning to the valley, the idealized pastoral is made precise, so that where the first dive is a romantic, symbolic, slow-motion leap into the unknown, the second is a splash. The second verse consists entirely of facts recalled in finical detail ending with the four negatives, the only point where melody pre-empts the chorus line. The first verse is more complex, with three different kinds of time tossed together as if in a conversation: the general past ('when you're young they bring you up to do . . .'), narrative past ('we met in High School . . .'), and narrative conditional or mythic past, which is careful nevertheless to recall the past tense of fertility, now that 'the river is dry':

> We'd drive out of this valley down to where the fields were green.

The generalized past returns at the question about dream and lie, an open question for all time, while the narrative skips from 'just seventeen' across the mythic past of the first verse and its chorus into verse two: 'we met in High School . . . then I got Mary pregnant'.

In the joined third and fourth verses the song is a play between definite and indefinite report. The third verse begins in the past, 'I got a job . . .', and moves forward to 'lately'. At 'now', point y as described above, he fidgets: things that 'seem' so important, presumably everything so far, 'vanish', and what is left is pure fiction. Note the tiny difference between his 'just' acting and Mary's actually acting. Of course, as we saw at the beginning, where the verses collide without chorus, he is not just acting that he doesn't remember, he is lying: he does remember. Perhaps this is what *The Language of Psychoanalysis* defines as screen memory, 'a formation produced by a compromise between repressed elements and defence' (Laplanche and Pontalis 1973: 410–11), or maybe here's a selective amnesiac, careful in editing what he chooses to remember into the clarity and precision of the bizarre, perhaps of the guilty:

> But I remember us riding in my brother's car,
> Her body tan and wet down at the reservoir

As this x—transposed from E–F sharp–G to G–A–B—moves to y, what happens? Did he 'lay awake'? No:

> At night on them banks I'd lie awake
> And pull her close just to feel each breath she'd take

Here is the source of his being haunted by a curse, into something worse where, forced to confront the futility of existence, we might perhaps conceive, given that 'most important pun in the language' (Ricks 1975: 123), of the missing 'lie' rhyme, 'die'. The chorus is always hinting: we'd dive, we'd ride, river is dry, baby and I, we ride. And all those i,i,i's, coming after the d of ride. We'd dive : : ride die. It's a lot of d and i. The song is gloomy enough: remember 'put it all to rest' (like sick dogs, put to rest), 'vanished right into the air', and especially 'each breath she'd take'. The evidence is purely circumstantial, but this bar-talk has certainly led to a moment of extreme self-revelation.

'The River' encapsulates a lifetime. In that finical, factual second verse, x, y, and z are writ large. The first line is the mistake which this man never really comes to terms with:

> Then I got Mary pregnant and man that was all she wrote.

By z, he has reached nothing:

> No wedding day smiles, no walk down the aisle, no flowers, no wedding dress.

In between, $x-y$, $y-x$, the whole gamut: birth, union, wedding (coat/court), judgement, a higher authority, rest:

> And for my nineteenth birthday I got a union card and a wedding coat,
> We went down to the courthouse and the judge put it all to rest.

References

Barthes, R. (1977). *Image-Music-Text: Essays Selected and Translated by Stephen Heath* (London).

Cone, E. T. (1974). *The Composer's Voice* (Berkeley and Los Angeles).

Dean, W. (1969). *Handel and the Opera Seria* (Berkeley and Los Angeles).

Empson, W. (1935). *Some Versions of Pastoral* (London).

Laplanche, J., and Pontalis, J.-B. (1973). *The Language of Psychoanalysis* (London).

Lewin, D. (1968). 'Inversional balance as an organising force in Schoenberg's music and thought', *Perspectives of New Music*, 6/2: 1–21.

Ricks, C. (1975). 'Lies', *Critical Inquiry*, 2: 121–42, reprinted in *The Force of Poetry* (London and New York 1984), 369–91.

Tanner, T. (1979). *Adultery in the Novel: Contract and Transgression* (Baltimore and London).

Wimsatt, W. K. (1954). 'One relation of rhyme to reason', in *The Verbal Icon: Studies in the Meaning of Poetry* (Lexington, Ky.).

Discography

Dylan, B. (1975). 'Idiot Wind', *Blood on the Tracks*, CBS 69097.
—— (1978). 'True Love Tends to Forget', *Street Legal*, CBS 86067.
Springsteen, B. (1975). 'Thunder Road', *Born to Run*, CBS 69170.
—— (1980). 'The River', *The River*, CBS 88510.
—— (1982). 'Highway Patrolman', *Nebraska*, CBS 25100.

10
....
Pity Peggy Sue

BARBARA BRADBY AND BRIAN TORODE

Meaning in Rock Music

The sociologist Simon Frith identifies rock and roll as a hybrid music, which emerged in the American South of the mid-1950s as a grafting of puritan-ical 'white' country and western lyrics on to sexually explicit 'black' blues rhythms. While acknowledging cross-fertilization between black and white music 'since at least the middle of the nineteenth century', he states that since the Second World War,

> It is as dance music that black music has developed its meanings for white users. The most obvious feature of dancing as an activity is its sexuality. . . . Whereas Western dance forms control sexuality with formal rhythms . . . black music celebrates sex with a directly physical beat and an intense, emotional sound. It makes obvious the potential anarchy of sexual feeling. (Frith 1978: 180)

Frith appeals to an age-old metaphor: black nature is seen as fundamentally threatening to white culture. In modern popular music, this conflict is played out in terms of the liberation or the repression of sexuality.[1]

Dave Laing had earlier noted the challenge posed by rock music to tradi-tional Western song, specifically to the ballad, which until after the Second World War was the 'mainstay of popular song' (Laing 1969: 51). This ancient art form was

> among the last repositories of a complex of ideas and feelings about Love that derived ultimately from the Courtly Code of Love formulated in mediaeval Western Europe . . . [The Code's] main features include an intense, almost hyperbolic devotion of

---

[1] Frith is influenced in his view by Charlie Gillett's *Sound of the City* (Gillett 1970) which provides a history of rock music of the 1950s and 1960s in these terms. Of course this view corresponds closely with the repres-sive views of conservative white America. For a classic black liberationist statement of this position, see Cleaver 1968. For an alternative black interpretation, which views black popular music in terms of conflict between black and white *cultures*, see Keil 1966.

the protagonist for his mistress (a secularisation of the adoration of the Virgin Mary) . . . Love takes on similar heroic dimensions in the popular ballad. (Ibid. 57–8)

The ballad

has behind it a whole semi-articulate system of emotional situations, reactions, and relationships ready to flood forth . . . Magical status is conferred on the most prosaic occasion because the . . . ballad is rooted in a human universe towards which all the institutions of our culture are intent on propelling us. Each refusal of sentimentality in a popular song is in some way a refusal of that universe. (Ibid. 60)

For Laing, the line of pop music which begins with rock and roll 'constitutes a major contemporary refusal' (ibid. 60) of such sentimentality, hence of the universe of white Western Christian capitalist culture as a whole.[2]

Laing's interpretation has a grandeur which transcends Frith's account, but it lacks sufficient specificity. He specifies it in two main ways. First, he points out that the name of the new music derives from lines such as B. B. King's: 'Rock me baby, rock me all night long . . . Roll me baby, like you roll a waggon wheel.' Laing comments: 'These words were used in a hortatory way by black singers in the casual lyrics of songs meant for dancing. *Their function was merely to reinforce the rhythmic excitement*' (ibid. 63, emphasis added). As an account of musical meaning, this is similar to Frith's. Lyric is casual, its function to reinforce the rhythm of dance.

We diverge from this interpretation. The terms used in B. B. King's lyrics are not merely casual. They convey at least two meanings beyond the exhortation to dance. First, a 'baby' is an infant human being, and rocking is a sensual activity performed by its mother, day or night. Secondly, 'rock and roll' became in the US slang of the 1940s a metaphor for sexual intercourse and 'baby' the metaphorical term for sexual partner. We are interested in this metaphor, which has been repeatedly elaborated throughout the popular music which Laing celebrates in his book. So much so that in a sense the activity of 'rocking' and the self-identity as 'baby' constitute expressions of the very refusal of traditional culture which Laing described.

---

[2] Laing's 1969 statement implicitly promoted rock and roll in general, and Buddy Holly's music in particular, as an avant-garde art. In his *The Marxist Theory of Art* he presents Julia Kristeva's account of the challenge which the 'poetic language' of the literary avant-garde poses to Western culture. This challenge results from the way it contests the dominance of *symbolic* (verbal) language, instead privileging *semiotic* (non-verbal) communication, 'in the form of rhythms, intonations, and lexical, syntactical and rhetorical transformations' (Kristeva, quoted from Laing 1978: 101). However, he finds the thesis of a 'permanent contradiction' between the symbolic and the semiotic to be incompatible with 'the basic Marxist contradiction between forces and relations of production' (ibid. 102).

The second account of the refusal of sentimentality appears in Laing's discussion of Buddy Holly, whose work, he claims, 'represents the first important creative development of pop music' (ibid. 97). There was 'something new' in 'the interplay and intimacy between words, voice, and music in Buddy Holly's records' (ibid. 98). More specifically, Laing argues that Holly's distinctive vocal techniques undermine the coherence of the singing voice, on which the traditional ballad depends. 'The straight singing of a lyric is continually punctuated by exclamatory effects of various kinds. The voice suddenly swoops upwards or downwards, syllables are lengthened to cover three or more notes (as in 'ba-ay-by'), whole choruses are hummed or sung wordlessly, and sometimes phrases are spoken during instrumental solos' (ibid. 100). In his biography, *Buddy Holly*, Laing directly contrasts the traditional singer, who seeks 'to hold a note with maximum emotional effect', with Holly, who does not:

Few notes are held for more than one or two beats in Holly's records, so they avoid the overpowering emotion of the ballads of that period. Holly's listeners are not overwhelmed, as they are by a ballad, but continually have their attention redirected by the frequent changes of tone, pitch, and phrasing. Holly's music is, therefore, rarely sentimental. (Laing 1971: 68)

For Laing, Holly's wide variety of vocal techniques is radical in that it precludes the sustained unity necessary to the representation of an emotion in music. It is true that in ordinary usage an emotion, such as 'grief' or 'love', has to endure in time, unlike a sensation such as 'pain', which may be momentary (see Wittgenstein 1968: 174). So Laing seems justified in arguing that if Holly's style consistently avoids sustained notes, this constitutes a refusal of traditional sentimentality.

But Laing is led to value Holly's style for its own sake. A singing style which is 'dramatic' or 'trying to get something across to the listener' is deplored. By contrast, Holly, 'instead of trying to interpret the lyric . . . uses it as a jumping off point for his own stylistic inclinations. He uses it as an opportunity to play rock'n'roll music, instead of regarding his role as one of portraying an emotion contained in the lyric' (ibid. 70). The singer's personal style is not necessarily revealed in a single performance. It is an 'ensemble of vocal effects that characterise the whole body of his work' (ibid. 59). Ultimately, this approach reduces the interpretation of performed song to psychological considerations (whatever it is that unifies the person Buddy Holly over 'the whole body of his work') or even to physiology: 'Buddy Holly's singing voice was not strong, and this factor turned out to provide the basis for most of the vocal effects to be found on his records. Holly's voice was naturally higher pitched than those of many rock'n'roll singers and lacked the body and resonance of [others]' (ibid. 64).

Laing is highly attentive to Holly's vocal effects, but can offer no account of what the performer does with these devices, since he denies they are meaningful: 'many of the vocal techniques he employs cannot be said to have emotional correlates in real life' (ibid. 70). As a result, mere variety becomes the criterion for excellence in performance: the experience of 'Peggy Sue', for instance, is said to be 'like that of a roller coaster or switch-back ride' (ibid. 68).

In part, Laing's denial of meaning follows from the place he accords to rhythm in Holly's music. In describing Holly's most characteristic vocal technique, where one syllable is drawn out into several through a series of 'hiccoughs', Laing writes that 'instead of complementing the rhythm, Holly's staccato singing tends to imitate and parallel it' (ibid.). At times, Holly's hiccoughing voice may literally parallel a rhythm in the instrumental accompaniment; more usually, it is the rhythm of Holly's hiccoughing voice itself that disrupts the ordinary spoken rhythm of the lyric. In each case, the impression given is that both voice and lyric are dominated by the song's rhythm.

In the traditional ballad, the voice tends to approximate the ordinary speech rhythm of the lyric, and the rhythm and melody of any instrumental accompaniment tend to follow the voice.[3] The voice, therefore, appears to be master of the song, and is heard as equivalent to the lyric, presumed to be meaningful in its own right. But at least lyrics have meaning. If rhythm has none (and Laing avoids Frith's assumption that dance 'means' sexuality) yet is the *raison d'être* of the rock record, then the whole performance becomes meaningless.

This issue is central to the question of whether rock music represents sexuality and, if so, how its representations differ from those of traditional popular music. The Virgin Mary, that transcendent idealization of womankind of whom little is known, save her status as 'mother', is in Laing's account the

---

[3] Jean-Jacques Rousseau outlined a mimetic theory of musical meaning, in his *Essay on the Origin of Languages*, where he wrote: 'By imitating the inflections of the voice, melody expresses pity, cries of sorrow and joy, threats and groans. All the vocal signs of passion are within its domain. It imitates the tones of languages, and the twists produced in every idiom by certain psychic acts. Not only does it imitate, it bespeaks. And its language, though inarticulate, is lively, ardent, passionate; and it has a hundred times the vigour of speech itself. This is what gives music its power of representation and song its power over sensitive hearts' (Rousseau 1763: 57). Derrida commends this observation, not for its romanticization of music as superior to speech, but for its realization that musical and other non-verbal meanings are always imitating, and so substituting for, the verbal meanings communicated by the spoken voice (Derrida 1967b: 195–215).

prototype for the love-objects romantically celebrated throughout the ballad tradition. However, rock music, too, conjures up uninformative idealizations of woman, which can become transcendent objects of veneration. Famous among them is Buddy Holly's 'Peggy Sue'. As Jonathan Cott says, she 'is hardly there at all' in the song of that name, but is revived and recreated in a succession of other songs by Holly, and subsequently by Bobby Darin, Ritchie Valens, and the Beatles (Cott 1981: 80).

Unlike the heroines of traditional ballads, Peggy Sue is not described in Holly's song. Instead of focusing on the absent love-object, the song concentrates all its attention on the feelings of absence in the singer-subject. As Laing explains:

In the song, 'Peggy Sue', the title must be repeated at least thirty times, but on each occasion it is sung in a different way from the time before, so as to suggest the infinite variety of his affection for her . . . If the words suggest the ingenuity of his approach to the girl, the rhythm denotes the determined character of his pursuit of her. For this song, like so many others of Buddy Holly's, is the song of someone uncertain that his love will be reciprocated. (Laing 1969: 101)

Citing 'sudden changes of pitch' resembling 'the breaking voice of a young teenager', Laing concludes that 'the restlessness of the vocal style is the very incarnation of adolescence' (ibid.).

For us, this interpretation correctly observes only one role in a performance which dramatically and narratively relates it to several others. The verbal and rhythmic variations in Holly's song are not infinite, nor are they devoid of meaning. In our view, meaning should be sought within the performed song itself. Aided by many of Laing's observations, we shall therefore examine the meanings contained first in the lyrics and secondly in the rhythms of 'Peggy Sue'.

The Limits of Lyrics

We here reproduce the lyrics of the song, transcribed from Buddy Holly's record.[4]

---

[4] Lyrics and rhythms are transcribed from Buddy Holly, 'Peggy Sue' (Allison; Petty), on *Buddy Holly's Greatest Hits*, Coral Records CRLM 1001, Copyright Southern Music 1957. These are not 'pure' lyrics, since the structuring of words into lines, hence verses and refrains, already implies a certain rhythmic organization of the words. There is in fact no pure lyric: the voice is always already organized by some material representation of itself, but which is other than itself (see Derrida 1967a).

'Peggy Sue'

verse 1   If you knew
Peggy Sue
Then you'd know why I feel blue
Without Peggy
My Peggy Sue

refrain 1 Oh well I love you gal
Yes I love you Peggy Sue

verse 2   Peggy Sue
Peggy Sue
<u>Oh how my heart yearns for you</u>
<u>Oh-oh Peggy</u>
My Peggy Sue

refrain 2 Oh well I love you gal
Yes I love you Peggy Sue

verse 3   Peggy Sue
Peggy Sue
Pretty pretty pretty pretty Peggy Sue
Oh-oh Peggy
My Peggy Sue

refrain 3 Oh well I love you gal
And I need you Peggy Sue

verse 4   <u>I love you</u>
<u>Peggy Sue</u>
<u>With a love so rare and true</u>
<u>Oh Peggy</u>
<u>My Peggy Suh-uh-uh-uh-uh-uh-uh-ue</u>

refrain 4 Well I love you gal
I want you Peggy Sue
[instrumental break]

verse 5   Peggy Sue
Peggy Sue
Pretty pretty pretty pretty Peggy Sue
Oh-oh Peggy
My Peggy Sue

refrain 5 Oh well I love you gal
Yes I need you Peggy Sue

verse 6   I love you
Peggy Sue
With a love so rare and true
Oh-oh Peggy
My Peggy Suh-uh-uh-uh-uh-ue

refrain 6 Oh well I love you gal
            And I want you Peggy Sue
refrain 7 <u>Oh well I love you gal</u>
            <u>And I want you Peggy Sue</u>

key: _ _ _ _ _ _ = falsetto voice
       _ _ _ _ _ = deep voice

A division of labour between voices in the song accomplishes a specific meaning, which is worked out over the course of the performance as a whole. Verse 1 is sung *about* Peggy Sue as an absent third party, to an unspecified *you*. The absence is expressed (i) by use of the third person; (ii) in the assertion, 'I feel blue without' her. A conventional assumption (other assumptions being possible) would identify *you* as another boy, a buddy of the singer, able to sympathize with the 'blue' situation. In the refrain, the singer acts out how he would speak to the girl, were she present.

Verse 2 is directed to the absent love-object. The archaic 'yearning' is the biblical language of orthodox Protestantism. Both this sentimental lyric and the expression of love in the refrain are quite consistent with the love-in-marriage assumptions of Christian morality.

In verse 3 the object is imagined to be present, but in a special sense. Jonathan Cott provides an important suggestion here:

When adults communicate with infants, they use the language of *baby talk*, exaggerating changes in pitch, speaking almost in singsong, uttering their words more slowly, reduplicating syllables and rhymes, and employing simple sentence structures. It is clear that Buddy Holly absorbed, transformed, and revitalised this mode of expression in his use of . . . lines like 'Pretty pretty pretty pretty Peggy Sue' (reminding you of a child talking to a little animal in order to tame it) . . . and, most obviously, in his famous 'hiccup' signature, or in the sudden glides from deep bass to falsetto (and back again), revealing the child inside the man, the man inside the child. (Cott 1981: 78)

Cott, like Laing, is trying to characterize Holly's style as a whole, but we note his observation that baby talk is a specific feature of verses 3 and 5 of this particular song. In effect, the singer here enacts the role of father, addressing his baby child.

The refrain to verses 3 and 5 introduces a new term: 'need'. A parent is not physically dependent on a baby child, though the reverse is true, but emotionally and psychologically such dependence is essential to the structure of the family. Such dependence is equated with 'love' here.

The clichéd expression of 'rare and true' love in verse 4 is sung in Holly's high-pitched style. It is tempting to regard this as marking the uncertainty attaching to these words when first spoken by a teenage boy to a girl. They are romantic and conventionally 'feminine' words, hence the use of falsetto, the conventional male representation of the female voice.

Dave Laing acknowledges that, in the song which he calls 'Holly's most spectacular vocal performance', these lines contain an important innovation in style. This he describes, against his own general approach, in representational terms: 'The voice is . . . nasal and . . . "babyish" . . . It can be heard as a musical analogy to the private, intimate way of speaking two lovers might share; but it is only an analogy, not a representation of it' (Laing 1971: 66). If in verse 4 Holly sings as a lover, whereas in verse 1 he sang as a buddy, then there is clearly a narrative development in the song, which demands analysis. Laing however avoids this conclusion. He values Holly's performance purely for its novelty:

> This new intonation within the record increases the tension and excitement. In Peggy Sue the change of intonation is not related to the emotional mood or significance of the words, to reflect a particular feeling. It relates instead to the musical development of the record as a rock'n'roll performance. Holly changes his vocal tone to take the music higher, to make it more exciting, as he would at a live performance. (Ibid. 66)

This account is essentially incomplete. Unless we imagine that (live) rock musical performance simply takes 'music' (surely 'emotional mood' would fit Laing's argument more explicitly?) higher and higher without limit, then we must have other terms in our analytical vocabulary, to account both for the raising and lowering of tension, and for the opening and closing of the performance.[5] In our view, a narrative analysis can provide these terms.

Up to this point in the record, the song lyrics have performed a step-by-step narrative transformation, as follows:

verse 1 boy talks to boy about his loneliness;
verse 2 man expresses desire for woman in quasi-religious terms;
verse 3 father talks affectionately to baby girl;
verse 4 adolescent uncertainly confesses true love to girl.

In a sense, defences are progressively stripped away as the narrative approaches an actual encounter between boy and girl.

---

[5] Laing's appeal to the immediacy of the live performance (he even states that 'Peggy Sue' gives the impression of 'spontaneous creation': Laing 1971: 73) is at odds with his previous praise of Holly as pioneer of the integrated record production: 'All Buddy Holly's songs were conceived as records' (Laing 1969: 100).

Here analysis of the lyrics reaches its limits, since, verbally, verses 5 and 6 simply repeat verses 3 and 4. But, in fact, our analysis has already overstepped these limits, since the interpretation of verse 4 depends on hearing Holly's use of falsetto as representing the unbroken voice of an adolescent boy. This feature enables us to draw a contrast with verse 6, where the same words are sung in Holly's normal voice, so that the adolescent appears to have grown into a man. This impression is reinforced by the repeat of the refrain after this verse in a deep bass voice, an octave below the normal pitch of the refrain.

It is in the musical performance, then, that we hear the difference between verses 3–4 and 5–6. The singer's adoption of the position of father in verse 3 seemed a promising one from which to address Peggy Sue as his girl. But in verse 4, he fails to maintain this position. His falsetto voice mocks that of the father, and casts doubt on the sincerity of his own adoption of the adult position. His hiccoughs and stammering, particularly around the pronunciation of the name 'Sue', reveal him as only a nervous teenager, fearful of being rejected as too young and inexperienced.

Here a small verbal difference in the refrain of verse 4 becomes significant. The 'yes' of the refrain to verses 1 and 2 (which became 'and' in verse 3) is omitted altogether. The nervousness evidenced in the musical performance seems to centre around whether or not the girl will say 'yes'. In verse 5, the missing beat of the refrain is once again filled with a 'yes'. And in verse 6, the singer successfully maintains his fatherly voice in declaring his love to Peggy Sue. The repetition of Su-uh-uh-uh-uh-ue in line 5 is soothing, in contrast to the exciting performance of the same line in verse 4. These differences in performance make us hear verses 5 to 6 as ending the story of the song. The boy talking to his buddies about his secret crush is now the man, confident that his woman accepts him as such.

But if the singer's performance is what makes verses 5 and 6 different from verses 3 and 4, there is still a mystery as to why he is able to perform in this way in verse 6 but not in verse 4. The difference between boyhood and manhood has been exemplified, but the question of how a boy gets to be a man has not been answered. Two lines of analysis suggest themselves here. The first is to look more closely at the rhythmic variations used in the vocal performance as a whole, since the difference between verses 4 and 6 hinges partly on the rhythm of 'Sue' in line 5. The second is to look at what happens in the musical performance between verses 3–4 and 5–6, namely the instrumental break. We turn first to an analysis of the performance of Holly's vocal rhythms, which so fascinated Laing and other commentators.

Ex 10.1. Rhythm of sung verses of 'Peggy Sue'

Getting to Know Peggy

The vocal rhythms of 'Peggy Sue' are transcribed in Example 10.1. Modifications to the rhythm of each bar, which occur in successive verses, are shown vertically. This permits a reading of the rhythmic development of the song, which complements the narrative structure expressed by the lyrics and the voices in which they are sung. If we focus attention on the musical phrases whose rhythms are modified in the course of the song, it is clear that the most complex modifications all involve the title names of the song, 'Peggy' and 'Sue'. We shall therefore investigate whether the rhythmic changes introduced in the repetition of these names represent an unstructured show of 'variety', in Laing's terms, or whether they exhibit a narrative development of their own.

The name 'Peggy' occurs thirty times in all; of these, twenty are sung to an on-beat rhythm:

Ex 10.2.

Peg - gy

A further seven (one in each refrain) are sung to a modification of this rhythm involving the insertion of an extra quaver. Here too the emphasis is clearly on the beat:

Ex 10.3.

Pe-eg-gy

However, three occurrences involve an anticipation of the beat such that the first letter of the name appears on an off-beat:

Ex 10.4.

P' - heg - gy

These three are all in verses 1 and 2. The first is where the phrase 'My Peggy Sue' is used for the first time (bars 6–7). This is most naturally heard as following on from 'If you knew . . .' so that the singer is still talking *about* Peggy to the (male) 'you' of line 1. But 'My Peggy Sue' is separated off from the continuous lyrics both before and after it by rests in the vocal line in bars 5–6 and bars 7–8. Heard as an isolated phrase, it is ambiguous between the accusative and vocative cases, i.e. it could as well be spoken *to* her as *about* her. The refrain that follows clearly speaks *to* her as 'you gal'. The stuttering 'P'heggy' seems to signal the singer's ambivalence over which 'you' the phrase is addressed to. He is excitedly anticipating the transition from talking about 'My Peggy Sue' to calling her that to her face.

The same happens in bars 6–7 of verse 2, where the phrase is similarly ambiguous in facilitating a transition from addressing Peggy Sue as absent in the verse, to addressing her as present in the refrain. Here the excitement is increased by the further off-beat 'P'heggy' in the preceding phrase (the 'Oh P'heggy' of bars 4–5). *But after bar 6 of verse 2, the off-beat 'P' never reappears.* If the transformations of the rhythms are part of the narrative structure of the song, we can ask what has happened between bar 6 of verse 2 and the same bar of verse 3, where 'Peg' is sung on the beat.

The most significant rhythmic modification to occur in between these two bars is also one of the most striking verbal modifications in the whole song, namely the repetition of 'Pretty, pretty, pretty, pretty' in bar 3 of verse 3.[6] As already noted, the babyish connotations of such repetition have often been commented on. But repetition of words by adults to infants is usually to teach the child the sound. Here the phrase involves the rhythmic sounding of 'p' on each on-beat of the bar. The repetition of this rhyme in effect teaches the singer to pronounce the 'P' of 'Peggy' on the beat. Cott described this phrase as like a child taming an animal, but animals do not learn to speak.[7] A better analogy would be that of an adult teaching a child a mnemonic such as 'Peter Piper picked a peck of pickled pepper' as an aid to the correct positioning of certain consonants. Stuttering is a common problem of children learning to speak and can be taken as an indication of nervousness. In this song, the stuttering pronunciation of 'P'-heg-gy' is corrected by the repetition of 'Pretty, pretty, . . .'.

The association of 'pretty' and 'Peggy' appears very close because the sung rhythm of 'pretty' is that of 'Peggy' in normal speech, whereas 'Peggy' is never in fact sung as it would be spoken. The song sets up a context of speech rhythm with its opening line, 'If you knew'. This phrase is sung much as it would be spoken as part of the clause 'If *you* knew Peggy Sue' in normal speech, which could be written as:

---

[6] The bar is made additionally conspicuous to the listener by the only deviation in the whole song from a basic three-chord harmony. The chord appears to be F major (taking the tonic as A major).

[7] An exception, of course, is the parrot. The 'pretty Peggy' phrase is indeed suggestive of the 'pretty Polly' that parrots are often taught to say. But here again the analogy is clearly that of a language lesson, not that of taming a wild beast.

Ex 10.5.

If you knew Peg-gy Sue

The song follows this rhythm for 'If you knew', but deviates from it on the word 'Peggy' whose first syllable is drawn out to double its spoken length, so that the sung rhythm becomes:

Ex 10.6.

If you knew. . .   Peg - gy Sue

The expectation created by this 'If *you* knew' rhythm for the 'Peggy' of normal speech (Ex. 10.5) is fulfilled by 'pretty':

Ex 10.7.

Pret - ty, pret - ty, pret - ty, pret - ty

Since the rhythms of 'pretty' and 'Peggy' are virtually identical in normal speech, and since 'pretty' is sung as it would be spoken, 'pretty' appears here to stand in for 'Peggy'.

In this way the singer 'learns' not to anticipate the 'P' of 'Peggy'. This reveals a new meaning in the song's first-line invitation to get to know 'Peggy Sue'. The line not only advertises Holly's woman to his buddies, but also acts as an advertisement for the song.[8] (In ordinary usage the question 'Do you know Peggy Sue?' now refers to the song of that name, not to the woman.) The ambiguity in the invitation to *you* the listener is paralleled in the singer's own relation to the name: he himself is getting to know how to say 'Peggy Sue' in a particular way, in the course of the song.

---

[8] According to the well-known argument of Theodor Adorno, pop records resemble radio advertising jingles, and their frequent repetition of titles and first lines serves to advertise themselves as commodities (Adorno 1978). Adorno's argument is developed and criticized in Bradby and Torode 1984.

Getting over Sue

Getting to know 'Peggy Sue', then, involves getting to know how to say 'Peggy' in a way which elongates the first syllable so as to make both syllables fall on separate crotchet beats of the bar. 'Peggy' is therefore the paradigm for the on-beat marching rhythm, which occurs first in the four-bar instrumental introduction and which continues in the bass throughout the whole song. By contrast, the name 'Sue' commences on an off-beat each of the twenty-four times it occurs. Its frequent repetition makes it the paradigm for the syncopated rhythms in the song. These rhythms occur exclusively in the voice and lead guitar. Through their interruption of the on-beat rhythm they set up a conflict which is played out between the two names.

The rhythm of 'Peggy' deviates only three times out of thirty from the basic pattern of Examples 10.2 and 10.3, and the deviations have all been ironed out by the middle of verse 3. That of 'Sue' varies throughout the whole song, with the most complex elaborations being from verse 4 on. But, as with 'Peggy', it is in the phrase 'My Peggy Sue' at bars 6–7 that the major variations occur.

The simplest rhythmic element of 'Sue' anticipates the third beat of the bar:

Ex 10.8.

It is introduced in bar 2 of the first verse, and is heard eleven times in all. Musically, the syncopation is here left unresolved, making 'Peggy Sue' sound like a question, or a call expecting a response. The closing line of the refrain of each verse provides a resolution of the syncopation, more appropriate as a musical 'ending':

Ex 10.9.

This is also the rhythm of 'Sue' in bars 6–7 of the first three verses, where the singer is establishing the correct rhythm of 'Peggy'.

However, the resolution of Example 10.9 is weak in that it ends on the second beat of the bar, leaving the strong third beat empty. In verse four the 'Sue' of bars 6–7 is developed still further, creating an expectation that this and the subsequent strong first beat of bar 8 will be filled. In the event, the third beat of bar 7 is silent, and the first beat of bar 8 is occupied by one of Holly's famous hiccoughs, indicated by an 'h' in Example 10.10:

Ex 10.10.

Suh - uh-uh - uh - uh - h - h-uh - ue (Well I)

Rather than occupying the strong beat, the hiccough seems to emphasize its absence. The momentary resolution reached on the third beat of bar 8 is cut short by the 'Well I' of the refrain. The effect is one of prolonged tension, paralleling tension in the verbal narrative at this point.

As already noted, the words of verses 5 and 6 repeat those of verses 3 and 4. Rhythmically, however, these verse-pairs differ, the principal difference still affecting the word 'Sue' in bars 6–8.[9] In verse 5, the final crotchet of Example 10.9 is held over for a further two beats, achieving a conventional musical 'ending':

Ex 10.11.

Suh - uh - ue......

But this still employs the weak second-beat resolution. Only in verse 6 is a strong resolution finally achieved. Here the phrase starts to develop as it did in verse 4, but it eliminates the 'hiccoughs', fills the third beat of bar 7 and comes to a dignified ending on the strong first beat of bar 8:

Ex 10.12.

Suh - uh-uh - uh - uh - ue......

[9] Other differences relate to the progressive elimination of the syncopated beats that in verse 2 had preceded the syncopated 'P'heggy'. In verse 3, the 'oh' of bar 4 and the 'My' of bar 6 are still syncopated. By verse 4, they are sung on the beat; this is carried over into verse 5, creating two small differences between verses 3 and 5. Another small difference is the pronounced hiccough after 'I love you' in bar 1 of verse 6—the last one of the song.

218   BARBARA BRADY AND BRIAN TORODE

Rhythmically, as verbally, a heightening of tension in verses 3 to 4 is followed by its lowering in verses 5 to 6. The lyrics could give us no clue to the transformation between these verses, which was nevertheless 'heard' to take place, as the teenage falsetto voice 'breaks' into that of a man. But in the case of the rhythms, it makes sense to ask what has occurred between verses 3 to 4 and 5 to 6 to allow of the transformation, since the instrumental break between verses 4 and 5 is essentially a *rhythmic* interlude.[10] We can therefore turn to the break and see whether the resolutions of Examples 10.11 and 10.12 are produced there in anticipation of their use in verses 5 and 6.

The Lyrics of Imagination

Our analysis so far has been of rhythms accompanying verbal modifications, since the singing voice is articulating words. But the instrumental break is non-verbal. The possibility arises that rhythmic elements of the break can be identified with words sung to the same rhythms in the verses so that the guitar break evokes a sequence of 'imaginary' words. As Example 10.13 shows, such identifications can be made for the whole rhythmic sequence of the break, and, in all but a few cases, they occur at unique points in the structure. Once this is done, it becomes possible to analyse the instrumental break as if it were another verse of the song.

Our procedure here, which discovers verbal messages hidden in musical rhythms, resembles the method used by psychoanalysts to discover verbal messages hidden in visual imagery. For instance, Freud argued in the case of Dora's second dream that a verbal motif organized the visual material: *Bahnhof* and *Friedhof* were named in the dream, so that *Vorhof* was implied verbally (Freud 1977: 39). Similarly, Victor Burgin analyses a Gary Winogrand photo of four elderly women as sexist on the grounds that they are shown walking past four refuse sacks, implying the hidden verbal cliché 'old bags' (Burgin 1982: 206). What appears to be non-verbal visual material is here made sense of by imaginary words: in the same way, the discovery of imaginary words can make sense of the apparently non-verbal rhythms of the guitar break in 'Peggy Sue'.

---

[10] The harmonies of the instrumental break offer no variation on the very simple three-chord structure of the verses. The melody, too, is extremely simple, consisting only of four notes. The rhythms, on the other hand, are complex and varied, and appear at first hearing to be a completely new departure from the rhythms of the sung verses.

Ex 10.13. Instrumental break: rhythmic sequence
Notes: 1. We have taken a rhythmic sequence from the second half of the bar as equivalent to the same rhythm in the first half. 2. We have not transcribed the ornamental roll heard on each of the syncopated crotchets in bars IB3–IB4.

The first bar of the instrumental break (IB1) quotes the 'Peggy Sue' rhythm from the last line of refrains 1–6. Bar IB2 repeats this. Bar IB3 opens in the same way, but is interrupted by six repetitions of syncopated crotchets in the longest syncopated sequence of the song. In fact, the rhythmic phrase of bars IB3–IB5 can be identified with that of bars 9–10 of the refrain, with an inserted bar of syncopated crotchets. The six syncopated beats then correspond to a threefold repetition of the words 'gal, yes'. The first of these overlaps with and displaces the expected 'Sue' in bar IB3. The insistent repetition of 'gal, yes' will ensure that the 'yes' that was mysteriously lost from the refrain before the break will be forthcoming in the one after it.

After this, the rhythm shifts back to the on-beat at the beginning of bar IB5, from 'gal, yes' into the 'I love you, Peggy Sue' that follows it in the sung refrain. Once again, the expectation of 'Sue' on the last quaver of the bar is forestalled by a repetition of 'gal, yes'. It seems that 'Sue' is losing her distinctive name and becoming an indistinct 'gal'.

This time the syncopation is not prolonged, but is followed by the 'I love you' of bars 9–10. We expect this phrase to be completed with the 'Peggy Sue' rhythm that follows it in the refrain. But this has already been played in the first two bars of the break. Instead of going back to the beginning in this way, bar IB7 makes a new start. It takes the rhythm of the opening words of the song, which reappears at the beginning of verse 4 as the words 'I *love*'. The opening of verse 4 (repeated in verse 6) is the only place in the song where the word 'love' occurs on the off-beat. This syncopation of 'love' appears at the very point in the song where the singer as teenage boy confesses his love directly to the teenage girl. This rhythm is repeated twice in bar IB7, the resulting 'I *love*, I *love*' having almost the quality of a performative, suggesting a sexual *act*.

Up to this point, the syncopated phrases, taken in isolation, convey the following imaginary lyrics:

> Sue, Sue, (Sue),
>> gal, yes, gal, yes, gal, yes (Sue)
>>> gal, yes, love, love,

It is tempting to see the association of 'Sue', 'gal', and 'love' as indicating the femininity of the syncopated rhythms, with 'yes' being Sue's verbal response to the singer. However, this 'Sue' and her response are constituted only by the performance of the male musician.

A similar analysis shows that the on-beat rhythms of these bars convey the lyrics:

Peggy, Peggy, Peggy,
(love you), I love you, I love you, I, I,

This pattern seems to enact the subject position of the male performer of the song. 'Peg-gy' then represents what can be contained within the main masculine beat of the song, while 'Sue' is what continually eludes containment. One might be tempted to go further, and to regard 'Peggy' and 'Sue' as the names of two discourses, respectively masculine and feminine, which encircle one another and attempt to trap one another in the song. But this would be to ignore the fundamental inequality of these two sides. Rhythmically, the 'feminine' syncopation is never allowed to be more than a temporary interruption to the male beat: however often it reasserts itself, its attempts to disturb are overcome. In the lyrics, feminine speech scarcely appears at all. The words 'Sue' and 'gal' are his words for her. The only word she could be said to utter, and this only in what we have called an imaginary lyric, is 'Yes', i.e. his fantasy of her affirmation of him.[11]

The song therefore develops only one explicit verbal discourse, namely that of the male singer expressing his name for her, 'Peggy', in his confident on-beat rhythm. But a rival rhythm does challenge this one throughout the song, particularly in the singer's efforts to articulate her name 'Sue'. In the instrumental break, the two rhythms are replayed in a way which suggests the possibility of an inexplicit verbal dialogue, in which a female discourse rivals the male one. But, as we have shown, this inexplicit discourse is really only an echo, and a reaffirmation, of the explicit one.

In bar IB8, the 'pretty, pretty, pretty, pretty' rhythm restores the on-beat after the repeated syncopations of the previous bars. However, this regular rhythm is interrupted on the last quaver of the bar by an emphatic syncopation held over for half the following bar. The associated lyric appears to be a sustained 'Sue'. But 'Sue' will not be held for this length until the verse *after* the break. At this stage, the sustained minim is a new rhythmic element, introduced in the break and taken up in the subsequent verse (see Example 10.11).

By bar IB10 all syncopation has been eliminated. An on-beat minim provides the basis for the similar rhythmic resolution of 'Sue' in bar 8 of verse 6 (see Example 10.12). From here on, the texture of the instrumental break merges into the regular quaver rhythm heard in the short break between sung verses. The rhythmic work of the instrumental break is complete. The old ways

---

[11] The strength of this fantasized female 'yes' in the male imagination is shown by the difficulty that anti-rape movements have experienced in challenging the dictum that 'no means yes'. The reduction of 'Peggy Sue' to the repetition of this one word is strikingly similar to Joyce's ending of Molly Bloom's soliloquy (and of his book *Ulysses*) with her 'Yes' (1969: 704).

of saying 'Sue' have been displaced by her becoming 'gal' in an act of love; her 'yes' has been emphatically affirmed; and a new rhythm has been suggested for 'Sue' that will be taken up and developed in the verses after the break.

Meaning in Rhythm

Analysis of the instrumental break shows that the work it does is not purely rhythmic. If the rhythmic development is what is immediately apparent to the listener, it can be shown to contain an imaginary verbal level which connects the rhythms to the words of the verses before and after it. As a sequence, the words evoked on the imaginary level do not themselves make sense. It is the organization of the rhythm that makes them do so. For instance, interruption and overlap of one rhythmic phrase by another enable the name 'Sue' to be eclipsed by her status as 'gal'. And if 'gal, yes' means nothing specific, its rhythmic repetition as 'gal, yes, gal, yes, gal, yes' seems unmistakably sexual. But the major feature of the rhythm is its division into syncopated and unsyncopated accents. As the two rhythms continually interrupt each other, 'Peggy' is set against 'Sue', 'I' against 'gal', and the verbal declaration 'I love you' against the achievement of bodily union in the 'yes' that the masculine discourse speaks for the woman.

The rhythmic development of the two names over the song as a whole confirms this division of the verbal 'Peggy' from the bodily 'Sue'. The singer's initial problem with saying 'Peggy' was the separation of the 'P' from the rest of the word on an anticipatory off-beat. The hiccough in the enunciation 'P'heggy' is indeed a physical, bodily interruption of the *word*: it seems to remind us that the spoken word is material. But it is corrected by a purely *verbal* exercise—the repetition of 'P' on the beat in the 'pretty, pretty' phrase. By verse 3, the singer 'knows' 'Peggy'. The problem then arises of how to say 'Sue' in line with this 'Peggy', and the first attempts to solve it only make the matter worse. The prolonged 'uh-uh-uh-uh . . .' phrase of verse 4 does involve hiccoughs, but as a whole evokes another bodily activity, that of crying. In effect, the singer makes 'Sue' cry in his own crying performance.

By verse 5, the singer appears to have 'got over' 'Sue', in that he can say her name without it evolving into the sobbing and hiccoughs of verse 4. In getting to know 'Sue', he has quietened her crying. But, as distinct from the case of 'Peggy', no learning of verbal rhythms has taken place between verses 4 and 5. The instrumental break employs only the non-verbal rhythms of Holly's guitar. One possible interpretation would be that indeed the crying of a baby is silenced not by words, but by the union of the bodies of mother and baby in a rhythmic rocking motion. 'Rock and roll' songs take this bodily relation between mother and baby as a metaphor for the sexual relation between man and woman, in which the man rocks his 'baby', the woman, in order to silence her crying. This might lead us to a position similar to that of Simon Frith's, in which the rhythms of rock music would directly *represent* the physical motions of dancing or of sex, so long repressed in Western culture.

However, our analysis of the rhythms of 'Peggy Sue' shows Frith's idea of a 'directly physical beat' to be an illusion. The rhythms do not represent anything directly, physical or otherwise. The rhythms of the song are the rhythms of *verbal images* which are reworked and repeated in the instrumental break. Such verbal images can represent sexuality: here, they perform the silencing of 'Sue' in an act of love. Similarly, the relation between 'rock' music and 'blues' is not a purely rhythmic one. The rhythmic metaphor is also the powerful verbal one that came from 'blues', in which 'man' stands in for 'mother' and 'woman' for 'baby' in the 'rocking' relationship. It is the imaginary performing of this act in the instrumental break that creates the difference between the performance of verses 3 and 4 and verses 5 and 6.

This difference, although it is rhythmic, cannot be reduced to the 'rhythmic variety' that Dave Laing considered to be the radical innovation in Holly's music. Indeed, the difference lies partly in the use, in singing 'Sue', of sustained notes, the absence of which, Laing had argued, distinguished Holly's musical style from that of the traditional ballad. Such notes are in fact used in 'Peggy Sue' in a quite conventional way, to convey the ending of the musical narrative. Contrary to Laing, we consider the disruption of the coherence of the voice in the 'Su-uh-huh . . .' of verse 4 is not lasting. It is only one moment in a dramatic performance, which concludes with a strengthened and deepened male voice affirming 'I want you'.

We therefore disagree with Laing's claim that rhythm in Holly's music is a thing-in-itself, autonomous from the explicit representation of feelings. The verbal rhythms of 'Peggy Sue' represent and develop the emotions of the singer. We can even suggest a name for the emotion the song expresses for Peggy Sue.

Our rhythmic analysis has so far concentrated on the syncopations made by voice and guitar. These syncopations are all heard against the steady on-beat of the rhythm and bass section in the band. Only in bar 3 of the song does the voice consistently align itself with this underlying beat. The words sung to regular crotchets in this bar (running on into bar 4 in the first verse) are as follows:

1.	Then	you'd	know	why	I	feel	blue
2.	Oh	how	my	heart	yearns		
3.5.	Pretty	pretty	pretty	pretty	Peg		
4.6.	With	a	love	so	rare		

The verbal image of 'my heart' accompanying this regular beat in verse 2 suggests that the underlying on-beat rhythm can represent the singer's beating heart. Holly's own song 'Heartbeat', which is contemporary with 'Peggy Sue', employs this imagery. Here, Laing does acknowledge a form of representation at work: '[In] "Heartbeat" . . . the basic rhythms of singing and playing have a dramatic function, to suggest a pounding heart' (1971: 71). In this song the performance of the lyric indicates its own meaning: ' "Heartbeat why do you *miss*/When my baby *kisses* me". In the first line there is an almost imperceptible pause after "you", and "miss" is jerked out emphatically' (ibid. 74). In 'Peggy Sue', the syncopation of 'Sue' (and also of 'you' and 'true' in the continuations of the lines quoted above) can likewise be heard as the singer's heart missing a beat in the presence of the female other.

In 'Heartbeat', the metaphor of a mother being kissed by her baby is used for the singer being kissed by his lover. Literally, the steady heartbeat, and the words addressed to it, belong to the mother: the singer takes them as a metaphor for his own. Similarly the words 'Pretty, pretty, pretty, pretty' addressed to Peggy Sue are literally the words spoken to a baby by its mother, here repeated metaphorically by a man to his lover. The regular heartbeat of the mother underlies the repetition of 'p' on each beat which is crucial to learning to say 'Peggy' without stammering. In verses 4 and 6, the same beat is associated with 'a love so rare', again suggestive of a mother's love, in marked contrast with the syncopated 'true' that follows. ('True' can be a clichéd description of love between man and woman, but is not appropriate to mother–child love.)

These verbal images of bars 3 and 4 appear to have a narrative structure of their own. In verse 1, the regular beat evokes the monotony of 'blue' feeling when Peggy Sue is absent. In verse 2, the singer expresses desire for Peggy Sue from a distance, by establishing the regular beat as representing that of his heart. In verse 3, the regular heartbeat recalls that of his mother, which underlay the repetitive language she used in teaching him to talk; here he repeats this language to teach himself how to address Peggy. In verse 4 he addresses her, describing his love in words he could use to describe his mother's love for him.

In this way, the mother's heartbeat, language, and love are used successively to move the singer from the absence of Peggy Sue in verse 1 to approach
her presence in verse 4. This movement involves establishing the mother as
absent. 'A love so rare' could be spoken about a dead, or distant, mother; it
could even be sent on a Mother's Day card; it could hardly be used to her
face. But Holly makes the mother present in her absence, as she speaks through
him and for him to Peggy Sue.

Jean-Jacques Rousseau named as *pity* the fundamental, and in his view,
natural, affection of a mother for her child. In invoking his mother's love for
him to express his love for 'Peggy Sue', Holly constitutes 'Peggy Sue' as an
object of pity. And we can imagine him to be singing 'Pity pity pity pity Peggy'
in the manner of an adult adopting the baby-language of a child unable to
pronounce its 'r's.[12]

Strictly speaking, Dave Laing's argument should lead him to condemn this
expression of emotion. In fact, Laing praises Holly for breaking with the tran-
scendentalism of the traditional ballad, modelled on songs of love for the Virgin
Mary. It is true that, in this song, the male singer grows from stuttering boy
(verse 1) through eager anticipation of fatherhood (verse 3) to self-confident
man (verse 6) by reducing the stature of his girl from that of quasi-religious
object of yearning (verse 2) through crying baby (verse 4) to silence (instrumental break). Initially, her rhythm disturbs his. By the end of the song it
does not. It is not clear that this represents any departure from a conventional model of male socialization.

Both Frith and Laing praise rock music as a whole for liberating rhythms
from subservience to the singing voice. For Frith this enables these rhythms
to express sexuality directly. For Laing it enables them to express themselves
alone. We affirm that in a song such as 'Peggy Sue', the role of rhythm in
the dramatic representation is crucial. But its role is to intervene in and
to transform the meaning of the lyrics. In itself, it is meaningless: which is
why, almost without exception, instrumental rock music is so banal. The
fetishization of rhythm which is a hallmark of much rock aesthetic writing
is escapist. The origins of the rhythms are inevitably thought to be physiological, as we have shown in the case of both the writers we have discussed.
Appeal to rhythm against language is ultimately an appeal to biology and

---

[12] For Rousseau, pity 'is a natural feeling, which, by moderating the love of self in each individual, contributed
to the preservation of the whole species' (quoted from Derrida 1967*b*: 173). Amorous love is for Rousseau the
perverse imitation of this feeling, by culture (ibid. 175). Precisely this imitation is at work in the song 'Peggy
Sue'.

natural forces against a concern with culture, ideology, and the social forces which language describes and expresses.

In our view rock music is pre-eminently a reworking of social forces, and above all, of socialization. The song lyrics constantly reiterate a parallel between the infant's situation as a learner of language in early childhood, and the adolescent's situation as a listener to the song, learning the adult language of love. This parallel is not merely portrayed in the lyrics, but is also dramatically performed in rhythms whose names are given explicitly by the song itself.

In fact a repertoire of rhythms is returned to repeatedly in rock music. These rhythms represent a stylized re-enactment of the life of the child within the domestic scene, a life which the infant is—with intense excitement—preparing to enter, and which the adolescent is—with equal excitement—preparing to leave. They are the rhythms of 'talking', 'walking', 'crying', 'hearts beating', 'babies rocking', and the like. This limited range permits an economy of expression, a density of cross-reference both within and between songs, and an intensification of experience which must always be at once absolutely familiar and yet absolutely new. Of this genre, 'Peggy Sue' provides a paradigm.

References

Adorno, T. W. (1978). 'On the fetish-character in music and the regression of listening', in *The Essential Frankfurt Reader*, ed. A. Arato and E. Gehbardt (New York).

Bradby, B., and Torode, B. (1984). 'To whom do U2 appeal?', *Crane Bag 8/2* (Dublin).

Burgin, V. (ed.) (1982). *Thinking Photography* (London).

Cleaver, E. (1968). *Soul on Ice* (London).

Cott, J. (1981). 'Buddy Holly', in *The Rolling Stone History of Rock and Roll*, ed. J. Miller (London).

Derrida, J. (1967a). *Speech and Phenomena* (Paris, trans. Evanston, 1973).

—— (1967b). *Of Grammatology* (Paris, trans. London, 1976).

Freud, S. (1900). *The Interpretation of Dreams* (Vienna, trans. London 1953).

—— (1977). 'Fragment of an analysis of a case of hysteria ("Dora")', in *Pelican Freud Library*, Vol. 8, *Case Histories I* (Harmondsworth).

Frith, S. (1978). *The Sociology of Rock* (London).

Gillett, C. (1970). *The Sound of the City* (London).

Joyce, J. (1969). *Ulysses* (Harmondsworth).

Keil, C. (1966). *Urban Blues* (Chicago).

Laing, D. (1969). *The Sound of Our Time* (London).

—— (1971). *Buddy Holly* (London).

—— (1978). *The Marxist Theory of Art* (Hassocks, Sussex).

McCabe, C. (1979). *James Joyce and the Revolution of the Word* (London).

Rousseau, J.-J. (1763). *Essay on the Origin of Languages* (Paris, trans. New York, 1966).

Wittgenstein, L. (1968). *Philosophical Investigations*, 2nd edn., trans. G. E. M. Anscombe (Oxford).

Part 3

Modes of Representation

If pop really is to be seen as 'inextricably entangled in the secular life-processes of real people' (p. 16 above), it seems likely that it is capable of *representing* aspects of those processes to us. With once-popular realist theories (that is, theories of 'reflection') long since abandoned, the question then becomes how best to conceive the routes through which the myriad layers of mediation are traversed; not to mention how best to deal with the possibility (broadly structuralist in provenance) that songs not only represent to us how things are but also help to construct the very categories of identity through which we experience them. Progress here might permit us to start talking once again about how in some sense music 'shows' us how we live (or might live).

At a very general level, songs—through their musical style, their mode of performance, use, and interpretation—do seem to point towards particular historical moments, knots of collective experience, cultural traditions, and so forth. At this level—the level of style-indicators and cultural codes—music can be taken to represent to us the features of a specific conjuncture (neo-Gramscianism), structure of feeling (Raymond Williams), or chronotope (Bakhtin). It is in this way that Sheila Whiteley's study of Jimi Hendrix records can present them as belonging to a favoured 'expressive form' of the sixties counter-culture: they encapsulate key values, namely, artistic 'progressiveness' and drug-related experience. But Whiteley, not content to rest there, asks what mechanisms produce this connection. The answer comes on various levels: anaphonic musical signs (i.e. signs that work through structural analogy with non-musical experiences of time, space, movement, etc.);[1] culturally mediated semiotic coding (musical features that work through comparison with other, familiar effects in different styles); intra-cultural interpretation (what counter-cultural listeners said); cultural resonance (analogy between aspects of the music and of the cultural context); technological innovation. Overall, though, the method lies close to approaches centred on the idea of *structural homology*.

Implicit in Whiteley's account is that this particular conjunctural representation finds its most striking focus in the persona of Jimi Hendrix himself. And here, inscribed on the musical and performing body of this remarkable musician, we find intersecting discourses not only of 'progressiveness' and 'psychedelia' but also of race, gender, and sexuality. Given pop's orientation to the star performer, this structure of representation, not surprisingly, is

---

[1] See Tagg (1992), 372–5.

commonplace. Its lineages go back some way—for instance, to the torch singers discussed by John Moore. The songs he analyses concern, clearly, key themes relating to the social changes of the 1920s and 1930s, in particular as these affected conceptions of class, gender, sexuality, and ethnicity. But the representations of these themes offered in the songs (which, basically, are songs of 'unrequited love') cannot be understood except in the context of the overall personas constructed for and by the singers (through visual images, journalistic comment, their own words, performance styles). What is interesting too is the element of negotiation and even contestation within the representations, as songwriters and singers work in variable ways at the discursive topography of the torch-song genre.

At issue there were the possible dimensions of this genre (which defined itself against and in relation to 'flapper songs' and 'blues'). Genre is always important for representational strategies, defining what can and cannot be said, and in what ways.[2] But genres in pop are exceptionally fluid and polyvalent, the representational spaces they cover governed by a multitude of factors. One of these, as just suggested, is performance style, which can in important ways help *produce* the text—or even *rewrite* it. Charles Hamm pursues this point in relation to early songs by Irving Berlin, where it appears that the published texts are often of little help in deciding the genre to which the song belongs. Far more use are the meanings attributed to the song at the time, in relation to contemporary social debates; and of particular importance there are the identities of the song's protagonists, as mediated by performance style. Thus the meaning of 'suggestive songs' turns on nuances of class-coded sexual behaviour, as represented in performance, and similarly 'coon songs' can change into nostalgic ballads if stereotypes of African-American performance are replaced by different norms.

The relationship between performance and pop songs' representational work crystallizes in particularly strong form in the career of Hank Williams. Williams is important historically for his role in the shift of country music from a limited regional context to a national, and international music with a mass audience. But on paper his songs break little new ground. For Richard Leppert and George Lipsitz, his importance lay in *how* he sang them, what they could be made to mean, and how this meshed with and reshaped discourses of age, gender, and class at a moment of profound social change. Williams, they argue, 'remained part of the crowd by letting its diverse

---

[2] On genre in pop, see Fabbri 1982; Frith 1996, ch. 4.

currents flow through him'; yet this required a cross-cutting of themes, images, and singing voices which could convey a flux of 'shifting subjectivities', but which, playing into widely available narratives and images of 'Hank Williams the man', could reground popular memories in opposition to emergent, 'modernizing' cultural rupture: he 'constituted his own voice and body as sites of resistance'.

Though the subject-matter of this essay, as indeed of Hamm's and Moore's, predates the beginnings of rock and roll, many of the themes continue to resonate, just as the methodologies of the writers offer themselves readily for application to more recent material. Interestingly, too, the subjects of all three essays are situated at historical moments of great danger—when, within the USA in particular but also in the Western world more generally, profound changes to the cultural field, and the wider social formation, were in train. Ellie Hisama's study of 'orientalism' in three songs of the 1980s locates them in a moment of similarly deep threat, at the point of a reconstituted musical colonialism in a supposedly post-colonial world. On the analytical level, what emerges strongly here is the importance not just of the performer but of other protagonists in the songs. In music, lyrics, and performance, the Western musicians construct themselves as dominant, but in relation to the figure of a desired Other—exoticized representations of stereotyped Asian women—a scenario confirmed in visual and video images. Reading 'against the grain' of this dominance, Hisama's polemic in a sense redraws the boundaries of these texts to include her own mediation.[3]

If the 'narratives' offered in the songs that Hisama discusses only pretend to 'dialogue', an important issue is nevertheless raised here, namely the part played by narrative in the functions of representation. How 'characters' and 'voices' are shaped through the passage of musical time, and in relation to other protagonists, is crucial to songs' effects. The personas constructed in the songs of Jimi Hendrix, Hank Williams, the torch singers, and others do not just exist in particular settings, they *act*, and *interact*. But so, on a variety of levels, do the various voices and features of the musical textures: in songs, narrative operates in a variety of overlapping, and sometimes contradictory ways. As if combinations of lyric, musical, and performance structures did not offer complexity enough, accompanying videos often amplify this still further. Alf Björnberg analyses four early 1990s songs/videos from the point

---

[3] On its first publication, her essay stimulated considerable debate among the Asian-American community—and a public apology from John Zorn, one of the musicians involved.

of view of the interacting musical and visual narrative structures. The interactions move across a spectrum, from parallelism to contradiction; and since, Björnberg argues, the available narrative modes *within* music are themselves numerous, the resulting range of possible relationships is large. He does not interpret the semantics to any extent—concentrating on narrative structure—but the implications are considerable, and available to future work. At the same time, his recasting of the 'textual' in terms of the shaping of temporal experience succeeds, one might say, in arresting the flow—as textual analysis must—while at the same time insisting upon it.

References

Fabbri, F. (1982). 'A theory of musical genres: two applications', in *Popular Music Perspectives*, ed. D. Horn and P. Tagg (Gothenburg and Exeter), 52–81.

Frith, S. (1996). *Performing Rites: On the Value of Popular Music* (Oxford).

Tagg, P. (1992). 'Towards a sign typology of music', in *Studi e Testi 1: Secondo Convegno Europeo di Analisi Musicale*, ed. R. Dalmonte and M. Baroni (Trento), 369–78.

11

Progressive Rock and Psychedelic Coding in the Work of Jimi Hendrix

SHEILA WHITELEY

But like, the blues is what we're supposed to dig . . . sometimes the notes might sound like it, but it's a different scene between those notes. (Hendrix quoted in Pidgeon 1967: 2)

Discussion of the 1960s generally identifies progressive rock as the prime organ of communication within the counter-culture. At the same time, musical analysis of the genre is an underdeveloped field of study, including only an identification of musical characteristics (Willis 1978), Mellers' analysis of the Beatles (1973) and Middleton and Muncie's analysis of five representative songs in the Open University's course, *Popular Culture* (1981). As a particularly heterogeneous genre (compared with, for example, rock 'n' roll and r&b), definitions of progressive rock equally raise problems: to what extent does the variety of styles reflect the variety of radical movements contained within the overall term counter-culture; alternatively, given the variety of styles, can progressive rock be considered a single phenomenon and, if so, to what extent does it have musical codes in common?

Although it is possible to isolate music from its social, cultural, and ideological context, progressive rock was located where particular sociological factors and musical developments crossed. The question thus arises as to whether progressive rock can be interpreted as a particular expressive form of the counter-culture's social and material life experience and, if so, the extent to which it can be considered as containing cultural values and social meanings.

Grateful acknowledgement is made to Peter Winkler, State University of New York, Stony Brook for his help in transcribing 'Purple Haze' and 'Love or Confusion'.

With progressive rock standing in a contradictory position to mainstream pop conventions, the critical imperative rests on the degree to which the music can be read as 'oppositional'. How does progressive rock, from within its musical structure, articulate the socially mediated subjective experience of the different groups within the counter-culture? Is it a simple contestation of existing musical frameworks and how can a musical language express an alternative 'progressive' viewpoint? To what extent does this rely on personalized intuitional breaks, inflections, and the breakdown of structures?

While my initial analysis of Hendrix addresses the problem of the music itself—how it is arranged, instrumentation, style etc.—the problem remains as to *how* it can provide social and cultural meanings. My starting point has been that musical facts are socially grounded: that 'the socially constructed codes which are responsible for musical structures set the limits of meaning, but the music is actually created in concrete cultural situations, and these orient its received meaning in particular ways' (Willis 1978). However, while it can be argued that the sense of innovation in progressive rock challenged the more standardized structure of pop songs and as such provided a musical analogy for the counter-culture's search for alternative cognitive and social modes beneath and outside the framework of the dominant culture, the area of signification presents problems. In particular the level of denotation seems lacking or at best unclear as there is very little sense of objective reference to concepts and perceptions. On the other hand, it is possible to discuss connotation, in that music was recognized, by the counter-culture, as a symbolic act of self-liberation and self-realization in which reality and musical experience were fused. As such the sound-shape, together with the socio-cultural element superimposed upon it, consolidate to form a distinct form of communication.

As the counter-culture was largely concerned with alternative modes of living which involved, to a large extent, the use of drugs as a means towards exploring the imagination and self-expression, Hendrix's music is analysed for psychedelic coding. Focused by a reading of Joel Fort's *The Pleasure Seekers: the Drugs Crisis, Youth and Society* (1969), this analysis explores the way in which progressive rock conveys a musical equivalent of hallucinogenic experience through the manipulation of timbres (blurred/bright/overlapping), upward movement (and its comparison with psychedelic flight and the 'trip'), harmonies (oscillating/lurching), rhythms (regular/irregular), relationships (foreground/background), and collages to provide a point of comparison with the more conventionalized, 'normal' treatment inherent in rock.

At the same time, it is recognized that such associations quickly become conventionalized. As Middleton and Muncie (1981: 87) point out,

psychedelic elements in musical style are typically interpreted as such by reference to a sub-culture of drug usage; in other words they are defined in this way primarily because hippies said they should be. A whole group of connotations, arising from our knowledge of the drug culture, then settles on the music. But this culture has already been defined in this way partially because of the existence in it of this particular kind of music. The meaning of drug-usage is affected by the meaning of the associated music . . . The system is perfectly structured internally . . . but has no necessary connection to anything outside itself; there is no purchase on it from without.

While my analysis of Hendrix has been influenced to some extent by this awareness of intra-cultural interpretations, I have tried to establish the meaning of psychedelic elements through an examination of the musical codes involved and, more important, their relationship to each other.

This essay suggests a possible approach towards correlating cultural and musical characteristics and, in particular, the correspondence in Jimi Hendrix's music between its 'progressive rock' and its 'psychedelic' associations. In particular, it explores how the emphasis on self-expression, improvisation, and experimentation, implicit in progressive rock,[1] related to the counter-culture's emphasis on the immediacy of the experiential here and now of psychedelic experience.

Jimi Hendrix: The Relationship between Structure and Psychedelic Coding

Prior to his move to London in 1966, Hendrix's musical career in the United States had included package tours with Solomon Burke and Wilson Pickett. His strongest influence came from the serious blues musicians who came out of the South—Muddy Waters, Willie Dixon, and Little Walter—and on one occasion he backed his idol, B. B. King. Other temporary engagements included backing Little Richard, Jackie Wilson, Wilson Pickett, and Curtis Knight and for a time he played with the Isley Brothers, the first band to give him a chance to play lead guitar. This broad-based experience in the clubs made him equally conversant with jazz, saxophone swing, r&b, gospel, and soul.

---

[1] My own research, of which the analysis of Hendrix constitutes only a small part, indicates that progressive rock was characterized by a sense of creative development from a base style and involved an underlying sense of uncertainty and surprise through extensive improvisation; that performance (live and recorded on LPs) would demonstrate both originality and self-expression.

Hendrix was brought to England by Chas Chandler who saw him playing at the Cafe Wha in Greenich Village. Chandler took him back to London where they auditioned a rhythm section which resulted in the engagement of Noel Redding (bass) and Mitch Mitchell (drums). Calling the band the Jimi Hendrix Experience, they played their first public engagement at Paris Olympia.

'Hey Joe', with flip side 'Stone Free', was the group's first single, and was released on 16 December 1966. By this time Hendrix had spent four months playing the London clubs: the Marquee, the Upper Cut, the Bag-O-Nails, and the short-lived 7½ Club. A review in *Melody Maker*'s 'Caught in the Act' section focused on his powerful psychedelic blues style, but the press generally wrote him off as so much loud, useless noise, calling him 'The Wild Man from Borneo' or 'The Crazy Black Man'. Rather than fight the image the group encouraged it, hoping it would increase their following in the underground. 'Hey Joe', musically reinforced the image.

Mysterious, menacing and dynamically very well paced, the record in effect picked up on the blues where the Rolling Stones had left the idiom after topping the British charts with 'Little Red Rooster' in 1964, and 'Hey Joe' . . . made the British top ten early in 1967. Just as Britain was beginning to feel the reverberations of the drug culture of San Francisco, here was a young black man from the West Coast with frizzy hair, outrageously colourful clothes, and no inhibitions about using the guitar as a sexual symbol. (Brown and Pearce 1978: 13)

But, as Mike Clifford points out, Hendrix had everything going for him—he had a supremely cool vocal drawl, dope-and-Dylan oriented lyrics, the acid dandyism of his clothes and the stirring element of black sexual fantasy (Gillett 1970: 385).

'Hey Joe' is based on a simple repetitive harmonic structure (see Example 11.1a). The introduction establishes the inherent menacing mood of the song with a moody, blues-like riff (Example 11.1b). The vocal is based on a heavily repetitive falling motif, coloured by inflection and muttered comments (Example 11.1c). After a shouted 'I Gave Her the Gun/I Shot Her/Yes, I Did./ I took the gun and I shot her' the second verse leads into Hendrix's guitar solo. This is based on scale figures which move around the principal chord structure: three bars on G major, two bars on E minor. The effect of the simple repetitive harmonies is to free the melody line (the structure is easily extended to create breaks of an irregular length) while the form itself is not constrained by a set harmonic sequence (such as the twelve bar blues). At the same time, the progressions provide harmonic motion under the strongly

Ex 11.1.

Ex 11.2.

rhythmic figures which are themselves punctuated by Hendrix comments: 'Shoot her one more time baby' (Example 11.2).

Progressive Elements

Hendrix had first heard 'Hey Joe' when jamming with Arthur Lee of the group Love, but whereas Lee relied on a mixture of muttered vocals and a guitar line borrowed from Jackie DeShannon's 'When You Walk in the Room', Hendrix shows more the influence of two of his guitar heroes, John Lee Hooker and Albert King. The introduction, for example, with its heavily accented G, the underpinning in the vocal line with the long decay on the D over which Hendrix mutters 'I said', reflects the moody and menacing style of Hooker, while the casual dexterity in the lead break is more reminiscent of Albert King. The influence of B. B. King is also present in the sensuous articulation in the break, the flurries of quick notes contrasting with the sustained G and glissando fall in bar 7. The basic falling pattern which was established in the vocal is also there, and is a typical r&b formula. However, as Hendrix himself once replied to an interviewer who was comparing his style with Clapton: 'but like, the blues is what we're supposed to dig . . . Sometimes the notes might sound like it, but it's a different scene between those notes' (quoted in Pidgeon 1976: 62). Thus, while there are blue notes, pitch inflection, 'vocalized' guitar tone, triplet beats, and off-beat accenting and a call-and-response relationship in Hendrix's own commentary to his guitar solo and verse line, the way in which these elements are pulled together is typically Hendrix. The sustain tone, which originated with B. B. King, takes on an even more overt sexuality, which was particularly evident in live performances by Hendrix where he would play the guitar with his teeth or with strongly masturbatory connotations to feed both the rhythmic emphasis of the guitar line and the words themselves: 'I caught her messin' with another man.'

In January, 1967 Nick Jones's article in *Melody Maker*, 'Hendrix—On the Crest of a Fave Rave' provided a formative account of the basic ingredients for progressive rock: 'The Hendrix sound is what England hasn't yet evolved—but desperately needs. It's a weaving, kaleidoscope of tremor and vibration, discords and *progressions*.'

The album *Are You Experienced* was released in September 1967. The single 'Hey Joe' appeared on side one and two other tracks also became chart hits: 'And the Wind Cries Mary' and 'Purple Haze'. The album focused on the psychedelic, with the title pulling on drug connotations.

'Purple Haze', the name given to a particular brand of the drug LSD, is overtly concerned with hallucinogenic experience:

> Purple Haze was in my brain
> Lately things don't seem the same
> Actin' funny, don't know why
> 'scuse me while I kiss the sky

The energy, use of distortion, fuzz (see Appendix), wah wah, and loudness coupled with precise and sinuous scalic riffs are comparable to 'Hey Joe', but this time the sexual focus, the betrayal of the male by the female and the violent consequences are shifted to pull on a sense of timelessness:

Purple Haze all around
Don't know if I'm coming up or down
Am I happy or in misery
Whatever it is, that girl put a spell on me

Ex 11.3.

Ex 11.4.

'Purple Haze' begins with a bass pedal E under A♯ on bass and lead guitar, the two bars creating an underlying beat, a common pulse, which works to establish a bonding between performer and audience (Example 11.3). The pulse-like beat continues in the next two bars, but here the A♯ disappears as Hendrix moves into the opening riff with its characteristic bending up of notes and dipping vibratos. Whilst this is basically a pentatonic blues riff, the extremes of distortion blur the actual pitching of the notes and the discordant partials make it practically impossible to hear the pitch. However, given the blues logic of Hendrix's other songs it is probable that the underlying structure is based on the chords of E–G–A which support the earlier vocal line (Example 11.4).

Ex 11.5.

The riff has the typical feeling of muscle and crunch common to most Hendrix numbers, and this comes through particularly in the tonal quality created by the electronic distortion, the fuzz, and the resultant discordant partials. The expectations generated in the opening riff are also picked up in the main break which moves towards an overt theatricality with its hammered and pulled-off notes, the jittered bursts of broken words over the free-flowing improvisation with its wild yet controlled sense of energy. In particular, the logic of the melodic shape of the line, the downward curve from C♯–B subtly supports the more overt frenzy of the delivery itself (Example 11.5). Throughout the entire solo the impression is of doubling at the octave above, a possible effect of electronic distortion or alternatively some sort of partial harmonic. In some bars the lower octave predominates, in others the upper, with the clearest 'shifts' to the higher octave occurring at bars 2 and 8.

Psychedelic Coding

As an acid track, the torn sounds and muttered syllables work within the overall shape of the lead guitar line which moves from top C♯ to B (Example 11.6a). The movement into the *trip* is accompanied by upward moving figures (Example 11.6b). The drums gradually moving from a highly active and syncopated rhythm into a fast but even pulse in quavers (Example 11.6c). In the lead break, high notes, sliding amplifications, and the sheer volume of noise move against the continuous arterial throb of the rhythm to juxtapose two realities—the throb of the continuous bass heart beat against the exhilarated high of Hendrix's guitar solo, which is intensified by the doubling at the octave effect.

For the listener, the sheer volume of noise works towards the drowning of personal consciousness. The simultaneous underlying pulsating rhythm and the heightened sensation of raw power rips through the distorted amplification of the guitar sound with its sinuous *tripping* around the basic notes (Example 11.7).

The melody line is simple and based on a recurring motif (Example 11.8) which moves towards an incantatory, mesmeric effect. Again there is an indication that the song reflects the state of mind on a hallucinogenic trip. Under the influence of acid, a particular word or phrase can take on an unreal significance to become totally absorbing and dominant within the new state of consciousness. When the passage is played at half-speed on a tape-recorder, the word 'haze' in particular vibrates, dips, and moves upwards to

Ex 11.6.

Ex 11.7.

Ex 11.8.

Pur-ple Haze___ was in my brain   Late-ly things don't seem the same

Act-ing fun-ny   But I___ don't know why_   'scuse me__ while I   kiss the sky___

Ex 11.9.

Act in' fun-ny   But I___ don't know why_   'scuse me__ while I   kiss the sky___

Ex 11.10.

(blue note)

You've got me blow-in' Blow-in' my mind_   Is it   to-mor-row   or just the

end of time (tell me   tell me   tell me)

suggest a sense of fixation, and this particular effect is also present on 'funny' and 'sky' where the dip shapes create a strong feeling of floating around the beat (Example 11.9).

Overall, the use of repetition in the song works towards a mood of obsessiveness and absorption. This is reflected in the motif which constitutes the total melodic structure of the vocal line, and while there are minor variations based on inflection which bend with the words, its constant use moves ultimately towards a sense of fixation and total absorption within the 'purple haze'. The final vocal phrase (Example 11.10), for example, with its strong dip shapes and muttered comments is supported by an accented F chord over a pulsating beat which stops suddenly as Hendrix mutters 'tell me, tell me, tell me'. The effect is one of loss of time, the underlying beat has gone and all that remains is the distanced voice and a sense of other-worldliness.

The total effect of 'Purple Haze' is one of drifting and while the lead break, for example, is fairly metrical with most of the bars being in eights or sixteenths plus ornaments, the deflection of accents from weak to strong beats in bars

Ex 11.11.

3–5 create a feeling of being within a different time-scale (Example 11.11). The sensation of drifting is equally fed by phrasing and articulation. In the lead break the guitar meanders in an almost raga-like noodling around the notes, again suggestive of a state of tripping where a fixed idea/concept/point takes on a new reality. In conjunction with the feedback and distortion there is a feeling of incoherence. In particular the high registers are almost pure noise and as such resonate with the imagery of the words:

> Purple haze was in my eyes
> Don't know if it's day or night
> You've got me blowing, blowing my mind,
> Is it tomorrow or just the end of time?

Progressive Elements

While 'Purple Haze' makes use of many blues features, the basic falling shape of the vocal, the repetitive phrases and short motifs, the somewhat tuneless melodic line, the call-and-response between the vocal and guitar, there is over-all a sensation of anti-structure which comes through in the aural experience of the delivery, the dense sound, the distorted slide notes, the muttered broken questions:

> Tell me, tell me

and the deep/throated answer:

> Purple haze, Purple haze
> you go on and on till the end of time
> oooh noo, oooh noo . . .

and the final rising crescendo of the high-pitched E vibrato.

Hendrix's extreme use of a fuzz effect whereby even the slightest sound of the guitar gives off a full-volumed sound also feeds the underlying sense of disorganization. The effect was increased by his standing close to a speaker so that when a string was plucked, the guitar would pick up the sound which would then become amplified and come out of the speaker. As the sound wave

Ex 11.12.

Ex 11.13.

would make the string vibrate at the same frequency as before, the positive interference would have the effect of making the string vibrate indefinitely, which fuzz alone could not do. Then, by using filters, Hendrix would make the feedback occur on the second harmonic, so that when the string was plucked and the guitar was held near the speaker the note would jump up an octave, maintaining itself at a much higher frequency and causing the sound to become even more piercing. This effect occurs, for example, on the second 'help me, help me' which leads into the lead break. As such, while Hendrix is basically repeating the riff, the effect is one of added intensity (Example 11.12).

Other effects used in 'Purple Haze' are the wah pedal, reverb, echo, phase, and tremelo, all of which are common today but were relatively new at the time. Although not used as extensively as fuzz, they allowed him to extend on the expressive potential of the blues and, in conjunction with the psychedelic connotations of the words, the song moves towards a theatrical enactment of a drug-induced state.

In contrast to the raw power of 'Purple Haze', 'The Wind Cries Mary' is far more gentle in effect. The haunting guitar motif which opens the song (Example 11.13) has an echo effect which resonates with the evocative 'and the wind whispers/cries/screams/Mary' to create an innate sense of understanding. While 'Purple Haze' evokes a powerful acid experience, 'Mary' (marijuana) is a much milder drug and as such the gentler pacing of the song elicits a sense of complicity between Hendrix and the audience. There is a muted understatement. Hendrix's voice is at its most evocative, the words

Ex 11.14.

A-af-ter all the Jacks are in their box-es   And the clowns have all gone to

bed   you can hear hap-pi-ness stag-g'rin' on   down the sheet

foot-prints dressed in red

Ex 11.15.

Lead Guitar

Rhythm Guitar

are spoken rather than sung out with an off-the-beat inflection, against a gently moving melody which pulls on the mood of serenity and well-being that can accompany shared 'smoke' (Example 11.14).

The basic chord structure is simple, moving through a repetitive C : B♭ : F until the evocative:

> Footprints dressed in red
> And the wind whispers Mary . . .

where the move to G7–B♭ has an underlying darkness which is immediately counteracted by the brighter sound of the lead break which moves upwards in fourths, with a gentle bending of slide notes to effect a musical equivalent of floating (Example 11.15). There is an ease in tension on the penultimate note, a sudden stillness before the haunting lyrics of the last verse:

Will the wind ever remember
The names it has blown in the past
And with this crutch, its old age and its wisdom
It whispers, 'No, this will be the last'.

Ex 11.16.

Ex 11.17.

'And the wind cries Mary' is then picked up by the guitar motif which gently bends the last note (Example 11.16).

Overall, 'The Wind Cries Mary' encodes the effect of marijuana through the gentleness and inner-directedness of its style. The timing is subtle, with the inflections in the melody line meandering just off the beat (Example 11.17). In conjunction with the gentle drift of the key link motif: C : B♭ : F the effect is one of easy well-being. The wind can blow anywhere, and the marijuana experience is universal.

Ex 11.18.

'Love or Confusion' has an equally simple harmonic structure and is based on the chords of G–G6–F–F6. The effect is to free the vocal line, which follows the natural inflection of the words with accents both on and off the beat (Example 11.18). The rising and falling phrase-shapes and the muttered asides equally support the underlying meaning of the words, rising on the word 'burns' and 'love', sinking on 'cold', circling 'round and round', and

Ex 11.19.

distanced on 'confusion' (Example 11.19). The sense of confusion is intensi-fied by Hendrix's guitar playing which appears to be superimposed on the vocal. It is neither in dialogue with the voice, nor does it fill in gaps as in the blues, but instead provides its own vocal line. The effect is of two simultan-eous melodies, both in the G minor pentatonic blues scale. At the same time, the chromaticism in the bass line provides a certain 'dizziness' in effect, which again feeds the connotations of confusion (Example 11.20).

The overall effect of the passage is one of noise which is generated in the main by Hendrix's use of fuzz tone which sounds at times almost like snare drum accents. This functions to articulate the beginning or end of a section and here the fuzz, together with the low grinding sound of the bass guitar, moves against the rests and the drum roll. At the same time, the other instru-ments come briefly into focus, doubling the bass line to create a moment of coherence. The rhythm guitar, for example, actually doubles the snare drum part, but since it is so sustained and relatively free of high frequencies, the sounds are distinct. The vocal line bends heavily with the muttered 'or is it confusion' acting almost as commentary on the sounds of the passage.

Psychedelic Coding

The words are strongly psychedelic in their associations of colour and confusion:

> Must there be all these colours without names
> without sounds
> My heart burns with feelin' but
> Oh! My mind is cold and reeling
>
> Oh, my head is pounding, pounding,
> going round and round and round and round
> Must there always be these colours?

Ex 11.20.

and in conjunction with the acute distortions of fuzz sound and the tripping around notes in the lead break, move towards a sensation of movement through time and space. The endless feedback and distortion move the listener into an equivalent state of incoherence, the montage of sound effects, reverb, echo, tremelo, and fuzz, resonating with the vocal message 'pounding, pounding, going 'round and round and round and round'.

Hendrix's lead break with its bend-up notes and glissandos equally suggests flight. It is here that the psychedelic fuses with space rock: the electronically distorted notes encoding both the unpredictability of hallucinogenic search, the lack of certainty of a good/bad trip with the unknown element in space travel.

Hendrix's exploration of space reads like a negative reaction to the mainstream rather than a positive move towards engaging in cultural quest. The use of distortion and fuzz creates an unknown element which can connote a sense of uncertainty. This also comes through in the way in which he tuned his guitar. The top string was often tuned to D or E♭ and the excessive bending and the use of the wah wah pedal served to obscure the actual notes played. At the same time, Hendrix's use of a conventional guitar, similar to that of Hank Marvin, but played upside down, can be read as a turning upside down of the conventional world of such groups as The Shadows. Clearly, Hendrix could have bought a left-handed guitar (as he himself was left-handed), but his playing of the instrument upside down helped to construct his image of an inverter of norms.

At the same time, the extreme use of noise, in conjunction with the hypnotic nature of the Hendrix sound with its overwhelming sense of energy and drive, created a means through which he could tune into the 'collective unconscious' of his audience. This provoked the mass sexual ecstasy often associated with his concerts which moved towards a corporeal sense of tribal unity. At this point, Hendrix's personal expansion of human consciousness would fuse with the collective experience of the hallucinogenic in the exploration of the self through mind-expanding drugs:

> Is that the stars in the sky or is it raining far from now?
> Will it burn me if I touch the sun, so big, so round?
> Will I be truthful, yeah, in choosing you as the one for me?
> Is this love baby, or is it—a just confusion?

Mild physical sensations particularly in the limbs, occur, but the main dimensions are perceptual . . . primarily visual, but also (including) the other individual sensory modalities and sometimes a blending or synesthesia so that one 'hears' something seen or 'tastes' something touched. With the eyes closed, kaleidoscopic colors and a wide array of geometric shapes and specific objects . . . are often seen . . . Illusions can occur and sometimes, depending on the interaction of the many important human and drug variables, hallucinations. (Fort 1969: 182)

In conjunction with the overwhelming sense of energy and drive in his guitar playing, allied to unusual sound effects (running his hand up and down the fretboard, banging the guitar and feeding these sounds through fuzz) there is, then, the implication of a new language of sound which equates with the sense of hallucinogenic exploration implicit in the lyrics.

Progressive Elements

While 'Love or Confusion' continues to draw on blues resources, particularly in the single note attack with long decay and glissando fall, the basic melodic falling pattern—for example, 'Is this love, baby, or is it confusion'—is equally typical of r&b. The forcefulness in Hendrix's guitar style can be traced back to his early experience in r&b and rock 'n' roll, but generally structures and style are growth points rather than working barriers.

In particular his use of effects works to support the sense of the unknown, the 'confusion' in the lyrics:

> Is this love baby, or is it—a just confusion
> Oh, my mind is so mixed up, goin' round 'n' round
> Must there be all these colours without names
> without sounds?

The improvisations and the often incoherent instrumental melody/sound, the apparently disordered, random, and electronically dominated noise, the never-ending effect of the reverb, create a kaleidoscopic effect. Layers of sound appear to grow out of one another in a continuous flow to provide a musical metaphor for the endlessness of space itself. The emphasis on noise and the apparently chaotic sound of Hendrix's playing equally support the idea of confusion:

> Oh, my head is pounding, pounding,
> going round and round and round

The overall effect is anarchic, a move against reality (with its emphasis on logic) and as such there is a fusion with the psychedelic, the unpredictability of hallucinogenic search, the juxtaposition of unknown colours with chaos and confusion.

Ex 11.21.

(a) 'Long Hot Summer Night'

(b) 'Foxy Lady'

'Hey Joe', 'Purple Haze', 'The Wind Cries Mary', and 'Love or Confusion' were constantly performed by Hendrix in concert and appeared on seven of his LPs including the live recording *Woodstock*. As such they would appear to be representative not only of his particular style of performance, but also of his particular focus on the psychedelic, space rock, and sexuality. 'Foxy Lady', 'Fire', 'Red House', 'Long Hot Summer Night', 'Gypsy Eyes', and 'Dolly Dagger', for example, show a comparable sensuality in vocal delivery and performing style to 'Hey Joe'. There are the characteristic muttered asides (Example 11.21) to evoke an erotic intimacy which is intensified by the pounding beat and sensuous guitar style. 'Gypsy Eyes', for example, has the characteristic sliding glissandos and bent-up notes in the guitar introduction

Ex 11.22.

(a) no chords

(b)

Well, I   re - al - ize,___ that I've been   hyp - no - tize;___   I love you   Gyp-sy   Eyes_____

I love you   Gyp - sy   Eyes_____ _____

Ex 11.23.

Here comes

Dol - ly   Dag - ger___   Her love's so heav - y it's gon - na

make you   stag - ger   Dol - ly_____   Dag - ger___

Ex 11.24.

She ain't sat - is - fied   'til   she   gets what   she's   af - ter
She drinks her   blood   from a   jag - ged_____   edge
You'd bet - ter watch out,   ba - by,   here comes your mas - ter

(Example 11.22a) but the opening vocal has no supporting chords, and as such the focus is on Hendrix's slow sensual delivery (Example 11.22b). The overt sexuality of 'Dolly Dagger' is intensified by the pounding rock beat and bass riff (Example 11.23). In particular, the repetitive blues-like delivery of the coda in conjunction with the strongly bent-up chords moves towards an assertion of dominance and self-gratification which, in live performance, would have been intensified by the explicit masturbatory connotations of Hendrix's guitar style (Example 11.24).

Ex 11.25.

(a) 'Spanish Castle Magic'

It's ve-ry far a-way___ It takes a-bout half a day to get there

If we tra-vel by my___ dra-gon fly No it's

not in___ Spain___ But all the same you know it's a groo-vy name

(b) 'Are You Experienced?'

Ah!___ but are you ex-per-i-enced Have you ev-er been ex-

-per-i-enced spoken: not ne-ces-sar-i-ly stoned but beau-ti-ful.

'Spanish Castle Magic' and 'Are You Experienced' exhibit comparable techniques both in vocal delivery and guitar style but this time draw on a psychedelic vocabulary (Example 11.25). Initially, it is the lyrics that point to the psychedelic. 'Are you Experienced' invites hallucinogenic exploration:

> If you can get your mind together
> then come across to me
> We'll hold hands
> an' then we'll watch the sun rise
> from the bottom of the sea.
> But first, are you experienced?
> Have you ever been experienced?
> Well, I have.
> I know, I know, you'll probably scream 'n' cry
> That your little world won't let you go . . .

The 'are you experienced', in particular, points to the need for guidance by a trained, trusted person for the first-time user of LSD.

The underlying personality, mood, attitudes, expectations and setting in which the drug is taken have proven to be far more important as determinants of an LSD experience than with drugs such as alcohol, marijuana, barbiturates, or amphetamines . . . Because of the intensity and complexity of the experience, it can . . . be disorganizing and upsetting. (Fort 1969: 181, 183)

With Hendrix as a 'trusted' and 'experienced' guide (in the sense that he was both a loved and respected performer) the experience is promised as beautiful: 'Have you ever been experienced? Well, I have. Ah, let me prove it to you.'

> Trumpets and violins I can hear in the distance.
> I think they're calling our names.
> Maybe now you can't hear them,
> but you will if you just take hold of my hand.

'Spanish Castle Magic' extends the 'experience' itself:

> The clouds are really low and they overflow with cotton candy . . .
>
> Hang on, my darling, yeah, hang on if you want to go.
> It puts everything else on the shelf
> with just a little bit of Spanish Castle Magic

but in both songs the lyrics imply knowledge: 'candy' = 'sugar' = LSD, 'stoned' = 'high', pulling on the effects of LSD, the sensation of floating. Coupled with the overwhelming sense of energy in Hendrix's guitar playing and the sheer volume of noise generated by the fuzz tone there is then an implicit drowning of individual consciousness, an invitation to 'experience', which is reflected in the name of the band itself.

Space rock also required experience, with the form of the music depending upon comparison. As such its form of communication is symbolic and preconditioned by the structures of previous symbolic transfer. Unlike Pink Floyd, however, whose space rock (e.g. 'Astronomy Domine', 'Set the Controls for the Heart of the Sun') is melodically and rhythmically simple, relying on electronically produced sounds to create a dramatic realization of the vastness and potential beauty of space, Hendrix appeared more intent on *destroying* conventional reality (with its emphasis on logic), to constitute instead a sense of the anarchic through the mutation of sound. With both bands, space rock exhibits a comparability with psychedelic rock and hallucinogenic experience: both talk of flight, of colours, of the *extra*-ordinariness of experience.

Ex 11.26. 'Up from the Skies'

In 'Up from the Skies', Hendrix again makes use of spoken dialogue to effect a sense of personal experience which, coupled with the use of fuzz and distortion and the upward moving figures, suggests flight and disorientation (Example 11.26).

Thoughts which are ordinarily suppressed or repressed from consciousness come into focus and previously unseen relationships or combinations between these are recognized . . . Ordinary boundaries and controls between the self and the environment and within the self are loosened . . . mood changes or swings can occur and sometimes intense pleasurable or esthetic experience . . . On other occasion or with other individuals, the mood changes can be highly unpleasant and labile. (Quoted in Fort 1969: 182–3)

The songs analysed suggest, then, knowledge and experience, not only of psychedelic drugs and their potential effects, but equally of musical style. For example, while Hendrix made use of blues resources in the repetitive structure of the riffs, the repetition of phrases and short motifs, the use of blue scales, the falling shapes of the vocal, the use of call-and-response between the vocal and the guitar, the Jimi Hendrix Experience was ultimately based on an immense vocabulary of sound. Volume affecting sustain, wah wah pedal, fuzz tone, and reverb (see Appendix) are especially important in a consideration of style and Hendrix's experience in rock 'n' roll and r&b is equally apparent in the forcefulness of his playing and the emphasis on an essentially rhythmic rather than lyrical guitar technique. Overall, harmonies, melodies, and lyrics would appear to be secondary to a consideration of *effect* as what are often simple deep structures are masked by the incredible energy and forcefulness of the guitar style and the dynamics of the electronic effects themselves.

'Love or Confusion' for example, is based on the chords of G, G6, F, and F6, the phrases are repetitive and memorable, but overall the effect is one of anti-structure which is due to the aural experience of the delivery, the dense sound, the feedback and distortion which move toward pure noise. 'Purple Haze' is also based on a repetitive riff over a simple harmonic structure: E, G, A, but again the underlying logic of the chord progressions is transformed by Hendrix to produce a feeling of intuitive incoherence and lack of rationality through the use of fuzz tone which distorts the hammered and pulled-off notes.

The blues, then, is a growth focal point rather than a working barrier and Hendrix's guitar style, while reflecting the influence of B. B. King, John Lee Hooker, and Albert King, demonstrates his own physical feeling for sound, not only in the virtuosity of technique but also in the use of electronic effects which enhance the feeling of raw energy which characterizes all his songs.

The muttered vocals which are common to all Hendrix songs, also demonstrate a physical feeling for sound rather than melody and as such make their impact musically rather than semantically. In 'Love or Confusion' for example, the musical effect of 'or is it, or is it confusion' is to focus the confusion in the sound itself, the fuzz tone, the low grinding sound of the bass guitar against the roll on the cymbal. In 'Long Hot Summer Night' the muttered 'I'm so glad that my baby's coming to rescue me' again works as a sound source to effect a strongly sexual rhythmic focus before the lines are repeated twice to an upward melodic line to suggest, in context, an orgasmic high. 'Foxy Lady' again focuses on a repetitive rhythmic motif: preceded by the highly charged 'give us some', the repeated 'foxy' symbolically moves to an expression of the rhythm of the sexual act itself. The falling shape on 'Ah' in 'Are You Experienced' followed by the muttered 'but you are experienced' is also rhythmic in effect, the lack of melody moving towards an underlying intimacy and sense of personal hallucinogenic knowledge which is finally focused by the spaced out utterance: 'Not necessarily stoned, but beautiful.'

The muttered vocals show, then, a comparability with Hendrix's essentially rhythmic guitar style. To quote Greil Marcus, the 'words are sounds we can feel before they are statements to understand' (quoted in Frith 1978: 176). While it is difficult to describe verbally the aural quality of the rhythmic delivery and the sensuality in the vocal style, the overall effect is to give an underlying rhythmic weight to the content of the words and as such there is a parallel with the blues where repetitive lines are coloured by inflection to impart an underlying expressive tension.

Like their close contemporaries, Cream, the Jimi Hendrix Experience show a development of blues resources, and while both Clapton's and Hendrix's guitar styles show the influence of B. B. King there is nevertheless a difference in delivery—'where Clapton played with attack and tension, Hendrix tended to take his time and stay relaxed' (Gillett 1983: 385), relying more on electronic effects to create the effect of raw energy. At the same time, contemporary reviews of the two guitarists were curiously similar. 'Hendrix: Progressive and beautiful in his ideas': 'Clapton: Progressing with ideas and techniques' (*Melody Maker*, June 1967). As such it would appear that the concept of progressiveness was strongly determined by the way in which the two musicians could take on the basic resources of the blues and produce new and unexpected developments. As Zappa said at the time: 'If you want to come up with a singular, most important trend in this new music, I think it has to be something like: it is original, composed by the people who perform it, created by them.'

Appendix: The Technology of Fuzz

The 'fuzz' effect, so important in Hendrix's music, is effectively a severe distortion. The first deliberate distortion of this type was produced in the mid-1960s by damaging the speaker cones of an amplifier system. This meant they could no longer give a true response and thus introduced some distortion. The first properly controlled fuzz was produced in much the same way as it is today, except that valves were used rather than transistors. The input signal from the guitar is greatly amplified to push the signal level above the supply voltage. As this is not possible, the signal becomes saturated at the supply voltage level. This has the effect of clipping the top of the wave form to produce the distortion (see Figure 11.1).

This effect was used by rock musicians to produce an 'aggressive' quality through the introduction of many high frequency harmonics. Naturally produced sound waves have only a few harmonics, but these 'clipped' waves have many, especially at a high level and this is what gives off the piercingly painful effect. Natural guitar sounds at loud volume are not nearly so painful to listen to, and hence far less aggressive.

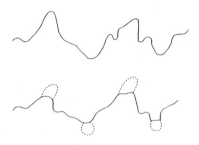

Figure 11.1

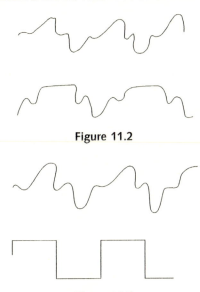

Figure 11.2

Figure 11.3

Hendrix took this use of fuzz much further by using amplifiers with a much higher gain. This meant that most of the signal was clipped, leaving only the bass part (see Figure 11.2). This greatly increased the effect by making the signal much harsher. At times he also used extremely high-gain fuzz which left practically none of the original signal and the output was similar to a square wave (Figure 11.3). It is probable that Hendrix later used transistors in his fuzz box. These have much higher gain than valves as they saturate faster, giving very square cut-offs as opposed to valves which tend to saturate more slowly, thus giving a more rounded and softer fuzz.

References

Brown, H., and Pearce, D. (1978). *Jimi Hendrix* (London).

Fort, J. (1969). *The Pleasure Seekers: The Drug Crisis, Youth and Society* (New York).

Frith, S. (1978). *The Sociology of Rock* (London).

Gillett, C. (1983). *The Sound of the City*, rev. edn. (London).

Mellers, W. (1973). *Twilight of the Gods* (London).

Middleton, R., and Muncie, J. (1981). 'Pop culture, pop music and post-war youth: countercultures', in *Politics, Ideology and Popular Culture (1) (Popular Culture, Unit 20)* (Milton Keynes).

Pidgeon, J. (1976). *Eric Clapton* (London).

Willis, P. (1978). 'The Creative Age', *Profane Culture* (London).

12

....

'The Hieroglyphics of Love': The Torch Singers and Interpretation

JOHN MOORE

The first law of love is subjective: subjectively, jealousy is deeper than love, it contains love's truth. This is because jealousy goes further in the apprehension and interpretation of signs. It is the designation of love, its finality. Indeed, it is inevitable that the signs of a loved person, once we 'explicate' them, should be revealed as deceptive: addressed to us, they nonetheless express worlds which exclude us and which the beloved will not and cannot make us know . . . Love's signs . . . are deceptive signs which can be addressed to us only by concealing what they express: the origin of unknown worlds, of unknown actions and thoughts which give them a meaning. They do not excite superficial, nervous exaltation, but the suffering of a deeper exploration. The beloved's lies are the hieroglyphics of love. The interpreter of love's signs is necessarily the interpreter of lies. His fate is expressed in the motto: to love without being loved. (Deleuze 1973)

The origins of the term 'torch singer' remain obscure. Several partisan writers have claimed the term was coined to describe their particular favourite, but with no historical evidence to support their contentions.[1] Whatever its source, however, several facts regarding torch singers and torch songs are incontrovertible.

The torch song's origins are readily apparent. The song 'Mon Homme' caused a sensation in France just after the first World War. With English lyrics adapted by Channing Pollock, 'My Man' became an instant success in America when presented by Fanny Brice in the 1921 edition of the Ziegfeld Follies,

---

[1] Contemporary observers were at a loss to ascertain the provenance of the term. One critic, for example, introduces his résumé of the topic with the words: 'Another innovation was called, for whatever reason, "torch singing"' (Sullivan 1935: 485). Marjorie Farnsworth (1956: 119) claims that Helen Morgan was 'the girl for whom the name "blues-" or "torch-singer" was created'. Ronald L. Davis (1981: 329) calls Morgan 'the queen of the torch singers'. Roger D. Kinkle (1974: iii. 861, 1307) describes her as the 'prime example' of the 'popular image' of the torch singer, and yet calls Libby Holman 'the epitome of the torch singer'.

and provided the formula for the torch song. To appreciate the significance of this formula, the contemporary circumstances of the music publishing industry must be understood.

During the nineteenth century, a semi-monopoly in sheet music publication had been created by a cluster of corporations centred on New York's Union Square. Until the end of the century, it was almost impossible for a composer to publish his music elsewhere. The flaw in Union Square's monopolistic practices resided in the fact that each company contracted with independent songwriters, and then possessed exclusive rights to market the material composed by the latter. While this eliminated competition, it also made companies reliant on the vagaries of the composers' creativity, and thus was not regarded as uniformly productive. At the turn of the century, some renegade firms took advantage of this flaw by converting songwriters into employees who composed on company premises, and whose continued employment depended on a constant creative flow. These firms centred on New York's Twenty-Eighth Avenue, which was nicknamed Tin Pan Alley after the sound of the partly muffled pianos upon which employees, under the constraint of continual production, composed songs with an inevitably standardized format. Tin Pan Alley replaced the 'inefficient' production procedures of Union Square with composition methods analogous to the assembly lines developed contemporaneously in other American industries. And in the process, it formed and discovered several skilled songwriters, who proceeded to lucrative careers on Broadway, but continued to work within the standard styles and formulas developed by the Alley. But in breaking Union Square's monopoly, Tin Pan Alley evolved its own monopolistic practices. During the 1920s, when torch songs were popular, the industry was in its phase of maximum growth. While, by the outbreak of the First World War, 'Tin Pan Alley had become a well organised, efficient factory, capable of producing songs on every conceivable subject on an assembly belt', by 1930 this monopoly had been swallowed up by even bigger monopolies created by movie, radio, and gramophone conglomerates.[2] The torch song formula, therefore, should not be regarded so much as a tradition, as a manufactured commodity, mass produced by an industry that initiated assembly line procedures to facilitate massive increases in productivity and profit, and employed composers to write songs that combined a standardized form and content with sufficient novelty to appeal to certain consumers. The fact that the torch singers, rather than merely promulgating

---

[2] Ewen 1957: 29. On Tin Pan Alley, see pp. 164–209.

these products, converted them into areas of contestation, and used the lyrics as instruments with which to probe power relations, remains central to their historical significance.

In terms of lyrical content, a torch song can be characterized as a lament sung by a woman who desperately loves a commonplace or even brutish man. The latter treats her badly, leaves her or no longer cares for her. Occasionally, he ignores or rebuffs her tentative advances. And yet she remains inexplicably enslaved to him. In short, a torch song is an elegy to unrequited or no longer requited love. Its concerns are entirely romantic, and do not include the earthiness or playful eroticism of contemporary blues lyrics.

And yet, particularly in their formal aspects, there are distinctly blues elements in torch songs. Generally, the latter remain within the parameters of Tin Pan Alley's standardized forms: 'The mature style of Tin Pan Alley . . . drew its formal structures from earlier generations of popular song writers in America, and its harmonic and melodic language from Western European classical music, particularly the German, Russian, and French composers of the second half of the nineteenth century and the very first years of the twentieth.' But many torch songs sound bluesy because, like other Alley products, they incorporate 'rhythmic patterns originating in ragtime' and 'the syncopated dance music played by early black jazz bands' (Hamm 1979: 372). The relationship between torch songs and the blues, however, remains deceptively complex. Objectively, the two traditions remained separate throughout the 1920s. Female blues singers were black, and their material was composed by and for Afro-Americans. In contrast, torch singers were white, and their material was composed by Tin Pan Alley songwriters for a particular stratum of white society. But, to complicate matters, what contemporary white mainstream discourse designated as blues or jazz could in fact refer to many types of music, from race records through to some Tin Pan Alley products. Because the Alley incorporated elements from black music into its compositions, no distinction was made between the different styles. Reviewers, for example, suggested that the torch singer Libby Holman possessed 'a remarkable blues voice', performed 'Coon songs', and was the 'Queen of the Blues' (Bradshaw 1985: 74, 68). This may not be surprising, given that Bessie Smith, whose performances she had attended, was a 'passion' for Holman, and that Ethel Waters, whom she saw perform frequently, had been a longstanding 'idol' for the torch singer (Bradshaw 1985: 53, 63). But, to cloud the issue even further, many torch songs were to be incorporated into the blues canon during the 1930s when they were widely performed and recorded by Billie Holiday.

But the relations between the two traditions extend beyond mere formal concerns into a whole series of issues which imperceptibly merge into one another. Foremost, at least in the minds of many white contemporaries, must have been the shared exoticism. This aspect of the response to black cultural insurgency remains outside the main focus of the present article. But it remains central to any examination of the torch singers, who were exotic in at least three respects: in terms of visual appearance, vocal production, and musical accompaniment. And in each case, the exoticism was characterized by a radical ambiguity.

Visually, the torch singers are linked through images of urban sophistication. These images—projected by the singers on stage and constructed for them in promotional material—are deliberately contrived to convey the impression that these women are urbane, worldly-wise, but hence rather world-weary, and possessing a deep sadness edging toward despair. But even in this condition there remains a hint of narcissism which suggests that in some way they are rather enjoying their emotional agonies. Certain characteristic images stay in the mind because they capture this state so poignantly. A full-length photograph of Fanny Brice shows her with her head tilted back, her chin pointing to the camera, her left hand clutched to the top of her head, her face (with her eyes directed at the viewer) a picture of despair. And yet the angle from which the photo is taken, with the right side of Brice's torso toward the lens, brings out a deliberately voluptuous curve, which is accentuated by a slight bending of the right knee. These two aspects of the shot mutually contradict, and yet simultaneously confirm each other. Similarly, a promotion portrait photograph depicts Libby Holman in profile, posing with a cigarette in her right hand. Again, the head is slightly tilted back and Holman is pouting mistily upward. But the effect remains the same: the subject appears lost in the smoke supposedly emanating from the tip of the cigarette, but she is simultaneously aware of the regard she is receiving, and pleased with this attention. Alternatively, there is the typical Helen Morgan pose. She often appears in a plain, low-cut black evening dress, offset by a simple string of pearls and her raven hair, aptly described as having the appearance of a mop of chrysanthemums.[3] Her performance trademark was, attired thus, to perch on a grand piano and sing torch songs with only a pianist for accompaniment, all the while nervously twisting a black silk handkerchief in her

[3] The comparison appears in Farnsworth 1956: 118. Although in their early to mid-twenties, the torch singers projected images of a greater maturity than their Flapper counterparts, with their contrived teenage (or collegiate) look. All of the former had fashionably short hair, but none had the classic Flapper bob.

**Figure 12.1 Fanny Brice
(from *Ziegfeld* by
Charles Higham)**

hands. The handkerchief, of course, provides the finishing touch: it sub-
liminally hints at the self-consciousness that remains characteristic of the
torch singers' visual appearance.

But apart from such poses and gesticulations, these performers were also
linked through an exoticism even more intimately bound up with their persons. This exoticism was derived directly from their features. Fanny Brice was
a Jewess, which was no doubt exotic enough for many white Americans,

Figure 12.2 Libby
Holman (UPI/Bettmann
Newsphotos)

particularly the wealthy, given the striking otherness of the contemporary
Jewish ghetto in New York. But photographs suggest that her image alone
was not sufficient to identify her ethnicity. To a certain extent, she remained
difficult to place with any precision, yet evidently exuded an aura of exoticism. And this aura was even more pronounced in other torch singers. Helen
Morgan came from Irish-American stock, but was brought up in Canada,
and started singing French-Canadian folksongs in the French quarter of
Toronto at the age of twelve. Perhaps this Gallic connection accounts for her
exoticism. But, anyway, she was often thought to be a mulatto, a mistaken
identification that no doubt contributed to her landing the role of Julie in
Showboat, the innovative stage musical which tackled the theme of misce-
genation. Playing a stage mulatto in a hit show probably increased the
identification for the public, particularly when Noel Coward then wrote a song
entitled 'Half-Caste Woman' especially for her. But in Libby Holman's case, the

Figure 12.3 Helen Morgan (Universal Studios. Photograph courtesy New York Public Library)

identification was even more explicit. Although of German-Jewish parentage, she was teased at school for her 'Moorish blood'. Many critics made comparisons between her and Ethel Waters, not only in terms of their voices, but also their skin colour. She was offered the lead role in an all-black musical because the producers were convinced that she could pass for black. She performed what critics called 'Coon songs' at the Apollo Theatre in Harlem. In *The Little Show*, she played a high-yellow prostitute almost raped and beaten up for hiding part of her earnings from her pimp. Reviewers referred to her with adjectives like 'Creolesque', 'dusky', 'sultry', and described her as a 'dark-eyed houri'. And she often played up to this identification. One

Figure 12.4 Helen Morgan (from *Ziegfeld* by Charles Higham)

**Figure 12.5 Libby
Holman**

of many tinted or underexposed monochrome photographs is inscribed: 'To
Amy, my *white* sister.' And she reportedly told columnist Walter Winchell that
'Her primary passion was the blues song, which, for Libby, symbolized the
pain and hope of the entire colored race'.[4]

The exoticism inherent, or perceived, in many torch singers' features was
enhanced by cosmetics and costuming. Libby Holman, for example, posed
for a publicity shot wearing Chinese silk embroidered pyjamas, and elsewhere
wore make-up which gave her eyes a distinctly oriental slantedness, her hair
frizzed and lacquered into an imitation conked Afro style.[5] This personal exoticism was frequently reinforced by musical accompaniment. On stage, many

---

[4] On Morgan, see Maxwell 1974, *passim*. On Holman, see Bradshaw 1985: 28, 63, 71, 73, 74. The inscribed
photograph is reproduced on p. 130.

[5] See photographs reproduced in Bradshaw 1985: 129, 133.

torch singers performed merely with a jazz pianist, though even this was something of an innovation at the time. But on record, they often employed a variety of accompanists.

Documentary evidence to indicate how much control individual artists maintained over the presentation of material in stage and recording contexts remains singularly lacking. But the recordings themselves testify to the amount of thought invested in the production of a single number. The styles of musical accompaniment preserved on record are enormously diverse. Helen Morgan's accompaniments are invariably in the conventional European-derived romantic ballad mode. But Lee Morse used white jazz musicians, including high calibre players such as Benny Goodman and Tommy Dorsey, to provide a more syncopated accompaniment. And Libby Holman's basically conventional orchestration not only incorporated jazz syncopation, but an entire range of exotic instruments (e.g., banjos and Hawaiian guitars) and effects (stylized musical phrases designed to evoke images of exotic 'primitivism': the rhythm of Arabian caravans or Amerindian wardrums, the melody of an Indian snake charmer's pipe, and so on). Taken as an entirety, these accompaniments constitute a collage of diverse musical elements, a combination of supposedly primitive musical cultures (Afro-American, Amerindian, Arabian, Oriental, Pacific Islanders) with the sophistication of the European. Such a blend would necessarily incorporate a potent affect in a post-War America at the peak of its insularity and isolationism.

But the musical accompaniment's exoticism is complemented and reinforced by the singularity of most torch singers' vocal performances. Unlike their contemporaries, the Flapper singers, with their cute baby voices and spirited up-tempo numbers, the torch singers were characterized by their deep voices and doleful songs. Recordings indicate that the latter performers possessed substantial vocal ranges. Their normal registers were very low for women, and contemporary critics most frequently described their voices as throaty or husky. However, torch songs are characterized by trilling climbs up the octaves from the lowest through to a piercingly high register. As this style remains absent from early recordings of 'My Man', its exotic origins can perhaps be traced to Lee Morse, who during the mid-1920s developed the practice of 'whooping', which sounds like a cross between yelping and (most significantly) Tyrolean yodelling. The yodel's alternation between a low masculine register and falsetto may well have fed directly into the torch song style. The ensuing quavering effect provides a sense of trembling appropriate to the genre's lyrical content, and reinforces the despairing vocal tone. But exotic elements other than the Tyrolean were also deliberately incorporated into vocal style. The critic Brooks Atkinson referred to 'the dark purple menace of Libby Holman in the blues,' (Perry 1983: p. vii) and the singer herself explained her vocal technique:

What I'm singing is always a very present thing. It's here, it's now, it's what's happening at the moment. That's what makes my songs so vital. When I sing, I never spare my vocal chords. My singing is like Flamenco. Sometimes, it's purposefully hideous. I try to convey anguish, anger, tragedy, passion. When you're expressing emotions like these, you cannot have a pure tone. (Bradshaw 1985: 92)

And Walter Winchell referred to the torch singers as:

those female Troubadours with voices of smoke and tears, who moan and keen love's labours lost in the rhythm and boom of the Roaring Twenties. (Bradshaw 1985: 73)

Visually, vocally, and in the overall recorded sound, the image projected by or for torch singers was unmistakably exotic. Moreover, in the crucial registers of race and gender, these images contained a radical ambivalence. Were these women white, black, mulatto, creole, or from some other mysterious ethnic group? And what did that combination of low and high octaves indicate about their sexuality? These ambiguities were fascinating, and necessarily implied a highly-charged erotic interest for both men and women. The female response will be considered later, but the male response can be gauged from the remarks of Whitney Bolton in his column in the New York *Herald Tribune*. 'The newest of the ladies who croon forlornly from husky, stirring throats is Miss Libby Holman. The possibility that some may be confused by the expression [torch singer] demands an explanation. The carrying of a torch means that a person is miserable because a still adored lover has deserted, leaving one desolate and brokenhearted.' Bolton is unfamiliar with the work of this particular singer, and is informed that:

Miss Holman had been the pet of the disco record set [*sic!*] for months. It seems she had made a series of torch-song records for phonograph reproduction and that her thrilling plaints are bringing life to remote villages.
    She becomes, therefore, one of the treasured sisterhood that has been my solace for countless weeks. The first of these to coo miseries in a provocative key was Miss Ruth Etting. I burned sacred oil there with undivided allegiance until Miss Helen Morgan began to hum the throaty 'Can't Help Lovin' Dat Man of Mine'. The third chauntress to join the purling group was Miss Helen Kane, whose torches were more

vigorous and less dolesome than the Etting and Morgan flambeaux. Now, there is a fourth—come to titillate Broadway with enticing murmurs of dejection, sad, but ravishing whispers. Maybe an expert forger of jests can make up one about a torch-lit procession.[6]

Beneath the façade of blasé cynicism, the sexual attraction remains easy to discern. The language alone indicates that the fickle columnist is rather ironically enamoured of the whole bunch of singers whose lyrics reveal their devotion to one man.

Direct male intervention in the lives of the torch singers remains important because men controlled the performance contexts (the theatres, radio stations, record companies, and most importantly the night clubs) in which the singers worked, and the production mechanisms for stage and phonographic performance; they also constituted a sizeable part of their audience. The torch singers' spatial coordinates can be specified with some precision. If the prototypical torch song appeared in 1921, these singers were at the peak of their popularity during the last few years of the 1920s. Their performances centred on New York, especially the Broadway area. Although the exact dimensions of the phenomenon are difficult to assess, the biographies of a core of successful performers of this genre illustrate the archetypal pattern of the torch singer's road to success.[7] After preliminary employment for several years in vaudeville, chorus lines, and bit parts, each performer received national recognition through appearances in Broadway musicals and revues, particularly Ziegfeld productions. From these and other shows —including each other's—torch singers extracted apposite numbers and appropriated them for their own uses. This act of appropriation remained central to the creation of a torch singing identity. For if these performers' national recognition as stars of the musical stage—or even as singers of specific torch numbers—was achieved on Broadway, their torch singer identities were established elsewhere.

The daily patterns of their lives were largely determined by the requirements of their audience. During Prohibition, the night life of the typical New York reveller began with a dinner at one of the city's thirty thousand speakeasies, extended through a Broadway show, and continued in one of

---

[6] Bradshaw 1985: 66–7. Another columnist characterized Holman as a singer of 'sullen sex hymns' (ibid. 73). Bolton's implicit reservations about Helen Kane were justified. His libido evidently clouded his judgement. Kane was in the Flapper mould, and by no means a torch singer.

[7] Other than the texts by Bradshaw, Perry, and Maxwell noted above, see Machlin 1980, and Kinkle 1974: ii. 1123 (Libby Holman), iii. 1472–3 (Helen Morgan), ii. 620–1 (Fanny Brice), and ii. 879–80 (Ruth Etting).

the seventy or more night clubs around midnight.[8] The torch singer regularly participated in at least the last two stages of this progression. After performing in a show, she would often proceed to a night club and in the process be transformed from Broadway star to torch singer. The night clubs were often openly or covertly financed by gangsters. Hence, once again precise information about artistes' control over their material and performance format remains scanty. But other relevant aspects of the night club environment are relatively well documented.

Night clubs needed gangster backing, not merely for protection against other mobsters and to forestall police raids for bootleg alcohol, but also for financing. 'The average Broadway place costs twenty-five thousand dollars to start, and fifteen thousand of it has to be in cash . . . The overhead of a first-class place with an ace attraction runs to at least five thousand dollars a week.' Given that 'torch numbers' were one of the great contemporary 'drawing cards', torch singers could command substantial salaries (Durante and Kofoed 1931: 193). Helen Morgan and Libby Holman, for example, received five to six hundred dollars a week at the peak of their careers for cabaret work alone. The clubs, however, could be very profitable concerns for their owners. The Morgan Club, which featured Helen Morgan as its star attraction, had takings of ten thousand dollars on the admittedly exceptional night of New Year's Eve, 1928.

Nonetheless, given the smallness and intimacy characteristic of the night club, and hence its limited clientele, prices—which included substantial cover charges, the cost of meals, and surreptitious liquor—had to be high, and this limited the patrons, for the most part, to a wealthy elite. Other, more down-market establishments catered to those with smaller pockets, but these were not the places where the top-flight torch singers performed. The elite clientele consisted of socialites, celebrities, showgirls, top-drawer racketeers, high-class prostitutes, a few intellectuals, and a peppering of the notorious 'butter-and-egg men', out-of-town businessmen on a spree. As Lewis A. Erenberg has demonstrated (Erenberg 1981), within these limited parameters, nightspots provided a context within which barriers between classes, genders, married and unmarried women, and even ethnic groups were lowered. Nevertheless, whatever their fields of endeavour, the majority of patrons came from an elite, whether it be of stage, society or the underworld. And, with only a

---

[8] On the shape of the reveller's night life, see Morris 1951: 326 and 317–37 *passim*. Morris's retrospective reconstruction should be compared with F. Scott Fitzgerald's story 'May Day'.

slight intensification, this group—Café Society—reflected the wider audience
to which the torch singers appealed:

It seems fair to generalize that Tin Pan Alley songs were for white, urban, literate,
middle- and upper-class Americans. They remained practically unknown to large
segments of American Society, including most blacks . . . and the millions of poor,
white, rural Americans. (Hamm 1979: 379)

At one point when Libby Holman was temporarily unemployed, she was
engaged to sing for three weeks at a small honky-tonk, accompanied only
by a pianist. But she was released from her contract after one night, as 'the
audience, most of whom appeared to be truck-drivers and their wives, all
but ignored her' (Bradshaw 1985: 69). Torch singers and their songs were
neither recognized nor popular amongst working class audiences.

Erenberg suggests that for the female members of the audience, night clubs
provided a context for a degree of personal emancipation. But this was not
equally true for women who worked in such environments.

Don't let anyone tell you that the night club is an easy spot for a girl. It's a tough
racket, no matter if she is in the chorus or is an entertainer, cloakroom attendant,
cigarette-girl, or hostess. Every man on the loose figures she is there to be made, and
some have persuasive tongues and pocket-books. It takes a jane with a lot of deter-
mination to keep the chisellers away. (Durante and Kofoed 1931: 58)

The sexual threat must have been even more intense for torch singers, given
the exoticism and fascinating ambivalence of their images, the alluring-
ness of their voices (they were predictably characterized as sirens), and the
response these elements evoked in men like Whitney Bolton.

As a consequence, many women involved in the night club world developed strategies designed to forestall or dispel this concentration of accumulated passion. The most famous example remains the hostess Texas Guinan's
opening address to her male audience, 'Hello, suckers!' This remark was so
effective because it blatantly acknowledged a fundamental truth: namely, that
these patrons were paying excessive amounts for not much at all. But it also
subtly informed the men that she was in on the game, wise to all the tricks,
and hence implied that they had better not try anything unless they really
wanted to be fleeced. This provided her with sufficient space within which
to control the proceedings. But for torch singers circumstances were rather
more complex. For their songs to succeed, they could not afford to project
such strident personalities. However, this essay's concern is not so much with

the ways in which they coped with this environment, as with the response they evoked in their audiences, and the reasons why their songs were so effective in this respect.

Within the club circuit, torch singers were a speciality act. Seeking the rationale for the cabaret's popularity, Durante (ibid. 39, 40) suggests:

> When the sun goes down and the moon comes up, people like to make whoopee. They want to forget they've had a tough day, that the mortgage is due and some time pretty soon they'll be laid out in rosewood boxes with silver handles. These are not pretty thoughts and the only way to wash them away is with plenty of laughs.

And he continues: 'The basis of all whoopee is wine, woman, and song', which provides people with 'the chance to get away from themselves and the dullness of everyday life'. The boredom and meaninglessness of existence within a hierarchical, competitive society constitutes the objective basis for the function of night clubs. The latter provide a context in which alienation is temporarily effaced, rather than confronted. But clearly not all Durante's formulations apply to the torch singers. Their performances—in an intimate setting, amidst an alcoholic haze, and the simplicity of a pianist, his instrument, and a spotlit singer—include all the requisite components of 'whoopee', and yet rather than produce 'plenty of laughs', they created a diametrically opposite effect. In these emotionally charged environments, they warbled their elegies of retrospection and loss, with the result that 'the combination of sentiment, liquor, dim lights, and smoke-filled air was too much for many of the customers and tears rolled down their cheeks'.[9] Why did certain patrons respond so effusively to such performances? And why did they deliberately seek out these performers, rather than confine themselves— as many contemporaries evidently did—to cabarets featuring comedians, song-and-dance men or scantily-clad nubile chorines? In short, other than the elements enunciated above, what were the contemporary bases for the appeal of torch singers and torch songs? These are the questions the remainder of this essay will attempt to answer. For, to create such a response, not occasionally, but regularly, demands more than an appropriate location, a conducive atmosphere and the right material. To evoke such intense reactions, torch singers tapped associations deep within the contemporary American psyche, or rather within the subconscious of a certain sector within American society.

---

[9] Andrist 1970: 171. Other than instances cited elsewhere in this essay, more detailed documentary evidence of audience response remains lacking.

In order to account for this complex phenomenon, approaches to the material will be made from three angles. The first approach examines the connotations of the term 'torch singer' in relation to contemporary psycho-social structures. It aims to examine the principal subconscious motifs of the 1920s as they converge on the torch singer complex. The second approach comprises an explication of the most typical and popular torch song lyrics. And the third approach considers the symbolic value of the torch singers to a contemporary audience—not so much the connotations they unconsciously derived from, as the emotional investments they made in, this figure. Only through such a multiple approach can an adequate understanding of the torch singer phenomenon be attained.

....

In determining the connotations of the torch singer appellation, all concrete and individual details should be dismissed, and a purely abstract figure conjured up by the term alone should be held in mind. Once this abstract picture has been attained, two methods of deriving appropriate connotations are available.

The first connotative method poses a relationship of externality between the torch and its bearer. A torch singer carries a torch—or more precisely a flambeau—for her love. In other words, she loves a man who does not return her love. The act of bearing the flambeau alone, however, elicits specific resonances. Since 1886, in American iconography—and especially in New York, the provenance of torch singing—this image unequivocally suggests the Statue of Liberty. Contemporary critics readily grasped the connection when they rather predictably characterized Libby Holman as 'the Statue of Libby'; one columnist, writing about the musical *Rainbow*, indicated that Holman 'sang a torch that made Liberty's enormous flambeau seem like a charred and whittled match stick' (Bradshaw 1985: 67, 73).

Thus, at a basic subliminal level, the torch singer represents the icon Liberty and hence embodies the political value, liberty. This equation is reinforced by certain of the statue's details. For instance, the statue's sculptor, Bartholdi, modelled Liberty's face after that of his mother, whom he perceived as a victim of the vast political upheavals of nineteenth-century Europe. Thus, 'unlike other representations of liberty, Bartholdi's expresses not only triumph but embittered desire'—a quality eminently appropriate for a torch singer. Moreover, 'with just broken shackles at her feet . . . her grim face the picture of suffering, Bartholdi's *Liberty* is a martyr' (Trachtenberg 1976: 60, 72). Similarly, the torch singer remains a martyr to her love.

But such a simple bi-univocal correlation between Liberty and the torch singers disguises the complexity of the relationship. Even before her unveiling, Liberty constituted a site of contestation on a minimum of three interrelated levels. Firstly, the ideological meaning of the statue remained problematic. Originally designed to symbolize 'international revolution', there were doubts whether it commemorated the bourgeois revolutions of the past or prefigured the proletarian revolutions of the future. Secondly, the connotations of the torch were similarly ambiguous. The statue was originally entitled 'Liberty Enlightening the World', but could be interpreted as a dangerous incendiary as much as a Promethean figure. And, thirdly, uncertainties concerning the significance of the statue for women were voiced. On the one hand, a group of feminists attempted to appropriate the symbol as their own at the unveiling ceremony in 1886. On the other hand, however, as one historian suggests, 'for a fee' Liberty remains 'open to all for entry and exploration from below' (Trachtenberg 1976: 60, 72). The torch singer, iconographically identified with the statue, inherits all the ambivalences of these two eidetic chains. Is she a conservative, an enlightener, and a whore? Or a revolutionary, an incendiary, and a feminist? If she enlightens, whom does she educate and to what ends? If she is a revolutionary, upon whose behalf does she revolt? These questions remain unresolved at this level, and can only find their solutions on another connotative level.

The second connotative method rejects the literalism of its precursor. The torch singer only metaphorically carries a torch. The latter really represents her heart: metaphorically speaking, she is burning with desire, aflame with love. Fire, the source of light and heat, remains the central, linking metaphor. For Gaston Bachelard, fire equals 'one of the principles of universal explanation' (1964: 7). Its basic chemical properties have been overlaid with so many mythological layers that it can be interpreted to mean almost anything. One element in all mythological interpretations of fire remains constant, however: fire and sex are always correlated. In America during the 1920s this metaphorical correlation manifested itself in a specific paradigmatic mode. Politically, this decade represents a period in which revolt was compelled to assume new and startling forms, for two reasons. On the one hand, the repression of domestic dissent during the war and immediate post-bellum years shattered the organized radical movements that had developed over the previous two decades. On the other hand, the sectarian and totalitarian visions which replaced them were ideologically repellent and organizationally sterile. For these and other reasons, the decade represented a hostile environment to many people, especially the young (Mottram 1971: 233–62). Those who sought psychic nourishment and social renewal found little to sustain themselves other than a range of mass produced commodities. Insatiable hunger could not be satisfied with such meagre fare, and the ensuing frustrations bred the urge to revenge at any cost. Through despair, creative activity was replaced by self-immolating nihilism, and one of the decade's central themes was formulated. Due to lack of adequate psycho-social nourishment, many perceived that the only way to destroy constraints and oppressions of all kinds was through self-consumption—through partying, drinking, and any kinds of excess. In a string of metaphorical connections, such people turned in on themselves, hoping to consume the consumer society by consuming themselves. Not surprisingly, the central metaphor for this act was fire. By setting themselves ablaze, they aimed to set society on fire and burn it down. These incendiaries were collectively baptized 'flaming youth'.[10] Bereft of nourishment and hence energy, they literally and symbolically galvanized themselves into activity with illicit alcohol. Alcohol—the liquid that can be set on fire—burns the gullet, blunts moral perceptions, and lights the sexual fires. In the ensuing carnality, male and female members of the 'flaming youth' ignored disparities in power relations between the sexes. The aim was oblivion: an immersion in alcohol and pleasure with the intention of bypassing or overcoming repression by forgetting it. The consequences of such activities were regarded as irrelevant: the point was to overcome inhibitions and achieve an intensity of experience unavailable to others.[11] Any resistance to this hedonistic surge—be it a legitimate complaint regarding disparities of power in sexual relations, divergent emotional priorities, or an actual repression—was automatically condemned and indiscriminately lumped under the debased Freudian rubric of inhibition. The forces of inhibition were conceived as external in origin and assailable through

---

[10] Warner Fabian's best-selling novel *Flaming Youth* (1920) originally coined the term. The book was made into a film in 1923.

[11] Lewis Mumford recreates and analyses the 'flaming youth' mood in his autobiography:
'The 1914 war had left my generation, even those who had taken no active part in it, in a state of shock; the unthinkable had happened, and from now on nothing would be quite unthinkable. As is natural in shock, we withdrew into a dugout of our own making; and as so often has happened in such a compensatory response to the horrors of war, that private retreat set the stage for a public orgy. The conventions and ideals that hitherto had been accepted as a normal and necessary covering for the raw *id* were flung aside as hypocrisies and frauds; no longer rejected merely as ideas, but rejected in practice. All the joys of life were reduced to liquor and sex: drink to the point of anaesthesia, sex to the point of impotence or fretful exhaustion. . . . The immediate moment was what counted: to drink life to the dregs and to pretend that the dregs were particularly to one's liking' (Mumford 1982: 377–8).

an alcoholically-induced lowering of psychic thresholds and a subsequent release of sexual energy.

Within this wider context of unfocused revolt, the position assumed by the torch singers—through their appropriation of torch song materials for their own uses—becomes evident. Although operating within the same mythological region (i.e., sharing the fire imagery) their emphases and methodology remain far more sophisticated than the complementary elements deployed by the 'flaming youth'. Rather than converge on a fixed point of sexual intensity, through their assembled corpus of torch songs they emphasize emotional retrospection. Instead of sublimating disparities in power relations in a shared experience, they stress these inequities and try to analyse their structure and meaning. Rather than shatter externally-imposed restraints, they use torch songs to explore the paradoxes of self-repression. And, as a consequence of these divergences, they pursue the mythological cycle to cathartic ends, postulating an ideologically meaningful life beyond the intense sexual experience advocated by members of the 'flaming youth'. The latter accompanied the cycle from its alcoholic departure point up to the apex of sexual consummation, at which juncture they intimated that further experience remained irrelevant. In contrast, the torch singers insist that the cycle will continue to unfold: alcoholic dissipation will inexorably result in a hangover and lust, transformed into love, will discover loss and sorrow. The liquor which was ignited will be transformed back into liquid in the form of tears, and out of the anguish and yearning elicited by recollection will develop analysis and understanding.

In mythological terms, then, the torch singers reacted to the oversimplifications proposed by the 'flaming youth'. In musical terms, however, they responded to a group of performers who, in a modified form, also participated in the cultural mythos of fire. Although practically contemporaneous with the torch singers, the red hot mamas—performers such as Sophie Tucker and Belle Baker—can in a sense be considered as their precursors. The earthy and physically robust red hot mamas are a phenomenon almost as complex as the torch singers, and cannot be treated in any detail here. But to provide some indication of their characteristics, the lyrics of one red hot mamma song will be examined. Any distortions this analysis accidentally introjects into the interpretation of the mama canon remains regrettable but perhaps inevitable.

In 1930, Sophie Tucker—who was variously billed as 'The Original Red Hot Mama' and as 'The Last of the Red Hot Mamas' (Farnsworth 1956: 163;

Kinkle 1974: iv. 97) during the 1920s—recorded a song entitled 'If Your Kisses Can't Hold the Man You Love'. This particular song becomes relevant in the present context because it deals with the calamity that remains the central torch song subject: abandonment by a lover. Tucker's response to this situation remains diametrically opposite to that of the torch singers. Rather than remain enthralled by her faithless partner, and pursue catharsis and analysis through weeping, she philosophically accepts the situation, as the song's constant refrain suggests: 'If your kisses can't hold the man you love/Then tears won't bring him back.' Instead of brooding on the past, she uses this basic acquiescence as a basis from which to launch alternative sexual activities. In a long recitation, or spoken passage, at the song's centre—a passage all the more daring because it deals with marital infidelity—Tucker lectures the weeping wife:

And what are you crying about?
You might as well be crying for a broken china cup,
'Cause when your red hot papa's steam pipe gets cold,
Cold tears won't heat it up.
And there's nothing like a weeping wife to drive a man from home.
Laugh and the world laughs with you, weep and you sleep alone.

Love is like home cooking, good and wholesome,
But all men like a little piece of mutton on the outside now and then.
And if you find your husband *is* cheating,
Go out and do the same, old dear.
Why he's only giving you the chance you've been waiting for for years.
My goodness, tears won't get you anything—just a shiny red nose.
So come on, paint up, powder up, put on your swellest clothes.
Go out and make whoopee. Men? You'll get 'em by the score.
Neglected wives should worry—that's what God made sailors for.[12]

For Tucker, relationships are based in sexual compatibility. Emotions are a flimsy superstructure built on a sexual infrastructure. And once this compatibility ceases, the entire structure collapses. Desire remains subject to entropic processes. The 'red hod papa's' phallic 'steam pipe' will inevitably cool. Kisses—in other words, sexual activity—can postpone but not halt this dissolution. Tears only accelerate the process. Concomitantly, infidelity

---

[12] Tucker 1982. The line which closes the first part of the quoted passage mordantly parodies the most famous line of the best-selling poet Ella Wheeler Wilcox, who wrote 'Laugh and the world laughs with you, weep and you weep alone'. All transcriptions of lyrics, and hence any errors, are mine.

also remains inevitable. Men may insist upon monogamy, but the entropic nature of love ensures that they will be unable to maintain their resolutions. And this feebleness gives the woman the moral initiative: she now has the excuse to match her partner's infidelity. In fact, she can far surpass his timid philandering by embracing a multiplicity of partners and indulging in the excitements of transient relationships that never sexually decompose because they are too brief for familiarity to develop. Hence, given the sexual basis of relationships, the inevitability of desire's dissolution and infidelity, and the opportunities for augmented sexual activity such decompositions imply, tears and emotional enslavement are inappropriate.

But while the torch singers accept that male desire tends to diminish and hence men are therefore more likely to be unfaithful, they reject any suggestion that relationships are sexually based, and consequently repudiate the proffered sexual opportunities infidelity creates. For them, love remains the basis of any relationship, and any betrayal of this feeling provokes sorrow and anguish, not elation at the prospect of freedom. Through a catharsis of tears they begin the work of interpretation. While the red hot mama remains a sexual butterfly, fluttering from encounter to encounter, enjoying herself but never questioning the order of things, the torch singer broods over a single experience until it yields some significance. She interprets the hiero-glyphics of love.

The torch singers' repudiation of a sexual basis to relationships remained firmly based in an accurate perception of contemporary constructions of male sexuality. While the persona in Tucker's song launched herself into the sea of sexual exploration from a position of strength—she was an experienced woman who had known conjugal love but retained no illusions about men —the inexperienced torch singers are buffeted and almost drowned by men's incessant sexual demands. Figuratively speaking, no man could take advantage of a robust red hot mama. But a fragile torch singer remains an easy victim for predatory male desire.

But before examining the lyrics of the most characteristic torch songs, it is worth noting a certain disparity between the composers and the performers of these pieces—namely, the fact that the former were male, and the latter were female. This inevitably introduces a note of ambiguity into any interpretation of lyrical meaning. Did male composers, for example, merely intend to reinforce notions of monogamy when writing torch songs? Or did the men involved in the production mechanisms—the producers, managers, and agents whose precise degree of influence remains so difficult to reconstruct —impose material that lyrically promoted gender constructions supportive of the status quo? And if so, what are the connotations for the interpretation of the material by performers, and of the torch singer phenomenon by later analysts? Again, lacking any specific documentation on the structure of the interrelations between an artiste and her male associates, these issues remain difficult to resolve. Nevertheless, certain indications suggest that many key songs were not imposed upon passive and helpless performers. Some of the major torch songs were written in collaboration with their singers, or at least with their participation and approval. For example, Libby Holman, dancer Clifton Webb and composer Howard Dietz worked together on 'Moanin' Low', and Dietz 'constantly rearranged and restaged' the song 'Body and Soul' for a dissatisfied Holman, even to the point of writing an entire new set of lyrics at her insistent instigation. Similarly, Jerome Kern and Oscar Hammerstein wrote 'Why Was I Born?' (and other songs) specifically for their close friend, Helen Morgan, who greatly approved their work.[13] Secondly, in the case of many *recorded* torch songs, it remains difficult to determine the definitive lyrical 'text'. Often, lyrics are altered, or modified through phrasing, to achieve quite diverse and delicately nuanced meanings. It remains conceivable that such shadings and re-emphases were multiplied in performance. And, of course, it is precisely through such techniques that torch songs were converted into an area of contestation.

Such contestation remained necessary given the construction of contemporary gender roles and sexuality. In a song with the self-explanatory title 'I'm Good for Nothing but Love', Ruth Etting reveals how constant harassment makes it easy for a woman to a accept men's evaluations of her:

> Try to be sweet, but I'm bound to be molested.
> If I'm discreet nobody is interested.
> They make it plain I'm good for nothing but love.
>
> All eyes keep leering and look wise and sneering
> When I try being just a friend.
> How soon they forget me,
> Right after they've met me,
> And turn away to somebody they respect,
> While I suffer from neglect.

---

[13] On Holman, see Bradshaw 1985: 71, 86; on Morgan, see Maxwell 1974: 97.

Maybe I'm worse than others whose charm is mental
Gee, it's a curse to make people sentimental.
Am I to blame?
I'm good for nothing but love.

Lips pressing me, hands caressing me, arms brushing me,
Seems I'll go mad.
Men winking, I know what they're thinking—
I'm only good to be bad.

(Etting 1980*a*)[14]

The naive yet sophisticated Etting tries to initiate a range of amicable relations with men, but they uniformly ignore or rebuff these invitations to friendship, monotonously insisting that the only possible relationship depends solely on their sensual gratification. When she rejects these advances, they disregard her, yet if she accedes to their demands they spurn her immediately afterwards, preferring women who are not such easy conquests. She is cursed by the capacity to make men feel 'sentimental', and this capacity allows them to persuade her, and eventually convince herself, that she is good for nothing but 'love'. But the love she inadvertently arouses remains debased. This love merely consists of the cynical protestations of men who want to inveigle her into bed. And at this point, the reasons for the torch singers' rejection of sexually based relationships and their deification of love become transparent. True love, no matter with how imperfect a partner, and no matter how gruelling or painful, remains infinitely preferable to becoming the humiliated victim of male sexual strategies.

The truth of this contention can be seen in the original torch song, 'My Man', where Fanny Brice sings of her eponymous hero:

He's not much for looks
And no hero out of books—
He's my man.

Two or three girls has he
That he likes as well as me,
But I love him.

---

[14] The major torch singers recorded all the main torch songs. Hence, there are multiple versions of songs like 'Moanin' Low' and 'Body and Soul'. Some of these different recordings have modified lyrics, but all contain differing accompaniment styles and vocal nuances. My selection of versions is based upon what I consider to be the most characteristic in terms of lyrical content.

I don't know why I should.
He isn't good, he isn't true,
He beats me too—what can I do?

Oh my man I love him so,
He'll never know
All my life is just despair.
I don't care. When he takes me in his arms
The world is bright alright.

And what's the difference if I say I'll go away,
When I know I'll come back on my knees some day?
For no matter what he is, I am his forevermore.

(Brice 1980)

All the essential elements of the torch song are assembled here. Also, the crucial, obsessive question asked by the torch singers receives its initial formulation. Brice's man is not good looking or heroic. He sees other women, does not treat her well, beats her, and does not possess the intelligence to perceive her despair. And yet she loves him: only he can brighten her world, and should she desert him she would soon return, begging him to take her back. The question immediately arises: why does she love him? Her devotion cannot be explained in terms of the torch singers' emphasis on love at the expense of sexual relations, for such a relationship remains as exploitative and degrading as the carnality demanded by predatory men. Yet this kind of devotion remains central to the torch singer identity. A dissatisfied red hot mama would dismiss the incident as a regrettable but not irreparable loss, and pass on to the next candidate. A torch singer, however, tries to extract some significance from the event, to explain a paradoxical act: an act of enslavement where no external constraints are visible.

The urge to achieve a satisfactory explanation pervades Helen Morgan's 'Bill'. Before meeting her eponymous hero, she dreamed of discovering the 'perfect lover', but instead ended up with Bill. In addition to many of the unamiable traits enumerated by Brice, this mediocre individual cannot play sports or sing, is not handsome or grateful, and dresses appallingly. And yet Morgan remains enthralled by him. At one point, out of sheer frustration, she protests: 'Oh, I can't explain why he should be/Just the one man in the world for me.' But eventually, she provides the following formulation: 'I love him because he's wonderful, because he's just my Bill.' In short, part of his attraction lies in his very mundanity. He is, in Morgan's words, just 'an ordinary man' (Morgan n.d. *a*). His very mediocrity allows her to shine in comparison: it gives her the scope in which to express her deepest feelings. While this formulation partly explains the attraction of this type of relationship, it also grossly overestimates the amount of freedom accorded to the female partner. Essentially, the torch singer remains a slave to love, and the helot, already mystified by the lack of visible coercion, cannot explain away her servitude by asserting that she deliberately selected a bland nonentity for a master. When unexpectedly stricken with love for her ordinary man, she does not have a choice. Her dreams of a perfect lover, whom she would have chosen, are replaced by an inexplicable reality: loving enthralment to an undistinguished individual.

'Can't Help Lovin' Dat Man' by Helen Morgan provides a timely corrective to any ideas of feminine free will in these relationships. The song adumbrates two deterministic explanatory grids. On the one hand, Morgan's love for her typically 'lazy', 'slow', and 'crazy' man remains part of the natural order:

> Fish gotta swim, birds gotta fly,
> I got a love that's meant till I die.
> Can't help lovin' dat man of mine.

Love constitutes her mode of locomotion, her way of progressing through life, and will cease with her death. Motion and emotion are inextricably linked, and any divergences from this order are impermissible. On the other hand, however, Morgan proposes a supernatural origin for her love:

> Oh listen sister!
> I love my mister man,
> And I can't tell you why.
> There ain't no reason why I should love that man.
> It must be something that the angels done planned.
>
> (Morgan n.d. *b*)

Rather than genetically programmed, her love remains divinely preordained. In short, in trying to explain the basis of her feelings, she repudiates explanations based around the character of her lover in favour of interpretations which increasingly centre on her personal psychological motivation. This shift in emphasis becomes apparent in the song. While the natural and the supernatural orders appear external, in reality they are nothing other than mental projections of order on the ephemera of perception. The apparent movement from characterological to extrinsic interpretative modes thus actually disguises a shift toward a psychological explanatory grid. When Morgan proclaims that there is 'no reason' why she loves her man, she indicates that explanations based on reason and rationality are inadequate to account for her apparently unwarranted feelings. She thus abandons the rational for the irrational, the conscious for the unconscious.

But before proceeding, the valuable clue this song provides regarding the torch singers' ideological orientations should be noted. Significantly, just as Morgan shifts her attention toward the unconscious, she incidentally discloses the audience at whom torch songs are targeted. The 'sister' she enjoins to listen to her song constitutes one of the sorority of womanhood. Earlier, it became apparent that at a basic subconscious level the torch singer represented the Statue of Liberty, and hence embodied the political value, liberty. Now, the liberty she symbolizes can be clearly identified with the liberty of women. Her torch enlightens her benighted sisters.

In order to gauge the depth and power of her unconscious motivations, the torch singer allows them free reign. In the depths of servitude into which her unconscious impels her, she seeks an explanation for her irrational desires. In 'What Wouldn't I Do for that Man', Ruth Etting releases all inhibitions and discovers a surprising joy in complete degradation:

> Life was blind to me, now it's kind to me,
> Love has opened my eyes.
> Since it came to me, life's a game to me,
> With the sweetest surprise.
>
> I never knew how good it was to be
> A slave to one who means the world to me.
>
> I loved that man from the start
> And way down deep in his heart
> I know he loves me, heaven knows why.
> And when he tells me he can't live without me,
> What wouldn't I do for that man.

> (Etting 1981*a*)

Love, and the servitude it elicits, appears all the more inexplicable because it provokes happiness. Although her man, with all his customary 'faults', remains the object of her affections, it is the love she nurtures within herself that enslaves her. And, furthermore, self-enslavement exhilarates her. Paradoxically, in slavery she discovers kindness and playfulness for the first time. But the mere assertion that she will do anything for her man disguises a subtle shift in power relations. From the beginning, the question posed by the torch singers was: Why do I love a worthless man? Now, the terms of the enquiry are reversed. The relevant question now becomes: Why does he love a worthless woman like me? If love opens her eyes, it also provokes self-deprecation. But this new question remains as unanswerable as its precursor. 'Heaven knows why' he loves her, but as he is 'not an angel or saint', her inarticulate lover remains unable to explain his feelings. The supernatural explanatory grid remains inadequate but again points to a more satisfactory psychological explanation: 'He must be mad to be crazy about me' (Etting 1981*a*). If insanity can account for his feelings, however, it remains insufficient to explain her more complex reactions. While he may love her, he does not experience the paradoxical desire to enslave himself.

Etting failed to discover the reasons for her love because she did not penetrate deep enough into self-deprecation and degradation. In 'I'm Yours' she sinks further into the morass:

> Ask the sky above and ask the earth below
> Why I'm so in love and why I love you so.
> Couldn't tell you though I tried, dear,
> That's why, dear, I'm yours.
>
> When you went away you left a glowing spark.
> Trying to be gay is like whistling in the dark.
> I am only what you make me,
> Come take me, I'm yours.
>
> How happy I would be to beg and borrow
> Or sorrow with you,
> Even though I knew tomorrow
> You'd say we were through.
>
>   (Etting 1981*b*)

Initially, Etting rehearses the by now familiar arguments concerning the inadequacy of the supernatural ('sky') and natural ('earth') grids in explaining her love. To compensate for this insufficiency, she makes a positive virtue out of inexplicability and proposes this as the impetus for her love. Beneath this conscious interpretation, however, unconscious tendencies impel her toward further degradation and thus nearer to an adequate explanation. The image of the 'glowing spark', a clear visual representation of the torch singer's flambeau, presages a more vital, psychological interpretation. If slavery provokes a surprising joy, this happiness remains dependent on the continued presence of the master. Should the latter abandon his slave, she would be heartbroken. Sorrow shared with her master remains happiness, but intimations of sorrow in and because of abandonment starkly prefigure the agony of separation. Realization of this fact provokes further dependence. Etting no longer retains any autonomy. Her entire being can be moulded by her man: 'I am only what you make me.' Furthermore, this truly slavish dependence makes separation rather than love appear predestined. And this sense of predestination, in turn, increases her dependence: even knowing he will leave her tomorrow, she will do anything for him today.

In the inevitable ensuing break-up, the theme of predestined love again arises, but this time it forms the basis for a wider pessimism. In 'Why Was I Born?' a despairing Libby Holman sings:

Why was I born? Why am I living?
What do I get? What am I giving?
Why do I want a thing I daren't hope for?
What can I hope for? I wish I knew.
Why do I try to draw you near me?
Why do I cry? You never hear me.
I'm a poor fool, but what can I do?
Why was I born to love you?

(Holman 1978)

An initial enquiry into the aleatoric nature of love produces a proliferation of existential questionings, which in the long term can only prefigure a transvaluation of values. But in the short term, the fact that Holman has been reduced to tears constitutes the most important element. The act of weeping signifies that her journey through degradation has reached its nadir: joy, transformed into sadness, becomes suffering.

The torch singer loses her lover, and a thousand existential questionings crowd her mind. In the process, however, the original question becomes irrelevant and is lost. It no longer matters why she loved her mediocre man while he was there: all that matters is that she loves him now he has gone. In 'Body and Soul', perhaps the quintessential torch song, Ruth Etting transforms the nihilistic questioning of 'Why Was I Born?' into a paradoxical affirmation of female integrity:

I'm lost in the dark,
Where is the spark for my love?
I'm lost in the night,
Holding the light of my love.

The heavens opened and closed,
As well I might have supposed,
And I am lost in this abandon
So far removed from all I had planned on.

My days have grown so lonely,
For I have lost my one and only.
My pride has been humbled,
But I am his body and soul.

I was a mere sensation.
My house of cards had no foundation.
Although it has tumbled,
I still am his body and soul.

(Etting 1981*c*)

While the song's opening stanza provides a vital visual image of the torch singer, the second stanza approaches the familiar interpretative grids only to find them transformed by loss. When the god withdraws, the interpretative machinery becomes meaningless or prosaic, and dislocation and rupture replace continuity. Predestination and free will are briefly countenanced, but separation rather than love appears preordained (what she 'might have supposed'), while free will becomes irrelevant in a universe where prediction and planning are impossible. Similarly, the image of the pulsating heavens refers not to the natural or supernatural interpretative grids, but to rainfall and thus metaphorically to the cathartic tears wept by the torch singer. Out of the wreckage of betrayal and loss, however, she manages to retrieve her integrity. The assertion of her love for the absent lover can become a militant affirmation of her integrity because of its very gratuitousness. There can be no necessity in proclaiming one's fealty to a master who has voluntarily decamped. And yet such an assertion creates an ethical victory. For Gilles Deleuze, 'The interpreter of love's signs is necessarily the interpreter of lies. His fate is expressed in the motto: to love without being loved' (1973: 9). This motto eminently expresses the torch singer's predicament. But she transcends this fate, the requirement to interpret lies endlessly, by investing her love in a figure no longer actively involved in her life. She has interpreted the beloved's lies and discovered their deceptive nature. To select another lover would mean merely starting the interpretative cycle all over again. But to assert one unassailable truth about love—the fact that her love survives the agony of loss—transcends the regimen of infinite interpretative repetition.

Paradoxically, such an assertion provides her with a margin of freedom. Through choosing enslavement to an absent master, she becomes free to love, but in a manner that repudiates the fervid interpretation of love's signs. Ruth Etting's 'Easy Come, Easy Go' expresses this tranquil, easy-going approach to love:

> Easy come, easy go,
> That's the way, if love must have its day,
> Then as it came, let it go.
>
> No remorse, no regret,
> We should part exactly as we met,
> Just easy come, easy go.
>
> Love has fooled us, it has cooled us,
> Once it ruled us, but now we're free.
> We'll be happy
> In remembering that we found love easily.
>
> (Etting 1980*b*)

Love's passage through Etting's life does not ruffle her serenity and calm. Her attitude to love remains one of tolerant inevitability: 'if love must have its day', let it pass with the minimum of disruption. If love's signs deceived and hence ruled her, once their deceptive nature becomes apparent the fire engendered by incessant interpretation dies down, and emancipation occurs. Freedom consists in remembering love, not with remorse and regret, but with happiness. Falling in and out of love becomes so painless and frequent that regret remains inappropriate. But affairs of the heart should never be forgotten. Unlike the red hot mamas, who lustily leap from partner to partner, torch singers always emphasize and assimilate the emotional aspects of experience. In a sense, the mamas and the torch singers are complementary: one advocates sexual freedom, while the other recommends liberation from constraining emotions. In the end, however, the torch singers deploy the more incisive methods, for three reasons. First, because they examine the mechanisms of self-imposed enslavement. Second, because they retain an emotional emphasis, and thus do not exclude a vital component of interpersonal experience. And, finally, because they propose an alternative praxis which incorporates their accumulated knowledge. They make an emotional investment in memory, and use this energy to nurture the future.

....

An explication of torch song lyrics reveals many important details but fails to illuminate the essence of the torch song phenomenon. Something intangible escapes any mere assemblage of the lyrical skeleton. This missing component is the mood, which even recordings can only partly recapture, for the mood coalesces on the interface between the songs, with their evocative capabilities, and the audience, who invest both singers and songs with emotional associations which are formulated deep within the contemporary unconscious, and thus are only partly retrievable by later analysis. Nevertheless, to understand the popularity of the torch singers, it remains necessary to try to reconstruct this mood and thus understand what the torch singer phenomenon meant to a contemporary audience.

In *The Golden Day*, Lewis Mumford provides the instruments with which to probe this phenomenon. In his study of pre-Civil War New England culture, he notes that it cannot be accidental that the most sentimental American popular songs originated in the first half of the nineteenth century. Songs such as Stephen Foster's 'Jeanie with the Light Brown Hair' and 'Gentle Annie' are songs of lost love, but their popularity and efficacy in provoking tears was due, not to an epidemic of failed love affairs, but to the contemporary technological depredation of the psycho-social environment. The ante-bellum audience cried, not over lost love, but over a lost way of life. In short, Mumford provides two instruments with which to probe popular musical phenomena (Mumford 1957: 32–3). Firstly, he suggests that on one level a song's lyrics possess no intrinsic importance. Lyrics are signs or indicators that are not necessarily seen to possess any inherent significance, but are to be followed, like signposts. The sign's importance resides in its ability to point to the song's major component: the atmosphere its performance creates. The sign acts as a catchword which automatically provokes an unconscious train of feelings and associations, and which is reinforced by the purely musical aspects of the composition. Secondly, he indicates that the meaning of the atmosphere or mood evoked by the song should be sought, not in the lyrics, but in a wider, socially-derived feeling, which the song reflects, encapsulates, and releases. The key to the torch singer phenomenon thus appears to lie in discovering the social basis of the sadness that torch songs evoked in a contemporary audience.

Before ascertaining the sources of this melancholy, however, it remains necessary to enquire more closely into the characteristics of the torch singer and her audience. While Mumford, with a smaller, more homogeneous nineteenth-century populace as subject, did not need to specify the age, gender, race, and class status of the sentimental song's audience, this becomes imperative given the more complex context in which the torch song developed. The fact that the torch singers' night club audiences were white and mostly middle or upper class remains unimportant at this level. But age and gender differentials are crucial in this instance, and share a common structural organization. Except for Fanny Brice, who was thirty years old in 1926, the torch singers were all in their twenties at the peak of their fame. They spoke primarily to and for the young generation, even though their audiences were composed of adults of varying ages. Similarly, as the injunction in 'Can't Help Lovin' Dat Man' implied, the torch singers primarily addressed the women in the audience, although the sentiments aroused by their performances were shared by members of both sexes. Thus, in accounting for the torch singer phenomenon, it becomes necessary to interpret a message designed to provoke a specific response in women, particularly young women, but which also aroused comparable affects in some men of all ages. In short, the sources of the torch singers' popularity must be sought in an experience shared by all Americans, which affected the young generation especially, and young women in particular. The immediate, facile answer to this enquiry would be the First World War. And, indeed, this holocaust had a profound effect upon the generation who reached maturity during the 1920s. But if the war, with its technological and moral changes, and resulting psycho-social dislocations, provided many reasons to grieve, it cannot in itself account for the popularity of the torch song. The complexity of the message promulgated by the latter indicates the necessity to discover a more satisfactory answer.

The sentimental songs considered by Mumford were sung in a variety of contexts by a range of performers. Consequently, no subconscious associations could be attached to the singers, and because of the songs' relatively straightforward content, the subconscious links forged between the analogous sentiments of lost love and a lost way of life were easily made and relatively unambiguous. In contrast, the torch song phenomenon remains characterized by a pervasive ambiguity. In connotative terms, the torch singers inherited all the ambivalences that inhered in the Statue of Liberty. Their visual and vocal projections were characterized by a fascinating and radical ambiguity in the crucial registers of race and gender. Their songs explored the paradoxical pleasures derived from blithe self-enslavement, often to a mediocre nonentity. The characteristic shifts displayed in this corpus, from loving enslavement through painful separation to liberation, are only undertaken with extreme reluctance. And, furthermore, these shifts result in the ambiguity of a major emotional investment in a partner from whom the torch singer will in all likelihood be permanently separated.

This pervasive ambiguity, however, provides the key to the wider social significance of the torch singer phenomenon. This ambivalence, centred on the interface between interpersonal relations and various psycho-social definitions of liberty, reflects—or rather refracts—the equivocal response to increased sexual freedoms made by middle class youth in the 1920s. Such a response can be seen, for instance, in Lewis Mumford's autobiography. Mumford bemoans that in the post-War years 'all the joys of life were reduced to liquor and sex', a reduction which constitutes the characteristic act of the 'flaming youth' encountered earlier. But almost immediately, he admits that 'the postwar *mores* brought a welcome measure of open-eyed frankness, hitherto conspicuously lacking in both our life and our literature' (Mumford 1982: 377, 379). Similar examples of ambivalent feelings can be found in many other reminiscences and contemporary statements.

The feelings evoked by torch songs are thus much more complex than those aroused by early nineteenth-century sentimental songs. In the latter compositions, the contemporary psyche readily condensed the emotions associated with lost love with those excited by the passing of a way of life through a common concern with unmitigated loss. In the torch song, however, conflicting tendencies within the unconscious simultaneously direct energies into the past, toward the old lover and enslavement, and into the future, toward emotional convalescence and liberty. In the sentimental song, the listener feels unmitigated loss, and cries tears of pure sorrow; in the torch song, the auditor, pulled in opposite directions by ambivalent feelings, cries bittersweet tears. While torch songs could evoke such ambiguous emotions in all who had lived through these years of accelerated sexual change, the reasons for their especial significance for young women now becomes apparent. The latter, supposedly in the vanguard of the movement for sexual liberation, must have felt the conflicts between the longing for sexual and emotional stability, and the desire for emancipation from self-induced affective slavery, in a very acute manner.[15] The torch singers assembled the various components of this dilemma and presented it back to their feminine audience in an intelligible format. In stylized form, their songs encapsulate the wealth of post-War youthful female experience in the affective realm. At every stage in the presentation of this experience, even (or especially) while exploring its most

---

[15] Many of Dorothy Parker's tales from the 1920s focus on precisely this conflict. See Parker 1973, *passim*.

paradoxical aspects, they never ceased to arouse conflicting emotions in their feminine audience. This systematic deployment of emotional ambiguity facilitated the achievement of a specific result. At no point could the female listener comfortably relinquish her critical faculties. The torch singer ensured that her listeners could not become mindless, obedient campfollowers. The contradictory options she presented to her auditors were too divergent and emotionally-charged to allow unthinking acceptance. At every juncture, the listener was impelled to interpret her own feelings and formulate her own strategy. In the end, the torch singer gave her audience a gift—the gift of interpretation. Impelled to interpret her own feelings in terms of the torch singers' experience, she worked through her emotions, learned to evaluate and discriminate, and began to understand some of the psycho-social structures which ordered contemporary sexuality. Through constantly interpreting the 'hieroglyphics of love', she was able to distance herself from overwhelming nostalgic emotions, and for the first time perceive the full extent of love's mosaic.

References

Andrist, R. K. (ed.) (1970). *The American Heritage of the 20s and 30s* (New York).

Bachelard, G. (1964). *The Psychoanalysis of Fire*, trans. C. M. Ross (Boston).

Bradshaw, J. (1985). *Dreams That Money Can Buy: The Tragic Life of Libby Holman* (London).

Davis, R. L. (1981). *A History of Music in American Life*, vol. iii: *The Modern Era: 1920–Present* (Malabar, Fla.).

Deleuze, G. (1973). *Proust and Signs*, trans. R. Howard (London).

Durante, J., and Kofoed, J. (1931). *Night Clubs* (New York).

Erenberg, L. A. (1981). *Steppin' Out: New York Nightlife and the Transformation of American Culture, 1890–1930* (Chicago).

Ewen, D. (1957). *Panorama of American Popular Music* (Englewood Cliffs, NJ).

Farnsworth, M. (1956). *The Ziegfeld Follies* (New York).

Hamm, C. (1979). *Yesterdays: Popular Song in America* (New York).

Kinkle, R. D. (1974). *The Complete Encyclopedia of Popular Music and Jazz, 1900–1950*, 4 vols. (New Rochelle).

Machlin, M. (1980). *Libby* (New York).

Maxwell, G. (1974). *Helen Morgan, Life and Legend* (New York).

Morris, L. (1951). *Incredible New York: High Life and Low Life of the Last Hundred Years* (New York).

Mottram, E. (1971). 'The hostile environment and the survival artist: a note on the twenties', in *The American Novel in the Nineteen Twenties*, ed. M. Bradbury and D. Palmer (London), 233–62.

Mumford, L. (1957). *The Golden Day: A Study in American Literature and Culture* (Boston; first published 1926).

—— (1982). *Sketches from Life: The Autobiography of Lewis Mumford—The Early Years* (New York).

Parker, D. (1973). *The Collected Dorothy Parker*, ed. B. Gill (London).

Perry, H. D. (1983). *Libby Holman: Body and Soul* (Boston).

Sullivan, M. (1935). *Our Times: The United States, 1900–1925*, vol. vi (New York).

Trachtenberg, M. (1976). *The Statue of Liberty* (London).

Discography

Brice, F. (1980). 'My Man', *The Original Torch Singers*, Take Two Records.

Etting, R. (1980a). 'I'm Good for Nothing but Love', *The Original Torch Singers*, Take Two Records.

—— (1980b). 'Easy Come, Easy Go', *The Original Torch Singers*, Take Two Records.

—— (1981a). 'What Wouldn't I Do for that Man', *Ten Cents a Dance*, Living Era.

—— (1981b). 'I'm Yours', *Ten Cents a Dance*, Living Era.

—— (1981c). 'Body and Soul', *Ten Cents a Dance*, Living Era.

Holman, L. (1978). 'Why Was I Born?' *Vintage Libby Holman*, Take Two Records.

Morgan, H. (n.d.a). 'Bill', *Helen Morgan Sings*, Audio Rarities.

—— (n.d.b). 'Can't Help Lovin' Dat Man', *Helen Morgan Sings*, Audio Rarities.

Tucker, S. (1982). 'If Your Kisses Can't Hold the Man you Love', *Flappers, Vamps and Sweet Young Things*, Living Era.

13

Genre, Performance, and Ideology in the Early Songs of Irving Berlin

CHARLES HAMM

Irving Berlin's 200-odd songs written between 1907, the date of the first one, and late 1914, when his first complete show for the musical stage (*Watch Your Step*) opened at New York's Globe Theatre, are virtually identical to one another in their published piano/vocal format. Like other Tin Pan Alley songs of the early twentieth century, most of them consist of a brief piano introduction, a few bars of vamp, then several verses, each followed by a chorus. All are in major keys and most have a tempo marking of moderato. Piano introductions are drawn from either the first or last phrase of the chorus, the vamp anticipates the melodic beginning of the verse, and both verse and chorus are usually made up of four 4-bar phrases in $\frac{4}{4}$ or four 8-bar phrases in other metres.

But despite this apparent homogeneity, publishers advertised these songs under different rubrics and we know from comments by songwriters, journalists and audiences that one song could be perceived in one way and another in quite another way. In other words, various kinds—or genres—of songs were recognized at this time.

Genre and Music

Genre has been a major fascination of literary criticism for much of the twentieth century. The construction of taxonomies based on close textual analysis occupied many scholars of the modern era, while postmodern criticism has

This essay, first presented at the annual meeting of the American Musicological Society in Montreal on 5 November 1993, is dedicated to my friend and one-time colleague Wilfrid Mellers. Though he has not yet written at length about Irving Berlin, his remarks in Mellers (1964), including the observation that '[Berlin's] lyrics and tunes went straight to the hearts of the millions who were like him, except that they lacked his talent' (p. 383), seem to me to capture the essence of Berlin and his world better than any subsequent literature.

tended to deconstruct the process of genre construction itself—that is, to ask *why* the exercise is undertaken, not how—or to emphasize the flexibility and overlap of genres. As Jorge Luis Borges parodies the complexities of genre construction:

> Animals are divided into: (a) belonging to the Emperor, (b) the embalmed, (c) tame, (d) suckling pigs, (e) sirens, (f) fabulous, (g) stray dogs, (h) included in the present classification, (i) frenzied, (j) innumerable, (k) drawn with a very fine camelhair brush, (l) *et cetera*, (m) having just broken the water pitcher, (n) that from a long way off look like flies. (Quoted in Perloff 1989: p. vii)

British and American historical and critical writing on music has tended to ignore genre, though, at least until recently. There is not even an entry for the term in *The New Grove Dictionary of Music and Musicians*, the *New Harvard Dictionary of Music*, or *The New Grove Dictionary of American Music*. But German scholars have been much more concerned with the topic. Carl Dahlhaus, for instance, insists that genre must be approached from the intersection of occasion and technique, or context and text; and since he sees a general weakening of the social role of music from the late nineteenth century onwards, he argues that genre becomes progressively less important in the modern era.[1] Adorno, representing another German intellectual tradition, sees genre formation as a dialectic between Universal and Particular, with deviations generating new forms; 'Universals such as genres . . . are true to the extent that they are subject to a countervailing dynamic', he argues (Adorno 1984: 242; see also Samson 1989: 214).

More recent musicological literature agrees that genre should not be defined by description or analysis of stylistic features alone. In a study of Chopin's Nocturne in G minor, Jeffrey Kallberg contends that while musical analysis may succeed in 'provid[ing] factual information about a term, classify[ing] it, [it] does not explain its meaning . . . [which] must emerge from the context of the term'. Defining genre as a 'communicative concept' through 'the reconstruction of contexts and traditions, and the perceptions of composers and their audiences, both historical and modern', he puts forward the notion of a 'generic contract' between composer and listener. The composer signals his choice of genre by means of title, metre, tempo, or characteristic opening gesture, establishing a context in which '[he] agrees to use some of the conventions, patterns, and gestures of a genre, and the listener consents

---

[1] See Dahlhaus (1967) and Dahlhaus (1983). For an exhaustive bibliography on genre by Dahlhaus and other German scholars, see Kallberg (1988: 258).

to interpret some aspects of the piece in a way conditioned by this genre' (Kallberg 1988: 243). Robert Pascall, discussing the final movement of Brahms's Fourth Symphony, takes four categories of 'generic difference and development' to be 'fundamental and unalienable'; in addition to description and analysis of the music itself ('its diachronic structure, with continuity and development'), one must also take into account performance site, performing forces (the 'instrumentarium') and a definable expressive code (Pascall 1989: 234–5). Jim Samson, exploring the relationships and differences among genre, style, and form, posits that 'the repetition units that define a genre, as opposed to a stylistic norm or a formal schema, extend beyond musical materials into the social domain so that a genre is dependent for its definition on context, function, and community validation and not simply on formal and technical regulations' (Samson 1989: 213).

Underlying most musicological writing on genre is the assumption that both composer and listener have a technical understanding of the genre in question, and a knowledge of relevant social and historical issues, equal to that of the scholar. While it is not my intention here to agree or disagree with this assumption, I will suggest that it is of limited use in dealing with genre in popular music.

Most of the literature on genre in popular music distances itself even more vigorously from dependence on musical factors alone. Franco Fabbri, after objecting that 'in most musicological literature which has tackled the problem of genres . . . formal and technical rules seem to be the only ones taken into consideration, to the point where genre, style and form become synonymous', then offers a definition of genre as 'a set of musical events (real or possible) whose course is governed by a definite set of socially accepted rules' and suggests that semiotic, behavioural, social, ideological, economic, and juridical dimensions must be considered as well (Fabbri 1982: 55–9). Robert Walser argues that 'musical meanings are always grounded socially and historically, and they operate on an ideological field of conflicting interests, institutions, and memories . . . This is a poststructural view of music in that it sees all signification as provisional, and it seeks for no essential truths inherent in structures, regarding all meanings as produced through the interaction of texts and readers . . . Ultimately, musical analysis can be considered credible only if it helps explain the significance of musical activities in particular social contexts' (Walser 1993: 29, 31). Or, even more bluntly: 'the purpose of a genre is to organise the reproduction of a particular ideology' (Walser 1993: 34).

The Flexibility of Genre

Many recent critics emphasize the flexibility of genre. As Jacques Derrida puts it, 'every text participates in one or several genres, there is no genre-less text; there is always a genre and genres, yet such participation never amounts to belonging' (Derrida 1980: 65), and Frederic Jameson agrees: '*Pure* textual exemplifications of a single genre do not exist; and this, not merely because pure manifestations of anything are rare, but . . . because texts always come into being at the intersection of several genres and emerge from the tensions in the latter's multiple force fields' (Jameson 1982: 322). Robert Walser extends this view to popular music: 'Nowhere are genre boundaries more fluid than in popular music. Just as it is impossible to point to a perfectly exemplary Haydn symphony, one that fulfils the "norms" in every respect, pieces within a popular genre rarely correspond slavishly to general criteria. Moreover, musicians are ceaselessly creating new fusions and extensions of popular genres' (Walser 1993: 27).

In setting out to construct a taxonomy of Berlin's early songs,[2] not as an abstract intellectual exercise but as a way of getting at their meaning, I found this concept of flexibility to be absolutely indispensable. The further I proceeded with my taxonomy, the more evident it became that a given song by Berlin could be perceived as belonging to two or more genres, or as lying between several of them. It also became clear that genre was defined more importantly by a song's intended and received meaning that by its compositional style and structure, and that two factors previously disregarded in the literature could be crucial in defining meaning and therefore genre —the identity of a song's protagonist, and performance style.

Genre, Meaning, and Ideology in 'Coon' Songs

Berlin wrote each of his early songs as the expression of some protagonist, whose identity was encoded into the text and music, then projected, clarified, or even changed in the act of performance. To take the most obvious example, any song with an African-American protagonist was immediately recognized by its audience as a 'coon' song. This identity could be established in the text by proper names already associated in popular culture with black characters (Alexander or Liza, for instance), by dialect purporting to represent black speech patterns and usage, by code words ('honey' or 'baby'), or

---

[2] This taxonomy was undertaken in connection with my complete, critical, three-volume edition of Berlin's early songs, *Irving Berlin: Early Songs* (Madison, WI, 1994).

by turns of speech thought to reflect black practice; it could be suggested in the music by syncopated rhythmic patterns or melodic contours supposedly derived from African-American music. This racial identity was further ensured in performance by the singer's use of dialect, whether or not already present in the written text, by the interpolation of spoken dialogue clarifying the ethnicity of the song's characters, and sometimes by make-up, costume, and stage deportment.

The African-American identity of a song's protagonist would then be a key factor in the perception of its meaning. For instance, both text and music of Berlin's 'When The Midnight Choo Choo Leaves for Alabam' (1912) imply a black protagonist:

> When the midnight choo-choo leaves for Alabam'
> I'll be right there. I've got my fare.
> When I see that rusty-haired conductor-man,
> I'll grab him by the collar and I'll holler 'Abraham! Abraham!'
> That's where you stop your train, that brings me back again.
> Down home where I'll remain,
> Where my honey lamb am.
> I will be right there with bells, when that old conductor yells,
> 'All aboard! All aboard! All aboard for Alabam'!'

Hints of 'black' dialect in the text ('honey lamb' and the elision of 'Alabama') and passing suggestions of syncopation in the music may seem subtle clues today, but would have conveyed a clearer message in 1912. Beyond that, this vignette of a black man who has decided to return to his home in the South, and to stay there, takes on a more specific meaning when placed in the context of a racial issue of the day with relevance to the patrons of vaudeville houses in the urban North: resistance to the first mass migration of African-Americans from the South, where they 'belonged' and where they had been happy, at least according to minstrel and 'coon' songs by white songwriters.

'Midnight Choo Choo' is not an isolated song of its sort. Together with dozens of similar pieces, it forms a 'back-to-Dixie' sub-genre of 'coon' song with black protagonists, often identified by even more overt references to their race than in Berlin's song, happily headed South.[3] Any possible ambiguity

---

[3] For instance, the sheet music cover of another song of this type, 'All Aboard for Alabam' (George Mann and Walter Esberger, 1912), shows a black man astride a toy train. Other songs in this sub-genre, which traces its origins all the way back to such mid-nineteenth century minstrel songs as Dan Emmett's 'Dixie's Land' and Stephen Foster's 'Old Folks At Home', include 'I Want to be in Dixie' (Irving Berlin and Ted Snyder, 1912), 'All Aboard for Dixie Land' (Jack Yellen and George L Cobb, 1913), 'I'm Going Back to Carolina (Here Comes My Train, Ding Dong, Toot Toot)' (Billy Davis and Ernie Erdmann, 1913), and 'I Guess I'll Soon be back in Dixieland (Hear the Whistle, Hear the Bell)' (Jack Rogers and Will Rossiter, 1915).

of racial identity is dispelled by period recordings, for instance the performance of Berlin's 'Midnight Choo-Choo' by Arthur Collins and Byron Harlan
(Indestructible Columbia Cylinder 3289, recorded in September 1912) in
which the two singers assume broad 'Negro' accents and interpolate 'comic'
dialogue unequivocally intended to designate African-American characters.[4]
However, if 'Midnight Choo-Choo' is performed in such a way that the
race of the protagonist is changed or obscured, as in the performance by Fred
Astaire and Judy Garland in the film *Easter Parade* (1958) or as recorded by
Max Morath on *Irving Berlin: The Ragtime Years* (Nonesuch Records), the song's
meaning, and thus its genre, is altered. No longer a 'coon' song, it now shares
characteristics of two other genres, the ragtime song and the rustic ballad,
the latter a favourite of such songwriters as Charles K. Harris and Paul Dresser,
featuring a protagonist who is nostalgic for his or her childhood home in
Indiana or Virginia or Michigan or New Hampshire or wherever.

In a tradition of the popular stage going back to the early nineteenth
century, textual references to 'serious' literature or musical references to
the classical repertory can be comical touches if the protagonist of a song is
lowerclass and ethnic. The resulting satire is double-edged: the protagonist
is mocked for his or her pretensions to elite culture, which is itself mocked
for the benefit of the working-class audiences of the popular theatre through
parody by an unlettered protagonist. The intended meaning of Berlin's 'That
Mesmerizing Mendelssohn Tune' (1909) revolves around the appropriation
of the melody of Mendelssohn's 'Spring Song' by a black protagonist:

> Don't you stand there, honey, can't you hear me sighin'?
> Is you gwine to wait until I'm almost dyin'?
> Ummm! Ummm! Oh, that Mendelssohn Spring Song tune:
> Get yourself acquainted with some real live wooin'.
> Make some funny noises like there's something doin'.
> Ummm! Ummm! Oh, that Mendelssohn tune . . .

The identity of the protagonist is unequivocal in a period recording by Arthur
Collins and Byron Harlan (Columbia A801, Mx. 4328-2, January 1910). But
this point is lost and the meaning, genre, and ideology of the song are
changed if it is performed so that 'black' dialect disappears, sections of
the text with overt reference to the racial identity of the protagonist are

---

[4] 'Gee, I'm Glad that I'm from Dixie' from the revue *Shuffle Along* by Noble Sissle and Eubie Blake, available
on *Shuffle Along* (New World Records NW 260, 1976), is a recent reissue of a 'back-to-Dixie' song.

omitted, and voice production invokes only 'white' performing traditions.[5] The song becomes a romantic ballad, with the quotation from Mendelssohn serving to suggest a 'refined' protagonist.

The 'Suggestive Song': Performance and Ideology

In a number of Berlin's early songs, protagonists are members of the bourgeoisie or elite classes, and they engage in drinking, smoking, gambling, adultery, premarital sex, and other acts contrary to the dominant public morality of the day. The identification of these protagonists as white and privileged, made clear by their British-American names, their activities and occupations, their manner of speech, and the absence of ethnic tinges in the music, is crucial to their meaning.

In the Victorian era, songs dealing with socially unacceptable behaviour followed one of two scenarios: either the moral transgression was condemned and punished, as in 'A Bird in a Gilded Cage' (1902) by Arthur J. Lamb and Harry von Tilzer, in which a young woman's greed in marrying a much older man for his money, rather than for love, brings her isolation and death; or the protagonist was a member of a lower-class, ethnic group, as in Hughie Cannon's 'Bill Bailey, Won't You Please Come Home' (1902), a tale of marital strife and separation in an African-American family. But Berlin's protagonists, as noted above, belong to America's privileged classes, and these songs, humorous rather than tragic, are thus socially subversive.

Most popular songs of the Victorian era, written to be sung in the bourgeois parlour, had a didactic as well as an artistic function: their texts urged their well-to-do performers and listeners 'to work hard, to postpone gratification, to repress themselves sexually, to "improve" themselves, to be sober [and] conscientious' (Howe 1976: 17). But Berlin was not a product of American Victorianism. A member of an immigrant family struggling to rise above poverty, forced to take to the streets to earn pennies while still a child, he began singing ribald parodies of popular songs in bars and restaurants. When he began writing his own songs, it was from the perspective of the people he had known in New York's streets and working-class places of amusement, for whom the privileged classes were a fair target.

In 'Call Me up Some Rainy Afternoon' (1910), for instance, Nellie Green meets Harry Lee at a masquerade party and promptly invites him to drop

---

[5] As in Joan Morris and William Bolcom, *Blue Skies: Songs by Irving Berlin* (Nonesuch Digital 9 79120-1 F, 1985).

by her house for a 'quiet little spoon'. When he shows up one afternoon, he overhears her giving an even warmer invitation to another man, and also learns that promiscuity is a way of life in her family, and by implication her social circle:

> Call around tomorrow night,
> We can then put out that fire in the furnace . . .
> My Mama will sure be out of town,
> She'll be entertained by Mr Brown,
> My Papa won't be round,
> He will call on Mrs Brown . . .

The singer has a double task in projecting the intended meaning of this song: to make it clear through diction, voice quality, and demeanour that Nellie is white and from a privileged class, and also to leave no doubt about the nature of the 'fire in the furnace' she intends to put out.[6]

Publishers, songwriters, and audiences recognized a genre known as the high-class ballad, exemplified by such classics as 'The Rosary' (1898) by Ethelbert Nevin and 'I Love You Truly' (1906) by Carry Jacobs-Bond. Berlin wrote a handful of such songs, marked by sentimental and chaste texts and somewhat pretentious harmonic and melodic language. As with other genres, the high-class ballad was defined not only by its text and music, but by performance, with 'cultured' diction and vocal production stressing precise pitch and a voice quality invoking the concert or recital rather than the vaudeville stage.[7] But many of Berlin's other ballads, among them 'Stop, Stop, Stop (Come Over and Love Me Some More)' (1910) were intended to be teasing, playful, and provocative, and in fact belong among his 'suggestive' songs.

> Cuddle and squeeze me honey,
> Lead me right to cupid's door,
> Take me out upon that ocean called the 'Lovable Sea',
> Fry each kiss in honey, then present it to me—
> Cuddle and please me honey,
> Anchor at this kissing shore;
> My honey stop, stop, stop, stop, don't dare to stop,
> Come over and love me some more.

---

[6] Ada Jones accomplishes this in a recording of the song made in June of 1910, released on Victor 16058-B.
[7] Henry Burr's recording of Berlin's 'When I Lost You' (Victor 17313-B, 1912) illustrates this style of 'high-class' performance.

The challenge for the singer is to make it clear that this song is neither a sentimental ballad nor an ethnic song, by projecting a protagonist who has more in mind than cuddling and kissing, yet is white and privileged. Elida Morris does this by singing with considerable rhythmic and melodic freedom, though still in a somewhat 'cultivated' style, and speaking the key words 'Stop, stop, stop . . .' in an obviously provocative way.[8]

The subversive nature of such songs did not go unnoticed by public defenders of America's morals, who attacked them in the press and from the pulpit, and succeeded in getting them banned in Boston. As one journalist indignantly put it, 'suggestive songs'

laugh openly at the sacred institutions of marriage [and] frankly praise and encourage the faithlessness and deceit practised by . . . friend, husband or wife. What has come over us anyhow? Decent women and girls with their men folks sit in theatres and applaud vociferously, amid their boisterous laughter, some singer who with well-studied indecency proceeds to gush forth songs of the most vulgar and immoral character . . . If I had my way I would appoint a rigorous censorship upon all so-called 'popular song', and make it a criminal offense to publish such songs as I have mentioned.[9]

Performance and Genre in Ragtime Songs

The role of the performer was crucial in shaping the genre of 'ragtime' song. One writer remarked in 1916 that 'now, everything that carries the jerky meter, or an irregular meter that possesses a pleasing lilt, is called ragtime' (Wickes 1916: 33). Ragtime manuals demonstrate how popular and classical pieces could be played in ragtime style, and Wickes observes that 'a clever pianist can "rag" the most sacred song ever published' (Wickes 1916: 33).

Many of Berlin's songs with no hint of syncopated rhythms in their music and no mention of ragtime in their titles or texts, 'I Want to be in Dixie' and 'When the Midnight Choo-Choo Leaves for Alabam', for instance, were perceived as ragtime songs because of the style in which they were sung and played on stage and recorded on phonograph discs and cylinders. British journalists identified the former as 'one of [Berlin's] most popular rag songs' when he performed it in London, and Berlin himself includes both in his ragtime medley 'They've Got Me Doin' it Now'. Almost any song, then, might be perceived by audiences as a 'ragtime' song if performed in a 'jerky' style.

---

[8] Victor 17787-A (9146), recorded 13 September 1910.
[9] Alexander Blume, in an unidentified newspaper article from 1913 included in a scrapbook kept by Irving Berlin, now in the Irving Berlin Collection in the Library of Congress, Washington.

Conclusions

Performance flexibility in classical music is limited to narrow decisions of tempo, dynamics, phrasing, and articulation. Genre is defined by the form and style of composition and the circumstances of reception, and is negotiated by composer and audience. Performers play little or no role in genre formation. Performers of popular music, on the other hand, work within a tradition that allows and even demands flexibility and creativity in shaping a piece. Genre is not determined by the form or style of a text itself but by the audience's perception of its style and meaning, defined most importantly at the moment of performance. Performers can thus shape, reinforce or even change genre.

Flexibility of genre in popular music extends beyond the fact that a given piece can belong to two or more genres or fall somewhere between several of them: genre can also change from performance to performance.

References

Adorno, T. W. (1984). *Aesthetic Theory*, ed. Gretel Adorno and Rolf Tiedemann, trans. Christian Lenhardt (London).

Dahlhaus, C. (1967). *Musikästhetik* (Cologne).

—— (1983). *Foundations of Music History*, trans. J. B. Robinson (Cambridge).

Derrida, J. (1980). 'The law of genre', *Critical Inquiry*, 7 (Autumn), 55–81.

Fabbri, F. (1982). 'A theory of musical genres: two applications', in *Popular Music Perspectives*, ed. D. Horn and P. Tagg (Gothenburg and Exeter) 52–81.

Howe, D. W. (1976). 'Victorian culture in America', in *Victorian American*, ed. Daniel Walker Howe (Philadelphia).

Jameson, F. (1982). 'Towards a new awareness of genre', *Science Fiction Studies*, 28.

Kallberg, J. (1988). 'The rhetoric of genre: Chopin's Nocturne in G Minor', *19th Century Music*, 11/3 (Spring), 238–61.

Mellers, W. (1964). *Music in a New Found Land: Themes and Developments in the History of American Music* (London).

Pascall, R. (1989). 'Genre and the Finale of Brahm's Fourth Symphony', *Music Analysis*, 8/3: 233–45.

Perloff, M. (ed.) (1989). *Postmodern Genres* (Norman, Okla., and London).

Samson, J. (1989). 'Chopin and genre', *Music Analysis*, 8/3: 213–31.

Walser, R. (1993). *Running with the Devil: Power, Gender, and Madness in Heavy Metal Music* (Hanover, NH, and London).

Wickes, E. M. (1916). *Writing the Popular Song* (Springfield, Mass.).

14

'Everybody's Lonesome for Somebody': Age, the Body, and Experience in the Music of Hank Williams

RICHARD LEPPERT AND GEORGE LIPSITZ

'He was so ordinary he merges with the crowd in my memory.' (Mrs Lilly McGill, teacher, Georgiana, Alabama, on her former pupil, Hank Williams.)

Houston Baker locates the blues at the crossroads of lack and desire, at the place where the hurts of history encounter determined resistance from people who know they are entitled to something better (Baker 1984: 7, 150). Like the blues singers from whom he learned so much, Hank Williams (1923 to 1953) spent a lot of time at that particular intersection. There he met others whose own struggles informed and shaped his music. Williams's voice expressed the contradictions of his historical moment—post-Second World War America—a time when diverse currents of resistance to class, race, and gender oppressions flowed together to form a contradictory, but nonetheless real, unity of opposites. Standing at a crossroads in history, at a fundamental turning point for relationships between men and women, whites and blacks, capital and labour, Williams's songs about heartbreak and failed personal relations indentified the body and the psyche as crucial terrains of political struggle in the post-war era.

Hank Williams was an extraordinary artist, a songwriter with a gift for concise yet powerful expression, and a singer with exceptional phrasing and drama. Yet we miss the point if we view Williams solely as an individual genius who rose above the crowd; the real story of Hank Williams is how he remained part of the crowd by letting its diverse currents flow through him. His extraordinary popularity, his success at introducing country music to new audiences, and his influence on an astonishingly diverse range of popular musical artists and genres all stem from Williams's ability to understand and articulate the blasted hopes and repressed desires of his audience.

Above all, Hank Williams understood that the profound changes in American family life during the 1930s and 1940s had ushered in a new era, fundamentally altering old categories of age, gender, and romance. His songs soared to popularity in the early 1950s, a time often hailed as the 'golden age' of the family (see May 1988; Mintz and Kellogg 1988). Yet Williams's narratives exuded a fatalism and despair about personal relationships. They resisted romantic optimism, and also avoided the kinds of closure and transcendence historically associated with male subjectivity. In this way, they expressed what Tania Modleski has described as a refusal to be oedipalized (Modleski 1982: 74), and what Fred Pfeil calls the 'de-oedipalisation of American society' (Pfeil 1988: 395–6).[1]

This is not to argue that Hank Williams found his way to an emancipatory political programme or even to a cultural vision completely free from dominant constructions of gender, sexuality, and romance. Far from it. But it is to claim that Williams's music and lyrics represented a significant refusal to accept dominant cultural narratives, and that they gave voice to potentials for resistance that remain important to this day. People can be imprisoned by cultural stories as easily as by iron bars and stone walls. Indeed, the core insight of contemporary cultural studies has been the understanding that people are more frequently contained within cultural narratives than within jail cells. In this context, all refusals are important because they represent a challenge to the prisons of mind and spirit that repress emancipatory hopes. Our exploration of the music of Hank Williams focuses on the ways in which he gave an individual voice to collective fears and hopes about the body, romance, gender roles, and the family. We wish to locate these issues variously in the site/sight of his physical body, his voice, his lyrics, and his music.

Age and Historicization of the Body

Hank Williams began his career as a child prodigy and ended it as a still young man who appeared years older than his age. At thirteen, he won an 'amateur hour' contest in Montgomery, Alabama with a song protesting against the conditions facing labourers for the federal Works Progress Administration. Williams's singing and songwriting immediately earned him a spot

---

[1] We use psychoanalytic language here as a shorthand way of describing our culture's dominant narratives about the construction of subjectivity, not because we believe in any innate or transcendent human personality.

as 'The Singing Kid' on a local radio show featuring 'Dad' Cryswell and his band (Caress 1979: 25). But his first recording session did not come until 11 December 1946 and he attained his first hit record in 1947 (Kingsbury and Axelrod 1988: 247). His last recording session occurred on 23 September 1952, slightly more than three months before his death in the early morning hours of 1 January 1953. Thus his career as a country singer spanned only six years, beginning when he was twenty-three and ending with his death at twenty-nine. Despite Williams's short life and the relative brevity of his career, among the more striking aspects of his work as a lyricist, composer, and performer were the multiple and complex encodings of both age and experience as played out on the ground of the individual human body, both physically and psychically. Significantly, he located his work within a context that invariably posited that body not in the transcendence of timeless/universal humanism, but in the history of rural southern poor and working-class America in the mid-twentieth century.

The concept of youth is largely taken as a 'natural'—and not constructed —category in American middle-class culture today. But in the early post-war years (especially among the rural poor) the concept had little bearing on life as it was lived, as Williams's own typical experience as a child labourer illustrates. To be young was essentially to be an even less reliable wage slave than one's parents, in a setting when obtaining work at all ages was a necessity for survival. Hank Williams lived out his short life within this larger reality; he lived out his decade as an 'official' of-age adult under still more complex circumstances, during a decade of traumatic post-war change in America in general, and in the rural south in particular. In this respect, his experience paralleled that of a generation of young men—and women—who came of age during the war (where, in the field, a twenty-six-year-old might commonly be referred to as the Old Man) and who confronted the jolting realities of an atomic peace immediately redefined in terms of Cold War and economic upheaval, massive migrations from the land to the emerging suburbs, and changing prescriptions for family life and for relations among races, classes, and genders.

Hank Williams was heard as 'authentic' at a time when authenticity was a prime determinate in the success of in-person and radio performers. (Like other country singers of his time, Williams never pulled back from the live-performance circuit; audiences were built and maintained by visual contact and live radio, without which recording careers could not develop, and 'in his prime, Hank was doing two hundred one-nighters a year' (Koon 1983:

Figure 14.1 Hank Williams in performance. Photograph courtesy of the Country Music Foundation Inc.

88; see also p. 93).) There are several interlocking reasons why this is so, among which the 'age' of the experiences his lyrics described and the 'age' of his voice were of special importance. At a more immediate—and pre-musical—level, his appearance played a part as well.

At twenty-three, as at twenty-nine, Williams was a chronologically young man long past youth—indeed, a man who seemingly never experienced youth, as was borne out by his physical appearance. At six feet in height he was not especially tall, but his thin body (140 lbs), and the hats he perpetually wore (to cover his thinning hair about which he was sensitive (Williams 1981: 144)), made him look taller: he stood out. Toward the end of his life he was haggard, gaunt, physically wrecked. He began drinking by the time he was eleven (ibid. 15), a habit he continued with few interruptions for the rest of his life, compounded by drug use in his later years (amphetamines and Seconal, the sedative chloral hydrate, and morphine). He had a form of spina bifida which exacerbated his chronic back pain and, near the end, hepatitis,

Figure 14.2 Hank Williams in performance. Photograph courtesy of the Country Music Foundation Inc.

Figure 14.3 Hank Williams in performance. Photograph courtesy of the Country Music Foundation Inc.

and a heart condition; and he suffered from malnutrition—when drinking heavily he did not eat, sometimes for days on end (ibid. 175, 205, 207; Koon 1983: 50). His body could never properly fill out his expensive tailor-made suits (evident even in the posed publicity shots).

The appearance of Williams's body marked the urgency of age as a central category in his work, especially in a culture where increasingly pre-scriptive post-war expectations of bodily and behavioural propriety were being forged. It was well known that Hank Williams lived his life on the edge. His music masked none of it. His songs about failed love followed closely the dismal history of his marriages—and his innumerable one-night stands—just as his obsession with death and repentance (of which more follows) confirmed that he knew the price he was paying both in this life and, unless he was careful, likewise the next. Williams referred to himself as 'ole Hank' both on the air and in private.[2]

Audiences were by no means amused by or even tolerant of his most drunken performances, especially when he failed to remember lyrics (see Williams 1981: 180). His increasingly debilitating alcoholism culminated in his being thrown off the Grand Ole Opry in 1952 (ibid. 172–3, 191, 196–8); his trips to sanitariums for drying out 'became almost routine' (ibid. 194). Nevertheless, audiences 'loved Hank partly *because* of his problems', accord-ing to Frank Page, associated with Shreveport's KWKH Louisiana Hayride (ibid. 198).[3] For those who saw his live performances, drunk or sober, his physical vulnerability was both obvious and affecting. In body he confounded the model of the self-reliant, self-contained in-shape, and battle-tested post-war male ('He'd come slopping and slouching out on stage, limp as a dishrag' (ibid. 140, quoting *Montgomery Advertiser* columnist Allen Rankin)).

Hank Williams's lyrics and music, like his physical appearance, reflect age and the historicization of the body in love songs and gospel numbers alike. In the first instance, his subjects invariably exude a spoken or unspoken his-tory. His upbeat love songs ('If You'll be a Baby (to Me)') characteristically refer to a rural timelessness, a pastoral imagery that pulls back from post-war futurism ('I can plow and milk the cow . . . [You] keep the homefires burnin'') but which, by recalling agrarian cyclical chronology, confront the

---

[2] See the examples quoted by Williams's second wife Billy Jean in Horstman 1975: 194.

[3] His chronic back problem, for example, was explained on a pre-recorded-for-broadcast apology that Williams produced from his hospital bed when he had to miss a December 1951 appearance in Baltimore. It is reproduced as the final cut on *Hank Williams: I Won't Be Home No More (June 1952–September 1952)*, Polydor 833 752-1 Y-2, volume 8, and the last, of Polydor's comprehensive, retrospective series of Williams's recordings.

sense of the real (not imagined) loss of that way of life.[4] To be sure, images of the man in the field and the woman in the kitchen correspond roughly to the Levittown ideal of suburban social organization, but only to an urban/suburbanite. The rural reality encoded here is one of shared labours: the woman is not kept cosy by her man's work; she is a labourer as well. She heats her cookstove with wood and coal, and she does the wash with her bare knuckles. In this way Williams's lyrics, built on traditional domestic rural social organization, incorporate simultaneously an ancient and recent past that his listeners clearly recognized, that most had lived or were still living, but which they also knew was ending in favour of a future that was profoundly uncertain. In this regard, Williams when he sang about love, voiced more than the desire for partnership: he voiced the pain of loss for a way of life that could already be described with the anxiety of ending.

As regards gospel, the fact that a young man in the 1940s might sing of Jesus (and in 20 per cent of his repertory (Koon 1983: 81)) is not in itself particularly surprising, at least in the rural south, though the numbers of Williams's gospel tunes may be unusual (some were recorded under his own name, others under the pseudonym of his alter-ego Luke the Drifter). In many respects a tune like 'How Can You Refuse Him Now?' is quite an ordinary, even conventional piece of white gospel. But in other ways, this song and others like it exceed conventions. Unlike contemporaneous southern black gospel, his tunes are seldom upbeat; neither musically nor lyrically do they convincingly encode happiness, let alone ecstasy. Instead, they fixate on death (as in 'We're Getting Closer to the Grave Each Day', recorded when he was twenty-six, and 'Mother is Gone') and on death rituals ('The Funeral'; in this instance that of a black child[5]). Williams's religious lyrics speak to life's suffering and failures, often without recourse to the promise of an afterlife. As such they tend to exceed and politically subvert the generic passivity encoded especially into much white gospel music. (The musical and performative vitality of black gospel, by contrast, acts to undercut the other-worldly fixation of the lyrics, re-establishing the physical present, as well as the spiritual future, in the lives of believers.) That is, once the hope of after-life is pushed aside, the terrain that matters is located in the concrete personal and social body, not in the abstract soul. Thus even in 'I Saw the Light',

---

[4] The loss of home through the upheavals of war and migration are a recurrent theme in Southern culture beginning with the Civil War, and become more intense after each of this century's two world wars. One price paid for migration was guilt for not remaining to 'share the common burden'. See Horstman 1975: 3–5.

[5] See further Hume 1982: 94–6, 'Dead Kids and Country Music'.

perhaps his best known gospel song—but certainly not his best—the most Williams can offer for accepting Jesus fails to exceed this life, as it vaguely conjures up the rather tired imagery of smiling in the face of adversity (as the phrase now runs: 'Don't worry, be happy'). The text proffers consolation, and consolation is the only reward; the reserve with which Williams sings the words only confirms the limits of hope offered, all the more given his 'biological' youth from which conventional 'idealism' and future directedness are already stripped.

'Men with Broken Hearts', a Luke the Drifter (non-gospel) recitation (recorded 21 December 1950), locates the terrain of failure in particularly dismal (and unrelenting) fashion, calling forth rhetorically to God at the end, but without hope for redress. The text speaks of defeat in the metaphor of men's broken bodies—stooped shoulders, heads 'bowed low', vacantly staring eyes—walking allegories of what Williams calls 'living death', relief from which can only come via death itself.

At the level of an unconscious politics lies the gesture of recognition that to have failed in this life is to have failed: it carries its own punishment and there is nothing more beyond it, or at least nothing one can safely predict. In 'We're Getting Closer to the Grave Each Day', Williams reiterates the theology of Christ's redemptive death and, to be sure, he makes passing reference to the Judgement Day. But the image that incessantly repeats is that of the approach to the grave. In 'How Can You Refuse Him Now?', the image of Christ crucified is not that of the redeemer, but of a man suffering. It is His suffering that should trigger our response, not our own fear of death or a hope for afterlife. Christ, in essence, becomes one of us, a man in trouble.

Hank Williams's singing voice registers differently from his [FM!-] radio-perfect speaking voice. There is an aura of careworn exhaustion even in his quasi-upbeat tunes. Thus in the 56-second fragment 'If You'll be a Baby (to Me)', a lyric essentially proposing marriage, Williams does not sound like a teenager in love, nor even a twenty-year-old. There is no sense of passionate sensuality in either the words or the voice. There is instead a textual promise of peace ('no quarrellin' ') and a vocal—explicitly timbral—expression of hope for refuge. That is, the putative subject of the tune has all the naivety of uncomplicated first-love-and-family aspirations ('I'll be your baby/And I don't mean maybe'), but Williams's voice encodes something more complex. The delivery is subdued, the words slightly swallowed, the overall acoustical affect establishing associations less of first love than of trying-once-more. It is a voice of knowing, not anticipating, confined to a narrow range (a major sixth), middle register (the high note is A below middle C), and a middling dynamic. The enthusiasm presumed by the lyrics is undercut by the doubtfulness of the delivery.

In 'A House without Love is Not a Home', the narrative plays off a long-time relationship now failed, its imagery repeatedly referring to the passage of time and loss. The timbral difference from Williams's deep, resonant speaking voice is striking. The voice is thin—and, characteristically, his pitch wavers on held notes, especially in the upper half of his narrow register. It is a voice lacking certainty—but gaining thereby in credibility. The melodic structure produces a different affect from that of 'If You'll be a Baby (to Me)'. In the earlier tune, Williams's upper register is not called upon and most of the intervallic relationships are seconds, apart from the major/minor thirds and a single perfect fourth. In 'A House without Love' the range extends over a tenth (to E above middle C), and the tune is largely constructed around the interval of a fourth: that is, it is far more disjointed, providing the opportunity/ necessity for him to connect the two pitches of the interval with a slurred slide (in instances where the interval is falling, as the majority of them do). And though, to be sure, this is a musical gesture characteristic to much country music, it is a musical practice—outside country music—more commonly located in the singing of women than men. Combined with the other vocal features we have described, it registers uncertainty, vulnerability, and—given the lyrics—the sorts of failure that only age can produce.

Both tunes are in the key of C and neither uses any chromatic inflection: the melodies are musically straightforward, 'guileless'. Indeed, Williams characteristically keeps melodic, rhythmic, and harmonic surprises to a minimum —the arch-shape of his melodies is sufficiently predictable that committing the tunes to memory is easily accomplished on one or two hearings. All of this affects the reception of Williams's music. Taken together, the appeal is that of a boy-man; the musical vocabulary encodes a simplicity on the verge of the child-like; contrarily, the voice is marked by uncertain age. The contradiction results in the ambiguity and complexity of audience reactions, especially when combined with his physical performance image. He is to be mothered, but also to be erotically loved, and above all to be heard as one's own: a capsulized history of a self-consciously regionally-ghettoized people.

If we look at Williams's gospel tunes, the same features are found ('We're Getting Closer to the Grave Each Day', 'How Can You Refuse Him Now?'); indeed, the distinctions between these two primary genres of his work are few.[6] Notable among them are the frequent shift from the duple time characteristic of the secular tunes to a lilting 3/4 in gospel; in the religious tunes, he uses a more pronounced slur-slide on downward moving intervals; and here too the famous vocal 'tear' (as in both weeping and pulling apart) appears: the voice momentarily breaks, in a convention of pathos which Williams perfected (this device occurs repeatedly in 'We're Getting Closer to the Grave Each Day').

There was a considerable rift between Williams's deep, resonant speaking voice and the thinner, more nasal, crooning quality of his singing, a rift notably widened by the accompanying change in his physical appearance when, from standing before the microphone conversing, he shifted into song: 'It was like a charge of electricity had gone through him' (Allen Rankin, quoted in Williams 1981: 140). (Between songs Williams enjoyed folksy bantering with his audiences; indeed such contacts were conventional in gigs and radio shows alike. And many Luke the Drifter bits were essentially monologues with musical accompaniment.) Minnie Pearl was struck by his stage presence from the first time she encountered it: 'He had a real animal magnetism. He destroyed the women in the audience' (ibid. 144).[7] He knew how to use his body; hunching forward into the mike, 'He'd close his eyes and swing one of those big long legs, and the place would go wild' (ibid. 145, quoting Don Helms).[8] He played on a sexuality that was exciting precisely because of the contradictions it contained. Minnie Pearl suggests that Williams appealed to women's maternal instincts. Others suggest a far more sensual dimension, though both reflected his true character—a womanizer nevertheless dominated by his strong mother. This contradiction engenders an ambiguity of a simultaneously exciting but politically dangerous sort. It constitutes a partially masked refusal to adhere to standards of propriety established for a post-war culture of redomestication, a culture built on self-contradictory and increasingly complex erotic economies of controlled role-playing. Williams —like Elvis soon after him—marked with his bodily gestures a language of difference and demand, just as one might expect (or hope for) in the young

---

[6] The other genres being the Luke the Drifter accompanied monologues, and the occasional novelty songs like the slightly bizarre 'Indian' love song 'Kaw Liga' or the famous 'Jambalaya'.

[7] On Williams's securing of women following show dates, see ibid. 164. Nor was his stage presence effective only on women: 'He quickly became the favorite act on a military entertainment entourage to Europe in 1951. [Moreover, o]n a celebrity-studded touring show known as the Hadacol Caravan he upstaged such luminaries as Jack Benny, Milton Berle, and Bob Hope, and eventually took over the closing spot' (Blaser 1985: 17, n. 18). For details of the Caravan tour, see Williams 1981: 150–5; Koon 1983: 36, 38.

[8] Cf. Frank Page: 'He was just electrifying on stage. . . . He had the people in the palm of his hands from the moment he walked out there' (Koon 1983: 74; see also p. 28).

—thereby accounting for the insistence then, as now, that youth be tightly controlled, especially physically. Yet his speaking and singing voices also referenced acoustics culturally characteristic of middle age and beyond, just as his love songs consistently dealt with the failures of middle age, and his gospel tunes with death. In sound and sight alike, he encompassed the experiences of life's full range of contradictions, hopes, and failures for a society which unquestionably recognized in him both what they loved and hated of themselves.

Gender Difference and Social Class: Identity by Alienation

America as a social and political organization is committed to a cheerful view of life. (Film critic Robert Warshow)

That's just it, Minnie, there ain't no light. (Hank Williams to Minnie Pearl)

Kent Blaser points out that forty-five of Williams's fifty most important songs deal with relationships between men and women, and that fifteen of these complain about being abandoned by one's partner (Blaser 1985: 23). From 'Lovesick Blues' to 'Your Cheatin' Heart', his most popular songs articulate loneliness, frustration, and despair as necessary parts of the search for love. This pessimism made a break with the traditional romantic optimism of popular music as crafted in Tin Pan Alley, but in the context of post-Second World War America it held special significance.

After the Second World War, Americans married earlier and in greater numbers and had more children than had been true in the past. This extraordinary increase in marriages and births brought with it an unprecedented focus on the family by both private capital and the state. The nuclear family emerged as the primary social unit, a unit whose true home was the suburban shopping mall (see Leo 1988: 31), and everything from the Cold War to the growth of suburbs to increases in private debt and consumer spending drew justification from uncritical celebrations of the nuclear family and heterosexual romance (see May 1989: 155). In that context, Hank Williams's fatalism and existential despair rebuked dominant social narratives and spoke directly to the internal psychic wounds generated by the gap between lived experience and an ideology that promised universal bliss through the emergence of romance and the family as unchallenged centres of personal life.

Hank Williams's own life experience allowed him precious few illusions about the nuclear family, and in that respect he exemplified a broader social and historical experience. The Great Depression of the 1930s had undermined both the theory and the practice of the nuclear family. Unemployed fathers deserted their families in large numbers; by 1940 1,500,000 married women lived apart from their husbands. Many families formed extended households by moving in with relatives, but in the mid-1930s an estimated 200,000 vagrant children roamed the country. Women and children once again entered the workforce in large numbers, and their earning power undercut the previously unchallenged authority of male breadwinners (Mintz and Kellogg 1988: 137–8). Mobilization for the Second World War accelerated these trends. During the war, six million women workers entered high-paying production jobs in industry. Sixteen million Americans left their homes to join the armed forces, and another fifteen million travelled to new jobs in war production centres. Under these conditions, old ties of family and community broke down, and Americans experimented with new gender and family roles (ibid. 155).

Hank Williams's family life reflected these larger social trends. His father had suffered shell shock in combat during the First World War and, after a series of short-term jobs in the late 1920s, was committed in 1930 to the Veterans Administration Hospital in Biloxi, Mississippi where he stayed ten years. Thus for most of the time between his sixth and sixteenth birthday, Hank Williams was raised by his mother and his sister. His mother assumed an awesome presence in his life and career, supporting her children with her own labour during the hard years of the Great Depression, and managing her son's entry into show business. Like many working class children, he also spent considerable time with relatives outside his nuclear family, living for a year when he was six with his cousin J. C. in Monroe County, Alabama, so that J. C.'s sister could go to school in Georgiana by living with Hank's mother and sister (Caress 1979: 12). Lilly Williams moved her family to Montgomery in 1937 when Hank was fourteen, and she ran a boarding house there that exposed her son to yet another extended household.

There was little in Hank Williams's personal experience that conformed with the reigning cultural optimism about the nuclear family. He started dating Audrey Mae Sheppard, a married woman with a daughter at home and a husband overseas, in 1942. Sheppard's father threatened to kill Hank over the relationship, and when Hank first brought Audrey home to meet his mother, Lilly asked 'Where'd you get this whore?', a comment that provoked a fistfight between mother and son (ibid. 35–6, 38). In a culture that increasingly lauded motherhood in the abstract while imposing ever-greater burdens on it in practice, not every son could use the words Hank Williams employed to speak about his mother to Minnie Pearl, 'Minnie, there ain't nobody in the world I'd rather have alongside me in a fight than my mama with a broken beer bottle in her hand' (Pearl 1980: 213). Hank married Audrey in 1944 before a Justice of the Peace in a Texaco station in Andalusia, Alabama, but the marriage was illegal because it came too soon after Audrey's separation from her husband to satisfy the requirements of Alabama law (Koon 1983: 19). Hank and Audrey were divorced in 1948, but reconciled after the birth of their son Randall Hank (Hank Williams, jun.) in 1949 (ibid. 29–30). The tempestuous relationship led to another divorce, and his remarriage (in 1952) to Billie Jean Eshlimar (who had been abandoned by her first husband) led to constant bickering among Williams, his mother and both his wives (Caress 1979: 189).

Biographer Jay Caress locates the roots of Williams's personal problems in the singer's distance from the experience of a nuclear family, arguing that Williams 'never made the normal psychological transfer from what psychologists call dependent mother love to assertive, independent (father emulating) mother love' (ibid. 12). Yet Hank Williams's experiences with strong-willed and competent women left him with a deep respect for women and a powerful desire for connection to them. His 'failure' to make the oedipal break led him to remain in dialogue with all of the significant women in his life, and led him away from the dominant 'heroic' image of masculinity.

In an age when cultural voices ranging from the masculinist rhetoric of Mickey Spillane novels and John Wayne films to the conformist and paternalistic pressures of outer-directed corporate culture to the hedonistic appeals of *Playboy* magazine all encouraged men to widen the distance between themselves and women, Williams presented a masculine voice that longed for reconnection with the feminine, that refused the oedipality of the dominant culture in favour of an almost pre-oedipal craving for intimacy, pleasure, and reconnection with women (see Modleski 1982: 72–9). Of course, even this refusal could be channelled into the kind of flight from the family and responsibility that Barbara Ehrenreich describes as an important factor in sexualizing and engendering male consumer desire in the 1950s (Ehrenreich 1984). The pre-oedipal stage might be seen as the perfect model for the needy narcissism vital to consumer desire. As Fred Pfeil explains, 'the increasing

number of de-Oedipalized middle-class male subjects, even ostensibly politically progressive ones, in no way guarantees any decrease in their fear of and
hostility toward women' (Pfeil 1988: 396). But the rise of a de-oedipalized
subjectivity does constitute the body and psyche as sites for political meaning,
and it also evidences a kind of subjectivity that seeks connection rather than
separation, that disconnects ego and identity from hatred of a (proximate)
mother and identification with a (distant) father. Collective social problems can
never be solved by purely individual responses, but individual predispositions
can often disclose contradictions and interruptions in dominant ideology that
prefigure the sites where resistance might emerge. In Hank Williams's case,
resistance to the oedipal narrative reveals structural weaknesses within the
idealized nuclear family and its promises of happiness, as well as the existence
of a popular desire for something better.

Hank Williams not only refused a narrowly oedipal definition of masculinity,
but in fact he spent most of his life as a fugitive from nearly any stable
identity. As a child he attached himself to black street singers Rufus Payne
(known as Tee Tot) and Connie McKee (known as Big Day) who became his
first strong adult male role models. Before deciding on a life as a musician,
he tried out for the rodeo, and while working as a shipfitter's helper in
Mobile, Alabama took a secret trip to Portland, Oregon in 1944 to try his
luck in the Kaiser shipyards in that city. Even after achieving stardom, he
went to work under the pseudonym Herman P. Willis for Dallas nightclub
owner (and later assassin of Lee Harvey Oswald) Jack Ruby (Koon 1983: 34).
As a young musician, he formed a country and western band with 'Indian
Joe' Hatcher on lead guitar and 'Mexican Charlie' Mayes on fiddle. He adopted
the pseudonym 'Luke the Drifter' for a series of recitations, and repeated the
'drifting' theme by naming his band of Alabama-born musicians the 'Drifting
Cowboys' (Caress 1979: 20, 22, 26, 17; Koon 1983: 34). While on tour with
his band, he loved to listen to baseball games on the car radio, but had no
favourite team (Williams 1981: 135). He sang religious hymns to his audiences, but lived a decidedly non-religious life.[9] This refusal to accept any

[9] His contradictory relationship to religion is encapsulated in what is probably an apocryphal story about a
young fan who admitted to not being a 'God-fearing boy', and found Hank piping up 'Don't let it trouble you
none. I ain't afraid of God, either' (Caress 1979: 81–2). Koon quotes the very authoritative Bob Pinson as saying that the Shestack interview, from which this story is taken, is 'all fiction; it never happened' (Koon 1983:
94). Yet the quotation seems to capture correctly something about Williams's view of religion. Roger M. Williams
notes, 'Hank, after his childhood, never demonstrated an interest in organized religion. But he had flashes of
intense personal feeling about spiritual matters, which led to some of the finest songs he ever wrote. Further,
he knew that "sacred songs" always find a ready market in country music' (Williams 1981: 57).

permanent identity also characterized Williams's view of class which he interpreted through the frame of gender. As Dorothy Horstman notes,

The farmers and labourers who made up the original market for country music were for the most part dirt-poor, bypassed by the American dream and the means of achieving it. Burdened with poor land, a poor economy, and hostile natural forces beyond their control, many felt they were, indeed 'born to lose'. . . . A tragic love affair, then, is the final insult—and perhaps the focus for economic and social frustrations it would be unmanly to admit. (Horstman 1975: 140)

Country musicians in general, and Hank Williams in particular, locate the politics of gender on the terrain of social class difference, but less on the overt ground of society and its institutions than on the privatized body, particularly its psyche. In the process, Williams gives sight to the unseen, especially in love song laments about infidelity and failed relationships.

Marital cheating was a taboo subject in country music recordings prior to the social upheavals of the 1940s, so that Hank Williams's 'Your Cheatin' Heart', among the classics of the genre (recorded in his last session—23 September 1952—together with another tune of the same sort, 'Take These Chains from My Heart', and two others), was a type of song having a very short history. When Williams wrote these tunes, their subject rang true, not as repetitious or timeless commentaries, but as expressions of profound and shattering change. They caught on precisely because he was able to locate the societal in the most personal and private terrain of sexual love. It was not that infidelity never occurred in the rural south prior to Williams's generation; it was rather that infidelity was admitted for the first time among the expressible catalogue of failures. By inscribing the rising stakes of societal suffering in infidelity, by locating that suffering in the psyche, he undercut the final refuge for resistance. The soul of the privatized body could no longer be separated, refuge-like, from the larger social economy: cheating songs confirmed devolutionary change.[10]

Similarly, songs of unrequited love ('I'm So Lonesome I Could Cry'; 'Cold, Cold Heart'), though excluding the sin of adultery, preserve the political essentials of songs about cheating, even if they accomplish their politics of emotion in a slightly different fashion. By emphasizing a love that is never

---

[10] 'Inevitably, in the upheaval of a wartime society, with women working, husbands and wives separated, easy social and geographical mobility, and honky tonks no longer populated exclusively by women of easy virtue, country writers began to flirt with, then to address directly, the subject of cheating' (Horstman 1975: 182; see also Hume 1982: 84–5).

responded to, as opposed to a love that once was but is now lost, unrequited love songs fundamentally account for an equally defeating—if not necessarily worse—sort of failure: the inability to find love in the first place, to love but not be loved in return, to be rejected. It is in songs of unrequited love that the work of Hank Williams approaches black music most directly, and where it crosses gender lines into emotional ground more commonly occupied by women, and notably by women who are black (e.g. Billie Holiday, Nina Simone). As Billie Holiday, dying, gravel-voiced, movingly—and pathetically —sang in 'Glad to be Unhappy', one of her last recorded songs, when someone you adore fails to love you back, 'It's a pleasure to be sad'.

The emotional intensity that Billie Holiday accorded to this topic,[11] via her vocal/timbral inscription of failure (as well as by the words), bears a distinct similarity to that achieved by Hank Williams, though musically by quite different means. The difference can be stated quite simply: the musical and cultural traditions that would allow a black woman to produce this lament generally affect men in a quite dissimilar way. For a man to utter similar sentiments, in this society, reflects a more extreme degree of failure and frustration. The fact that Williams wrote and sang such tunes, in other words, produces affect by collapsing the distinction not only between genders, but between races as well (southern whites, after all, heard blues music). Not only with subject matter, but also with what might be termed the politics of timbre, an acoustic solidarity is implicitly forged: between genders, between the races, and among the poor. Black audiences recognized elements of their

[11] See also the work of Nina Simone, ten years Hank Williams's junior, for example, on her live album, *Little Girl Blue*, especially 'He Needs Me (He doesn't know it but he needs me)'.

It is worth noting the correspondences and, especially, the differences between Hank Williams's songs of failed love and some of the early recordings of Patsy Cline (all songs written by others, whereas Williams mostly performed his own material). 'If I Could Only Stay Asleep' moves slowly, underscoring the sense of loss inscribed by a vocal line repeatedly leaping to high notes only to slide back as if in defeat. 'I'm Blue Again' registers the vocal 'tear'—perfected by Williams—to help mark a text entirely about loss, but this effect (and others) acts in contrast to the tempo, oddly upbeat, and to Cline's vocal delivery which breathes an air of confidence seriously undercutting the text's defeatism. Indeed, time and again in Cline's work, discrepancies occur between the putative subjects of the lyrics and her delivery of them. Among the reasons Patsy Cline is such an exciting singer is that, like Hank Williams, she pushed hard against the margins of musical conventions—stretching semiotic possibilities, introducing contradictions and unexpected tensions, and, in particular, refusing to be bound by conventional expectations of vocal delivery located in gender distinction. Thus whereas Williams voices feminine identity, mediating traditional masculine vocal qualities, Patsy Cline voices a masculine identity, notably by mediating the passivity that tunes of loss commonly inscribe lyrically and often musically. The loss of a man may be getting her down, so her words go, but she won't be down for long, so her voice encodes. She subscribes to the potential joys of men and women relating to each other but she refuses (not textually but vocally) to be overwhelmed by the absence or failure of the experience. It is very difficult to listen to 'I've Loved and Lost Again' and really believe that the pain will be permanent. She will be up and dancing soon, playing a profoundly (vocally) liberated role: her vocal-gutteral growls on 'Gotta Lot of Rhythm (in My Soul)', a thoroughly upbeat number, echo an effect heard commonly in early rock-'n' roll singers (both male and female).

own culture in Williams's music, and in large numbers attended the Louisiana Hayride when he was on the bill.[12] Blues singer B. B. King remembers paying special attention to the songs by Hank Williams that he heard on the radio while working on a Mississippi plantation because:

Like Hank Williams, man, when he wrote 'Cold, Cold Heart', tunes like that, that carried me right back to my same old blues about 'don't answer the door' and all that kind of stuff. 'Cause this is a guy hurting. He's hurting from inside. And 'Your Cheating Heart', many things of this sort are just to me another form of blues sung by other people. (Redd 1974: 97)

The sound of a white man's voice singing about these subjects, hence crossing gender and racial boundaries, inscribes a socio-cultural disruption of the most encompassing finality, at precisely the instant that it offers the specifically *acoustic* opportunity to establish a relationship of resistance with another socially alienated group.

Finally, even in tunes of courtship or proposal, like 'If You'll be a Baby (to Me)', conventional romantic love is not part of the equation;[13] instead there is an offer of a partnership for mutually-supporting labour, and the extent of the male singer's love is promised in terms of the work appropriate to her that he's willing to shoulder: if she cooks, he'll plough and *even* do the churning. He loves her and considers doing 'women's' work a gesture of his devotion.[14] This may not be in the depoliticized tradition of romantic love, but it *is* romantic love of the most meaningful and committed sort. It openly

---

[12] On these shows Williams typically included one or two Luke the Drifter recitations that specifically addressed black subjects, such as 'The Funeral'. This recitation, to the accompaniment of Hammond organ and steel guitar (recorded 10 January 1950), tells of the narrator, a white man, coming upon a humble country church and witnessing the funeral service for a black child. To be sure, Williams repeats racial stereotypes and dialogue embedded in southern racism (the child is described as having 'curly hair, protruding lips'; the black preacher's speech includes 'sho 'nough'); on the other hand, Williams in effect absents himself as narrator almost from the start, giving sole voice to the preacher whose sermon he repeats at length. That is, a white man takes a pew to witness a funeral and thereafter tells his story: he tells his (primarily white) audience that he has learned something from what he describes as the 'wisdom and ignorance of a crushed, undying race'. (See Williams 1981: 74–5.) Hank Williams's own funeral, held in Montgomery auditorium, included about two hundred blacks —seated in the segregated balcony—among the three thousand mourners who managed to squeeze inside; moreover, the music was provided in part by a black quartet, the Southwind Singers, in addition to various white country music luminaries (see Koon 1983: 54).

[11] Indeed, romantic love is generally in short supply in the country music of Williams's day, precisely because it could have had little ring of credibility in the circumstances of its hearers. See Horstman 1975: 119.

[14] Occasionally Williams confronted the politics of class more directly; perhaps the best example is 'A Mansion on the Hill' (recorded 7 November 1947). Audrey Williams has said that (Chicago, urban-bred) Fred Rose gave Hank the title and sent him off to see what he could do with it. The result was an explicit articulation of high–low class hierarchy invited by Rose's title—the lyrics employ a binary opposition between the mansion on a hill and the narrator's cabin in a valley. (See Horstman 1975: 165.)

recognizes the mutuality of marital labour and the urge to take on more than what society conventionally identifies as the man's share. (It is arguable that, under these conditions, what otherwise passes for romantic love might flourish past the stages of passion characterizing young relationships.) Lyrics of this sort are all the more striking given the national phenomenon in the early post-war years of a return to 'traditional' pre-war gender divisions, articulated especially in the domestication of the suburb with its removal of women from the labour force, as well as in a broad range of popular cultural expressions built upon the assumption of innate antagonisms between men and women, ranging from commercial television programmes and film noir motion pictures to the lyrics of most popular songs.

Yet for all his shifting subjectivities, a remarkable consistency character-izes Williams's voice, and that consistency is connected to his class and regional identity. There is no discernible difference between his earliest recordings and his last, and the same holds for his unsophisticated, elementary, essentially three-chord guitar strumming. The voice is common, untrained. The deliv-ery is inevitably straightforward, without pretence, without acrobatics or tricks—unless one counts the country-conventional vocal 'tear' mentioned earlier. The upper range, which Williams uses to good effect in producing acoustic tension, is thin and often strained, the latter quality exacerbated by a notable and fast vibrato; the low and middle range is both rich and firm, like his speaking voice. Together these variant timbres produce a comfort in the latter, inevitably undercut by the vulnerability of that comfort in the former. Moreover, he typically gives accentual and dynamic emphasis to his high voice, that is, to that part of his range that semiotically undercuts the culturally coded paternal assuredness of the deeper male sounds.

Williams's slightly nasal twang is especially obvious in the higher register —the locus of tension—thus most evident in precisely the acoustic space that best identifies pain and its politics. The country twang, in other words, locates him as one of his listeners' own, a man who shares their experi-ences. Nasality in other circumstances provides the southern rural poor with subcultural/community identity, like any other accentual or dialectal effect. But in extra-regional popular culture (notably the movies, often in grotesquely exaggerated burlesques like *Ma and Pa Kettle*, and in later televi-sion shows like *Beverly Hillbillies*) that effect becomes a weapon for derision, a fact never lost on any poor person. Hank Williams exploited that sound in a timbral expression of class and regional solidarity, though to be sure he was not unique in this regard. To similar, if more obvious, purpose is his swallowing of word endings at phrase ends ('quarrellin'', 'churnin''), and regional pronounciations ('yer' for 'your' and so on). In his Luke the Drifter recitation 'Beyond the Sunset' (recorded 10 January 1950), he tells of a man's vigilant loyalty to a woman preceding him in death; it is his memory of her that gives him the strength to go on. The recitation depends on an implicit understanding of the uses of memory as regards its connection to history, issues that go far beyond the narrower topic of this small piece. As 'Beyond the Sunset' has it: 'Memory is a gift from God that death cannot destroy'. The politics embedded here grow from the fact that Williams recognized less that songs are social constructions and more that society itself is constructed by the songs we sing, the stories we tell, and the *sounds* we voice in the narration.

Everybody's Lonesome for Somebody

I'm so lonesome I could cry. (Hank Williams lyric)

What prepares men [*sic*] for totalitarian domination in the non-totalitarian world is the fact that loneliness, once a borderline experience usually suffered in certain marginal social conditions like old age, has become an everyday experience of the ever-growing masses of our century. (Hannah Arendt in *The Origins of Totalitarianism*)

Goodbye Hank Williams, my old friend, I didn't know you but I've been the places you've been. (Tim Hardin lyric)

Hank Williams you wrote my life. (Moe Bandy lyric)

The extraordinary popularity of Hank Williams's songs in the late 1940s and early 1950s played a crucial role in transforming country music from a regional and class-bound genre to a staple of mass popular culture. Along with related developments in popular speech, dress, and dance, the rise to national prominence of country music reflected the emergence of a prestige from below in which cultural hybrids emanating from intersections of race, class, and gender articulated a new basis for American commercial culture.

Class, race, and gender all contributed to the grounding of Williams's music in oppositional cultures and practices. His songs resonated with the materials memory forged in previous popular struggles against hierarchy and exploitation. But as a creation of a distinct historical moment, he added a new element to the historic struggle for the good life. In an age of renewed racism, he created a music that underscored the connections between whites and blacks. At a time of upward mobility and cultural assimilation for much of the working class, he affirmed his standpoint as a worker and an ordinary citizen. In an age of resurgent patriarchy, he lamented the schisms between men and women, resisted the dominant oedipal narrative, and sought closer connections to women. Finally, he foregrounded existential despair in an age of exuberant and uncritical 'progress', countering ubiquitous romantic invocations of the superiority of the nuclear family with honest words and deep emotions drawn from the hurts of history and the experiences of everyday life. As modern life became increasingly characterized by 'the policing of families' as part of capital's project to colonize the psyche and the body, Williams constituted his own voice and body as sites of resistance. Millions of fans could feel that he 'wrote their lives', because even when they did not know him, they could feel that he knew the places they had been.

References

Baker, H. (1984). *Blues, Ideology, and Afro-American Literature: a Vernacular Theory* (Chicago).

Blaser, K. (1985). ' "Pictures from Life's Other Side": Hank Williams, country music, and popular culture in America', *The South Atlantic Quarterly*, 84/1: 12–26.

Caress, J. (1979). *Hank Williams: Country Music's Tragic King* (New York).

Ehrenreich, B. (1984). *The Hearts of Men: American Dreams and the Flight from Commitment* (Garden City, NY).

Horstman, D. (1975). *Sing Your Heart Out, Country Boy* (New York).

Hume, M. (1982). *You're So Cold I'm Turnin' Blue: Martha Hume's Guide to the Greatest Country Music* (New York).

Kingsbury, P., and Axelrod, A. (eds.) (1988). *Country: The Music and the Musicians. Pickers, Slickers, Cheatin' Hearts & Superstars* (New York).

Koon, G. (1983). *Hank Williams: A Bio-Bibliography* (Westport, Conn.).

Leo, J. (1988). 'The familialism of man in American television melodrama', *South Atlantic Quarterly*, 88/1: 31–51.

May, E. T. (1988). *Homeward Bound* (New York).

—— (1989). 'Explosive issues: sex, women, and the bomb', in *Recasting America*, ed. L. May (Chicago), 154–70.

Mintz, S., and Kellogg, S. (1988). *Domestic Revolutions* (New York).

Modleski, T. (1982). 'Film theory's detour', *Screen*, 23/5: 72–9.

Pearl, M., with Dew, J. (1980). *Minnie Pearl: An Autobiography* (New York).

Pfeil, F. (1988). 'Postmodernism as a "structure of feeling" ', in *Marxism and the Interpretation of Culture*, ed. L. Grossberg and C. Nelson (Champaign), 381–405.

Redd, L. (1974). *Rock is Rhythm and Blues* (East Lansing).
Williams, R. M. (1981). *Sing a Sad Song: The Life of Hank Williams*, 2nd edn. (Urbana, Ill.).

Discography

Cline, P. (1985). 'Gotta Lot of Rhythm (in My Soul)', 'If I Could Only Stay Asleep' and 'I've Loved and Lost Again', *Patsy Cline: Today, Tomorrow & Forever*, MCA-1463 (all songs first released 1955–9).
Holiday, B. (1987). 'Glad to Be Unhappy', *Lady in Satin*, Columbia CK 40247 (first released 1958).
Simone, N. (1958). 'He Needs Me', *Little Girl Blue-Nina Simone*, Bethlehem BCP 6028.
Williams, H.

Note: All Hank Williams's songs mentioned in this essay were included on the eight-volume comprehensive series issued on Polydor (PolyGram Records) between 1985 and 1988. The discography, drawn exclusively from Polydor's retrospective, indicates the date of the original release, when we could establish it, or instead lists the date of the recording session. In the years immediately following Williams's death, many home recordings (Williams accompanying himself on guitar without back-up) were released in over-dubbed versions. A number of years sometimes intervened between the original recording date and the over-dubbed issue. The Polydor set made available for the first time many of Williams's home recordings in their original, undubbed state. For additional information see the discographies in Williams 1981 (compiled by Bob Pinson), and Koon 1983.

—— (1985). 'I Saw the Light' (recorded 21 April 1947), *Hank Williams: I Ain't Got Nuthin' But Time (December 1946–April 1947)*, Polydor 825 548-2.
—— (1985). 'Lovesick Blues' (first released 1949) and 'A Mansion on the Hill' (recorded 7 November 1947), *Hank Williams: Lovesick Blues (August 1947–December 1948)*, Polydor 825 551-2.
—— (1986). 'A House without Love is Not a Home' (recorded 30 August 1949), 'How Can You Refuse Him Now' (first released in 1954; over-dubbed home recording), 'If You'll be a Baby (to Me)' (first release of original home recording; over-dubbed version released previously), 'I'm So Lonesome I Could Cry' (first released 1949) and 'We're Getting Closer to the Grave Each Day' (first release of original home recording; over-dubbed release in 1957), *Hank Williams: I'm So Lonesome I Could Cry (March 1949–August 1949)*, Polydor 825 557-1 Y-2.
—— (1987). 'Cold, Cold Heart' (first released 1951), 'Beyond the Sunset' (by Luke the Drifter; recorded 10 January 1950), 'The Funeral' (by Luke the Drifter; first

released 1950), *Hank Williams: Long Gone Lonesome Blues (August 1949–December 1950)*, Polydor 831 633-4.

—— (1987). 'Men with Broken Hearts' (by Luke the Drifter; recorded 21 December 1950), *Hank Williams: Hey, Good Lookin' (December 1950–July 1951)*, Polydor 831 634-1.

—— (1987). 'Kaw Liga' (first released 1953), 'Mother is Gone' (first released 1955; over-dubbed), 'Take These Chains from My Heart' (first released 1953), 'Your Cheatin' Heart' (first released 1953), *Hank Williams: I Won't Be Home No More, June 1952–September 1952*, Polydor 833 752-1 Y-2.

—— (1988), 'Jambalaya' (first released 1952), *Hank Williams: Let's Turn Back the Years (July 1951–June 1952)*, Polydor 833 749-1.

15

·········

Postcolonialism on the Make: The Music of John Mellencamp, David Bowie, and John Zorn

ELLIE M. HISAMA

> China Girl
> Take me to your jasmine place
> Cool me with your subtle grace
> To know me is no sin
>
> And I won't break you, China Girl
> If you take me into your world
> It's been my good fortune to find you
> China Girl
>
> (John Cougar Mellencamp)

When we acknowledge that an idea, history or tradition is not ours, we distance our-selves from it. When we then proceed to use, incorporate or represent it, we arrogate the right to employ what we acknowledge as not ours. It is not something we do *despite* the foreignness of our subject; it is something we do because of our percep-tion of it as other. The implicit hierarchical nature of otherness invites seemingly innocuous practices of representation that amount to (often unknowing) strategies of domination through appropriation. (Dominguez 1987: 132)

Listening to John Mellencamp's 'China Girl', a pop song in which a white male narrator attempts to woo an Asian female, I, an Asian-American female,

I would like to thank Gish Jen, Greil Marcus, Susan McClary, and Peter Watrous for their encouragement and suggestions on this piece; the members of Susan McClary's 'Music and Postmodernism' seminar (University of Minnesota, spring 1991) for their warm response at its debut; Claudia Hasegawa for generously sharing her materials on Asian-American issues; and Anton Vishio and Loretta Malta for their support and insights. The initial version of this paper was presented at 'Bring the Noise: New Writing on Popular Music', Concordia University, Montréal in October 1991.

am feeling fairly troubled.[1] Yet many people will not share my discomfort: 'So it's a love song sung by a white guy to a Chinese girl, but what's wrong with a little interracial romance?'

To clarify just what I find problematic in this and other pop songs in which white men croon to Asian women about their racial virtues, I would like to begin by reading Mellencamp's piece through the lens of Dominguez's essay. (Lyrics for all songs discussed here are included in the Appendix.) 'China Girl' seems to me excellently to exemplify a work predicated on the strategies Dominguez describes. Addressing the object of his affections simply as 'China Girl', the narrator crows that 'stolen flowers/Are sweetest in the morning'. After informing her that to know him is 'no sin', in the chorus he promises that he will not 'break' her if she will take him into 'her world'. The narrator closes off the chorus by congratulating himself on his good fortune to have found her.

This 'chinagirl' is very much the innocent, shy female whose father governs her actions ('Your daddy tells you white lies/To keep you from my blue eyes').[2] That the narrator believes her to be sexually reserved is evidenced by his persistent attempts to convince her that it will not be a sin for her to take him to her 'jasmine place'.

What makes this song more than merely a male adolescent's whine for the girl to 'do it' is the element of race. Remaining nameless throughout the work, she is not just any girl; she is a '*China* Girl', a figure who inhabits a world separate and distinct from his own as the line 'If you take me into *your world*' suggests. She stands metonymically for the entire Orient, possessing a pastiched identity made up of Oriental women from 'Shōgun', *The Mikado*, 'Hawaii Five-O', and observations made by Archie Bunker.[3] The narrator's relationship to this chinagirl is composed not of simple binary opposites but of hierarchical ones: weak and strong, passive and aggressive, subtle and direct—as Edward Said argues in *Orientalism*, pairs that the Occident has generally ascribed to itself and the 'Orient', a region located vaguely 'over there' (Said 1978).

---

[1] By 'Asian-American' I mean persons of Asian descent who are citizens or residents of the United States. Asian-American groups include persons with origins in East Asia, Southeast Asia, South Asia or the Indian subcontinent. The three tunes I discuss in this article focus on Chinese and Japanese women; examples of other recent artistic representations of Asian women include Asian Indian women in Mira Nair's 1992 film *Mississippi Masala*, and Vietnamese women in the musical *Miss Saigon*.

[2] I refer to the concept of the mythical Chinese woman using the term 'chinagirl' in order to parallel the derogatory nineteenth-century American term for a Chinese man, 'chinaman'.

[3] Gish Jen (1991) and Irvin Paik (1971) discuss the portrayals of the stereotypical Oriental in American films and mass culture.

Yet Orientalism in a postmodern world diverges significantly from the brand of Orientalism that Said describes. He concentrates on British, French, and American representations of the Arabs and of Islam which tend toward the mythic, depicting the Orient as something quite distant. But in the age of the fax machine, satellite, and DC-10; of the recent surge of Asian immigrants towards Western shores; and of the subsequent increase in numbers of Asians who step into America's schools, neighbourhoods, and workplaces—in this century, the East has drawn increasingly nearer to the West. As Mellencamp puts it, 'Your silk's against my skin'.[4]

One response to this new proximity of the East, what the cultural theorist James Clifford calls the 'salvage paradigm', will initially inform my readings of Mellencamp's song, David Bowie's tune of the same name, and John Zorn's 'Forbidden Fruit'. The salvage paradigm recalls the 'salvage ethnography' performed by early twentieth-century anthropologists such as Kroeber and Malinowski who took it as incumbent upon themselves to 'save' vanishing cultures like those of the California Indians and the Trobrianders. Clifford defines the 'salvage paradigm' as 'a desire to rescue "authenticity" out of destructive historical change' (Clifford 1987: 121).

In 'China Girl', the narrator refuses to acknowledge that the world of the Oriental female may intersect or overlap with his world. These lyrics paint a one-dimensional image of the Asian woman he addresses by borrowing heavily from Western stereotypical notions of what constitutes Asian female identity. They present her as some sweetly perfumed, delicate blossom from the East who mysteriously exudes a certain 'subtle grace'; she is a fragile China doll whom he wants to possess.[5] The musical framework of Mellencamp's melodic lines, a pentatonic scale associated with traditional music of east Asia, is meant to evoke the 'sound of the Orient' and reinforces the narrator's dominant position.

In explicating these works I intend to demonstrate how Orientalism in a postmodern age functions in them with regard to their texts and music. But my purpose is not simply to declare that this body of music exists and then

---

[4] The 1980 US census estimated the number of Asians in the US at 1.5% of the total population, a figure which nearly doubled by the time of the 1990 census, to 2.9% (Barringer 1991).

[5] Puccini's *Madama Butterfly* exemplifies a Western masculinist representation of Asian female as exotic blossom, a fantasy David Henry Hwang confronts in his 1988 play *M. Butterfly*. Hwang's work was inspired by a news item about a French diplomat who discovered, at his trial for espionage, that his Chinese lover of many years was not a woman, but a man. This oversight was apparently due to the diplomat's belief that his lover was extremely modest, as was the way of all Chinese women (Hwang 1988). Dorinne Kondo (1990) analyses orientalism in both *Madama Butterfly* and *M. Butterfly*.

to analyse specific examples, confining my observations to what is evident
only in the musical texts; I want to examine, expose, and speak against the
social attitudes that spawn these compositions, attitudes that remain largely
unrecognized except by the women to whom they are directed. Because these
deeply held notions about Asian female identity tend to be received uncrit-
ically, they reinforce a pernicious racial and sexual stereotype that many of
us have to live within.

My Little Fortune Cooky

The 1980s proved to be the decade in which professional services that
served up Asian brides to Western men exploded into a multimillion-dollar-
a-year industry. The concept is simple: the prospective suitor orders a catalogue entitled something like *Jewels of the Orient* or *Lotus Blossoms* which
contains photographs, addresses and self-descriptions written in pidgin English
in order to ensure these women's authenticity. They market exotic Oriental
ladies guaranteed to happily perform traditional wifely tasks.

Ironically, the men drawn to mail order Asian brides seem to be driven by
a desire to have the kind of traditional marital relationship their fathers had.
According to some of the men mentioned by John Krich, Asian women
possess a distinctly refreshing femininity which Western women have
unfortunately lost:

American girls left me really disappointed . . . They look like tubs of lard stuffed into
Levi's. They're pushy, spoiled rotten and they talk like sailors. They're not cooperat-
ive, but combative—and they never appreciate what you do for them. In the morning you wonder how many guys before me? Was it the football team? Maybe it's our
fault, the fault of men for repressing them for so long. But they're not psychologically together. They just don't seem to know what they want. (Krich 1986: 36)

On the contrary: after the women's rights movement in the United States
emerged in the late 1960s and 1970s, women as a group formulated and
articulated *exactly* what they wanted—freedom from the oppression of ready-
made gender roles. The women's movement initially left many men frantic,
but the age of technology, which made it possible for exotic images to float
by on our television screens while we eat egg rolls from bright microwave-
able packages featuring modest, dark-haired, smiling women, cleared many
a bewildered man's head: to find the girl of his dreams, he simply had to leaf
through the latest issue of *Island Blossoms*.

As the mail order bride business began to prosper during the 1980s, the phenomenon of Asiophilia also surfaced in pop and postmodern music. Within recent years, several prominent artists have performed works laden with romantic longings for Asian women, a feature I might find less offensive than pitiable if not for the inequality of the relationship as they depict it. 'China Girl' by Mellencamp was released in 1982; David Bowie's 'China Girl' (written with Iggy Pop) in 1983; and John Zorn's many offerings, including 'Forbidden Fruit' and his New Traditions in East Asian Bar Bands, were performed or released during the late 1980s and early 1990s.

The narrators in both Mellencamp's and Bowie's works position her under their blue-eyed male gaze, enjoying the look. (The line in Bowie's 'China Girl' is 'I feel a-tragic like I'm Marlon Brando/When I look at my China Girl'.)[6] They rejoice that they have finally 'discovered' her, this ideal woman (Mellencamp's line is 'It's been *my* good fortune to find you'); neither mentions whether *she* is content with the relationship.

Yet Bowie's tune presents a different chinagirl from Mellencamp's.

> My little china girl
> You shouldn't mess with me
> I'll ruin everything you are
> I'll give you television
> I'll give you eyes of blue
> I'll give you man who wants to rule the world
>
> (David Bowie)

Rather than evoking jasmine, perfume and oriental exoticism, she, as an inhabitant of the Third World, lacks blue eyes and television—epitomized here to be the destructive, ruinous forces of the West.

When the image of the Asian woman first appears in the music video version, she is dressed in the loose, simple clothing of a Communist Chinese. Her hair is straight and her face fresh-scrubbed. As soon as she begins to march while waving a red flag, little doubt remains that she is meant to represent *Third World* China. As an Asian, she is assumed to have a particularly calming temperament; and as a Chinese, she supposedly possesses amazing,

[6] In the 1957 movie *Sayonara*, Marlon Brando was one of the two actors who broke the taboo in American films against on-screen sex between a white male actor and an Asian actress (before this watershed in movie history, Asian women were played by white women in yellowface). This event led to a slew of such films (*The World of Suzie Wong* (1961); *Diamond Head* (1962); *The Hawaiians* (1970)). Brando also starred in *The Teahouse of the August Moon* (1956) as a white man in yellowface (Paik 1971: 32).

mysterious powers unknown to the West which could greatly benefit from them, much like ginseng root or acupuncture.

This ability is aptly demonstrated in the music, which is introduced, as Mellencamp's was, with superficial notions of what constitutes 'oriental' music —here, parallel fourths played by the guitar. In the first two stanzas Bowie's vocal quality is relatively serene. In the third stanza, his melodic line rises in register and becomes more agitated. In the fourth stanza, after he stumbles into Chinatown with 'plans for everyone', his vocal quality gets increasingly aggressive, higher, and louder; he calms down in the fifth after locking his chinagirl into a long caress.

What precipitates her striking shift from tranquil and simple in the video's opening to angry and garish in the closing frame seems to be our blond narrator. After he seizes her, her world starts to spin, changing irrevocably from black and white into colour. Her skin begins to receive layers of make-up—lipliner, eye-shadow, foundation, and rouge—and the final image we are left with is of our formerly serene Third World member, attractive in her simplicity, having been transformed into a cross woman with heavy make-up and a bad perm.

Bowie's is a more complex piece to read than Mellencamp's in the context of Orientalist politics because its narrative of Western Man meets Asian woman seems so overdone, and thus done tongue in cheek. The act of stroking her hair while she is on her knees, as if she were an obedient dog; the photo of a debonair Bowie prominently displayed upon her bedside table; and the moment in which he lunges upon her passive body on the bed while he sings 'I'll give you a man who wants to rule the world' all contribute to an exaggerated, self-mocking portrait of white male–Asian female relationships.

Furthermore, the narrator seems to conceive of a role for her other than as demure virgin or sweet little housewife who cheerfully gets his bath ready: she could, to his mind, challenge Hitler's desire to 'rule the world'. Her way of being is so soothing, so antithetical to Western hegemonic energies that she need only whisper 'Oh baby, just you shut your mouth' and the visions of swastikas are scattered—powers of surely mythic proportions. Furthermore, as the line 'I'll ruin everything you are' indicates, the narrator manifests concern about corrupting her: this is new.

To read this work as a sardonic commentary on the practice of Asiophilia would be consistent with Bowie's interest in rethinking gender roles and with a statement he reportedly made regarding stereotypes of Asian women: in discussing the opening track of his album *Scary Monsters*, 'It's No Game', Bowie is said to have expressed a desire for the song to 'break down a particular kind of sexist attitude about women, and I thought the Japanese girl typifies it, where everybody sort of pictures her as the geisha girl—sweet, demure, and nonthinking. So she [Michi Hirota] sang the lyrics in a macho, samurai voice' (Hopkins 1985: 217).

Although reading his 'China Girl' as a brilliant piece of irony would leave my admiration for Bowie's work intact (his album *Low* is one of the finest recordings I own), I am still unable to convince myself to accept this interpretation. For while the song *seems* sensitive to the domination and corruption by white men of Asian women, it nevertheless homogenizes Asian female identity in a manner which I do not perceive as being critical. When the Western man laments to his little chinagirl that he will 'ruin everything you are', he takes one admirable step towards realizing that he is appropriating her. Yet she remains nameless, reduced to a sex and a race. And despite the narrator's claim that she has the power to get him to shut up, the chinagirl is never permitted to speak in her own voice—the first and only time she gets the opportunity to say anything, she mouths her line while Bowie delivers it in a monotone.[7] Thus, although their conversation seems to be interactive, it is actually monological. Bowie *appears* to allow an Other to speak, but the 'dialogue' only underscores his authority to represent, and at the same time confers upon himself the role of hero in a Kevin Costner-style rescue fantasy, thereby enacting a new form of colonialism.

Reaching for the Forbidden Fruit

New Yorker John Zorn qualifies as Asiophile *extraordinaire*. Although some critics have suggested that his music contributes to a better society through its attempts to break down boundaries between different cultures, I perceive his musical efforts somewhat differently. Zorn habitually performs works that are predicated upon this troubling gender stereotype about Asian women. Pieces like his New Traditions in East Asian Bar Bands and 'Forbidden Fruit' indicate a disturbing obsession with Asian women's sexual impact upon him.

Like many postmodern artists, Zorn freely borrows from musics he admires, either sampling the works themselves or drawing from their aesthetic. He

[7] Barbara Bradby has argued more generally that male rock performance 'makes the woman into a silent object of exchange among men' (Bradby 1990: 345); for example in 'That'll be the Day', Buddy Holly and a male chorus utter the woman's response *for* her, rather than letting her speak for herself.

has frequently acknowledged the extent to which many of his works are influenced by East Asian music styles or forms. According to his own account, when he visits Japan he likes to 'look at girls' and to get ideas from Asian music (Zorn 1987). Zorn seems not unlike a James Bond of the downtown music scene: he travels to exotic locales where he encounters numerous beautiful women; when he emerges triumphant at the end of the adventure, his exploits are routinely celebrated.

In many of his recordings and performances that call for Asian females' musical participation, they are assigned the role of either vocalist or narrator who evokes a 'pure' East Asian identity. For example, each of the three songs in his New Traditions in East Asian Bar Bands series (performed in the summer of 1991 as part of the New York International Festival of the Arts) requires an Asian female narrator to read a text in Korean, Chinese or Vietnamese (Rockwell 1991).

In these performances, Zorn offers no translations to the texts, and those who do not understand what is said are left with an impression of three beautiful Asian women who babble charmingly but unintelligibly. Furthermore, in each work Zorn pits two male instrumentalists (a pair of drummers, electric guitarists, and keyboardists) against each other in competition for the woman. Although Zorn has said that the three works are meant to pay tribute to the Asian actresses Que Tran, Jang Mi Hee, and Hu Die, the women after whom the pieces are named, I find it difficult to comprehend how works that require Asian women to be the prize in a struggle between two white men are supposed to function as any kind of 'homage' to them.

'Forbidden Fruit' (1987) also appropriates Asian female identity. Scored for string quartet, turntables, and female Japanese voice, it too was intended as a tribute piece. In the album's liner notes, Zorn identifies a specific image that inspired him to compose the work in honour of Ishihara Yujiro, a Japanese actor who died in 1987: a photograph of Ishihara, a second actor and Ishihara's wife, Kitahara Mie, whom Zorn finds 'unbelievably gorgeous' (Zorn 1987).

In the photo, Kitahara is sitting, foreground centre, in a strapless swimsuit. She is clearly braless and her silkily smooth skin glows. Both men in the photo are riveted upon her. But in contrast to the ready availability of her body, she sits shyly, modestly cupping her arm about her torso as if to shield her breasts from the camera; her eyes do not meet its gaze, but look somewhere beyond it. Her suit is edged with a row of innocent embroidered flowers, perhaps daisies.

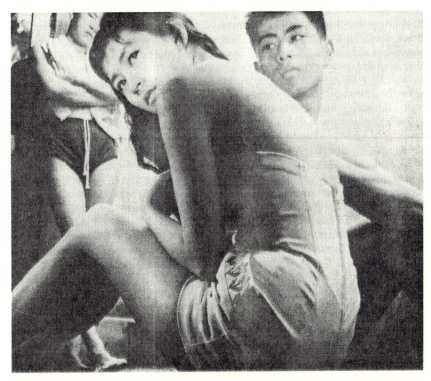

Figure 15.1 Ishihara Yujiro, Kitahara Mie, and Tsugawa Masahiko in *Kurutta Kajitsu* (1956). Picture used by permission of the Nikkatsu Corporation, Japan

Sexy but not sleazy, the irresistibly beautiful Japanese female represents to Zorn a space to which he is drawn over and over again, in his musical as well as personal life. Like the narrators in both Bowie's and Cougar's tunes, Zorn perceives the Asian woman's world as distinct from and opposite to his own. He eagerly wants to explore her world, and invariably ends up exoticizing it.

The text of 'Forbidden Fruit' intimates a sexual encounter between a Japanese female and some unnamed 'he'. Ohta Hiromi reads a narrative in Japanese in which 'You and I, sweat and sweat'; soon 'something happens/ He is coming'. Reassured that she can 'do it well', 'pain' ensues, followed by 'shine'. She concludes with the words 'I lick . . . I gnaw . . . I devour' in a sultry whisper.

As is characteristic of Zorn's compositions, 'Forbidden Fruit' is musical pastiche. Fragments of familiar musical themes fly by—Carmen's Habañera vamp; the opening of Mozart's Piano Sonata in B♭ major, K. 315; a phrase by the soloist in Bruch's G minor violin concerto—only to have their cadences smudged or snatched away. The vocalist, Ohta Hiromi, delivers the text with a soft, high, sweet vocal quality, and concludes with nonsense baby syllables.

This bestowing of child-like qualities on the Asian female is consistent with both Cougar's and Bowie's depictions of her as innocent little girl. The authenticity of Ohta's Japanese female identity in the piece is bolstered by her pronunciation of the text's English words—'slash', 'slowmotion'—with an unmistakable Japanese lilt, the equivalent of broken English in mail order Asian bride catalogues. But it is clearly not Ohta who is desired. Zorn reveals that he thinks of her as bodyless, calling her 'one of my very favourite voices in the world' (Zorn 1987). The photograph on the album cover serves as a constant reminder of just what Body we're talking about. Zorn's gaze is obviously as firmly fixed upon Kitahara as Ishihara's and Tsugawa's. But as composer, Zorn can take on the role of puppet-master and the Asian women whose vocal parts he writes will do anything he wants, including licking, gnawing, and devouring on command.

A Story

Growing up in southern Illinois as an Asian-American female was a rather repulsive experience. For Valentine's Day each year I was presented with the single card from those shiny red plastic-covered boxes in which a grinning, slanty-eyed Oriental wearing a kimono declared, in a bubble coming from her mouth, 'You're my cup of tea!' My classmates did not seem to intend offence; yet the Valentine I opened with dismay every year made all too clear what they perceived me as being—a kimonoed, tea-pouring Oriental. And as the early childhood ritual in which one is expected to declare affection for a particular person wore on, Valentine's Day also taught me that Asians are marked as romantically undesirable Others.

That is, until I turned ten. For our weekly music period my class merged with the other fifth-grade class down the hall. One week during a break I overheard a white boy boast to his friend that 'when I grow up, I'm gonna marry an Oriental girl'. The person to whom he was speaking pointed at me and asked him if he liked me. He said, yes . . . but did not know if he would marry me. His friend was clearly puzzled as to why a person with free choice would ever choose to marry an Oriental, but his bewilderment did not nearly match my own. How could this boy 'like me' when we had never seen each other before?

Sadly, this tale has been repeated many times, not only to me personally but to most other Asian-American females I have spoken with.[8] It happens at bus stops: a white man sidles up to you and strikes up a conversation in which he reminisces about the time he served in Korea—then the inevitable 'are you married?'[9] Often when I take a taxicab home alone at night, the driver muses on how fine the women from 'my country' are, or in the classroom, the professor announces he would like to call me by my Japanese middle name, Michiko, because he finds it 'much more beautiful'.

Let me try to express what I find so unsettling if it is not yet clear:

(1) To be rejected because of your race and to be desired for just the same reason are both forms of racism. But the latter is a tricky position to negotiate: I know of several women who willingly enter into relationships with Asiophilic men because they are attracted to them; refuse to believe that their individual identity goes relatively unnoticed; feel grateful to be finally accepted; or simply do not mind—in fact they feel proud of this interest in their culture.

(2) Asiophilia carries with it old-time sexism ('when women were women') as well as heterosexism: if one holds the Asian woman as the quintessential female, the Asian lesbian would be a paradox.

(3) The stereotypes imposed upon us force a loss of individual identity. A great many Asians living in the United States know that, to many non-Asians, we are all Chinese, and have been repeatedly told that 'All Orientals look alike'. (If this indeed were the case, it would surely be impossible for our family and friends to tell us apart.) This belief quickly goes beyond problems of physical differentiation and name confusion into more harmful realms such as not getting a job as a result of the widely held assumption that Orientals are naturally adept at maths but inevitably struggle with English. (I have been told on countless occasions: 'You speak English very well!!' or: 'You don't have *much* of an accent.' Once as an undergraduate I was questioned by a professor as to whether the writing in what he considered a particularly eloquent paper was 'really my own'.)

---

[8] Matsumoto (1989) and Wong (1983) provide other such accounts of males' sexual interest in the 'little Oriental woman'.

[9] In her essay 'G.I.'s and Asian Women' Evelyn Yoshimura relates how United States drill instructors during the Korean and Vietnam wars dangled images of Asian women as willing, immoral sex toys before the GIs in order to incite them to kill the less-than-human Oriental and to instil in them the desire to return to the good white women who were waiting at home (Yoshimura 1971: 27–9).

Two deaths of Asians in the USA within recent years speak to the frightening possibilities that can result from the homogenizing of Asian identity. In 1982, a Chinese-American, Vincent Chin, was clubbed to death in Detroit by two white autoworkers who said to him, shortly before smashing his skull with a baseball bat, 'It's because of you motherfuckers that we're out of work' (Takaki 1989: 481–4). And in February 1992, a Japanese businessman in California began receiving death threats from a man who claimed that the Japanese had caused him to lose his job; he was killed two weeks later (Mydans 1992).

(4) The 'pure' identity pre-formed for anyone who looks Asian poses a particular problem for those who are Asian-*American*. Depending on our hometown, many of us have grown up feeling that Asia is indeed the 'Orient'—distant and opposed to what constitutes our own identity: we too were born in the United States, know all the episodes of the Brady Bunch, and despise raw fish;[10] whether asked about Zen Buddhism or demanded to 'Speak some Chinese!', we feel as much at a loss as the next person—yet we are expected to *be* oriental and are thus doomed to disappoint and to shrivel into inauthenticity.[11]

Reading as a Postcolonial Diasporic

In her essay 'Who Claims Alterity?' the literary theorist Gayatri Chakravorty Spivak describes a historical shift in the early 1970s into what she calls transnationalism, and locates an economic catalyst for this shift—the computerization of the stock exchange. She argues that as the old empires get dismantled,

a softer and more benevolent Third Worldism [enters] the Euramerican academy . . . [Yet the postcolonial diasporic] can be uneasy . . . with being made the object of unquestioning benevolence as an inhabitant of the new Third World. (Spivak 1989: 275)

This is a sentiment that Trinh T. Minh-ha also describes in her recent book *Woman, Native, Other*:

[10] In his recent book *Turning Japanese: Memoirs of a Sansei* (1991), David Mura poignantly describes his own emotional and physical separation from Japan as a *Sansei* (a third-generation Japanese-American), a distance which began to close after spending a year in Japan.

[11] The assumption that all people of Asian descent are not *really* American was the US government's premiss in ordering persons of Japanese ancestry (including US citizens) to be incarcerated during World War II, but not those of German or Italian descent.

It is as if everywhere we go, we become Someone's private zoo. . . . We no longer wish to erase your difference, We demand, on the contrary, that you remember and assert it. . . . Now i am not only given the permission to open up and talk, i am also encouraged to express my difference. My audience expects and demands it; otherwise people would feel as if they have been cheated: We did not come to hear a Third World member speak about the First (?) World, We came to listen to that voice of difference likely to bring us *what we can't have* and to divert us from the monotony of sameness. (Trinh 1989: 82, 88, 89)

Like Spivak and Trinh, I find myself nowadays writing from a new, uneasy position. When I mention the practice of Asiophilia to some of my white friends, they quickly list Asian and white couples they know as if to prove that 'good people' partake of interracial romantic relations too. They seem to believe that I am arguing that *all* interracial relationships are based on domination and appropriation, which is *not* what I am saying; or that I am opposed to manifesting a curiosity about worlds other than the ones most familiar to us.

What I *am* protesting, again borrowing Spivak's elegant terminology, is the projection of a 'hyperreal Third world' or the 'comfortable Other' (Spivak 1989: 275). Images of Asian females in these works by Mellencamp, Bowie, and Zorn might satisfy their creators' personal longings but do they ask what the chinagirl herself wants? feels? needs? Having repeatedly been expected to play the role of chinagirl, I often feel as if I am being placed in Trinh's zoo, or gathered up as just another exotic, fetishized object to be installed in some museum to assure the collector of his own identity while leaving my own blank, without a personal history or time.[12]

Along with the three forces behind Asiophilia that I have mentioned (the quest for the Real woman, the yearning to preserve 'pure' cultures, and the urge to collect), I believe the desire to transgress also plays a part: historically, Asian women in the United States have been either invisible or inaccessible to non-Asian men, forbidden by both law and custom. Comprising less than 2 per cent of the current US population, they often remained in Asia while their male kin worked in the States, or they lived in tightly knit Asian communities; intermarriage between Asians and whites in the USA was illegal for a time in several states including California, whose antimiscegenation statute was declared unconstitutional less than fifty years ago (Osumi 1982). Furthermore, enveloped in a mythic sexual aura (the geisha

---

[12] In his essay 'On Collecting Art and Culture' James Clifford discusses collection-making as an appropriative act which creates the illusion of adequate representation while helping only to define the collector's self (Clifford 1988).

girl, the Singapore girl, the Thai prostitute who eagerly awaits the arrival of the US military), Asian female identity has long been linked with prostitution and naughty sex.

My own repeated experiences of being approached by innumerable white men who expect me to be demure, domestic, and doting are both fuelled by these tunes by Mellencamp, Bowie, and Zorn and depicted by them. In other words, the orientalist representations in these pop songs reflect a phenomenon that is fast becoming an American way of life, as well as stimulate the practice itself. (I fear that the high visibility of Woody Allen and Soon-Yi Farrow Previn's romance may have inspired many Asiophilic relationships, given Allen's near cult status in the USA.) Through its ability to reach more and more of the globe by means of increasingly more elaborate forms of mechanical reproduction, the popular music industry can instantly represent other worlds as its practitioners see fit. Whether they attempt to go beyond representation depends, I believe, on us, its consumers, to assess critically what we hear rather than to valorize it because we like the tune.[13]

Thus I conclude by suggesting the possibility of hearing the line in Mellencamp's chorus, 'I won't break you/China Girl/If you take me into your world', as a threat to an enemy as well as a clumsy attempt at reassurance; the suggestion that she 'take me to your jasmine place' as a demand. Interpreted in this way, the elements of coercion and inequality are thrown into relief: the fear of the East and of the Female invading his world incites our former hero to invade their world first—or rather, again.

Appendix

John Cougar Mellencamp, 'China Girl' (1982). By Joe New and Jeff Silbar.

> China Girl
> I met you on the sea sand
> You touch me with your cool hand
> Your perfume's in the wind
>
> China Girl
> Your daddy tells you white lies
> To keep you from my blue eyes
> To know me is no sin

---

[13] One critical theorist who has written quite perceptively on issues of race, sex, and class in popular music is Michele Wallace, addressing black male rap (1990*a*) and the Michael Jackson phenomenon (1990*b*).

I won't break you, China Girl
If you take me into your world
It's been my good fortune to find you
China Girl

Stolen flowers
Are sweetest in the morning
The Eastern sun is dawnin'
Your silk's against my skin

China Girl
Take me to your jasmine place
Cool me with your subtle grace
To know me is no sin
I won't break you, China Girl
If you take me into your world
It's been my good fortune to find you
China Girl

David Bowie, 'China Girl' (1983). Lyrics and music by David Bowie and Iggy Pop.

Oh-Oh-Oh-Oh
Little China Girl
I could escape this feeling with my China Girl
I feel a wreck without my little China Girl
I hear her heart beating loud as thunder
Saw the stars crashing

I'm a mess without my little China Girl
Wake up in the morning where's my little China Girl
I hear her heart's beating loud as thunder
Saw the stars crashing down

I feel a-tragic like I'm Marlon Brando
When I look at my China Girl
I could pretend that nothing really meant too much
When I look at my China Girl

I stumble into town just like a sacred cow
Visions of swasticas in my head
Plans for everyone
It's in the white of my eyes

My little China Girl
You shouldn't mess with me
I'll ruin everything you are

I'll give you television
I'll give you eyes of blue
I'll give you man who wants to rule the world
And when I get excited
My little China Girl says
Oh baby just you shut your mouth
She says . . . sh-sh-shhh.

John Zorn, 'Forbidden Fruit' (1987). Original texts by Reck.

Close my eyes
Take deep breath
My memories slash

You and I, sweat and sweat
Keeen . . . keeen . . . slowmotion
In my ears . . . endless echoes
color . . . empty . . . colors

Sitting still, listening still
Flowing, wrapped within
Something happens

He is coming. So beautiful
So I can do it well
I'm waiting on the beach

Soon I awake
Thirst and sigh
Dazzling and grow dizzy
Pain . . . shine

I lick . . . I gnaw . . . I devour

References

Barringer, F. (1991). 'Immigration brings new diversity to Asian population in the US', *New York Times*, 12 June.

Bradby, B. (1990). 'Do-talk and don't talk: the division of the subject in girl-group music', in *On Record: Rock, Pop, and the Written Word*, ed. S. Frith and A. Goodwin (London), 341–68.

Chuman, F. F. (1977). *The Bamboo People: The Law and the Japanese-Americans* (Del Mar, Calif.).

Civil Rights Issues Facing Asian Americans in the 1990s (1992). A Report of the United States Commission on Civil Rights (Washington).

Clifford, J. (1987). 'Of other peoples: beyond the "salvage" paradigm', in *Discussions in Contemporary Culture*, 1, ed. H. Foster (Seattle), 121–30.

—— (1988). *The Predicament of Culture: Twentieth-Century Ethnography, Literature, and Art* (Cambridge, Mass.).

Davis, F. (1991). ' "Zorn" for "anger": the composer John Zorn likes being the bad boy of new music', *The Atlantic* (January), 97–100.

Dominguez, V. R. (1987). 'Of other peoples: beyond the "salvage" paradigm', in *Discussions in Contemporary Culture*, 1, ed. H. Foster (Seattle), 131–7.

Hopkins, J. (1985). *Bowie* (New York).

Hwang, D. H. (1988). *M. Butterfly* (New York).

Jen, G. (1991). 'Challenging the Asian illusion', *New York Times*, 11 August.

Kondo, D. (1990). '*M. Butterfly*: orientalism, gender, and a critique of essentialist identity', *Cultural Critique*, 16: 5–30.

Krich, J. (1986). 'Here come the brides: the blossoming business of imported love', *Mother Jones*, 11/2: 34–46.

Matsumoto, V. (1989). 'Two deserts', in *The Forbidden Stitch: An Asian American Women's Anthology*, ed. S. G. Lim, M. Tsutakawa, and M. Donnelly (Corvallis, Ore.), 45–53.

Mura, D. (1991). *Turning Japanese: memoirs of a Sansei* (New York).

Mydans, S. (1992). 'Killing alarms Japanese-Americans', *New York Times*, 26 February.

Osumi, M. D. (1982). 'Asians and California's anti-miscegenation laws', in *Asian and Pacific American Experiences: Women's Perspectives*, ed. N. Tsuchida (Minneapolis), 1–37.

Paik, I. (1971). 'That Oriental feeling: a look at the caricatures of the Asians as sketched by American movies', in *Roots: An Asian American Reader*, ed. A. Tachiki, E. Wong, F. Odo, and B. Wong (Los Angeles), 30–6.

Pareles, J. (1991). 'Sound bites from Asia (composer John Zorn's group "New Traditions in East Asian Bar Bands")', *New York Times*, 7 June.

Rockwell, J. (1988). 'As important as anyone in his generation', *New York Times*, 21 February.

—— (1991). 'Evoking images of bars in Asian ports', *New York Times*, 10 June.

Said, E. W. (1978). *Orientalism* (New York).

Spivak, G. C. (1989). 'Who claims alterity?', in *Discussions in Contemporary Culture*, 4, ed. B. Kruger and P. Mariani (Seattle).

Takaki, R. (1989). *Strangers from a Different Shore: A History of Asian Americans* (Boston).

Trinh, T. M. (1989). *Woman, Native, Other: Writing Postcoloniality and Feminism* (Bloomington, Ind.).

Wallace, M. (1990*a*). 'When black feminism faces the music, and the music is rap', *New York Times*, 29 July.

—— (1990*b*). 'Michael Jackson, black modernisms and the "ecstasy of communication" ', in *Invisibility Blues: From Pop to Theory* (London), 77–90.

Watrous, P. (1989). 'John Zorn takes over the town', *New York Times*, 24 February.

Wong, N. (1983). 'When I was growing up', in *This Bridge Called My Back: Writings by Radical Women of Color*, ed. C. Moraga and G. Anzaldúa (New York), 7–8.

Yoshimura, E. (1971). 'G.I.'s and Asian Women', in *Roots: An Asian American Reader*, ed. A. Tachiki, E. Wong, F. Odo, and B. Wong (Los Angeles), 27–9.

Zorn, J. (1987). Liner notes to *Spillane*, Nonesuch, 9 79172-1.

Discography

David Bowie, *Low*, RCA CPL1-2030 (1977).

—— 'It's No Game', *Scary Monsters*. RCA, AQL1-3647 (1980).

—— 'China Girl', *Let's Dance*. EMI, America/SO 517093 (1983).

John Cougar Mellencamp, 'China Girl', *American Fool*. Riva Records, RVL 7501 (1982).

John Zorn, 'Forbidden Fruit', *Spillane*. Nonesuch, 9 79172-1 (1987).

—— 'Lotus Blossom', *News for Lulu*. Hat Hut, 6005 (1988).

—— 'Chinatown', 'Punk China Doll', and 'Saigon Pickup', *Naked City*. Nonesuch, 79238 (1989).

16

Structural Relationships of Music and Images in Music Video

ALF BJÖRNBERG

Introduction

In the course of the last decade, the body of writing on music video has grown to sizeable proportions. The reason for the present addition to this bulk of literature, in spite of the subject seemingly approaching the state of exhaustion, is that musical semiotics are still rarely applied to the field. It is a fact that pop and rock music have always been heavily infused with socially determined meaning such that an autonomous musical aesthetics appears clearly insufficient to explain their significance; however, to what extent and how this significance is linked in with particular musical structures as such is still largely uninvestigated. In my view, music video may perhaps be less interesting as a phenomenon in itself than as source material for an 'empirical semiotics' of popular music, shedding light on signification processes of a more general applicability. Furthermore, the distinctive features of music video may arguably be better explained on the basis of an understanding of the syntactical characteristics of popular music than by prevalent theories of postmodernism; the latter appear problematic not only due to their speculative and unsubstantiated nature with regard to media reception processes (cf. Frith and Horne 1987: 11), but their explanatory value as regards syntactic features of music video also seems to be limited (cf. Frith 1988: 207).

In an earlier work, I have presented a theoretical discussion of the characteristics of popular music syntax and their consequences for the analysis of music video, as well as a general typology of relationships between music and visuals (see Björnberg 1992a). The purpose of the present essay is to

An earlier version of this paper has appeared in the Working Paper Series of the Department of Music and Theatre, University of Oslo. Parts of the theoretical discussion are derived from Björnberg (1992b).

modify and substantiate in more detail this previous account, by way of an analysis of structural relationships of music and images in a number of music videos. This analysis is aimed at demonstrating both the range of possible different types of such relationships, the limitations imposed upon them by musical syntax, and their relative 'openness' to varying kinds of reception and interpretation, depending on the mode of listening/viewing applied.

Postmodern Society, Postmodern Media, Postmodern Audiences?

The specific characteristics of (the visual dimension of) music video attracting the attention of writers and scholars may be summarized as the breakdown of linear narrativity, of causal logic, and of temporal and spatial coherence. The apparently widely accepted mainstream line of explanation of these characteristic traits is based on the argument of *postmodernism*: the 'postmodern condition', pervading all of contemporary industrialized society, finds its most adequate representation in the fragmentary forms of music video, combining practices from Classical high art, avant-garde modernism, and popular culture (see, for instance, Aufderheide 1986; Kaplan 1987; Strøm 1989). The evaluation of the consequences of this situation varies among authors; whereas, for instance, Fiske (1986) regards the 'refusing of sense' as a practice potentially liberating from bourgeois hegemony of meaning, Tetzlaff (1986) is more pessimistic as to the existence of any such emancipatory potential. While postmodernism sometimes approaches the vague, all-embracing status of a *Zeitgeist*, many scholars relate it, and the characteristics of music video, to the development of the specific media codes of commercial television (Berland 1986; Jones 1988; Kaplan 1987; Larsen 1987), and especially, stressing the advertising function of music video, to the aesthetics of television advertising (Allan 1990; Frith 1988; Goodwin 1987; Kinder 1984; Laing 1985; Movin and Øberg 1990; Strøm 1989 and others). The loss, in this process, of rock music's presupposed 'authenticity' of expression is also commented upon (Grossberg 1988); this is described both in negative terms (Movin and Øberg 1990), and approvingly, as offering the means for a 'celebration of artifice' (Ihlemann 1992).

The explanations for the emergence of music video in its specific form also include references to the significance of the development of *technology*, both television (cable) and video production/post-production technology, as well as that of musical production and reproduction (Berland 1986; Goodwin 1987; Ruud 1988). Ruud (ibid.) also discusses the connections with video art, emphasizing the aesthetic quality of ambiguity inherent in the non-narrativity of music video (see also Strøm 1989).

Several explanations for non-narrativity from the point of view of the *audience* have also been offered. One line of argument apparently lying close at hand involves the view of the specificities of music video as a consequence of a general tendency, determined by social and media-technological developments, towards a Benjaminian 'distracted mode of perception', requiring a structure allowing the user to quickly catch the point of the message (Jones 1988; Larsen 1987; Movin and Øberg 1990); at times this view is extended into postmodernist speculation on the 'schizophrenic subject' (Jensen 1988). Another common explanation (presupposing the user's devotion of a more continuous attention) emphasizes the functions of fantasy, escape from everyday reality and imaginary problem solution provided by the incoherent and fragmentary structures of music video (Allan 1990; Aufderheide 1986; Morse 1986). The parallelisms between these structures and the workings of the primary processes of the psyche have been pointed out (Brown and Fiske 1987; Ruud 1988), as well as the potential of fantasy for exploitation for commercial purposes (Kinder 1984). In this context connections have also been made with the need-structures produced by the new, 'narcissistic' socialization patterns suggested by German socialization theory (Forsman 1986; Larsen 1987).

Music: The Missing Connection

Few of the theories related above can be totally dismissed as contributions to the understanding of the characteristics of music video. Nevertheless, in spite of the significant role of *music* in this context (if nothing else, as the alleged justification for the entire phenomenon), most of the authors cited have remarkably little to say about it. The opinion has been proposed that, for the user, the music is somehow 'dominated' by the visuals (Berland 1986; Kinder 1984; Tetzlaff 1986); this, however, seems to have little bearing on matters other than the individual mode of perception and musical preferences of these scholars. Others point out that historically, popular music performance has always been an audiovisual phenomenon, combining musical sound and visuals (Berland 1986; Goodwin 1987; Laing 1985), and several authors state that music is primary in relation to the visuals, although without elaborating much further on the nature and consequences of this primacy (Goodwin 1987; Laing 1985; Strøm 1989). Kaplan seems to regard music video visuals as mainly based on song *lyrics* (1987: 47 f.), restricting her discussion of musical characteristics to little more than one half page (1987: 123 f.).[1]

In several instances writers on music video have given indications of the position regarding the conditions for and/or operation of *musical signification* underlying their respective treatment of the subject. Ruud (1988) regards signification in music as mainly determined by social context and conventionalized. Movin and Øberg, following Adorno, characterize music as non-referential and experienced by way of 'emotional empathy' (1990: 127), while Brown and Fiske state that 'Rock videos, like rock music, work primarily on physical sensations and produce a physical pleasure that opposes the common sense of linear narrative in dominant ideology' (1987: 62). Morse, in her discussion of music video functioning as 'a form of magical thinking' (1986: 24), touches upon aspects of music as performed (the star-singer 'creating a visual world' by virtue of his or her privileged position in the musical as well as visual mode of communication) but does not relate this to other musical dimensions. Whereas these various positions indicate relevant aspects, they are hardly exhaustive on the matter of musical signification in music video, and in most cases seem not to inspire the undertaking of more detailed analyses.

Allan, in a discussion of correspondences between musical film and music video, identifies the functions of music as 'those of grounding, unity and resolution' (1990: 9), while Kinder (1984) states that the continuous flow of the music imposes unity on the video. These are among the rare instances of music video scholars approaching the significance of structural aspects of music; another example is Berland's (1986) somewhat impressionistic account of the relationship between formal song structure and visuals. Unfortunately, the embryo of structural analysis inherent in the latter approach is not followed up, probably due both to the author's Adornian view of popular music structures and to the visual domination postulated (cf. above).

On a theoretical level, Frith's (1988) discussion of structural characteristics of music video amounts to a well-considered counter-argument, based on musical facts, against postmodern theory speculation. Frith points to the general structuring principles of movement as 'the metaphor for sound' (1988: 216) and montage as representation of rock's musical experiential qualities, and also discusses the relationships between musical and visual

[1] For a discussion of the reasons for the sparse coverage of the subject of music in the literature on music video see Björnberg (1991: 64 f.); also cf. Nielsen (1991: 297).

repetitivity.[2] Although the arguments are coloured by the author's obvious dislike for music video in its currently dominant form, and may be criticized on some points (cf. Björnberg 1992*a*: 382, 386), this article remains an important corrective for writers on the subject. Frith's arguments have also been picked up by Nielsen, stating that music video images are subordinated to the music by way of 'a rhythmically determined pleasure principle' (1991: 299),[3] and Forsman, who adds to the montage/beat homology one between sound and an 'associative spatiality' (1991: 9).

However, despite these theoretical contributions, detailed analyses of music videos relating visuals to musical structure have been very sparsely presented. Ruud (1988) performs lengthy analyses of three videos; however, only one of these (Paul Simon's 'René and Georgette Magritte with their dog after the war') deals in greater detail with musical (mainly tonal) structure, thus emphasizing unique individual features rather than general structural principles, and giving an unfortunate bias to the study. Larsen (1987), basing his discussion on Greimas's narrative theory, analyses the relationship between musical and visual syntax in Phil Collins's 'Against All Odds'. The author convincingly relates visual structure to musical segmentation and intensity (dynamics and texture) processes. The implied seeds of a more general application of narrative theory to popular music are, however, not followed up; in a later work (Larsen 1988), the author restricts his discussion to Western art music and its derivatives in Hollywood film music, by implication dismissing contemporary popular music as generally non-narrative and not susceptible to this kind of analysis.[4]

Popular Music Form and Narrativity

In an attempt to remedy some of the shortcomings of the literature on music video recapitulated above, the analyses to be undertaken here will take

[2] The relationship between montage and musical beat is also touched upon by Goodwin, who refers this to the conditions of music video production: 'Directors working under enormous pressures of time will (. . .) often shoot some material that can be edited at random to the beat, without any great regard for realism or narrative closure' (1987: 26).

[3] At the level of visual content, Nielsen also connects this with Straw's argument that the fragmentary eclecticism of music video, rather than representing empty pastiche, constitutes a *reconstruction of pop music history* within traditional pop song forms: 'The relationship of song to visuals is (. . .) rather one between the basic demands of form (. . .) and the heterogeneity of codes and visual materials held in play by that form' (1988: 258; see also Berkaak and Ruud 1989).

[4] Most of the works cited here have been written by scholars in sociology, film studies, literary studies or mass communication research. Up to the present, the contributions of musicologists to the study of music video have been few and have also shown a general bias towards the perspectives of these other disciplines, this situation indicating the current embryonic stage of development of a structural semiotics of popular music.

as their theoretical point of departure the issue of *the potential for significa-tion in popular music syntax*. That is, I am concerned with 'primary' rather than 'secondary' musical signification (Middleton 1990: 220 ff.), and with the signification of *syntactical processes*, as opposed to particular, individual musematic meaning (ibid. 235). I would also like to make a distinction in favour of the *structural* rather than the (in a psychoanalytical sense 'more primary', i.e. related to primary processes of the psyche) 'physical sensation', *para-structural* signification dimension of music; although, as Middleton (ibid. 219) points out, these cannot be clearly separated, the latter aspect of musical communication appears as yet to have attracted considerably more attention from writers on music video than the former.

Differently phrased, this is a matter of the potential for *narrativity* in music. In this connection, Middleton suggests a general distinction between three modes of construction of musical syntax:

In contrast to the *narrative* category, which privileges difference, there is what we can call an *'epic'* mode, where the focus is on repetition and varied repetition; and in between comes a *'lyrical'* category (marked by symmetrical open/closed and binary structures). (Middleton 1990: 216; my italics)

The positing of 'narrative' and 'epic' as polar opposites may appear some-what confusing against the background of the everyday use of these terms in relation to literature and film; taking up the geometrical metaphors already hinted at by Middleton, a better terminology would perhaps be using 'linear' instead of 'narrative', 'circular' instead of 'epic', and maybe 'elliptical' (in the strictly geometrical sense) for 'lyrical', implying the dual aspects of movement and return inherent in the latter syntactical mode. Still, the categorization appears valid and potentially fruitful for the analysis of popular music syntax, and although these terms in this usage may primarily be comprehended as rather abstract structural analogies, they nevertheless also arguably indicate experiential correlates to models of musical syntax, that is, to musical *form*, in a general sense. The formal structures of popular music are usually con-ceived of and described in terms of standardized, 'neutral' structures, having achieved 'a naturalness' (Berland 1986: 44) to the listener; still, this does not render their intrinsic potential for signification non-existent.[5]

---

[5] Straw's (1988) emphasis on the recourse in the music video era to traditional pop structures (see note 3) seems to attribute a historically relatively stable and constant, and thus relatively vague and unspecified, nature to this potential ('the basic demands of form'); however, in view of the significant range of variation as regards formal construction in popular music it appears more relevant to speak of 'forms' rather than of one general 'form', and to investigate in more detail the potential experiential consequences afforded by this variation.

Middleton links the narrative mode of musical syntax construction with the absence of repetition, with the extreme variation of the 'infinite set', in which no musical element is repeated, the music continuously moving forward linearly and teleologically in a manner homologous to the structures of (verbal/visual) narrative. In order to investigate further the existence of homologies between music and narrative, structuralist narrative theory appears to offer some useful concepts.[6] A basic distinction made within this body of theory is that between *story*, the signified or content of narrative, and *discourse*, the signifier or structure of the narrative text (Chatman 1978: 19; cf. Barthes 1977: 87; Genette 1980: 27). While the semantic precision of musical narrative as to its content, its 'story', is low compared to verbal or visual narration, musical structure may be demonstrated to be capable of exhibiting several of the characteristics constitutive of narrative discourse. In a somewhat loose but helpful phrasing, Chatman (1978: 25) identifies the distinctive features of narrative as 'eventhood, characterhood, and setting-hood'. These concepts appear adequately applicable to musical discourse. A basic feature of Western music since the Renaissance, and particularly of popular music, is the structural dualism of melody and accompaniment (Maróthy 1974: 22; Tagg 1979: 123 f.). As Tagg indicates, this dualism is generally conceived in terms of a relationship between figure and background, or between individual/character and environment/setting. These are frequently consistently identifiable with separate musical 'voices'; however, the structural specificities and polysemic nature of music also allow for the same 'voice' to alternate between various functions, such as a guitar first playing a riff as part of the background, then switching to fill in the vocal line as a 'secondary character', and subsequently becoming the 'main character' in a guitar solo. As for the quality of 'eventhood', musical structure may appropriately be described as a succession (and/or simultaneity) of events, ranging from instantaneous changes to long-term processes. From this point of view, 'musical form' is defined by the particular nature of each musical event, by the temporal density of events and by their distribution throughout the duration of the piece in question.

For the purpose of investigating the *degree of narrativity* of particular musical structures a further distinction made by Chatman may be useful. Narrative discourse is characterized as being constructed from *statements*,

---

[6] My earlier discussion of this matter (see Björnberg 1992a: 380 ff.), while remaining, to my view, theoretically valid, is somewhat too generalized for the present analytical purposes.

which may be divided into *stasis* ('is') statements and *process* ('does') statements (Chatman 1978: 31 f.); a parallel distinction is the one made by Greimas between *radotage* and *affabulation* (cf. Larsen 1987: 89). Narrativity, in the common-sense meaning of the term, is linked to the quantity and density of process statements: a narrative where 'nothing happens' clearly has a 'non-narrative' character. Adequate musical analogies to this categorization exist both in Ruwet's (1987: 16) differentiation between *parametric* and *non-parametric* elements in music, and in Middleton's (1990: 215) distinction between *binary/digital* and *analogue selection*. Parametric elements are characterized by being constant throughout a piece of music or switching between the two poles of an opposition, i.e. being subject to binary alternation, while non-parametric elements are characterized by 'a fairly large number of internal distinctions of the same dimensions', i.e. they tend towards analogue selection. On the basis of the analogy between 'process statement' and 'non-parametricness', narrativity in music may thus be seen as related to the quantitative and qualitative significance of non-parametric organization/analogue selection, in agreement with the argument of Middleton related above.

Although, as Ruwet points out, it is impossible to determine *a priori* whether a particular musical dimension has a parametric or non-parametric organization, in Western music in general dimensions such as tempo, mode, instrumentation, and timbre tend to be parametric, while melodic pitch, surface rhythm, and harmonic tension are more or less non-parametric. Narrative qualities in Western music have thus primarily been associated with the dimensions of melody and harmony: melodic processes of aperture and closure combine with harmonic processes of tension and release, forming potentially long-ranging, forward-directed musical structures. Illustrative examples of this may be found in 'extremely narrative' music, such as, for instance, Wagner's operas; in popular music, however, a high degree of such narrativity is seldom the case. Generally, popular music is characterized by *strophic disposition*, i.e. repetition of a small number of well-demarcated sections, and *symmetrical construction*, i.e. larger units being constructed by binary combination of smaller units (cf. Björnberg 1992b: 4). These characteristics imply a predominance of the lyrical mode: the use of symmetrical structures, whose well-roundedness works against directional linearity, is distinctive of this mode, and strophic disposition involves processes of repeated return to an experiential focal point or 'point of departure', processes whose *reflective* character contrasts both with the linearity of the narrative mode and with the short-term repetitivity of the epic category. This lyricality is not, however, homogeneously prevalent across the popular music field; it is modified by different styles (and individual pieces of music) tending more or less towards linearity or circularity. It is also important in an analytical context to take into account the possibility for other dimensions than melody and harmony to produce narrativity in popular music, by virtue of being organized non-parametrically.

Analytical Concepts and Criteria

On the basis of considerations presented in the preceding discussion, in what follows I will propose a list of analytical dimensions relevant to the analysis of popular music form and its narrative characteristics. In the subsequent section, the concepts presented will be applied to the analysis of a number of music videos.

Discursive Repetition/Structure of Lyrics/Function

This dimension comprises most of the factors contributing to the constitution of musical form in a non-analytical, 'intuitive' sense. 'Discursive repetition' is a concept suggested by Middleton, and defined as 'the repetition of larger units, at the level of the phrase, the sentence or even the complete section' (Middleton 1990: 269). Finding the 'main sections' of a piece is largely a question of identifying the largest sections subject to (discursive) repetition. In principle, this could be done by using Ruwet's (1987) paradigmatic method of analysis; in practice, this would entail a number of problems concerning the 'equivalence' of sections (how much variation is allowed for one section to be considered a 'repetition' of another?), and an intuitive classification in most cases yields the same results, although much faster. Taking the temporal order of sections and the structure of lyrics into account, main and subordinate sections may then be classified according to their respective functions; these functions (cf. Björnberg 1992*b*: 4 f.) include *verse* (V), *chorus* (C), *bridge* (B), *solo* (S), *break* (Bre), *introduction* (In), *interlude* (Il), and *coda* (Co).

Demarcation

A basic, albeit somewhat crude, measure of the distinctness of demarcation of the sections of a piece is *the number of musical dimensions exhibiting change* in the transition from one section to the next: the more dimensions that are affected by change of some kind, the more well-demarcated the section will be perceived to be. The musical dimensions in which changes may occur include *lyrics* (L), *melody* (M), *harmony* (H), *vocal texture* (V), *accompaniment texture* (A), *instrumentation* (I), *dynamics* (D), *tempo* (Te) and *tonal centre* (To).

Symmetry

Symmetrical binary construction being the implicit norm of popular music, asymmetrical structures will be perceived precisely as deviations from a norm, that is, occurrences of asymmetry are perceptually marked as 'events'. In general, the experiential effect of a deviation from symmetry is inversely related to its size; deviations 'below bar-level' not only disturb period and phrase structure but also regular metre (cf. Björnberg 1987: 76 f.). The categories of deviation from the symmetrical norm include *prolongation* (P: addition of metrical units to a symmetrical structure), *truncation* (T: subtraction of metrical units), and *elision* (E: 'overlapping' of two symmetrical structures).

Musematic Repetition

This concept is defined by Middleton (1990: 269) simply as 'the repetition of musemes'; 'museme' is here to be understood in the sense used by Tagg (1979: 71) as 'the basic unit of musical expression', although, as pointed out by Middleton (1990: 189), 'the nature and size of the museme need to be regarded flexibly'. In comparison to discursive repetition, musematic repetition is thus characterized by the repetition of smaller units, and in most cases also a greater number of repetitions; still, the necessary flexibility some-times causes problems of delimitation between the two categories, problems which are best discussed in each particular context. According to the dimension affected, musematic repetition may be classified as *melodic* (M), *harmonic* (H), or *accompanimental* (A); however, in the interest of clarity of distinction it appears reasonable to exclude in this analysis those accompanimental parts which in popular music ordinarily feature musematic repetition to a considerable degree (i.e. drum, bass, and chordal accompaniment parts; cf. 'Motorial flow' below).[7]

---

[7] The presence of such parts would seem to bring popular music in general closer to the epic category (cf. Table 16.1 and the analysis section); it may also be pointed out that the *regular metre* characteristic of most Western music constitutes a constant element of musematic repetition, although on a rather abstract level.

Directionality

This dimension involves the sense of forward-directedness effected by the evolving of melodic and harmonic structures through time (a more complete designation would be *pitch-related directionality*). The proposal of this concept constitutes an attempt to summarize the effects both of parametric dimensions such as mode ('tonal language') and of non-parametric aspects of tonal organization. It is thus related to the amplitude and frequency of fluctuations of melodic/harmonic tension, and partly analogous to the concept of 'prolongation' proposed by Lerdahl and Jackendoff (1984: 242 ff.). While directionality in principle is a quantifiable dimension, a detailed quantification would seem to entail a high degree of subjective judgement. I will therefore in my analyses only estimate the degree of directionality on a coarse quantitative scale, a high degree being considered as related both to *the total number of different elements* (melodic pitches and chords) used, and to the degree of adherence to *the voice-leading principles of functional tonality* (melodic leading notes, melodic dissonance/consonance progressions, 'strong' harmonic progressions, e.g. involving descending-fifth root progressions, 'regular' use of chord inversions, etc.). The degree of directionality is also affected by *deviations from metrical symmetry* (e.g. prolongation increasing the directionality of a dominant chord) and by *musematic repetition* (a 'strong' progression, when repeated, gradually loses its sense of forward-directedness).[8] In connection with the analysis of directionality, occurrences of *closure* (cadential effects), classifiable as *melodic* (M) and/or *harmonic* (H), may also be conveniently identified.

Motorial Flow

The presence of an accompanimental 'motorial continuum', mainly effected by drums, bass, and chordal instruments, approaches the status of yet another popular music norm (cf. Brolinson and Larsen 1981: 200). Variations in the motorial flow are therefore also perceived as musical 'events'. As is the case with directionality, the degree of motorial flow is also quantifiable in principle but open to subjective judgement; the rough quantitative estimate in my analyses is based, on the one hand, on *the number of contributing layers of musical texture*, and, on the other, on *the temporal density and regularity* of the sound-events (beats) constituting the motorial continuum. It should

---

[8] The *number* of repetitions is crucial for this effect. While a large number of repetitions of directional musematic structures reduces directionality, a 'small' number (2–4) often serves to increase it by means of tension/release effects; cf. Tagg's (1979: 132 ff.) discussion of 'ready, steady, go'-patterns.

perhaps be pointed out here that such an analysis presupposes a mode of listening involving the expectation of an explicit 'spelling out' of motorial flow; such a mode of listening may arguably be assumed to be frequently applied to contemporary popular music, in contrast with, for instance, a jazz-oriented mode of listening enabling the experience of intense motorial flow as implicit in a single melodic line (cf. Durgnat 1971: 36 f.).

Dynamics

Changes in the overall dynamic level of the music are estimated on a coarse quantitative scale.

Sound Processes

This dimension involves changes affecting *the characteristics of the overall sound* or of *the sound of individual voices/instruments*, e.g. changes in timbral quality, amount of reverberation or echo, dynamic balance between individual voices/instruments, etc.

Individuality Predominance Factor (IPF)

This is a rough quantitative measure of *the significance of 'individuality'* in a musical piece, based on a reading of the dualism of lead vocal melody and instrumental accompaniment in terms of the individual/background relationship (cf. above; also see Björnberg 1987: 219). It is calculated in three ways: (*a*) as the ratio of the total duration of vocal phrases to the total duration of sections featuring vocal parts, i.e. the duration of vocal phrases plus the rests between them (IPF_{vs}); (*b*) as the ratio of the total duration of sections featuring vocal parts to the total duration of the piece (IPF_{st}); (*c*) as the ratio of the total duration of vocal phrases to the total duration of the piece (IPF_{vt}, equal to $IPF_{vs} \times IPF_{st}$).

The general relationships between these analytical dimensions and the three modes of musical syntactical construction discussed above are shown in Table 16.1. The table entries indicate how the analytical dimensions, each one viewed separately, are related to the syntactical modes; however, due to the multidimensionality of music, actual pieces of music offer several possibilities for tendencies in different dimensions to work in different directions. A thorough theoretical analysis of the overall effects of such conflicting tendencies being a very complicated task, in the present context I will restrict myself to a discussion of such conflicts appearing in the particular examples to be analysed.

	Narrative/linear	Lyrical/elliptical	Epic/circular
Discursive repetition	no	yes	some
Demarcation	variable	distinct	indistinct
Symmetry	low	high	high
Musematic repetition	no	some	yes
Directionality	high	variable	low
Motorial flow	variable	relatively constant	constant
Dynamics	variable	relatively constant	constant
Sound processes	short-term	long-term	long-term
IPF	high	relatively high	low

Table 16.1

For the sake of clarity of distinction, in what follows I will partially effect the change of terminology suggested above, using the terms 'linear', 'elliptical', and 'circular' when exclusively discussing musical syntax, while retaining the narrative/lyrical/epic triad when speaking of visuals, combinations of music and visuals, or experiential aspects of musical structures.[9] An initial hypothesis underlying my analyses is that the visual structures of music video are generally determined by, and reflect, the elliptical (i.e. non-linear) nature of popular music syntax, and the polysemic nature, or 'conditional referentiality' (Björnberg 1992*a*: 380), of musical denotational signification, rather than a 'postmodern fragmentation' of visual narrative. However, in light of the range of variation *per genera et species* characterizing the syntactical construction of actual popular music, the conclusion that 'rock music cannot *in principle* be illustrated with logical narrative processes' (Nielsen 1991: 298; my italics) appears too rash; furthermore, visualization in music video is of course not necessarily entirely determined by musical syntax. In the reciprocal interplay between musical and visual signifying systems there is scope for various kinds of relationships between the two (or three, including verbal lyrics), and one of the purposes of the analysis is precisely the investigation of the practical and aesthetic limitations on this scope.

The objects chosen for analysis are four early 1990s music videos recorded for MTV Europe. These have not been selected with an aspiration to any kind of statistical representativity, but with the aim of demonstrating a range of

[9] Jones (1988) distinguishes between 'mimetic', 'analog', and 'digital' (non-linear) narrative, where television and music video have been moving towards the third; however, these concepts do not appear immediately transferable to discussions of musical syntax (but may perhaps be seen as parallel to Middleton's concepts, and mine, as regards the ratio of 'narrative information' to total information).

possible relationships between musical and visual structures. The musical analyses are also presented graphically (see Appendix, Figures 16.1–16.4).

A Streetcar Named Defier

The first object selected for analysis is the video for Bruce Springsteen's 'Human Touch'. The song is a 'trad rock' number in medium tempo and 'VCB-form' (VVCVCBVCC; see Figure 16.1); however, this is interspersed with several instrumental sections (In, II, and S sections), giving the song an overall length of roughly 6′ 25″. The last C section (preceding the extended instrumental Co) is prolonged by way of varied repetition of the last phrase. Demarcation is generally distinct, with changes in vocal texture, instrumentation, and accompaniment texture supporting the segmentation defined by lyrics, melody, and harmony. Sections are mostly symmetrically constructed, but two-bar prolongations occur in the C, B, and S2 sections. Melodic musematic repetition is not very prominent; the V section melody may be characterized as using 'varied musematic repetition', with a small number of repetitions. The harmonic structure, though, utilizes musematic repetition for the most part of the song: the V and C sections are based on the two-bar Mixolydian chord sequences | I | ♭VII IV | and | ♭VII | IV |, respectively, the first of which is also used in the In, II, and S2 sections, while the second appears in the S1 section. The vocal sections, however, conclude with the sequence | ♭VII | ♭VII IV I |, producing a (weak) harmonic closure, combined with melodic closure in C sections. Directionality is thus fairly low throughout, except for the B section, featuring a more active (also Mixolydian) chord sequence; also, there is no final closure, since the song ends with a fadeout. Motorial flow and dynamics are highly variable, with variations reinforcing segmentation. Sound processes mainly concern the relative dynamic levels of lead vocals and lead guitar. The overall IPF stated is fairly low, due to the extended instrumental sections; however, an experientially relevant value would be rather higher, on account of these sections featuring improvisatory vocal elements.

All in all, the song exhibits structural features typical of the 'epic' (this time, in the sense 'heroic narrative') trad rock style characteristic of Springsteen. The basic conception is circular (the harmonic ostinatos and mainly low-directional melody), but this is modified by its adaptation to an elliptical framework (clearly perceptible, albeit weak, harmonic and melodic closures, discursive repetition of well-demarcated sections). The circular character, however, is also manifest in the relationship between the sections here termed 'verse' and 'chorus': the musical material of the C section mainly amounts to permuted V material (my identification of this section as a 'chorus' is based on temporal order of presentation, closure, and lyrics, the song's title appearing at the end of this section'; cf. Björnberg 1992*b*: 2 f.). Thus there is little of the contrast or directionality usually associated with verse-chorus progressions; the largest contrast in the piece with regard to tonal processes is produced by the B section. The returns (discursive repetition) of entire sections, being generally typical of the elliptical mode of musical syntax construction, have the effect of 'grounding' the processual flow by way of the 'reconciliation of difference' function discussed by Middleton (1990: 223 f.). Nevertheless, the song also has a distinctly narrative quality, effected by means of a cumulative succession of multiple circular/elliptical sections modulated by processes of variable motorial flow and dynamics (especially evident in the transition from I14 and I15, the most climactic point in the song), but this narrativity is thus of a particular, static, long-term, slowly evolving nature.[10]

The visuals of the 'Human Touch' video, as is the case with most music videos, are to a large extent structured by the segmentation of the music; hence the following account is arranged according to corresponding musical sections:

In: Nocturnal North American city street; approaching streetcar.

V1: Superimposition of image of Bruce Springsteen (hereafter, Springsteen1) lip-synching vocals, shower of sparks from trolley-wire on the word 'pretenders'; dissolve to streetcar, with man in window easily identifiable as Springsteen (Springsteen2).

V2: Intercutting between Springsteen1 and passengers of streetcar, including Springsteen2.

C1: Springsteen1 sings against indeterminable grey-brownish background; dissolve to streetcar running; sparks on the work 'touch'.

Il1: Rapid montage composed of shots of running policemen, guitar-player (Springsteen3) in tiled pedestrian tunnel or suchlike, Springsteen2 in streetcar and young people in nocturnal city street settings illuminated by flashing lights.

V3: As V2; rapid insert of indistinct close-up of woman on the word 'tonight'.

C2: Springsteen1 singing; lonely woman in room; Springsteen2 in streetcar exchanging smiles with little girl.

---

[10] This may be illustrated by the fact that with regard to motorial flow, the 'intro' (i.e. introductory) section of the song actually extends over the entire first 52 measures (cf. Brolinson and Larsen 1984: 345).

Il2: Rapid montage of Springsteen 3 and street scenes; restless camera; flashing lights.

B: Montage of Springsteen 3 lip-synching and street scenes; trolley-wire sparks on the word 'we're' ('. . . all riders on this train').

S1: Montage of Springsteen 3 and street scenes, ecclesiastical scenes (funeral, christening), mother with baby, little girls dancing, and wedding-couple.

Il3: Montage continued; cut to tilted-camera shot of shadow of streetcar moving on housefronts; cut to Springsteen 3.

V4, C3, C4, Il4: Intercutting between Springsteen 1 lip-synching and streetcar stopping, Springsteen 2 getting off, crossing street, entering building, climbing stairs, walking down corridor, knocking on door.

Il5: Rapid intercutting: Springsteen 3 shouts; woman runs towards door, bare-chested Springsteen 3 swings guitar; Springsteen 2 enters room; Springsteen 3; Springsteen 2 and woman embrace; Springsteen 1, now playing guitar, etc.

Il6: Springsteen 1 playing guitar; montage of this, caresses of naked body, and Springsteen 3 with hands lifted as if in prayer; cut to trolley-wire sparks with Springsteen 3 in background on percussion intro to next section.

S2: Montage continued, mostly featuring caresses and Springsteen 3; however, the video ends with Springsteen 1 smiling relaxedly and self-confidently into the camera.

As indicated by this recapitulation, the video is composed of three distinct visual components: an act of narration, a visual narrative, and a series of disconnected scenes in various settings, i.e. in agreement with Kinder's (1984) well-known categorization. Each of these three components features its own edition of Bruce Springsteen: Springsteen 1, the balladeer and narrator; Springsteen 2, the actor and protagonist of the narrative; and Springsteen 3, the 'guitar hero' from the streets. The first two components together make up the visuals during the In section, most of the vocal sections and the Il4 section (which may be regarded as a short 'coda' to the prolonged C4 section), while the third dominates the instrumental sections Il1–3 and S1, as well as the vocal B section. In the montage of the extended coda section (Il5/Il6/S2), the three components seem to merge and form a synthesis. Accordingly, the separate identities of the three Springsteens: the calm, controlled, and controlling narrator, the vulnerable protagonist travelling to see his loved one, and the defiant street rebel-musician, apparently move

towards becoming different aspects of one and the same identity (the variations of the clothing of Springsteens 1 and 3 are interesting in this respect),
although the concluding shot of the video indicates which of the three is to
be perceived as the 'real' one (cf. Frith 1988: 216).

In accordance with the general character of the musical narrativity of the
piece, the visual narrative is fairly low on process statements, i.e. not very
much 'happens': a man travels by streetcar to meet a woman waiting, they
meet and rejoice. Nevertheless, it forms a coherent 'logical narrative process',
at the same time as its openness and ambiguity (who are this man and this
woman? where does he come from? for how long have they been separated?
will they have to part again?) allows for a range of interpretations (cf.
Goodwin 1987: 26 f.). In the musical sections high in directionality and/or
motorial flow the visuals evolve into an 'elliptical' (this time, in the literary
sense) narrative, inviting paraphrases in the direction of 'it's a dangerous world
out there, but human touch is still essential in all stages of life'. Thus a conflict
is set up, musically as well as lyrically/visually, but this conflict is reconciled,
visually/narratively as well as musically, in the coda of the song.[11]

Blue Dolphin Beat

My second example is the video for Bryan Adams's 'Thought I'd Died and Gone
to Heaven'. This song is a mainstream rock ballad in 'VCB-form' (VCVCB-
VCC; see Figure 16.2), where the vocals of the first eight measures of the V3
section are replaced by a guitar solo. Demarcation is distinct: the segmentation defined by lyrics, melody, and harmony is reinforced by changes in vocal
texture, instrumentation, and accompaniment texture. Deviations from
symmetry are numerous in the form of $2\frac{1}{2}$-bar prolongations of V sections
(two bars by phrase repetition, one half 'extra' measure added) and one-bar
prolongations of C sections ($1\frac{1}{2}$ bar in C3). Musematic repetition is sparsely
used; the C sections feature the two-bar, four-chord vamp | I V | vi IV |, which
may be regarded as a 'border case' of musematic repetition (cf. Björnberg
1992b: 12), while the V_B sections contain a discreet guitar riff. Experien-
tially, the combination of In and the first eight bars of V1 also produce an effect
of harmonic musematic repetition, an effect not present in the following V

---

[11] The essence of the song and the video, like so much of Springsteen's production, appears to amount to
what Berland (1986: 44) ironically describes as 'the oldest tune in the book: big world, little me'. Existential
facts do have a tendency to sound trivial; the interesting point, however, is not so much the triviality of the
message as the signification potential (and pleasure) invoked by the specific way in which it is structured.

sections. Directionality is medium-high and fairly variable, with lows in V_A sections and a peak in the B section. No unambiguous melodic or harmonic closure occurs, and the song ends with a fadeout. Motorial flow and dynamics are nearly constant throughout, except for breaks at the ends of sections and the first four bars of the B section. Sound processes include a temporary echo effect on the first entry of the lead vocals, and a successive domination of accompaniment over lead vocals in the concluding C sections. The overall IPF is fairly low, in spite of vocal sections constituting the bulk of the piece, on account of the 'gaps' in the vocal line ($IPF_{VS} = .63$).

As is the case with most rock ballads, the song is predominantly elliptically constructed, with an orderly repetition of clearly demarcated sections. This, however, is imprinted with distinctly linear traits: the fairly high and variable directionality, and the frequent deviations from symmetry,[12] while motorial flow, dynamics, and sound processes support ellipticality. On the whole, the processual character of the song is thus mainly lyrical, i.e. reflective and self-contained, but with a not insignificant narrative potential, although this narrativity is primarily of a 'local', short-range nature, and accommodated within the larger elliptical framework.

The visuals of the video, arranged according to musical segmentation, are summarized in the following:

In: One continuous shot; camera, directed downwards, moves over grassy meadow at night but with blue-ish lighting (which pervades the entire video); camera tilts up to horizontal, dollying in on Adams, standing in the meadow.

V1: Shot continues; camera stops at m. 14; three dolphins jump out of the grass and fall back, in slow motion; camera dollies upwards and out; cut (for the first time, at m. 19) to medium close-up of Adams; cut to drummer, then Adams, camera dollying down/in, then out; cut to Adams from another angle, camera moving in; cut to close-up of Adams.

C1: Dissolve to distance shot of entire group, upwards down; camera dollies in while turning clockwise; dissolve to Adams, camera moving down/out, showing guitarist; wind moves the previously calm grass; at m. 33 camera stops and marathon runners (?) start appearing out of the grass at gradually decreasing distance; the last six or seven of these,

---

[12] Such deviations appear, in the popular music of the last three decades, to have gradually replaced tonal processes as a means of increasing directionality (in a general sense); whereas in a Tin Pan Alley ballad a sectional transition may be emphasized by a series of II–V progressions with chord substitutions, in a rock ballad one, or a half, extra bar is instead added to a symmetrical period (cf. Björnberg 1987: 77).

who resemble the dolphins by wearing sweaters pulled up over their heads, disappear at top of picture; camera continues to move out; cut to drummer, camera moving upwards and out while turning.

V2: Similar images of Adams and the other musicians, camera constantly in movement; at m. 47 a dolphin jumps up, falling down two shots later; last shot in section featuring bass player, with camera moving in, then around, then upwards and out.

C2: Similar images; section ends with fade to black.

B: Fade in to medium close-up of Adams superimposed on meadow with moon and clouds above; the musicians, superimposed, act swimming- (or stage-?) divers, fully dressed, at top of picture; from m. 69 montage as before, with flying birds superimposed from m. 73.

S: Dissolve to camera dollying in, through shrubbery, to guitarist with moon above; camera stops at m. 81, moon turns into strobe light and a dolphin jumps up and somersaults, landing with great splash of water; cut to close-up of Adams.

V3$_B$: Montage as before; in last shot of section, one dolphin jumps up.

C3: Similar montage; in second shot of section, three dolphins come down.

C4: Similar montage.

Co(C5): One continuous shot; dissolve to medium close-up of Adams; camera moves out, showing the other musicians; at m. 121 five dolphins jump out of the grass in front of group, the middle one, corresponding to Adams' position in the group, jumping later and higher than the others; at m. 123, the dolphins having disappeared, the camera sinks, still horizontally directed, down into the grass.

Obviously, this is not a 'narrative' in any unqualified sense. The main visual components remain the same throughout the video: the nocturnal setting in the meadow, the blue-ish illumination, and the musicians doing nothing but performing (or, rather, lip- and hand-synching the performance of) the song. The things actually 'happening', i.e. the appearance and movements of the dolphins, runners, and birds inserted by means of technical special effects, stand out as isolated occurrences seemingly impossible to relate to the other visual components (or to the song's lyrics) within any coherent and logical narrative framework. One 'narrative' element in the video, however, is constituted by the almost constantly moving camera, producing perpetual shifts in distance and orientation; still, the 'story told' by these camera movements remains completely static.

Of course, the video is not intended to present any independent narrative, but to be experienced in connection with the music of the song. In spite of my arranging the summary above by musical segmentation, the visuals of this video are not very clearly structured by this segmentation, nor by the motorial layers of the music. Visual transitions are produced by dissolves rather than straight cuts and often displaced in relation to the beat (which is continuously spelt out by the bass, playing straight quavers, and drums). Some transitions (C1–V2, V2–C2; cf. above) are marked by particularly energetic camera movements, but generally the visual processes (besides the camera work, also the slow-motion movements of dolphins and runners) emphasize continuity and constancy, in a 'relay' relationship with musical processes (cf. Barthes 1977: 38 ff.). In this way, the visuals underline the lyrical, reflective character of the elliptical musical structure, potentially opening up vast fields of association to the user. On the other hand, except for the work of the 'narrative camera', the narrative potential of the music is not realized in the video; this, however, is not so much a matter of the images 'dominating' the music as of the visuals focusing attention on some aspects of the music while concealing others.

Egyptian Divorce

The object for my next analysis is the video for Michael Jackson's 'Remember the Time'. The song is a typical Jacksonian hip-hop-influenced dance piece in 'VCB-form' (VCVCBCCCCC; see Figure 16.3). Furthermore, there is a soloistic/instrumental middle segment (the Bre and II sections; m. 73–104); these are peculiar to the video version, not being present in the CD album version of the song. Demarcation is fairly indistinct, with mostly only changes in instrumentation (in most cases rather subtle) and vocal texture supporting the segmentation defined by lyrics and melody. Sections are symmetrically constructed throughout the piece, exhibiting no deviations. Harmonic musematic repetition is prominent; except for the B section and the (implied) static harmony of the Bre section, the entire song is built on a four-bar V–i ostinato (with varying alterations of the V chord). Although the vocal line shows general repetitive tendencies, actual melodic musematic repetition (more or less varied) occurs only in the Bre, II, and concluding C sections. In spite of the strong V–i progressions, directionality is low, due to the large number of repetitions, and no melodic or harmonic closure occurs, the song ending with an echo effect on an altered V chord. Motorial flow and dynamics exhibit little variation, with the exception of the Bre section. Sound processes mainly affect presence and reverberation of the vocals. The IPF is high, due both to rests between vocal phrases being short and to most sections featuring vocal melody (Jackson's habit of singing all vocal parts himself renders a clear distinction between 'lead' and 'background' vocals problematic; the experiential effect is one of 'multiple lead vocals').

The song's structure takes a mainly circular form: the repeated harmonic riff and constant motorial flow, acting against any sense of processual development, serve to level out contrasts between sections; the 'verse'/'chorus' distinction therefore mainly depends solely on lyrics and, to a limited extent, melody. This renders the processual character of the song epic, i.e. static and 'mythic'. The Bre and Il sections provide some potential for the kind of long-range narrativity discussed in connection with 'Human Touch', but to a considerably lower degree than in that case.

As in many other Michael Jackson videos, the length of the 'Remember the Time' video significantly exceeds that of the song, due to the presence of a visual/dramatic intro and a (shorter) visual coda; these are denoted 'Vis. In' and 'Vis. Co', respectively, in the following summary:

Vis. In: Throne-room of Pharaoh in ancient Egypt, Pharaoh and Queen seated on thrones; hooded figure approaches; Pharaoh asks 'Now, what is it you're going to do?' (the only instance of spoken dialogue); hooded figure takes brownish dust from pouch and spreads it on the floor, where it moves into circular pattern; hooded figure steps onto pattern and disappears mysteriously through the floor, leaving only his cloak; where he's stood, an amorphous shining figure arises, eventually metamorphosing into Michael Jackson. The scene is accompanied by Phrygian 'suspense' underscore music played by strings and electric guitar, and by sound effects.

In: Shots of Jackson, moving rhythmically to the beat, alternating with countershots of Pharaoh and Queen.

V1: Jackson lip-synching vocals; countershots of Queen; Jackson kisses her hand; Pharaoh signals to his guards; Jackson turns and runs down the stairs from the thrones, leaving Queen with hand outstretched.

C1: Intercutting of guards running or pointing, Pharaoh, Queen swooning; at end of section cut to doorway where Jackson appears, swirling on percussion pick-up to next section.

V2: Intercutting of guards searching, Jackson with passing camel in front, Jackson in harem, snakes in basket.

C2: Jackson dancing in circle of women; at end of section continuity cut from veil of dancing women to drapery.

B: Pan from drapery to Queen on bed; zoom out reveals Jackson at other end of room; intercutting of Queen and Jackson.

C3: Queen on balcony, looking out onto pyramids; Jackson approaches; they embrace and kiss; at end of section cut to column, behind which arm protrudes making 'Egyptian' gesture.

Bre: Intercutting of guards and dancers emerging from behind columns; intercutting of Jackson and dancers; zoom out from Jackson revealing surrounding dancers.

Il: Dance scene; Jackson and dancers from various angles.

C4, C5, C6, C7: Dance scene continued; at end of last section cut to close-up of Jackson.

Co: Jackson swirls; cut during swirl to different background.

Vis. Co: (accompanied by percussion underscore in same tempo as song); Jackson stops and looks around, finding himself back in throne room; Pharaoh comes in from left; Jackson smiles impudently and makes a dash; menacing-looking guards approach; Jackson, finding himself surrounded, escapes by swirling and disappearing mysteriously.

In this case, there is no equivocality as to the narrativity of the visuals: a logically consistent narrative, with a considerable degree of temporal and spatial coherence, is presented by means of well-established filmic codes. Nevertheless, this narrative is clearly divided into segments exhibiting varying levels of 'realism'. In the first, and 'most realistic' segment, the narrative evolves in 'real time'; this segment constitutes the 'visual intro'. In the second segment, corresponding to musical sections In-C3, the realism is modified by a more ambiguous construction of temporal continuity. The third segment, starting at the beginning of the Bre section, dismisses realism completely, suspending the narrative flow throughout the remainder of the song; the second shot of the guards in that section constitutes the last 'realistic' element. The 'visual coda', by returning to the first level of realism, resumes and concludes the narrative.

This segmentation of the visuals is obviously related to musical segmentation. In effect, this video constitutes a condensed version of the classical Hollywood musical film (as seems to be a favourite procedure with Michael Jackson), underlining the parallelisms between the two forms discussed by

Allan (1990), and lying significantly closer to the Hollywood musical than Morse (1986: 23) considers typical of music video. The correlation, characteristic of the musical film, of 'realistic narrative' with absence of music and of 'fantasy' with its presence is, however, modified in the video by the establishment of two levels of realism in the former mode, one without music (except for the underscore) and one with music.[13] The 'fantasy' in the video (the dance scene), the transitions in and out of which are musically marked by echo effects (in the Bre and Co sections), corresponds in function to the musical number of the musical film. However, the connection of 'level 2' narrative with circular music structure means that the latter is not very clearly realized in the visuals; with a few exceptions, edits and depicted movements are not strongly coordinated with the music. Due to the 'narrative interest' of the images, there is thus, in this particular segment of this particular video, some reason to speak of 'domination' of the music by the visuals. The only 'narrative' musical element present here is the high IPF, enabling in a limited way a musical support for the evolution of visual narrative.

A Space Obscurity

My final analysis concerns the video for Snap's 'Rhythm is a Dancer'. This song is a pop-techno dance number;[14] the overall formal structure might be characterized as an instance of 'expanded standard form' (cf. Björnberg 1992b: 2) with the disposition VVBV (see Figure 16.4), although the construct is not supported by the tonal processes typical of that form-type. The S (or B) section is composed of eight bars of instrumental solo followed by a sixteen-bar rap. Demarcation is of medium distinctness, the segmentation defined by lyrics and melody being supported by changes in instrumentation and accompaniment texture. All sections are symmetrically constructed with no deviations. Musematic repetition predominates in harmony and accompaniment structure: the bulk of the piece uses the two-bar Aeolian chord ostinato |i ♭VI | ♭VII i|, spelt out by a synthesizer riff in quavers. The vocal melody, although exhibiting no clear musematic repetition, works repetitive

[11] This differentiation of realism levels underlines the structural, functional, and experiential differences between traditional film underscore music and the music of music video; however, a detailed discussion of these issues cannot be pursued in the present context (on underscore music, see Gorbman 1987).

[14] The video is based on the '7″ edit' version of the song, with a duration of 3′41″; the CD single also contains a 5′12″ version subtitled '12″ mix', and a 6′49″ 'Purple hazed mix', the latter with a considerably different and less mainstream-oriented harmonic, rhythmic, and formal structure.

tendencies into arch-shaped lines. Directionality is generally insignificant, with a low in the Phrygian-coloured static-harmony B section. The final tonic minor chord gives no strong sense of harmonic closure, since it appears in the same metric position as previously in the harmonic riff; the song ends abruptly with a percussion echo effect disrupting regular metre by a shift to a rhythm of dotted quavers. Motorial flow is built up in discrete steps up to m. 32, thereafter being mostly constant, with the exception of the Bre sections. Dynamics show little variation; sound processes primarily concern the amount and quality of reverberation applied to vocals and/or overall sound. The IPF is medium-high as regards both rests between vocal phrases and relative duration of vocal sections.

Thus, like the preceding example, this song too exhibits a circular structure based on repetitive harmony and fairly constant motorial flow. One important difference, though, is that the application of the 'verse/chorus principle' is even less distinctly manifest in 'Rhythm is a Dancer'. While the vocal melody effects a demarcation in the middle of the V section, implying a differentiation into a 'verse' (V_A) and a 'refrain' (V_B), this is not supported by any variation as regards lyrics between the different V_A sections (all lyrics remain identical in all three V sections). The epic character of the song is therefore somewhat more emphasized in comparison with 'Remember the Time'; however, by the alternation of sections and the variations of motorial flow, the song still provides some (small) potential for the previously discussed long-range type of narrativity.

The visuals of the video, arranged as before according to musical segmentation, are summarized below:

> *In*: Establishing shots and show pans of rocket launching site, illuminated by pale mauve-orange lighting and occasional white flashes and spotlights; rockets standing in background; smoke; superimposed sped-up moving clouds; female singer, in tight, shiny, black dress, on slowly-rising construction-elevator; surrounding people dressed in similar garments of dull metallic lustre.
>
> *V1*: Similar scenery; three persons holding huge spheroids over their heads; mechanical body movements; bass player on similar slowly-rising construction-elevator behind and to the left of the one holding the singer.
>
> *V2*: Cuts on downbeat of every second bar; on m. 33 to computer/paintbox graphics with symmetric mirror effect; on m. 35 to different graphics featuring moving clouds, human silhouette in slow motion, and CAD (computer-aided design) rotating wheel; on m. 37 to singer; on m. 39 to

graphics resembling the first but with two human silhouettes and moving 'atom' symbol; then to intercuttings of singer, lip-synching and gradually moving more intensely, and bass player.

Bre1: Scenery similar to that of the V1 section.

S: New graphics: superimpositions of human silhouettes running in slow motion, clouds and nautical charts, changing by quick dissolves in quaver rhythm; on m. 61 cut to graphics featuring zoom in on human silhouette in slow motion and CAD rotating sphere; from m. 65 montage of these elements, medium-close-ups of rapper lip-synching and humans moving mechanically; at end of section 'zoom in cut' on face of rapper on the word 'dancer'.

V3: Scenery similar to that of section V1; several slow pans.

Il: Cut to human silhouette/nautical charts graphics; on m. 101 cut to bass player.

Bre2: Cuts on downbeat of every second bar to various graphics; on m. 112 cut to CAD sphere with superimposed clouds.

Co: Sphere recedes into distance, rotating; fade to black.

As in the case of 'Thought I'd Died and Gone to Heaven', this video is manifestly non-narrative. Two main visual components are set up: on the one hand the launching site scenery, on the other hand various types of special-effect graphics, but none of these shows any significant tendency towards narrative evolution.

Thus, to an even higher degree than in the Bryan Adams example, the visuals of this video are dependent on the music. The movements depicted and the editing both work towards an emulation of musical rhythm, the superimposition of several different types of movement reflecting the latter's multilayered nature. Many of the cuts described above as 'on the downbeat' are actually placed fractionally *before* the beat, thus producing an off-beat effect entering into a relay relationship with, and reinforcing, the rhythmic flow of the music. No narrative components interfere with the alignment of the visuals with the epic character of the piece. The actual content of the visuals potentially opens up large fields of association, but these are not strongly structured by the visuals nor by the music of the video.

Towards a Typology of Structural Relationships

On the basis of the preceding analyses, I would like to propose a tentative typology of structural relationships between music and visuals in music video (see Table 16.2). The four types indicated in the table are, however, not

| | MUSIC | |
	Narrative	Epic
Narrative	'Film music' relationship, i.e. narrative processes in music and visuals interacting, but on terms set by the music rather than the visuals	Assignment of 'mood music' function to music, i.e. the music providing backcloth to the visual narrative
Epic	'Circularization' of music, i.e. focusing of attention on non-narrative aspects of the music, concealing its narrative potentials	'Musicalization' of visuals, i.e. the visuals primarily reinforcing musical experience by synaesthetic 'translation' and emulation of musical experiential qualities

VISUALS appears to the left spanning the Narrative/Epic rows.

Table 16.2

equally representative of contemporary music videos. As Middleton (1990: 217) points out, post-rock 'n' roll popular music has generally tended towards mixtures of the elliptical and circular modes of syntax construction. The music/visuals relationships of most music videos could therefore be expected to approach one of the two types in the right-hand column of the table. However, this typology, being rather schematic, cannot be expected to exhaust the range of possible relationships, and it evidently needs further modification and differentiation. In this context, it should also be noted that in relation to the videos analysed here, the concepts 'narrative music' and 'epic music' must be regarded on a relative scale, as each of the four songs is based on a clearly discernible elliptical structure; on the whole, decidedly linear or circular structures rarely appear in popular music (cf. above). Thus, it appears particularly pertinent for the further elaboration of this typology to focus on the elliptical mode of musical syntax construction, to which no obvious visual counterpart seems to exist. The musical function of providing 'unity', mentioned by Allan and Kinder (cf. above) is relevant in this context, but conceived in too general terms: since music always has a tendency to effect unity by means of sheer redundancy in comparison to other communicative modes (cf. Björnberg 1992a: 382 f.), the crucial point is rather *how* this unification is brought about in each particular case.

It appears, however, to make some sense to draw a parallel between the linear/elliptical/circular axis and Kinder's (1984) aforementioned 'narrative/performance/dreamlike visuals' axis. The alignment of 'linear' with 'narrative', and of 'circular' with 'dreamlike visuals', seems relevant, as indicated by my analyses. Furthermore, performance visuals in music video often appear 'neutral' with relation to the signification of musical syntax, and they may thus constitute a 'natural' or privileged mode of underlining the reflective, introspective, reconciliation-of-difference character of the elliptical mode of musical syntax construction. These musical characteristics, described by Moore (1993: 85) in terms of the 'fictionality' of the popular song as a 'self-contained entity', could thus be viewed as homologous to musical performance in its function as an 'irrational' aesthetic activity, detached from everyday reality.

The complexity of the issue should also be acknowledged by taking verbal *lyrics* into account. I have not commented much on the lyrics of the songs analysed here, since these seem to me to be more important to an analysis of content than to one of structure; still, the matter clearly calls for further attention. In this connection, it can be noted that music videos with a visual narrative are often based on narrative lyrics (or lyrics with some narrative 'seed' in them), to a large extent regardless of the degree of musical narrativity (cf. videos such as Rolling Stones' 'Under Cover of the Night', 'Small Town Boy' by Bronski Beat, and Tom Petty's 'Into the Great Wide Open'). Nevertheless, clear correlations as regards narrativity in different signifying systems appear to exist at least in some musical genres (notably the predilection for 'mythically' conceived narrative lyrics, narrative videos, and 'baroque' musical syntax in heavy metal music; cf. Walser 1992).

Conclusion

None of the music videos analysed in this essay is particularly exceptional in respect of aesthetics, neither as regards music nor visuals; rather, to my view, all four examples are (musically as well as visually) well-crafted, and quite effective, instances of mainstream forms of expression. The widespread reluctance to deal with such 'naturalized' mainstream forms, implicitly dismissing them as uninteresting and aesthetically deficient, seems to be partly rooted in a somewhat romantic belief in the subversive power of rock music (see, for instance, Berland 1986; Tetzlaff 1986). However, as Goodwin (1987: 31) indicates, the counter-cultural potential of pop culture is often exaggerated (especially, it seems to me, by US-American scholars and writers); furthermore, a full understanding of the subversive and the exceptional cannot be expected to be gained without also examining the 'ordinary' (cf. Tagg 1982: 63 f.).

To be fair, the confusions and theoretical disagreements discussed here concerning the characteristics of music video are partially dependent on the time of writing, as the dominant forms of music video have changed considerably over the years. Furthermore, music video being a very heterogeneous phenomenon, it sometimes also appears that 'anything can be proven', depending on how examples are chosen. This illustrates the extent to which the field of contemporary popular music is stylistically, socially, and semiotically fragmented; still, despite postmodernist prophecies of 'the destruction of meaning', users of music video and other popular cultural forms continue to derive pleasure from the production of (albeit temporary and volatile) meaning induced by these forms (cf. Straw 1988; Frith 1992).

In spite of the emphasis placed here on textual-structural analysis, it would seem unwise to deny that there are limitations to the explanatory value of such an analysis of music video. It appears equally unwise, however, to discard the possibilities of textual analysis before the nature of these limitations has been investigated by way of such an analysis taking all relevant dimensions into account. Syntactical characteristics are 'objective possibilities' (Willis 1978: 198 f.), subject to influence by varying modes of perception, contexts of use and other factors; these factors, as well as the ways in which the visualization of musical structures is shaped by genre-specific cultural codes of expression, remain to be examined in more detail by future research.

Appendix

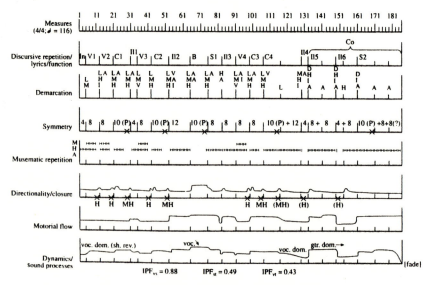

Figure 16.1 Bruce Springsteen: 'Human Touch'

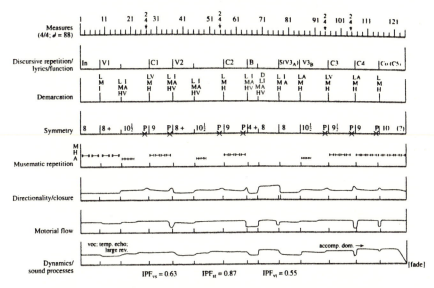

Figure 16.2 Bryan Adams: 'Thought I'd Died and Gone to Heaven'

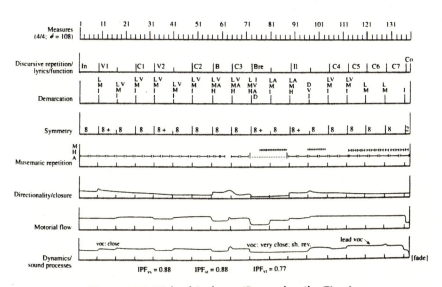

Figure 16.3 Michael Jackson: 'Remember the Time'

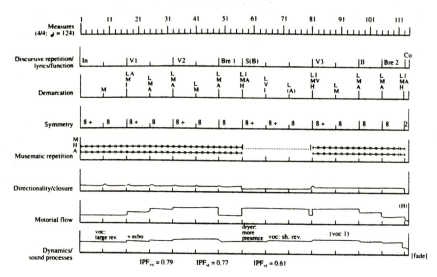

Figure 16.4 Snap: 'Rhythm is a Dancer'

References

Allan, B. (1990). 'Musical cinema, music video, music television', *Film Quarterly*, 43/3: 2–14.

Aufderheide, P. (1986). 'Music videos: the look of the sound', *Journal of Communications*, 36/1: 5–78.

Barthes, R. (1977). *Image—Music—Text* (London).

Berkaak, O. A., and Ruud, E. (1989). 'Rockeminner' ('Rock memories'), *Norveg*, 32: 205–17.

Berland, J. (1986). 'Sound, image, and social space: rock video and media reconstruction', *Journal of Communication Inquiry*, 10/1: 34–47.

Björnberg, A. (1987). *En liten sång som alla andra. Melodifestivalen 1959–1983* (A little song like all others. The Melody Festival 1959–1983) (Gothenburg).

—— (1991). 'Sign of the times? Om musikvideo och populärmusikens semiotik' ('On music video and the semiotics of popular music'), *Svensk tidskrift för musikforskning*, 72: 63–84.

—— (1992a). 'Music video and the semiotics of popular music', *Secondo Convegno Europeo di Analisi Musicale*, ed. R. Dalmonte and M. Baroni (Trento), 379–88.

—— (1992b). *Popular Music Form as Narrative Process*, Report series Ljudbilder, 1, Department of Musicology, University of Gothenburg.

Brolinson, P.-E., and Larsen, H. (1981). *Rock . . . Aspekter på Industri, Elektronik & Sound*, (Rock . . . Aspects of Industry, Electronics & Sound) (Stockholm).

—— (1984). 'Från början. Om "intro" och inledningsfunktioner hos ABBA' ('From the beginning. On "intro" and introductory functions in ABBA'), *Tvärspel—trettioen artiklar om musik. Festskrift till Jan Ling* (Gothenburg), 343–51.

Brown, M. E., and Fiske, J. (1987). 'Romancing the rock: romance and representation in popular music videos', *OneTwoThreeFour*, 5: 61–73.

Chatman, S. (1978). *Story and Discourse: Narrative Structure in Fiction and Film* (Ithaca, NY and London).

Durgnat, R. (1971), 'Rock, rhythm and dance', *British Journal of Aesthetics*, 11/1: 28–47.

Fiske, J. (1986). 'MTV: post-structural post-modern', *Journal of Communication Inquiry*, 10/1: 74–9.

Forsman, M. (1986). 'Det eviga nuet' ('The eternal now'), *Filmhäftet*, 54: 4–14.

—— (1991). 'Bilder av musik—om rockvideons formspråk' ('Pictures of music—on the form-language of rock video'), *Ung Film*, 9: 4–9.

Frith, S. (1988). 'Making sense of video: pop into the nineties', *Music for Pleasure* (Cambridge), 205–25.

—— (1992). 'Det gode, det dårlige og det ligegyldige' ('The good, the bad and the indifferent'), *Mediekultur*, 18: 45–56.

—— and Horne, H. (1987). *Art into Pop* (London and New York).

Genette, G. (1980). *Narrative Discourse* (Ithaca, NY).

Goodwin, A. (1987). 'From anarchy to chromakey: music, video, media', *OneTwoThreeFour*, 5: 16–32.

Gorbman, C. (1987). *Unheard Melodies: Narrative Film Music* (Bloomington and Indianapolis).

Grossberg, L. (1988). ' "You (still) have to fight for your right to party": music television as billboards of post-modern difference', *Popular Music*, 7/3: 315–32.

Ihlemann, L. (1992). 'Fra rockkoncert til musikvideo' ('From rock concert to music video'), *Mediekultur*, 18: 34–44.

Jensen, J. F. (1988) '. . . AND NOW . . . THIS:', *Kultur, identitet og kommunikation*, ed. H. J. Nielsen (Aalborg), 7–32.

Jones, S. (1988). 'Cohesive but not coherent: music videos, narrative and culture', *Popular Music and Society*, 12/4: 15–29.

Kaplan, E. A. (1987). *Rocking around the Clock: Music Television, Postmodernism and Consumer Culture* (London and New York).

Kinder, M. (1984). 'Music video and the spectator: television, ideology and dream', *Film Quarterly*, 38/1: 2–15.

Laing, D. (1985). 'Music video: industrial product, cultural form', *Screen*, 26/2: 78–83.

Larsen, P. (1987). 'Bortom berättelsen' ('Beyond narrative'), *Filmhäftet*, 55–6: 82–96.

—— (1988). 'Musik og moderne billedfiktioner' ('Music and modern visual fiction'), *Kultur & Klasse*, 15/4: 33–53.

Lerdahl, F., and Jackendoff, R. (1984). 'An overview of hierarchical structure in music', *Music Perception*, 1/2: 229–52.

Maróthy, J. (1974). *Music and the Bourgeois, Music and the Proletarian* (Budapest).

Middleton, R. (1990). *Studying Popular Music* (Milton Keynes and Philadelphia).

Moore, A. (1993). *Rock: The Primary Text. Developing a Musicology of Rock* (Buckingham and Philadelphia).

Morse, M. (1986). 'Post-synchronizing rock music and television', *Journal of Communication Inquiry*, 10/1: 15–28.

Movin, L., and Øberg, M. (1990). *Rockreklamer* (Rock commercials) (Viborg).

Nielsen, E. (1991). ' "MTV, MTV, MTV get off the air . . ." ', *Analyser af tv og tv-kultur*, ed. J. F. Jensen (Copenhagen), 281–304.

Ruud, E. (1988). *Musikk for øyet: Om musikkvideo* (Music for the eye. On music video) (Oslo).

Ruwet, N. (1987). 'Methods of analysis in musicology', *Music Analysis*, 6/1–2: 11–36.

Straw, W. (1988). 'Music video in its contexts: popular music and post-modernism in the 1980s', *Popular Music*, 7/3: 247–66.

Strøm, G. (1989). *Musikkvideo* (Music video) (Oslo).

Tagg, P. (1979). *Kojak—50 Seconds of Television Music: Toward the Analysis of Affect in Popular Music* (Gothenburg).

—— (1982). 'Analysing popular music: theory, method and practice', *Popular Music*, 2: 37–67.

Tetzlaff, D. J. (1986). 'MTV and the politics of postmodern pop', *Journal of Communication Inquiry*, 10/1: 80–91.

Walser, R. (1992). 'Eruptions: heavy metal appropriations of classical virtuosity', *Popular Music*, 11/3: 263–308.

Willis, P. (1978). *Profane culture* (London).

Discography

Bryan Adams, 'Thought I'd Died and Gone to Heaven', *Waking Up the Neighbours*. A & Records, 397 164-2 (1991).

Michael Jackson, 'Remember the Time', *Dangerous*. Epic, 465 802-2 (1991).

Snap, *Rhythm is a Dancer*. Logic Records, 665 309 (1992).

Bruce Springsteen, 'Human Touch', *Human Touch*. Columbia, 471 423-2 (1992).

Select Bibliography of Works Relevant to the Textual Analysis of Popular Music

The Introduction to this book implies that virtually any literature concerned with aspects of popular music can be relevant to analysis of the music. This view points towards an impossibly long Bibliography. Instead, the list given here offers a selection of writings whose main *focus* is on 'the music itself'—its structures, styles, performance, etc. Most are concerned with Western pop of the second half of the twentieth century; this simply reflects the fact (as does the content of this book) that most of the existing work has taken this repertory for its subject—there is little good interpretative writing on earlier styles. Similarly, increasing attention to pop music in other parts of the world has so far resulted in rather few studies with an analytical focus.

Adorno, T. W. (1990). 'On popular music', in *On Record: Rock, Pop and the Written Word*, ed. S. Frith and A. Goodwin (London), 301–14 (first published, 1941).

Bailey, P. (1986). 'Champagne Charlie: performance and ideology in the music-hall swell song', in *Music Hall: Performance and Style*, ed. J. S. Bratton (Milton Keynes), 49–69.

Bennett, T. (1986). 'Music in the halls', in *Music Hall: Performance and Style*, ed. J. S. Bratton (Milton Keynes), 1–22.

Björnberg, A. (1989). 'On Aeolian harmony in contemporary popular music', IASPM-Nordic Branch Working Papers, DK 1 (Gothenburg).

—— (1990). 'Sounding the mainstream: an analysis of the songs performed in the Swedish Eurovision Song Contest Semi-Finals 1959–1983', in *Popular Song Research: An Anthology from NORDICOM-Sweden* (Gothenburg), 121–31.

Bowman, R. (1995). 'The Stax sound: a musicological analysis', *Popular Music*, 14/3: 285–320.

Brackett, D. (1995). *Interpreting Popular Music* (Cambridge).

Bradby, B. (1990). 'Do-talk and don't talk: the division of the subject in girl-group music', in *On Record: Rock, Pop and the Written Word*, ed. S. Frith and A. Goodwin (London), 341–68.

—— (1992). 'Like a virgin-mother? materialism and maternalism in the songs of Madonna', *Cultural Studies*, 6/1: 73–96.

—— (1993). 'Sampling sexuality: gender, technology and the body in dance music', *Popular Music*, 12/2: 155–76.

Bradley, D. (1992). *Understanding Rock 'n' Roll: Popular Music in Britain, 1955–1964* (Milton Keynes).

Burns, G. (1987). 'A typology of "hooks" in popular records', *Popular Music*, 6/1: 1–20.

Chester, A. (1990). 'Second thoughts on a rock aesthetic: The Band', in *On Record: Rock, Pop and the Written Word*, ed. S. Frith and A. Goodwin (London), 315–19.

Cook, N. (1994). 'Music and meaning in the commercials', *Popular Music*, 13/1: 27–40.

—— (1996). 'Music minus one: rock, theory, and performance', *New Formations*, 27: 23–41.

Covach, J., and Boone, G. (eds.) (1998). *Understanding Rock: Essays in Musical Analysis* (New York).

Daley, M. (1997). 'Patti Smith's Gloria: intertextual play in a vocal performance', *Popular Music*, 16/3: 235–53.

Danielson, A. (1997). 'His name was Prince: a study of *Diamonds and Pearls*', *Popular Music*, 16/3: 275–91.

Durant, A. (1984). *Conditions of Music* (London).

Fabbri, F. (1982). 'A theory of musical genres: two applications', in *Popular Music Perspectives*, ed. D. Horn and P. Tagg (Gothenburg and Exeter), 52–81.

Floyd, S. A. (1991). 'Ring shout! Literary studies, historical studies, and black music inquiry', *Black Music Research Journal*, 11/2: 265–87.

Ford, C. (1998). 'Robert Johnson's rhythms', *Popular Music*, 17/1: 71–93.

Forte, A. (1995). *The American Popular Ballad of the Golden Era 1924–1950* (Princeton).

Fox, A. (1992). 'The jukebox of history: narratives of loss and desire in the discourse of country music', *Popular Music*, 11/1: 53–72.

Frith, S. (1988). *Music for Pleasure: Essays in the Sociology of Pop* (Cambridge).

—— (1996). *Performing Rites: On the Value of Popular Music* (Oxford).

Green, L. (1990). *Music on Deaf Ears: Musical Meaning, Ideology and Education* (Manchester).

Griffiths, D. (1992). 'Talking about popular song: in praise of *Anchorage*', in *Studi e Testi 1, Secondo Convegno Europeo di Analisi Musicale*, ed. R. Dalmonte and M. Baroni (Trento), 351–8.

Hamm, C. (1995). *Putting Popular Music in its Place* (Cambridge).

Hatch, D., and Millward, S. (1987). *From Blues to Rock: An Analytical History of Pop Music* (Manchester).

Hawkins, S. (1996). 'Perspectives in popular musicology: music, Lennox and meaning in 1990s pop', *Popular Music*, 15/1: 17–36.

Keil, C. (1991). *Urban Blues* (Chicago) (first published, 1966).

—— (1994). 'Motion and feeling through music', in C. Keil and S. Feld, *Music Grooves* (Chicago), 53–76 (first published, 1966).

Laing, D. (1969). *The Sound of Our Time* (London).

—— (1971). *Buddy Holly* (London).

—— (1985). *One Chord Wonders: Power and Meaning in Punk Rock* (Milton Keynes).

McClary, S. (1991). 'Living to tell: Madonna's resurrection of the fleshly', in *Feminine Endings: Music, Gender and Sexuality* (Minneapolis), 148–66.

—— (1994). 'Same as it ever was: youth culture and music', in *Microphone Fiends: Youth Culture and Youth Music*, ed. A. Ross and T. Rose (London), 29–40.

—— and Walser, R. (1990). 'Start making sense! Musicology wrestles with rock', in *On Record: Rock, Pop and the Written Word*, ed. S. Frith and A. Goodwin (London), 277–92.

Maróthy, J. (1974). *Music and the Bourgeois, Music and the Proletarian* (Budapest).

Marvin, E. W., and Hermann, R. (eds.) (1995). *Concert Music, Rock and Jazz since 1945: Essays and Analytical Studies* (Rochester, NY).

Mellers, W. (1973). *Twilight of the Gods: The Beatles in Retrospect* (London).

—— (1984). *A Darker Shade of Pale: A Backdrop to Bob Dylan* (London).

Middleton, R. (1983). ' "Play it again Sam": some notes on the productivity of repetition in popular music', *Popular Music*, 3: 235–70.

—— (1985). 'Articulating musical meaning/re-constructing musical history/ locating the "popular" ', *Popular Music*, 5: 5–43.

—— (1990). *Studying Popular Music* (Milton Keynes).

—— (1995). 'Authorship, gender and the construction of meaning in the Eurythmics' hit recordings', *Cultural Studies*, 9/3: 465–85.

Moore, A. (1992). 'Patterns of harmony', *Popular Music*, 11/1: 73–106.

—— (1993). *Rock: The Primary Text. Developing a Musicology of Rock* (Buckingham).

—— (1995). 'The so-called "flattened seventh" in rock', *Popular Music*, 14/2: 185–201.

Scott, D. (1994). 'Incongruity and predictability in British dance-band music of the 1920s and 1930s', *Musical Quarterly*, 78/2: 290–315.

—— (1989). *The Singing Bourgeois: Songs of the Victorian Drawing Room and Parlour* (Milton Keynes).

Shepherd, J. (1982). 'A theoretical model for the sociomusicological analysis of popular musics', *Popular Music*, 2: 145–77.

—— (1991). *Music as Social Text* (Cambridge).

Stefani, G. (1987). 'Melody: a popular perspective', *Popular Music*, 6/1: 21–35.

Tagg, P. (1979). *Kojak—50 Seconds of Television Music: Towards the Analysis of Affect in Popular Music* (Gothenburg).

—— (1987). 'Musicology and the semiotics of popular music', *Semiotica*, 66/1: 279–98.

—— (1992). *Fernando the Flute: Analysis of Musical Meaning in an Abba Mega-Hit* (Liverpool).

—— (1992). 'Towards a sign typology of music', in *Studi e Testi 1: Secondo Convegno Europeo di Analisi Musicale*, ed. R. Dalmonte and M. Baroni (Trento), 369–78.

—— (1994). 'From refrain to rave: the decline of figure and the rise of ground', *Popular Music*, 13/2: 209–22.

Titon, J. T. (1977). *Early Downhome Blues: A Musical and Cultural Analysis* (Urbana, Ill.).

Van der Merwe, P. (1989). *Origins of the Popular Style: The Antecedents of Twentieth-Century Popular Music* (Oxford).

—— (1996). 'The Italian blue third', in *Popular Music Studies in Seven Acts*, ed. T. Hautamäki and T. Rautiainen (Tampere), 55–67.

Vernallis, C. (1998). 'The aesthetics of music video: an analysis of Madonna's "Cherish" ', *Popular Music*, 17/2: 153–85.

Walser, R. (1992). 'Eruptions: heavy metal appropriations of classical virtuosity', *Popular Music*, 11/3: 263–308.

—— (1993). *Running with the Devil: Power, Gender and Madness in Heavy Metal Music* (Hanover, NH and London).

—— (1995). 'Rhythm, rhyme, and rhetoric in the music of Public Enemy', *Ethnomusicology*, 39/2: 193–217.

Waterman, C. (1990). *Juju: A Social History and Ethnography of an African Popular Music* (Chicago).

Wheeler, E. (1991). ' "Most of my heroes don't appear on no stamps": the dialogics of rap music', *Black Music Research Journal*, 11/2: 193–216.

Whiteley, S. (1992). *The Space between the Notes: Rock and the Counter-Culture* (London: Routledge).

Wicke, P. (1982). 'Rock music: a musical aesthetic study', *Popular Music*, 2: 219–43.

—— (1990). *Rock Music: Culture, Aesthetics and Sociology*, trans. R. Fogg (Cambridge).

Wilder, A. (1972). *American Popular Song: The Great Innovators 1900–1950* (New York).

Willis, P. (1978). *Profane Culture* (London).

Index

Note: Italic page numbers denote musical extracts and figures

Printed in the United States
21917LVS00002B/32

Printed in the United States
21917LVS00002B/32

9 780198 166115